THE ARCHITECTS OF EXISTENCE

THE ARCHITECTS OF EXISTENCE

ÀJẸ́ IN YORUBA COSMOLOGY, ONTOLOGY, AND ORATURE

TERESA N. WASHINGTON

ỌYA'S TORNADO

Copyright © 2014, 2015
Teresa N. Washington
All rights reserved

This book is a publication of
ỌYA'S TORNADO
Books To Blow Your Mind
Orífín, Ilé Àjẹ́
oyastornado@yahoo.com

ỌYA'S TORNADO™, Books To Blow Your Mind™, and all associated tornado logos are trademarks of Ọya's Tornado.

All rights reserved

No part of this book may be reproduced or utilized in any form or by any means, electronic or mechanical, including photocopying and recording, or by any information storage and retrieval system, without permission in writing from the author and/or publisher.

Washington, Teresa N.,
The Architects of Existence: Àjẹ́ in Yoruba Cosmology, Ontology and Orature / Teresa N. Washington.
p. cm.
Includes bibliographical references and index.
ISBN 978-0-9910730-1-6 (pbk); ISBN 978-0-9910730-3-0 (cloth)
1. Yoruba culture and philosophy. 2. Yoruba Gods and Creation. 3. Yoruba Mother Gods. 4. Yoruba women and power. 5. Yoruba mothers and sons. 6. Yoruba oral literature and women. 7. Yoruba rites and customs. 8. Yoruba secret societies. I. Title.

Revised Edition
Fourth Printing 2018

Frontispiece: *Odù-Ọbàtálá at Work: Cosmic Fundamentals*
2013 © Oyadare. Used by Permission

Manufactured in the United States of America

For Odùduwà

Mo ní Mọlẹ̀: Mọlẹ̀ ní mi

She conceived her Self
She nestled into my warm womb
empowered with the blood of the Gods
and she whispered, *Take care of me*

I birthed her
with help from no one
and attacks by everyone

I collected heads with Ọya's own sword
to protect her

I listened as she uttered
ancient wisdom through my labia
I deciphered the codes she murmured
while coaxing milk of my breasts
I chronicled her truths
because she said, *Take care of me*

I allowed no
vapid racist "editor"
to sully these sacred leaves with intentional errors
in hopes of turning this Power
against its Self
No.

I refused
to let an egomaniac smear
his name on her pristine face and body
prop his feet up on the fine latticework of her spine
and sear her immaculate melanin
with the whip scaring brands of
neoenslaving entitlement
No.

Like Òrúnmìlà, I am entrusted with the
invaluable
in/tangible
irrepressible
Soulforce of the Cosmos

Òrun's ìlà course
from Odù's womb
to my own
through my fingertips
from my bones
She comes
undiluted
unpolluted
boasting a glory of
"Perfect Imperfections"[1]
She
is
You
are
holding
in your hands
your own
healing truth
your breathing
living proof

Shimmering with womb-fresh fragility
reverberating with Cosmos-deep profundity
She commands you,
Take care of me

Your newborn
Power's request:
Take care of me

Onímọlẹ̀

TABLE OF CONTENTS

Acknowledgements / ix

Notes on Style / xi

Introduction: The Womb is a Cosmos /
The Cosmos is a Womb — 1

1. Odù: The Mother with a Womb Filled with Gods — 19

2. The Vagina Gives Birth to the World:
   Àjẹ́'s Signs, Symbols, and Orders of Operation — 58

3. Àwọn Ìyá Wa in the Ẹsẹ Ifá — 111

4. "The Left is for the Gods":
   Àjẹ́ in Secret Societies and Sacred Institutions — 152

5. The Mothers and Their Powers and Their Sons:
   The Influence of Àjẹ́ on Olatubosun Oladapo,
   Wole Soyinka, Fela Anikulapo Kuti, and Toyin Falola — 200

Conclusion: The Very Definition of Evil — 241

Notes / 254

Bibliography / 289

Index / 299

ACKNOWLEDGEMENTS

The radiance of the divine shined on me when I met Chief Ìyálájé Oyeronke Igbinola. Thank you for sharing your immortal wisdom with me. It does not matter that you will not be able to physically hold this book: It is because of you that this book exists. May this volume stand as a testament to your depth, power, and immortality. Àikú parí ìwà!

Samuel M. Opeola, your wisdom has been so influential to me in so many monumental ways: from my Ph.D., to my first book, to this one, and beyond. You have my eternal thanks and praise.

During a visit to the University of Ibadan, I was fortunate to meet renowned Yoruba poet and lyricist Olatubosun Oladapo who was kind enough to give me a signed copy of *Orin Odídẹrẹ́: Àjẹ́ Ọlọ́mọ*, a potent praisesong of profundity! Thank you for challenging me with your powerful ode. Your dynamic verses stand as examples of the immeasurably rich works that Yoruba visionaries have been undertaking in Yoruba language in the heart of the Yoruba world from time immemorial!

I am especially grateful to Rowland Abiodun: Everything I have written is undergirded with your wisdom. Thank you for sharing your rich knowledge with me—and with the world!

I am grateful to Kayode Adeduntan who was gracious enough to respond to my timid cyber greetings and generous enough to share with me his groundbreaking research on Àjẹ́.

I am most appreciative of James I. Adedayo a brilliant and innovative artist who shared with me vital information about the roles of Àjẹ́ in king-making.

I am thankful for the four winds of the world that coalesce around me to form Ọya's Tornado!

...

Writing a book: Difficult. Writing two books with one hand while cradling, nursing, and raising a child with the other: Impossible—unless the child is assisting and funneling wisdom, power, and divinity to the Mother as surely as she sucks sustenance, glory, and perfection from the breast...

This book is for you, Odùduwà. Arm Leg Leg Arm Head! The Ultra Dynamic! Ìyá Ọràǹyàn! Ọmọ Fela! Ọmọ Qaddafi! Ọmọ Miles! Ọmọ Ìyàmi Àbẹ̀ni! Ọmọgbọ́n! By growing in my womb, springing forth from my vagina, and claiming my breasts as your own you have taught me more about Àjẹ́ than I could have learned from any other source. You have taught me about myself as well. With you by my side, the impossible is so easy that I marvel at my productivity.

Everything I do is for you because you are Everything: Ayé mi, Òrìṣà mi, Òṣùpá mi, Ọ̀run mi, Ìráwọ́ mi. Not only are you the only family that I have, I now realize that you are the only family that I ever had. When you place your head between my breasts, wrap your arms around me, and squeeze, I know that there was no love before your love, ra ra. Thank you for choosing me. Thank you for teaching me: Every day you introduce me to another wonder! Ìwọ dá mi Abiyamọ gidi gidi. You make of my body a Shrine: Let us pray.

NOTES ON STYLE

African words and the author's neologisms are italicized in the first usage only. Proper nouns are not italicized unless they are italicized in a direct quotation.

Yoruba is an extraordinarily complex and fluid language. To avoid unintentional insult or error and to maintain consistency, with the exception of direct quotations, the proper names of academics and authors are not tone-marked unless such marks are necessary to avoid confusion.

INTRODUCTION

THE WOMB IS A COSMOS / THE COSMOS IS A WOMB

Despite all of the wonders of modern science and medicine—even the ability to create penises and vaginas and grant them to individuals desirous of obtaining the organs they were denied at birth—no man will ever know what a woman knows. No man will ever know the body's signal and celebration of its ability to create and sustain life, which is menstruation. No man will ever feel the subterranean twist of menstrual cramps, which are the womb's way of preparing itself and its owner for the contractions of labor. No man can be tickled by the silken whisper of the first drops of menses. No, no man will ever hear the conversation of the fallopian tubes as they usher sperm to a waiting egg or decree that the sperm and egg are not compatible and stymie fertilization. No man will ever feel the gentle expansion of the womb—from the size of a fist to the perfect arc of the most significant covenant on this Earth—as the body makes room for a life that it creates and nourishes spontaneously. No man will ever be privy to the conversation the unborn child has with her mother when she tells her: "I am perfect. My birth and life and destiny are assured. I cannot but be magnificent: I am you returning."

What man can boast knowledge of the gentle muted taps and pops that are the child's first movements? What father will ever feel his daughter's contained autonomy as she plays, giggles, and flips in the womb or as she sleeps inside of or along with mother while dreaming her own dreams? A father may hear his child hiccupping in the womb, but he cannot know what those gentle pitches feel like as they reverberate within. He cannot know the feel of the tickle of his daughter's delicate fingers trailing across the walls of the safest home she will ever know.

Mother's perfect body directs its own and all others' destinies. It expands from womb to hips to vaginal lips to accommodate the ultimate directive. Her womb fills with water of its own accord: No man can direct, dam, or diminish her flow. And when it is time for her daughter to leave the home and the womb of God and enter this world, only Mother can feel the velvet caress of the hair of her child's head as she emerges from the vagina.

Yes
Mother is God
Show me another
who can reproduce both
her Self and her fertilizing Other
You owe your existence
to the
choice
made by your
Mother

"In my womb there's a universe"[1]

"Mother" is the definition of "Creator," in both literal and divine senses. Every human being to ever exist on this Earth owes his life to the menses, ova, womb, and decisions of his mother. And it is because of her obvious yet understated numinosity and her complete control over life that organized religious fanatics have maligned, distorted, trivialized, and vilified the Mother and her truth, character, and definition.

Schoolteacher of Toni Morrison's *Beloved* decreed that "definitions [belong] to the definers—not the defined."[2] "The definers," bolstered by the power they vested in themselves, have sought to crush everything into linguistic-political submission. In *Yurugu: An African-Centered Critique of European Cultural Thought and Behavior*, Marimba Ani asserts that the compulsion to categorize, delimit, and control everything in the world is central to the Caucasian ethos.[3] This pathological obsession is evident in Judeo-Christian beliefs and the attempts of its mythmakers to dictate and even legislate that patriarchal fantasy take the place of scientific reality. Manufacturing male Gods who conjure something from nothing and create humans from ribs and Gods from beams of light all in the concerted effort to avoid the womb, which the Christian God and his saviors and apostles despise and abhor, is a study in self-hatred because it is not possible to love one's self while hating one's source, foundation, and cause of existence.[4]

The patriarchy's power probes and perambulations are most evident in its unflagging attempts to control the womb and its owner and its fruit through laws. The signature example of legalized domination is the institution of marriage. The Caucasian man created the patriarchal label or "brand" known as "surname" to extend his dominion over "his" wife and progeny.[5] Such domestic tyranny allows men to mitigate their feelings of inadequacy by claiming ownership of human beings and by "legitimizing" that which can never be illegitimate—human life.

After using laws and religion to enslave, colonize, and claim possession of and exert power over all life on Earth and the Earth itself, the

Caucasian man seeks to project his property line into the infinite. Eurocentric pseudoscience, with its roots firmly grounded in the ignorance to which it is dependent, has indoctrinated the world to believe that the most advanced and intelligent being on this planet and in the entire universe is the Caucasian male. This overwhelming desire to direct the course of and dominate everything that exists has led to stunning destructions and depravities and to telling silences in the face of readily observable facts.

The Earth is a living organism. Were it not living, humans, flora, and fauna could not gain endless sustenance, regeneration, and bounty from it. The living Earth supports the lives of infinite entities. There is life everywhere. It is neither possible nor necessary to create something from nothing because there is never nothing; there is always something—even if it is unseen, ignored, or misunderstood. Microscopic organisms are thriving on and in our bodies aiding digestion, creating cancers, and fighting infections. The air we breathe is filled with living organisms. Our clouds, stratosphere, thermosphere, exosphere and, yes, "space" are all living, life-supporting organisms.

Contrary to what Western science seeks to reify through vehement proclamation, "space" is not mere "space"; it is not a "void"; it is obviously not "empty"; and it is most definitely not a "vacuum." When viewing NASA's raw-feed videos of "space," including such space shuttle missions as STS-48, STS-63, STS-75, and STS-80, it is apparent that "space" is the home of diverse organisms that are constantly interacting, creating, fertilizing, enriching, and empowering.[6]

When observing the Earth's interactions with and within the Cosmos, the Earth appears to be a huge fertile egg revolving in perfectly black cosmic loam that nourishes, guides, motivates, and directs the movements of living forms and forces in the Cosmos that travel at varying rates of speed and throb, bob, weave, and pulsate with light. These forms direct their courses through, to, within, and around Earth in such a way that many resemble sperm, complete with flagellate, that sink into the Earth's upper atmosphere as if drawn to a waiting vibrating ovum.[7] However, if we are to envision the Earth as a life-giving egg, it is merely one tiny egg out of dozens of zillions that were given life by and are endlessly giving life within a grand cosmic womb.

The elegant dynamism of our galaxy exists within a gargantuan Cosmos that is shimmering, expanding, and throbbing with life, intelligence, and power. The Cosmos could and should be considered the Womb of Wombs. While the comparison of the universe to a womb highlights the significance of the womb of woman; the analogy is not merely for illustrative purposes. What happens in the womb of every woman reflects what is happening throughout the Cosmos.

The Africans of Kemet (Ancient Egypt) understood that Womb and Woman represent the Universe. This is apparent in the God Nwt who is depicted as the firmament with the Sun eternally cycling through her mouth, body, womb, and vagina.[8] Heralding the womb as Ilé Ọlẹ̀, the Home of Embryos, ancient Yoruba cosmologists, biologists, and scientists also understood the twinning of Woman and Cosmos: They are both teeming with life, and they are both sources of existence.

Just as the Cosmos contains infinite galaxies, each female is born with millions of eggs that collectively and individually represent infinite human possibilities. Each egg bears its own destiny and plots its own path in alignment with but also independent of the mother. In concord with the revolution and rotation of the Moon, eggs leave ovaries and journey through fallopian tubes to the womb. When applicable, the vagina ushers sperm along its silken path to unite with the eggs. The womb decrees if and when fertilized eggs should divide and multiply themselves exponentially in the supreme mathematics of existence.

Mother is Cosmos: The Cosmos is a womb: The womb is a miniature universe. Just as the Cosmos creates stars, supernovas, galaxies, and planets, so too does the diversity of humanity find its origin in the womb of woman. Every human being must sip, sleep in, and swim in the rich amniotic elixir of Mother. The uterine perfection that ensures existence finds its home in the core of the mother where it is hidden and its mysteries, innerworkings, powers, truths, and proofs are revealed only to its owner. No matter which secrets she chooses to share, one thing is certain: Only Mother is capable of creation. Only a mother can bring to life both another mother and a son. "Son" is the appropriate term for males because every male is the genetic offspring of and incomplete but independently-functioning aspect of Woman. Every man is but a son before every woman. The daughter fresh from the womb is a mother before her own father and grandfather because she holds within her body the forces that ensure their continuity. Mother is the only force capable of supporting life *in vitro* and ensuring the external survival of that life through her breasts alone for at least a year. Mother is perfect; she is complete. She has every tool that man boasts. She also has what man lacks.

That woman is the source of life and constitutes a complete and autonomous entity is reflected in her chromosomes. Each X chromosome is a sure, well-defined, and powerful signifying and vivifying force. The so-called Y chromosome is not a "Y" in fact; it is a deformed and incomplete X chromosome. Man's partial and malformed chromosome and his anatomy are indicative of his secondary role in the creative process: Men have breasts that do not normally lactate and that cannot nourish or sustain life; the protecting and guiding labia of women are the distended, fragile, and vulnerable testes of men; the penis is an elongated clitoris. While man's external genitalia serve as obvious reminders that the complete power of a full X chromosome is diminished and altered in him, man does not have a womb and there is no male equivalent of the womb.[9]

The cosmic decision-making and genetic processes that Mother undertook to create sons is, as of yet, unknown. Perhaps she determined that, rather than continue to do and be all, she should remold her self and reallocate power in such a way as to create a partner who would provide assistance and introduce the concepts of gender balance and complementarity to this world. The son could simply be a genetic mutation. Whatever his origin, his future is uncertain. Geneticists have found that the Y chromosome, already fragile and undefined, is degenerating:

> [T]he Y chromosome, which once contained as many genes as the X chromosome, has deteriorated over time and now contains less than 80 functional genes compared to its partner, which contains more than 1,000 genes. Geneticists and evolutionary biologists determined that the Y chromosome's deterioration is due to accumulated mutations, deletions and anomalies that have nowhere to go because the chromosome doesn't swap genes with the X chromosome like every other chromosomal pair in our cells do.[10]

The deterioration and, perhaps, termination of the Y chromosome and maybe even "man," as we known him, may elucidate why men felt it was necessary to create patriarchy, organized phallocentric religions, sexist language, genital excision and mutilation, femicide—whether through sex-selective abortion or so-called "honor" killings—and so much more. Perhaps these concerted actions are males' attempts, both unconscious and deliberate, to either secure their existence or reverse an irreversibly doomed destiny. The deterioration of the Y chromosome and many men's loathing of females are especially ironic in that the father's genetic contribution determines the sex of a child. Around the world, women are beaten, betrayed, and divorced for giving birth to girls whose gender was chosen at the dawn of their existences by their fathers.

Is man creating his own replacements in whole and empowered daughters? Could it be possible that God created man, as we know him, with an expiration date? Did she create man simply to fertilize enough eggs to bring the population of women to a tipping point where men are rendered obsolete and women regain full control from clitoris to continent to Cosmos? Has man either fulfilled or so corrupted his destiny that Mother Creator is recalling, recycling, refashioning, or reformulating him? Will she upgrade or eradicate him? If we are to use man's treatment of woman (in all of her forms: human being, earth, Earth, Cosmos) as an indicator of his fate, we will be bidding him *adieu*. Is there time for him to redirect his destiny by committing to his soul Mother's Law? If there is, then he can start by acknowledging the architect of his existence: Àjẹ́.

Although some geneticists, historians, and anthropologists are reluctant to admit it, the African woman is the mother of all. Known in Yoruba cosmology and science as Yewájọbí (The Mother of All of the Gods and of All Living Things) and "the Mother of All and the mother of mothers,"[11] and known to Western scientists and anthropologists as "mitochondrial African eve" (a term that reveals Judeo-Christianity's influence on Western "science"), an African woman is quite simply "the most recent common female ancestor of everyone alive today."[12]

The Yoruba assert that Ilé-Ifẹ̀ is the site of the world's origin and that the Yoruba are directly descended from the Gods. It is not uncommon for the Yoruba to describe themselves as a unique and superlative race of human beings.[13] Perhaps the chromosomal composition of the Yoruba can help elucidate these claims. In a study titled "A Map of Recent Positive Selection in the Human Genome," a team of geneticists found that the Yoruba "[appear] to have a greater number of signals on the X chromosome that map to genes compared with the other two populations [Europeans and East Asians]."[14]

That the Yoruba have a greater ability to map and select genes has profound biological and cosmological implications and may very well indicate not only superiority in genetic selection and biological creation but, perhaps, divinity. What is more, while hemoglobin variations are prevalent in the various melanin-rich peoples of the world, as their bodies boast unique defenses against malaria, a subset of Yoruba people boast their own unique variance, Hemoglobin C.[15]

It could very well be the case that the distinctions in the hemoglobin and the genes of certain Yoruba populations are the hallmarks of Yewájọbí and signify her select and direct progeny. This would be in consonance with the fact that the Yoruba woman bears the most elemental manifestation of Yewájọbí's biological and biochemical creative force: Àjẹ́. Àjẹ́ is a spiritual power resident in menstrual blood that can create lives, impart sacred genetic coding, and devolve destinies. Yewájọbí's blood is the source of Àjẹ́, and Yewájọbí's daughters are the very embodiments of her and the direct recipients of her divine blood. Consequently, when one sees an Africana woman, one is seeing Àjẹ́: the Source, the Creator, the God.

In traditional African societies, community members, especially African sons, are actively involved in maintaining the covenants of creation, creativity, and continuity within and outside of the womb. Sons logically herald their mothers as Gods because Divine Mother is neither mystery nor anomaly. She is not an imaginary vapor in the ether. She is right here offering her breasts, embraces, and endless bounty. By contrast, Christian Caucasian colonizers gazed upon the African woman and saw a power that they did not create, did not understand, could not define, and could not control. Upon deeper inspection, they realized that her force was also their source. Rather than celebrate their reunion, Caucasian colonizers turned their attention to crushing the quiet African dynamo who reminded them of the paradise lost many millennia ago.

Armed with diverse tools of subjugation, the Caucasian man introduced the Mother of All to what he claimed to be an accursed destiny: The African mother had to be made to know and assume her proper place as a subhuman subordinate in the Caucasian colonizers' world and worldview. To further the othering of Mother, Caucasian colonizing missionaries reached into their bag of tricks, pulled out Genesis 3:15, and began sowing diseased seeds of enmity among African women and men and children.

The founders of patriarchy realized long ago that one of the most effective ways to gain control over a woman's person and power is by convincing her that her womb, vagina, labia, fallopian tubes, and breasts are polluted and polluting sources of "original sin" and "evil." Caucasian scholars even projected their ignorance about and loathing of the womb into the image of Nwt cyclically giving everlasting life to the Sun.[16] Because they were unable to comprehend or unwilling to respect the dynamic interactivity of Kemetic medicine, early Caucasian physicians and psychologists divorced the esoteric from the exoteric and crafted a peculiar construct of a "wandering womb" that roamed throughout the body leaving disease in its wake. This perfect misunderstanding of human biology gave birth to the concept of *hysteria*, which is translated as "sickness of the womb" and has its root in the Greek word for womb, *hystera*.[17] The cure for hysteria, the disease caused by this roving rogue organ, is hysterectomy: removal of the womb. Hysteria was actually considered a bona fide psychological illness until 1980, and millions of women around the world were given—and are still given—hysterectomies to cure what pseudo-scientists determined to be their wombs' sickness.[18]

The concept of the uterus being sick and sickening is central to Christianity. Millions of converts are baptized every year in an attempt to rinse off the filth that patriarchy's self-loathing has injected into the womb, and, by association, humanity. Baptism is Christianity's ritualized, institutionalized, and internationalized womb-hatred. According to the Christian worldview, humanity's only hope upon emerging from the womb is in submission to a father and a dunking in or sprinkling of water he has decreed holy. Any woman not cleansed and approved by the patriarchy will be overcome by her filthy wandering womb and morph into a witch.[19] And, as the Bible informs us, a witch cannot be suffered to live.

Repeat After Me: There is No Such Thing as an African Witch

Àjẹ́, Ìyàmi Òṣòròngà, Àwọn Ìyá Wa, and other divine manifestations of the Mother are not synonymous with, akin to, or the equivalents of any type of "witch" or "witchcraft." "Witch" is a word and concept of Old English etymological, geographical, and cultural origin. The word specifically defines Caucasian cultural and religious concepts and preoccupations. The constructs of "witchcraft" and "witch" did not exist in any manner on the African continent prior to the Caucasian penetration, colonization, and ideological manipulation of Africa. There are no such things as "African witchcraft," "African witches," or "African witchdoctors"; all of these fictions sprang from the obtuse, morally bankrupt, and scientifically stunted minds of Caucasian missionary colonizers. Even though missionaries and scholars successfully globalized the "African witch" myth in their attempt to mystify and trivialize the scientifically, technologically, and spiritually superior Africans that they encountered, the only "witches" in Africa at present are those imported or held over from Caucasian nations and imaginations.

One gains greater insight about the origin of "African witches" by comparing their confessions and deeds to those of their Caucasian counterparts. African and Caucasian "witch" testimonies are often nearly identical because African "witch" confessions, accusations, trials, and lynchings commenced under the tutelage of Caucasians who used mistranslation, miseducation, capitalistic exploitation, and religious indoctrination to foment and justify the massacres of dissidents.[20]

In *The African Genius*, Basil Davidson hypothesizes that the economic, mental, familial, and cultural instabilities wrought by colonization facilitated the reification and concretization of the "African witchcraft" myth:

> Most observers seem agreed that witchcraft fears have much increased in Africa over the past fifty or a hundred years, and also that these fears are less controlled than they used to be by social restraints or other in-built protective mechanisms. . . . [T]he reason appears to lie in the disintegration of traditional structures and systems since the 1880s: in the passing of Africa's age of faith, and consequently in a growth of personal anxiety and alienation. No longer checked by the dykes of traditional precedent, witchcraft fears have fed on new or greatly increased mental and social strains.[21]

It is telling that Davidson links the spread of African "witchcraft fears" to the European colonization of Africa, which began in the 1880s and was formalized during the Berlin Conference of 1884–1885. Essential components of the colonization of Africa included not only the physical domination and enslavement of Africans in Africa but also the Christian indoctrination and crusade-mandated slaughter of Africans in Africa. The "personal anxiety and alienation" to which Davidson refers are two of the lesser ills born of the Caucasian colonization of Africa and its bloody battle to destroy African wisdom workers and knowledge systems.

Colonization wrought innumerable and seemingly unending disasters in Africa, and the "African witchcraft" construct is especially important to colonial and neocolonial objectives because it foments the destruction of African power, identity, and divinity at the source by literally and figuratively lynching the African mother.

When European colonizers probed, tricked, and schemed to arrive at the center of the African ethos, worldview, philosophy, culture, polity, and family they found what they feared the most: Woman. Fertile, over-abundant, aglow with undiluted melanin, and armed with an electric clitoris; ever-in-birth and always creating; the Divine Mother radiating Àjẹ́ in prismatic waves is the Truth. What is more, everywhere they looked, colonizers found exact duplicates of Divine Mother strolling around, nursing children, singing oríkì, harvesting crops, giving birth, hunting, and leading wars against oppressors when men offered sighs of resignation.

In order for the Caucasian conquest of Africa to be complete and include the colonization of the African mind, Mother, who served as the educator, physician, comforter, historian, empowerer, galvanizer, catalyst, and creator, had to be denuded of power. She had to be raped of her secrets and then reviled and renounced by not only her own husbands and children but by her sister-selves as well. The Mother who orchestrated existence effortlessly and perfectly had to be disgraced and replaced. With the memories of the stench of burning human flesh, the titillation of hyper-sexual confessions, and the images of the always-successful dunkings of their own "witch trials" dancing in their minds, Caucasian political and religious colonizers knew the tremendous damage that the "witch" construct could foment, and they deployed it.

The "African witch" myth was used to disgrace and the Caucasian father myth was appointed to replace the African Mother. Such gems as the mark of Cain and the curse of Ham reified the racist assertion that everything African, everything born of this Mother, was evil. While Maxim guns stood at the ready when racist myths failed, the "witch" concept proved especially expedient for Caucasian colonizers who fancied themselves more humane than King Leopold II and his massacring minion. Caucasian missionary colonizers need not dirty *their* hands by pointing out and slaughtering "African witches." Once the conversions began and indoctrination was complete, Africans would single out and turn upon their own mothers, daughters, sisters, aunts, and grandmothers—and fathers, brothers, and grandfathers as well. Having provided both the terminology and the methodology of eradication, Caucasians could sit back, point to the "Dark Continent" that they created, and muse, "Yes, here is a land of primitive, savage, superstitious, backward individuals: They actually still believe in and kill or ostracize 'witches.' Tsk, tsk, tsk."

Of all the propaganda introduced to Africa, the "African witch" earned a special place in the colonizers' curriculum of indoctrination. A comprehensive campaign—akin to a global gang rape—was mounted, and the results are stunning. The "African witch" is targeted in quiet communities and pilloried in local newspapers. She is the sensational star of multitudinous movies, and the she is the subject of unrelenting academic probes. Indeed, it would not be erroneous to posit that the reification of "African witchcraft" could not have occurred without the efforts of academic colonizers who published and consequently (and magically) made fact such fictions as African paganism, heathenism, cannibalism, and, of course, witchcraft.

What Fela Anikulapo Kuti might call "academic magic" has continued unabated. One can find any number of published works discussing "African witches" or describing Àjẹ́ as a malevolent and malignant force that is synonymous with "witchcraft." The casual way by which "African witchcraft" has been legitimized in many academic, religious, entertainment, and social institutions and publications is simply bizarre, and it is also profoundly contradictory, as Ayo Adeduntan elucidates in his perfectly titled and expertly argued exposition "Calling Àjẹ́ Witch In Order To Hang Her: Yoruba Patriarchal Definition and Redefinition of Female Power," which I discuss in chapter five.[22]

The pervasive and often default demonization of Àjẹ́ is especially disturbing in that Àjẹ́ is manifest in all Africana women, and to call one mother a witch is to condemn us all. I am the daughter of a mother who longed to have a daughter. I am the mother of a daughter whom I longed to have. The very thought that I or my mother—or anyone's mother—would be plotting to kill and devour—literally, figuratively, or spiritually—the very child whom she chose to have and whom she risked her life to push into this world is a heinous accusation from the most deranged of minds. However, academic books and articles offer such allegations as standard fare. The same researchers who would not have the courage to label all Caucasian women witches or who would cringe, be incensed, or laugh at the very thought of such an assertion, have no qualms about labeling Africana women in such an offensive manner.

Another tired workhorse that is routinely trotted out in discussions about Àjẹ́ is that the power and its wielders have the ability to do both good and evil. . . Who and what does *not* have the ability to be, be labeled as, and be used for both good and evil? Legions of priests, rabbis, pastors, imams, babaláwo, and popes can testify to the fact that anything and anyone—especially religions, religious leaders and figures, and actions undertaken in the name of an alleged God or for a supposed good—have been and will continue to be used to do the most evil most effectively.

The good/evil dichotomy does nothing more than serve as the carryall for the psychological baggage that colonizers and missionaries dragged with them to Africa and used to facilitate oppression. "Good" and "evil" are subjective constructs that reveal nothing about one's character, motivations, or intentions. To assert that Àjẹ́ can be both or either good and/or evil is a concession that cleverly extends tacit approval to accusations and definitions of "evil" while admitting that the elusive "good witch" might exist. The fact that a Western dichotomous delineation is completely inappropriate for such holistic African concepts as Àjẹ́ is routinely and intentionally ignored so that the most unabashedly infantile and derogatory terms and constructs can be employed to reduce complex and multidimensional African phenomena to utter nonsense.

Academic, religious, and economic colonizers did their work well. The fairytales of Europe have become reality in parts of Africa where "witch camps" have been established to house male and female elders who have been blamed for illnesses and accidents and been banished from their homes.[23] Conscientious Africans are debating whether they should renovate and modernize the "witch villages" so their inhabitants can live in peace, security, and comfort or whether they should demolish the villages and make the erection of such illegal, thereby forcing communities to find more sensible ways of handling grief and misfortune than picking out a scapegoat and creating more misery.

Hajia Hawawu Boya Gariba, the Deputy Minister for Women and Children's Affairs in Ghana, has taken a resolute stand against "witch villages":

> Gariba said the ministry would be doing everything that it could to ensure the practice of families and neighbors banishing women from communities whom they suspected of being witches is abolished by developing legislation that would make it illegal to accuse someone of being a witch and gradually closing down camps and reintegrating women back into their communities.
>
> "This practice has become an indictment on the conscience of our society," Ms. Gariba said at the conference called Towards

> Banning "Witches" Camps. "The labeling of some of our kinsmen and women as witches and wizards and banishing them into camps where they live in inhuman and deplorable conditions is a violation of their fundamental human rights."[24]

Unfortunately, in contemporary societies enslaved to capitalism and Christianity, the profitability of dehumanization often trumps human rights.

In Akwa Ibom in Cross Rivers State, Nigeria, some Christian evangelists have created a wildly lucrative business by accusing children in their congregations of being "witches."[25] These accusations lead families to abuse and abandon their children or pay thousands of dollars for exorcisms. So many children had been ostracized that in 2009 that the banished children united and drew up a proposal that would make it illegal to accuse someone of being a witch. The proposal is now a law in Akwa Ibom.[26]

One should not be so appalled by the modern phenomena of adult children accusing elderly parents; parents accusing infants, toddlers, and adolescents; and pastors accusing their flock of "witchcraft" that one fails to see both the similarities in these modern African accusations and those of early Caucasia and the financial motivations fuelling both Caucasian and African "witch" accusations.

Wherever Christianity exists there one also finds capitalism. This dynamic makes it possible for multitudes to profit off of various myths—such as "witchcraft"—and the profiteers include the sanctimonious contemporary Caucasian missionaries who create charities and secure donations to help the poor Africans find their way out of the psychological, cultural, and religious morass bequeathed them by their colonizing Christian forefathers. Many contemporary Christian churches, missionaries, ministries, and charities are not only as dependent on and in service to the myth of "witchcraft" as they were in the 17th century, but they owe their identities, careers, and wealth to this myth.

Perhaps you are wondering, is there not *some* truth in the gory accusations made about "African witches?" To that I say, think about your mother. You need not ponder anything more than the fact that you exist and are able to think. That alone should reveal to you the evil that lurks in her heart. You may never know the rapes, the hours spent sweating in fields and factories, the humiliation, the pain, the tears, the loneliness, the rage, the rapture, or the ruptures that she endured for you to have the luxury to ponder if she or another mother daydreams about sucking the soul out of you. If you, like all too many of us, have been raised on a steady diet of disrespect for Africana women fuelled by a global mass media that specializes in overt and covert Africana denigration, then think of yourself: How many times have you looked at your child and wondered what a tasty spiritual or actual meal he would make?

The Gods Who Give Birth to Gods

Àwọn Ìyá Wa are the superlative manifestations of our actual mothers. Our mothers do not plot to destroy, devour, or maim us. Were it not for them, we would not exist. Human life is dependent on the wombs and choices of our mothers, and this simple fact forms the foundation of the eternal bond between the African mother and child. This bond is so important that Àjẹ́ created essential social institutions—including polygamy—and various prohibitions to protect the ultimate dyad. The labors of Àjẹ́ are everywhere evident in traditional Yoruba society, and everything from ritual festivals to the Earth's topography, supports the fundamental dyad of mother and child.

In *A Mouth Sweeter than Salt*, Toyin Falola discusses the festival in honor of Òkè, the great hill of the town of Ìbàdàn who is Mother, God, Àjẹ́ manifest. With his description of Òkè, the reader better understands the organic, gentle, holistic, and undeniable force that is Àjẹ́ and its impact on men, women, children, and the Yoruba landscape:

> It was relatively easy to placate the hill. Men had surrendered their power to it, making the hill and the spirit who lives in it a woman with attractive breasts and gentle manners. The pot that contained the sacrificial food for the hill was shaped like a woman. To reach for the pot . . . was not only to pray but to take water from it. One could even buy small qualities of the water from the pot . . . to use for charms to end barrenness, request more children, and cure a variety of illnesses. The hill's breasts were abnormal in size and number. If the normal woman had two, the hill had sixteen because of the large number of children she must feed. And she fed them very well. The hill was presented as gentle, pro-family, kind, and favorably disposed toward women and children. The priests of the hill, though men, dressed like women, with plaited hair, fake breasts, and white wrappers. The priests carried both male and female attributes but presented themselves more as women so that the hill, now of the same sex, would be more merciful.[27]

It is not the case that men need surrender their power to Òkè. Male priests are cognizant that they derive infinite power and sustenance from Òkè and her monumental breasts and healing vaginal waters, which are replicated in every woman. Rather than emasculate men, Òkèbàdàn moves men to access their inner Àjẹ́ and adorn themselves with the symbols of biological and divine perfection so as to be as close to the Mother as possible. Rather than threaten or devour her children, Àjẹ́ Òkè has sixteen breasts to ensure their vitality. Women gaze upon Òkèbàdàn and witness the magnified reflection of their own numinosity. Everyone has a space of honor and respect before Òkè Àjẹ́, and Mother has breasts, milk, love, and room for all because everyone is the result of and responsible for the evolution of Àjẹ́. Rather than destroying, maiming, and coercing, Àjẹ́ Òkè protects and uplifts everyone in the community, and everyone heralds her eternal efforts.

The Òkèbàdàn festival features the celebration and appreciation of the genitals, which are rightly honored for they are the storehouses of existence from whence many Divinities spring. During the festival, every aspect of human procreation is heralded, teased, taunted, embraced, and explicated by everyone. While the songs Òkè's progeny sing might shock those who have been trained to be ashamed of the human body and the undulations that bring human beings into existence, these songs reveal how African societies in general and Yoruba societies in particular encourage the formation of healthy relationships with one's own body, with the opposite sex, and with the delights of sex. The songs also reveal how openness and exploration prevent such Western problems as generation gaps, frigidity, and self-loathing from forming.

The songs are logical in their explanation of the supreme mathematics of existence: "Penis times vagina equals penis / Vagina times penis equals vagina."[28] Onomatopoeia is employed to reproduce the sound of a vagina being hit by a long penis. Men are mocked for having "dangling, dangling, dangling" scrotums; women are teased for opening their vaginas "too wide."[29] Songs describe the genitals reflecting the occupations of their owners: "Teacher's penis / Enveloped in chalk. / Mechanic's penis / full of oil."[30] Every member of society without exception, from the ditch digger to the king, is subject to be described in song because every member of society comes to this world thanks to copulation and nurturance in arc of the Mother's covenant. Furthermore, everyone will use his and her empowered genitals to engage in sex and conceive new Gods in the form of children who are so dynamic they can walk the day after birth.[31] In celebrating Òkè, one is celebrating Life. In celebrating Life, one is celebrating Àjẹ́. The songs sung during Òkèbàdàn festival reveal how healthy and logical this society is, especially when compared to cultures that describe the genitals as dirty and polluting "private parts."

The key celebrant of Òkèbàdàn is Òkè, who could be considered a magnificent clitoris resonating with accessible and diverse power. The clitoris is made up of the same tissues as the penis and responds to stimuli in the same manner, indeed, some women ejaculate as do men, but the clitoris is perhaps 100 times more sensitive than the penis.[32] Just as the clitoris is a tiny electrifying reminder of woman's inherent comprehensiveness, Òkè is heralded as a consummate creator. In addition to the maternal attributes of multiple breasts and a fecund vagina, Òkè is also "the possessor of the penis," and it is a "tough" and "big penis" that she uses to both playfully hit men and enter the vagina with vigor.[33] Everything one finds in humanity, one finds in this God, Òkè Àjẹ́. And rather than despising the genitals, asserting that knowledge of them brings shame and evil, or demanding that the genitals be neutered during worship, Òkè encourages sex, sexual knowledge, sexual banter, and sexual play: The passion-play of man and woman and the frolicking of the child *in vitro* are re-membered holistically by the creation-oriented community.

Ever-birthing and ever-nursing, Òkè is a repository of a divine amniotic fluid which is a healing elixir and fertility aid, and while Òkè is "the one with the biggest breasts," they are not for sexual play, but for the sustenance of children.[34] The Yoruba woman's goal is to become like Òkè in every way and to be the God who gives birth to Gods. Consequently, when she successfully conceives a child, woman is complete and her status is reflected in the songs sung to tease her:

> Thou pregnant woman
> What a pity
> Your vagina has gone on leave
> For three years
> Your vagina is on leave.[35]

Mother turns her attention away from sex to focus on the most important job in the world—creating life. To assist the expecting mother in her sacred labors, her body's hormones decrease her sex drive, and this physiological shift works in conjunction with the Yoruba cultural prohibition that forbids men from having sex with pregnant women.[36] As the life developing in the core of her being directs mother's womb to fill with the richest and healthiest waters in the world and expand in the sacred arc of creation, mother becomes Òkè; her own life-filled hill is proof of her power.

In traditional African societies, post-partum sex is prohibited immediately after birth for obvious reasons: Mother's body needs time to fully close, contract, and recover, and this process can take approximately one year. However, the traditional ban on post-partum sex is extended indefinitely because nursing mothers are forbidden from having sex. This prohibition ensures the sanctity and integrity of mother's milk, and this is of paramount importance to both mother and child for breast milk can be contaminated by semen-borne diseases.

Many mothers choose to breastfeed for several years, and the ban on sex works in concert with polygamy to provide these mothers with all the time and space they desire to nurse their children. Mother's body also assists her in the goal of fortifying the world's most important union. Because the hormone oxytocin is released during breastfeeding (as well as during orgasm and labor—so efficient, considerate, and well-made is the female body), the lactating mother is suffused in physiological and spiritual satisfaction.[37] The breastfeeding mother finds completion within her self and her child, and vagina's three year sabbatical serves to create a foundation of perfection and power for the very individuals who sing the teasing song and for their children and for their children's children *ad infinitum*.

The focused devotion of mother and the resultant bond between mother and child are also described in a traditional Yoruba song:

>Mother is a precious gold
>That cannot be purchased with money
>She carried me in her womb for nine months
>She nursed me for three years
>Mother is a precious gold
>That cannot be purchased with money[38]

Traditionally, three years is the approximate, often the minimum, amount of time that children breastfeed. Children who are older than three are welcome recipients of the benefits of the bounty of the breast in many Africana communities.

In his autobiography *Of Water and the Spirit: Ritual, Magic, and Initiation in the Life of an African Shaman* Malidoma Somé reveals that although he had been weaned and was approximately four years of age, his mother would nurse him for snacks or when she sensed that he was in need of "tenderness and reassurance."[39] Julie Dash's *Daughters of the Dust* is the first full-length film by an African American woman, and it is a testament to African cultural, linguistic, and spiritual continuity in America, even in the minor character who is named "Ninny Juggs" because he continues to nurse at approximately five years of age.[40] Milkman of Toni Morrison's *Song of Solomon* earns his nickname at the breast in a scene that reveals the conflicts that ensue when "modernized" opinions meet ancient protections.[41] Also in *Song of Solomon*, Milkman's aunt Pilate constantly chews things throughout her life because her mother died before she was born and Pilate was not able to suckle at her breast. The bond that is established when the child's mouth latches onto the mother's breast is so important that Pilate spends a lifetime approximating what she was denied.

The African ancients' view on the importance of breastfeeding, the appropriate duration of breastfeeding, and the role of the father in breastfeeding is beautifully illustrated in a Kemetic frieze that depicts

Hathor nursing her son while they are both standing. Because he can stand and suckle, the son appears to be anywhere from eight to eleven years of age.[42] Not only does the child suckle publicly, but the community immortalized in stone and displayed for eternity the power of this elemental exchange. A significant but easily overlooked feature of this fundamental transference is the father who is depicted as patiently waiting off to the side. In traditional African societies, mother and child are supported by a father who understands that after he has fertilized the egg, man necessarily becomes secondary, even subservient, to the divine Mother and Child dyad which ensures his continuity.

We can learn a lot from the Gods, and they have always been eager teachers, for the wisdom that they share is our knowledge of self. The Gods—from Nwt to Odù to my daughter—teach us lessons about the logic and elegance of the female body and the fact that everything that a woman experiences every month, from water retention to menstrual cramps to menstruation, is preparation for pregnancy, vaginal birth, and breastfeeding. Furthermore, pregnancy, vaginal birth, and breastfeeding are all interactive and fundamental to the health and vitality of the mother and child.[43]

The traditional Yoruba social structure is centered on the protection of the divine dyad and the proliferation of Àjẹ́ because the cosmic directive could not be clearer: The objective of Àjẹ́ is to create more Àjẹ́; in other words, the goal of the Gods is to create more Gods. This work, Mother's ancient work, is the secret of life. Consequently, no matter the attacks engineered to destroy her, Mother and her wonder-working womb will be right here molding the heads of the Gods—gently, gently does she mold them.

. . .

My first book, *Our Mothers, Our Powers, Our Texts: Manifestations of Àjẹ́ in Africana Literature* (*Our Mothers*), explores the power of Àjẹ́ from the inside out to elucidate the undeniable and indelible impact of the Mothers on both Yoruba orature and the literature of men and women of the Pan-African world. With *The Architects of Existence: Àjẹ́ in Yoruba Cosmology, Ontology, and Orature* (*The Architects of Existence*), I move from the inside of this profound power to increasingly deeper levels within—for the study of Àjẹ́ is the study of the infinite. *The Architects of Existence* and *Our Mothers* are companion texts—twins which were conceived in the same intellectual womb; indeed, *The Architects of Existence* is born of the extensive data that I could not fit into *Our Mothers*. However, with its grounding in the ancient, the cosmic, and the fundamental, *The Architects of Existence* is very much the "mother" of

Our Mothers. The Architects of Existence explores the more esoteric aspects of Àjẹ́ that are, in many cases, heretofore unexplored, undefined, and, in some instances, intentionally obfuscated.

My goal is to offer a full elucidation and comprehensive analysis of the profoundly important and vastly influential power known as Àjẹ́. Consequently, *The Architects of Existence* is a study of marked philosophical, cosmological, and ontological depth that examines the power of Àjẹ́ in sacred institutions and secret societies; in the creation and dissemination of the Gods' words and writings; in the signs, symbols, and sons of the Mothers; and in the beginning of time, when the Mothers conceived and gave birth to the Cosmos.

CHAPTER ONE

ODÙ: THE MOTHER WITH A WOMB FILLED WITH GODS

In the Beginning, There Was Womb

Àjẹ́ is a force that is beyond definition, but English approximations for Àjẹ́ would be Power, Creation, Cosmos, and All. Yoruba spiritualist Samuel M. Opeola elucidates the definition and identity of Àjẹ́ in the Yoruba ethos by revealing that "Àjẹ́ actually is Odù."[1] In other words, Odù, the God, and Àjẹ́, the power, are one.

As do many Yoruba concepts and Gods, Odù has cosmic, biological, scientific, and terrestrial properties and manifestations. The mundane translation of odù is pot or caldron. Biologically, the pot symbolizes the womb. Scientifically and metaphysically, the womb represents the Womb of Creation, which rests in the core of the Mother of All.[2] The Womb of Creation is none other than the Cosmos in which the Earth is a microcosmic rotating and revolving sphere. To understand Odù, one must understand the Cosmos, for Odù is God as Cosmos. Àjẹ́ Odù is the infinitely empowered cosmic Blackness that gives form and life to power and light; Odù's vastness exceeds the imaginations and knowledge of most mortals. She is the mother of immeasurable depths who gave birth and gives life to our Earth and trillions of other planets, solar systems, and galaxies: To know Odù Àjẹ́ is to know infinitude.

Gazing into the night sky one sees not empty static space but the undiluted, fecund expansive Blackness of the Womb of Origins. The Cosmos is an immense organ and organism that nurtures and sustains infinite organisms, from the gargantuan to the infinitesimal. The fecundity of the Cosmos is not only analogous to that of human womb, but our inconceivably colossal Cosmos is Odù's womb: That is how vast Àjẹ́ Odù is. Indeed, Yoruba cosmogony reveals that, before they acquired human and divine identities and existences, many Òrìṣà were celestial bodies "representing parts of the heavens, connected with certain constellations."[3] With this information, the depth of the Yoruba understanding of and relationship to the Cosmos is revealed as is the scope and significance of Odù, who holds every constellation, galaxy, planet, and nebula in her womb.

The concept of God as Cosmos, as womb, as physics is also apparent in the cosmogony of the Kemites of Ancient Egypt, who depict the God Nwt as a naked woman stationed in the Cosmos through whose body the Sun travels.[4] A terrestrial perspective can be deceptive: The Sun does not rise or set, but it appears to do these things when viewed from the Earth. Likewise, the Earth appears to be stationary, and yet it is always rotating and revolving. While the classic image of Nwt can be interpreted as the Sun's apparent circumnavigation of the sky, Nwt's relationship to the Sun could reflect the movement of the Sun through the universe. In addition to the rotations and revolutions of the Earth and its solar system, the galaxy in which the Earth exists is also moving.[5] The entire universe is revolving and coursing like eggs through fallopian tubes, like the Sun through Nwt. Everything is cycling and revolving within the Great Womb that is Odù, and everything that occurs within the Mother is rich with relevance. Indeed, axial precession, one of the seemingly less significant movements of the Earth, is the reason that the celestial maps and orientations of ancient African astronomers, such as the Kemites, Kushites, Namortungans, and Nabta Playans, do not reflect the night sky seen in the 21st century, or the 1st century, or even 2000 BCE, but of the universe as observed by a most ancient and extraordinarily advanced people.[6]

The image of Nwt reveals many truths, and the concept of the Sun moving through her body offers an intimation of the scope of the Cosmos. Nwt's representation also has undeniable spiritual significance. As Anthony T. Browder confirms in *Nile Valley Contributions to Civilization: Exploding the Myths*: "This image of Nut is profound because it reinforces the Nile Valley concept of women being so significant that they are shown giving birth to the sun—an ageless symbol for God."[7] Through Browder's description it is clear that Nwt, identical to Odù, is the God who gives birth to All. Nwt, similar to Àjẹ́, is replicated in every mother bearing a child *in vitro*, and she is the mother protecting her children throughout their lives. In addition to her depiction as the God of the Sky, Nwt also takes many other forms—from animal to seemingly inanimate object—but no matter the form she chooses to adopt, she is always depicted as an immense motherly force who shields, protects, feeds, and soothes.

Nwt, in all her splendor and profundity, is merely a minute aspect of the immensity of Odù. Odù's womb is Ọ̀run, which is often translated as "heaven," but is more accurately the Spiritual Realm, the Universe, or the Cosmos. As Ọ̀run, Odù is, quite literally, the creator and maintainer of the Cosmos and everything in it. The creative labors ongoing in Odù's Ọ̀run are microcosmically replicated in human women who are the Odù of Earth.

Cognizant of the supremacy of the female genitalia, Yoruba wisdom keepers herald the vagina as the pathway to and from Ọ̀run and the Earth.

The vagina's role as gateway to the odù of the womb and the Odù of the Cosmos is evident in Yoruba *cosmontology*[8] which reveals that while some spiritual entities enter the Earth fully manifest, many others, including human souls, leave Ọrun, or the Womb of Odù, and enter the womb of an expecting human mother so that they can be born and experience the full spectrum of human existence and, thereby, further augment their divinity.

Because of the orientation and intentional disorientation to which earthlings are subjected, it may be difficult to conceive of the Cosmos as a womb from whence creation and existence come; however, this is precisely what Yoruba cosmontology posits. In *Ìwa-pẹlẹ: Ifá Quest* Awo Fá'lokun Fatunmbi explains the dynamism of Odù:

> In *Ifá* cosmology *Orisha* evolve from *Odu* through *Imole* and *Irunmole*. *Odu* are the primal principles that give structure to the Universe. *Imole* are those invisible forces that sustain creation. *Irunmole* are the dynamics and form within the Earth that give expression to the forces of evolution. It is the appearance of *Irunmole* that creates the environment that allows for the emergence of human consciousness.[9]

With Fatunmbi's delineation, the genealogy of the Gods unfolds with Àjẹ Odù as the Source of All who becomes All. Far beyond being a supreme or chief God; she is the reason there is any concept of God at all. Fatunmbi defines Odù as the "Spirit that generates form in the Universe";[10] this also serves as an appropriate definition of Àjẹ. Every concept, element, particle, planet, wish, will, being, and body is born through Àjẹ Odù. There is nothing that did not come from her womb. There is nothing that is not within her womb.

The wisdom keepers know Odù Àjẹ's infinite expansiveness. They also know that she created powers and technologies to help individuals translate, navigate, and activate divinity on Earth. One of the most important cosmic facilitators that Odù gave humanity is Ọrọ, Power of the Word. In "The Spider, the Chameleon and the Creation of the Earth," Modupe Oduyoye defines Odù as "oracular utterance"; this is also the definition of Ọrọ.[11] Odù shared Ọrọ, the manifestation of Àjẹ that she used to speak life into being, with humanity so that they could continue to ensure the sanctity of life, make effective medicines, and make curses take immediate effect.

Fatunmbi contends that Ọrọ and Àjẹ are complementary forces and that both originate in the womb and in menstrual blood.[12] Fatunmbi also makes the important observation that, "as a consequence of menstruation," women have a manifestation of Ọrọ called ọfọ àṣẹ which endows them with the power of effective prayer; by contrast, men can only receive ọfọ̀ àṣẹ through initiation.[13] This distinction, which recurs in Yoruba cosmontology, emphasizes the fact that Africana women, as manifestations and extensions of Odù, are equipped with Àjẹ́ and all its accoutrements, while men must organize initiations and manufacture synthetic facilitators to access Àjẹ́.

The significance of Odù Àjẹ́ and her administration of Ọ̀rọ̀ and ọfọ̀ àṣẹ are abundantly evident in the Odù Ifá, the Yoruba divination system. While some proponents of patriarchy have attempted to disassociate Odù Ifá from the God for whom it is named, the *da*, or creation, of Ifá can only occur with the permission of Odù. Babaláwo are the renowned vessels of the wisdom of Odù Ifá, and, in consonance Fatunmbi's findings regarding ọfọ̀ àṣẹ, the initiation process of the babaláwo, which Fatunmbi discusses below, involves men replicating, as best they can, and initiating themselves into the Womb of All:

> To become *Babalawo* requires a seven day ceremony that involves the use of a sacred ritual pot called *Odu*. The ceremony is called *Tefa* and it takes place in an *Ifá* grove called *Egbodu*. The *Odu* pot is placed on the head of the initiate at the end of the re-birthing process. *Odu* contains the *aṣẹ* of the first four *Odu* of *Dafa*. It is believed that all the remaining *Odu* evolve from these four. By placing the pot on the head of the initiate, he becomes *Babalawo* as a consequence of receiving the *aṣẹ* of *Odu*. This *aṣẹ* gives the *Babalawo* the power of the word needed to invoke all the spiritual forces recognized by *Ifá*.[14]

Unlike the Christian baptism which aims to remove what it considers to be the malignant influences of the womb and vagina, the babaláwo's initiation seeks to give him that which nature denied him—the womb and its extraordinary creative power. Because no internal reservoir is available, man's replica is temporarily stationed on his head. This synthetic womb will become his guide and Orí, the director and facilitator of his destiny.

The rituals that men must undergo provide clear evidence of the necessity and essentiality of Woman, Àjẹ́, Odù. These rites and initiations are designed to make men complete and worthy of receiving and dispensing Odù's divine communication. Man is not considered whole unless he has womb. By receiving the pot of Odù, the initiate becomes a man with a womb, a womb-man. Yoruba women do not undergo similar ceremonies in which they receive a womb or a symbolic penis because women are complete: The Africana woman is Odù's terrestrial manifestation who signifies at once the apex of humanity, elegant evidence of Divinity, and the embodiment of cosmic perfection.

Odù's Cosmic (Re)Creations

The religious terrorism wrought by colonizers has resulted in attempts to *degender*, or remove the gender of certain Gods, and to *patrify*, or make male, other Mother Gods. Patriarchally-motivated reconstitution attained formal reification with the translation of Yoruba orature into Romance languages. Yoruba does not have gender-specific pronouns. The Yoruba pronoun "ó" can mean "he," "she," or "it" depending on the context. As purveyors of patriarchy began imposing their culture of gender discrimination on Yoruba Gods, spirituality, and orature, they routinely translated the word "ó" as "he." When studying Yoruba orature (and that of many other African ethnic groups as well) the incongruity born of linguistic patrification is glaring. In addition to linguistic usurpation and misrepresentation, African Gods who are clearly Mothers in form, function, and fact are often patrified and minimized so that they can be deemed equivalents of organized religions' Jehovah and Allah.

In Yoruba culture, the patrification of gender-neutral pronouns facilitated attempts to denude Àjẹ́ of power and establish a Yoruba patriarchy. In order to fully understand Odù's sphere of influence and that of her Divine Daughters, it is necessary to peel back the layers of patrification; when this is done, what is revealed is a collective of Àjẹ́-rich Mother Gods who are prismatic manifestations of Odù with their own individual roles in the eternal work of creation and elevation. In the study of Odù's multitudinous forms, it is imperative to see through and beyond the mists and myths that envelop and distort her myriad images and to acknowledge the fact that what may have been introduced to the Western and academic worlds as an African Yahweh is actually a womb-bearing, clitoris-wielding, vagina-boasting Àjẹ́.

Odùduwà

As the galactic Mother of All, Odù is logically the source of all ìwà (identity, character, and existence), which finds its origin and apex in the undiluted power of pure cosmic Blackness (*Dúdú*). Odù is the perfect Blackness manifest in the melanin of the world's first nation builders, civilization founders, and life bearers. She is the Blackness of the infinite depths of the Cosmos that gives birth to constellations, nebula, and galaxies without end. Odù is so elemental a force that her resplendent Blackness identifies her and illuminates another divine manifestation of her Self—the God Odùduwà, who, as her name specifies, is The Immense Womb or Pot (Odù) of Infinite Depths and Blackness (Dúdú) that Contains all Attributes, Characteristics, and Identities (Ìwà).

While in some circles great effort is expended in attempting to disassociate Odù from Odùduwà, these Gods are as connected as the right and left sides of the human body. In *Religion of the Yorubas* J. Olumide Lucas confirms that "*Oduduwa, Odudua,* and *Odua,* refer to one and the same person."[15] Lucas traces Odùduwà to Kemet and argues that the name means "Lord of the Other World."[16] This translation correctly situates Odùduwà in the Ọ̀run within Odù. In "The Spider, the Chameleon and the Creation of the Earth," Oduyoye reveals the connectedness of these Gods by simply offering definitions of their names: He asserts that Odù means "oracular utterance," and that Odùduwà means "Oracular utterance created existence."[17] Oduyoye's translation also establishes a lineage relationship with Odùduwà being a specification of or an elaboration on the power of her mother, Odù. In *Olódùmarè: God in Yoruba Belief*, E. Bolaji Idowu offers a definition that is similar to Oduyoye's: Idowu defines Odùduwà as "The Self-existent chief who created being."[18]

Catholic missionary Noel Baudin describes Odùduwà as being both Odù and the welcoming womb for Odù's spark of creation: "Odudua, the great goddess of the blacks, seems to be considered as never having been created, but as eternal and coexistent with God. Odudua, who is also called *Iya Agba*, 'The mother who receives,' dwells in the inferior regions of the universe."[19] The latter assertion is indicative of the Caucasian proclivity to attempt to dichotomize and categorize everything hierarchically and racially—even the infinite ellipse that is the universe. But what is important in Baudin's discussion is the confirmation that Odùduwà, identical to Odù, has always existed. The manifestation of Odùduwà as Iyangbà, the Receiving Mother, is also profoundly important, for within Iyangbà is the Womb of Life, the Pot of Infinitude and Origins. The inexhaustible diversity of humanity finds its source in Iyangbà, the receiving womb, which is reproduced in human women. The search for the origin of Àjẹ́ leads to the Source of Existence and finds a womb that pulsates within a womb that throbs within a womb.

The symbiosis of cosmic and terrestrial Àjẹ́ that is articulated in the elaborations of Odù and Odùduwà is also elucidated by Samuel Crowther, who, in addition to describing "Odua" or "Odudua" as a God of Ifẹ̀ who is "said to be the supreme goddess in the world," explains Odùduwà's astronomical significance: "Heaven and earth are also called Odudua. Odudua igbá nlá meji adé iṣi, 'Heaven and earth are two large calabashes, which being shut can never be opened.'"[20] Here Odùduwà clearly represents the totality of Odù and embodies both Ọlọ́run, the calabash of the Cosmos, and Onílẹ̀, the calabash of the Earth.

Onílẹ̀ and Ọlọ́run are two harmonious and interconnected wombs of creation who have also attracted the attention of patriarchal mythmakers. While Onílẹ̀, the Owner of the Earth, has successfully weathered a recent attempt at degendering, which I discuss below, Ọlọ́run may be the first Yoruba victim of patrification. In the light of Odù's sphere and scope as defined by Crowther, Baudin, Fatunmbi, Idowu, and Oduyoye, Odù is, in fact, Ọlọ́run. Indeed, only Odù can be Owner of Ọ̀run, which is the Cosmos, the Womb of All. Because of religious colonization, Ọlọ́run became a patrified construct who is described as being the Yoruba equivalent of the Gods of Muslims and Christians. The patrification Ọlọ́run and placement of this remote, aloof, unknowable, omniscient construction in the same realm as Jehovah and Allah was a shrewd move for it allowed the Yoruba to continue worshipping their Gods while appearing to adhere to the same patriarchal monotheistic mores as their oppressors. However Ọ̀run is not synonymous with heaven or paradise, and Ọlọ́run has nothing in common with Christian and Islamic Deities.

Scientifically, Ọ̀run is the universe; spiritually and biologically, Ọ̀run is the Womb of Creation and the gateway to the human womb, vagina, and terrestrial existence. The female organs that the Gods of organized religions shun the most are precisely what Ọ̀run is and represents. Furthermore, rather than a mercurial unknowable Deity who only makes sense in a foreign land and religion, the Owner and Controller of the Cosmos is the Mother of the Receptive Vagina and Fecund Womb. Far from sinking into the anonymity of invisibility, Ọlọ́run emerges as a God who has the character, depth, compassion, and relevance of one's actual Creator, who is one's mother.

While the patrification of Ọlọ́run has been facile, Odùduwà's patrification has not been so successful. Depending upon the Yoruba ethnic group and its cosmological and political foundation, Odùduwà may be described as a female or a male God and/or creator of the world and/or founder of Ifẹ̀. A Yoruba oríkì of Odùduwà included in Ulli Beier's *Yoruba Poetry* solves the dilemma of having to choose one identity by embracing all of them. The orature says of Odùduwà: "[H]e sprinkles earth over the water. / Creator of land, / founder of cities."[21] These lines not only reveal the similitude between Odù, Odùduwà, and Onílẹ̀, as they are all credited with the creation of the Earth in different *itàn* (historical texts), but as the "founder of cities" Odùduwà's cosmic and historical attributes are combined.

Using seemingly deceptively references, the oríkì goes on to depict Odùduwà as a God who is the definition of holism, elegance, and essentiality:

> He is the husband,
> He is the wife.
> Warm like the sun,
> cool like the harmattan.

> He builds a house of parrot's feathers
> a wall of darkness
> that reaches into the sky.[22]

If this orature were rendered in Yoruba, the pronoun "He" would be the gender-neutral "Ó," and the need for gender neutrality is evident given Odùduwà's ability to be husband and wife and so much more. In addition to being the consummate spouse, Odùduwà is the meteorological harmony necessary for flora and fauna to flourish. Furthermore, using the signature symbol of Àjẹ́, the *ikó oódẹ* or *ikóódẹ*, the African Grey Parrot's crimson tail feathers which represent the Àjẹ́ of menses, Odùduwà builds a mansion of Àjẹ́ that transforms into the uterine calabash of Odù's infinite cosmic depths.[23] Odùduwà, with her unfathomable strength, creative abundance, and cosmic versatility is truly her mother's daughter.

While gender specific pronouns provide a clear source of confusion and conflict where Òrìṣà of Àjẹ́ are concerned, the force of the Mother is undeniable. Babatunde Lawal makes an important observation about Odùduwà that also surfaces in discussions about other Àjẹ́ who are threatened with patrification or gender excision. Lawal finds that "[o]ddly enough, those who regard Oduduwa as a male orisa still occasionally address him as Iya Imole."[24] While some segments of the Yoruba nation have always heralded Odùduwà as a Mother and an organic extension of Odù, even those factions swayed by the patriarchal shift are compelled to acknowledge Odùduwà as a primordial Mother of All (Ìyá Imọlẹ̀). This compulsion exists because the centrality and necessity of Mother is as irreducible a fact of existence as it is a central and defining element of Yoruba cosmontology. What the Mothers represent to the Yoruba nation is so fundamentally important that their sons cannot help but give them their proper respect.

Ọbàtálá

Another Àjẹ́ Odù who has become patrified in some regions is Ọbàtálá. To understand how and why the patrification of Ọbàtálá came about, one need only look upon "his" signature white cloth.

In order to reify the fabrications of Caucasian superiority and African inferiority, Caucasians found it effective to associate arbitrary values with colors and to relate those colors to ethnic groups. Despite the facts that Caucasians are not white and that the hue white has no scientific or universally recognized relationship to holiness, purity, or cleanliness, Caucasian myth makers conflated all of these concepts and related them to their ethnic groups so as to create a myth of superiority that they used to justify religious, territorial, and psychological colonization. In the dichotomous Caucasian worldview, white could only signify superiority in contrast to an inferior other. Consequently, Caucasian ideologues defined black as evil, wicked, devilish, and other concepts that did not exist in African cosmontology, and made their construct of "blackness" the marker for African people and the Continent as a whole. During the rush to equate complex African spiritual systems and Gods with parochial alien religions, Odù, the Àjẹ́ with the abundant Black womb of cosmic creation, became an "evil witch" while Ọbàtálá, who is heralded as the "Ruler of the White Cloth," became patrified, and the cloth was used to tie "him" to Christian Deities. Christo-Yoruba apologists could point to the reconstituted forms of Ọlọ́run and Ọbàtálá and assert that the Yoruba had been worshipping Jehovah and Jesus all along.

Jehovah and Jesus would be mighty uncomfortable in the blood-rich walls of the uterus, but Ọbàtálá is not only at home in the womb, "he," like all other manifestations of Àjẹ́ Odù, has a womb. Glistening with vaginal fluid and immersed in amniotic waters, Ọbàtálá does her most important work in the womb; there she harnesses the scientific properties of the hue white to combine, meld, direct, and reflect all colors, powers, identities, destinies, and characteristics. Every infinite possibility that swirls in Odù's immense Pot of Origins, Ọbàtálá selects and then projects into the *in vitro* human. Rather than curse the womb and seek every means to avoid it, the uterus is Ọbàtálá's art studio where she molds and shapes all human forms in their infinite diversity.[25]

Ọbàtálá's relationship with Odù and with light has even deeper esoteric levels of significance. In addition to being a God, Odù is also the way of knowing called Odù Ifá. The figures of the Odù Ifá are the literal and figural manifestations of Odù, and they contain the wisdom that is essential to the comprehension of identity and the determination and redetermination of destinies. Fatunmbi finds that each Odù of Ifá is related to an Òrìṣà, and at the heart of this coupling is the scientific and the cosmic dynamism of Ọbàtálá:

> Light is one of the fundamental expressions of energy in the Universe. *Ifá* describes the essential nature of light by saying that everything in the physical world, including consciousness, contains a spark of *Ọbatala's aṣẹ*. Different *Orisha* carry different *Odu* expressing different frequencies along the spectrum of light. *Ifá* considers all color as a form of spirit. Because all color is contained within white light, all *Orisha* are believed to be linked with *Ọbatala*.[26]

All forms are created in Odù's womb and are infused with their specific ìwà, Orí, and àṣẹ through Ọbàtálá white cloth which, not unlike a prism, refracts, reflects, and channels light.

Ọbàtálá works so closely with and within Odùduwà, giving and molding light and life, that these Gods are inseparable and nearly indistinguishable. Evidence of the twinning of these Gods is apparent in Ulli Beier's description of Odúà in "Gelede Masks":

> Odua is described as "the mother of all". She is alluded to as "the pure orisha" and like Obatala, she uses white cloth and her sacred metal is lead. She is called "the orisha who turns blood into children." The name Odua, of course, suggests relationship with Oduduwa, but the people consciously identify Odu with Obatala. Odua seems to belong to the group of "Orisha funfun" (white Orisha) and represents as it were, the female principle of the Obatala cult.[27]

The shared attributes and oríkì of Ọbàtálá and Odùduwà are profoundly important to understanding the holism and dynamism of Àjẹ́.

Given the curvilinear nature of divinity in the African worldview and the power of humanodivinity, the relationships between human beings and the Òrìṣà and the Ìrúnmọlẹ̀ are grounded in reciprocity and interdependence. The dynamic interactivity between human beings and Gods is evident in an oríkì Ọbàtálá recorded in *Yoruba Poetry* in which a woman challenges Ọbàtálá with the oríkì and attributes that she shares with Odúà:

> Obatala,
> you turn blood into children,
> come and create the child in my own belly.
> I own but a single cloth to dye with indigo.
> I own but a single headtie to dye with camwood.
> But I know:
> you have twenty or thirty children waiting for me,
> whom I shall bear![28]

The speaker of this invocation is very well aware of the alliance between Ọbàtálá and Odùduwà and that they will work together to grant her children. The speaker also makes it clear that money is irrelevant to her. She is not worried about the "cost" of raising a child, because she is not constrained by a Western capitalistic worldview. The thought of having twenty or thirty children is the modern nuclear family's and Western feminist's nightmare, but the speaker of the oríkì knows that by bearing life she is bearing Divinities, and she is cognizant that she has an entire community and nation to assist her in the monumental work of God-rearing. This mother-to-be has such confidence in her terrestrial and cosmic support that the conclusion of the oríkì exhibits her knowledge that her Ọ̀rọ̀ has been heard and is being actualized. While the oríkì for both Ọbàtálá and Odùduwà in *Yoruba Poetry* repeatedly refer to these Gods with masculine pronouns, their vaginas, wombs, and Àjẹ́ are resplendently and purposefully apparent.

Ọbàtálá and Odùduwà defy both the masculine gender forced on them and Western definitions of gender in general. Thomas Jefferson Bowen reveals the flexibility of gender and divinity when his description of Ọbàtálá becomes an organic ode to Odù-Iyangbà and her cosmic womb: "Ọbatalá is thought to be the first made and greatest of all created things. . . . His wife, Iyangbà, *the receiving mother*, is represented as nursing a child. But Iyangbà herself is Ọbatalá. The two are one, or in other words, Ọbatalá is an androgyne, representing the productive energy of nature as distinguished from the creative power of God."[29]

Although his discussion is marred by his struggle to define African holism in Western dichotomous terms, Bowen's description makes the same points and details the same cosmological melding as Beier in *Gelede Masks*. Bowen describes another dual but interconnected Motherforce that takes and gives to and from the immensity of the divine Self to create the varied and various beings and entities who comprise our world, galaxy, and Cosmos. Bowen also makes an important distinction in his description, for if Ọbàtálá is the "greatest of all created things," how magnificent must Ọbàtálá's creator be? How complete must she be?

The Creator of the Gods must function in accordance with the laws and logic of reciprocity. The Creator must be able not only to give but also to receive in order to create. The penis, with all of its might and turgidity, can only give, spew, ejaculate: Its flow is unidirectional. The vagina is a study in harmony as it, like the Cosmos, gives and takes, molds and shapes, births and creates. It is *the* reciprocal organ, and reciprocity is the cornerstone of existence.

The work, sensuality, copulation, creativity, and Àjẹ́ of Ọbàtálá and Odùduwà find a perfect terrestrial complement in the snail, which symbolizes and is a favorite of both of these Gods. The patient, ubiquitous, and Earth-loving mollusk has both male and female reproductive organs, and it proliferates as easily as it soothes and pacifies. The completion and wholeness of the snail is highly symbolic of Yoruba cosmogony, cosmology, and ontology. The importance of being both whole and holistic is apparent in numerous Yoruba Gods, including Èṣù Ẹlẹ́gbára, who boasts a massive penis as well as a tiny vagina, and Mother Gods such as Odù and Ọbàtálá-Iyangbà who bear both fecund vaginas and semen-rich clitorises.

The importance of being whole is everywhere evident in Yoruba life and iconography. And it is crucial to understand that the recurring and resonant recollections of woman-exclusive towns and the stunning images of bearded sword-bearing mothers and of ruling fathers who strut about in voluminous skirts and elaborately coiffed hair crowned with the ìkóódẹ of Àjẹ́ are not examples of transvestitism, homosexuality, androgyny, cross-dressing, queering, bisexuality, hermaphroditism, or any other Western construct or compartmentalization of gender: They are exhibitions of the manifest holism of Àjẹ́.

The Mothers' Máre

Another manifestation of Odù that is assumed to be male is Olódùmarè. "Olódù" means Owner of Odù, and only Mother Odù can be the owner of the primal Pot of Creation which is also the Womb of Existence and the Home of Àjẹ́. "*Áre*" means vindication, righteousness. Because of what it signifies, the word "áre" is found protecting and defending individuals through such names as Osundare, Obadare, and Oyadare; the word "áre" may also be promising protection through the Gods Olódùmarè and Òṣùmàrè.[30]

Òṣùmàrè is symbolized as a rainbow encircling the Earth and as a Rainbow Boa biting its tail often while encircling the Earth. These signs constitute a covenant of continuity that unites human beings with ancestors, Gods, and immortality.[31] Òṣùmàrè represents the curvilinear work of the Womb of Odù to usher spirits to the terrestrial world so that they can assist in the continual evolution and elevation of the Earth. She also represents the Earth's role in receiving the bodies and cosmically receiving the souls of human beings who become ancestors who are slated for rebirth. Fatunmbi finds that "[i]t is Òṣùmàrè's task to deliver a covenant between Ọlọdumarẹ and the people of earth," and that the rainbow is the visible reminder of the sacred covenant.[32]

As I discuss in greater detail below, Yoruba cosmology describes Olódùmarè as the child of Odù and Òṣùmàrè. Fittingly, Fatunmbi translates Olódùmarè as "The light of the Rainbow comes from the Primal Womb."[33] Olódùmarè could also be transliterated as the Owner of Odù Who Epitomizes Righteousness and Vindicates Her Progeny. Olódùmarè, as the progeny or, perhaps, as the amalgamation of Odù and Òṣùmàrè, provides humanity with another means by which to appreciate the eternal promise and power of Àjẹ́.

Olódùmarè is routinely depicted and described as a masculine God who is analogous to the male Gods of monotheism. However, Olódùmarè is another Mother-Creator Àjẹ́ who is eternally engaged in the womb-oriented labors of creation. In addition to her role in covenant-keeping,

Olódùmarè teaches an important lesson to patrifiers. The Gods of Àjẹ́ are extraordinarily flexible, multitudinous, and ubiquitous. Patrified creations do not boast these qualities, and that leaves them vulnerable to obsolescence. Idowu finds that the patrification of Olódùmarè has resulted in a telling reversal of fortune: "[T]he direct ritualistic worship of Olódùmarè as a regular thing is dying out in Yorubaland. In some parts it is no longer known; in some, it has become the cult of the women."[34] After the hue and cry of men and their attempts to crush divine infinitude into a one-dimensional alien definition, Àwọn Ìyá Wa quietly reclaim, assuage, and ensure continuity.

Odù and Her Offspring on the Earth

Àjẹ́ is elegant evidence of the completeness of Woman. From a matrix of wholeness and perfection, Odù reproduced herself as Odúà, Odùduwà, Ọlọ́run, Ìyàmi Òṣòròngà, Onílẹ̀, Olódùmarè, Ìyá Ayé, Imọlẹ̀, Òṣùmàrè, Ọ̀ṣun, Ọbàtálá, Ọya, Yemọja, and many more Gods. Indeed, every Yoruba Mother(ly) Òrìṣà could be considered a unique manifestation of Odù, complete with her own pot of Àjẹ́, her own destiny, and her own dominion. While Yoruba cosmontology often describes male and female Gods collaborating in the work of creation, the "male" construct of the terrestrial realm does not appear to be part of the creative matrix of the Cosmos: There is no wholly, predominantly, or even partially "male" God in Yoruba cosmogony.

The first wholly male Òrìṣà is Ògún. While Mother created him in the Cosmos, his heralded exploits occur on Earth and he resides on Earth. As the God of iron, weaponry, and technology, Ògún is essential to the development of terrestrial civilization. Such abilities as clearing and tilling land, building homes, and defending nations are Earth-specific. Furthermore, it is only on Earth that issues regarding masculinity and "man" as a separate gender arise. Ògún is directly related to the needs of a terrestrial community and to the men who would largely but not exclusively undertake Ògún-related endeavors. Ògún, as the quintessential masculine Òrìṣà, appears to have been created specifically to address the needs of the sons of the Mothers.

Odù did not need a penis to multiply and divide her Cosmic Self into multitudinous mothers or to create her sons. When Odù created Ògún, she extended and thickened her clitoris and rounded and filled her labia with seeds of life and gave these protrusions to her son. Odù filled his glands with testosterone so that his overwhelming urge and driving desire would always be to seek out his Source, enter its haven, and experience the bliss and wholeness of Woman, and, in the process, ensure human continuity.

While women are Àjẹ́ Odù and, consequently, the inherent owners and wielders of Àjẹ́, there are men and male Òrìṣà, such as Ògún, who are inherently endowed with Àjẹ́. Indeed, to undertake certain duties and fulfill certain roles, certain males *must* have Àjẹ́, and that power can only be obtained genetically from the Great Mother. Opeola explains why Àjẹ́ is a cosmobiological and sociopolitical necessity:

> Àjẹ́ is a power, is a knowledge. Anybody doing divination has Àjẹ́; any Òrìṣà regarded in creation, childbirth, protection of a town also possesses the power of Àjẹ́. That is why Ọbàtálá is said to have Àjẹ́ because he created humans; Ọbalúayé with prevention of disease and what not; war, defense, everything [associated] with Ògún; Odùduwà with growth, food supply, everything, giving birth, protection of crops, children—all are part of Odùduwà and they share part of Àjẹ́. It is only that Western beliefs gave the wrong impression of Àjẹ́.[35]

Rather than miserable hags ostracized from their communities, Àjẹ́ are the terrestrial architects of existence and reincarnations of their celestial progenitors. The Àjẹ́ of the Gods that Opeola discusses is essential to the labors they are called to undertake, and if they did not have Àjẹ́, they could not be involved in endeavors related to creation, defense, agriculture, and civilization. Furthermore there is no good "male" Àjẹ́ and evil "female" Àjẹ́ or vice versa: Àjẹ́ is Àjẹ́. The power's application relates to the ìwà and Orí of the bearer and the needs of the community. However, it is important to reiterate that the source of all Àjẹ́ is Odù whose living representatives are Àwọn Ìyá Wa and that all masculine entities are positioned as the sons of these Mothers.

My assertion that Àjẹ́'s social-spiritual relationship with men is articulated as a Mother-son dynamic is most evident in Ògbóni Ìbílẹ̀—one of the Yoruba world's most revered and seemingly patriarchal institutions. In "Ejiwapo: The Dialectics of Twoness in Yoruba Culture," Babatunde Lawal reveals important information about the reverence that Àjẹ́ receives in Ògbóni society: "[A]ll members of the society metaphorically regard themselves as Omo Iya ('Children of Mother Earth'), not as children of two parents, a father and a mother."[36] Yoruba cosmontology consistently highlights the fact that there is no "father": There is Odù Àjẹ́ and her innumerable reproducing reproductions, and there are the Mothers' sons.

Yoruba men do not view the designation of "son" or "child" as a demerit or a slight. They know that no position confers more safety, security, wisdom, protection, and power than being at mother's breast, enfolded in her arms, or frolicking in her womb. Not only is the Mother's son ever-protected by and girded in her power, but he is, historically, his

Mother's fiercest defender. The supremacy of the Mother and her ability to both encompass and protect all is evidenced in the Ẹdan symbol of Ògbóni, which is a brass icon of female and male figures presented back-to-back or joined at their heads by a chain. Lawal reveals that what may appear to be a connected pair is actually one, and both original and "reformed" Ògbóni society members "refer to the two figures as Iya ('mother'), treating them as one unit."[37] Mother is supreme; she is whole. She turns two into three into one. By acknowledging Mother, all is accounted for.

Odù on Earth: Effortless Exhibitions of Supremacy

Odù is the Gods' God who creates with Àjẹ́ and catalyzes and magnifies àṣẹ. In addition to her infinite gifts, forms, and functions, Odù is the prismatic Mother: When light shines on her, sixteen additional Divine Mothers are revealed and those sixteen reveal sixteen others, and so on and so on. Numerous Òrìṣà share attributes, ìtàn (biographies; historical texts), and oríkì (praisenames) with Odù. Ìyàmi Òṣòròngà, Òṣun, Yemọja, and Odù each have ìtàn that describe them as the founder, leader, and source of Àjẹ́. Yoruba ìtàn that recount the settling of the world and the sole female force capable of vivifying the acts of fifteen otherwise impotent male Gods may feature Ìyàmi Òṣòròngà, Òṣun, or Odù.[38] While her motherly forms are many, certain manifestations of Odù have become patrified; however, with a comprehensive understanding of Àjẹ́, the truths of the womb become elucidated.

Odù, in her immensity and multiplicity, is the root of Yoruba ontology, cosmology, and cosmogony which are as intricately interconnected and interdependent as Odù and her many manifestations. Odù's proliferation and distribution of Àjẹ́ through Òrìṣà, language, technology, and symbols are apparent in the numerous ẹsẹ Ifá: some of which detail her exploits as a God in Ọ̀run; some of which explore her life as a God in human form. Through the analysis of these verses it is possible to gain knowledge about Odù and Àjẹ́. Because the ẹsẹ Ifá are stored, by and large, in the memories and mouths of men, they can also reveal important information about a babaláwo's training regarding Àjẹ́; indeed, some verses appear to have been created specifically to malign Àjẹ́. However because Odù and Àjẹ́ are the sources of the Odù Ifá and the entire Yoruba world, those who attempt to denigrate Odù and Àjẹ́ eventually find themselves praising them.

While it is difficult if not impossible and unnecessary to determine when many works of oral literature were created, in some cases it is possible to trace the sources of patrification and patriarchal reification. Pierre Fatumbi Verger's article "The Rise and Fall of the Worship of Ìyámi Òṣòròngà (My Mother the Sorceress) Among the Yorùbá" ("The Rise and

Fall") includes an ẹsẹ of Òsá Méjì that recounts Olódùmarè giving Odù the power of Àjẹ́. In his analysis of the orature, Verger states that because Odù abused her power, Olódùmarè reclaimed it and gave it to Ọbàtálá, who is described as her male counterpart. In *Gẹlẹdẹ: Art and Female Power Among the Yoruba*, Margaret Thompson Drewal and Henry John Drewal repeat Verger's findings and assert that Odù was granted "control over the gods" but was warned to "use her enormous power with care, calm, and discretion. When she abused this power, Olodumare gave it Orishánlá [also Ọbàtálá], her male companion, decreeing that he would exercise it but that woman would retain control over it."[39] However, Verger and Drewal and Drewal are in error.

The ẹsẹ, which is transcribed and translated in the second part of "The Rise and Fall" titled "Texts and Translations," does not describe a patriarchal reclamation and redistribution of Àjẹ́. The only passage in the ẹsẹ that could be construed as a usurpation of power is the following interjection: "Olodumare first gave wisdom and the power of ẹlẹ́iyẹ to the woman. / But with intelligence and cunning the man takes it from the hands of woman."[40] However, the ẹsẹ, proper, does not reflect this claim any more than it reflects the assertions of Verger and Drewal and Drewal. Through discordant interjection, incongruous interpretations, and/or pseudo-academic mythmaking, a gift is portrayed as a cunning theft. What is more, the gift that Odù gives Ọbàtálá is not Àjẹ́ but Egúngún. In order to distinguish fact from fabrication, it is necessary to analyze the transcribed ẹsẹ of Òsá Méjì recorded in "The Rise and Fall." Upon analysis, a very different relationship between Àjẹ́, Odù, Olódùmarè, and Ọbàtálá is revealed.

The ẹsẹ of Òsá Méjì melds two well-known ìtàn: the transmission of Àjẹ́ from Olódùmarè to Odù and Odù giving Egúngún to Ọbàtálá, who is heralded as Ọbarìṣà in the ẹsẹ. The ẹsẹ offers detailed information about Odù's characteristics and methodology, and she is depicted as a wise, generous, and discerning Deity. However, throughout the ẹsẹ, unknown parties[41] consistently attempt to malign Odù and delimit her power. Strategically placed commentaries that run counter to the spiritual-historical events and facts are dispersed throughout the orature. For example, at one point, it is asserted that Odù "fell into disgrace" with misuse of her power,[42] but the ẹsẹ offers no evidence of this. Also worth noting are the many interjections from unknown parties that are designed to make it appear as if the patrified Olódùmarè repeatedly threatens to take Àjẹ́ from Odù. The fact is that no matter how she decides to use her power, it is *her* power. No one can take Àjẹ́ from Odù any more than anyone can take away her ìwà, Orí, or ẹ̀mí. Odù is Àjẹ́ and Àjẹ́ is Odù. As the ẹsẹ reveals, Odù "received the power called Odù."[43] The God receives and is empowered by Her Self.

As the consummate Creator, Odù's signature power is Creation. After noting that Ògún and a patrified Ọbàtálá both have unique gifts of power, Odù asks Olódùmarè what power she has, and Olódùmarè states that she *is* her power: "[Y]ou will be called their mother, forever."[44] Motherhood is Àjẹ́ is Divinity. In addition to being the Mother of the Gods, Olódùmarè reveals that Odù's responsibility is to "support the earth."[45] Here the important relationship between Odù and Onílẹ̀, the Mother of the Earth, is revealed, and the partnership between these Òrìṣà, as discussed by Crowther, above, is confirmed in various Yoruba orature which describe the world as being created and maintained by a collective of Àjẹ́ that includes Odù, Ọbàtálá, Onílẹ̀, Imọlẹ̀, Òṣùmàrè, and Olódùmarè, who have and fulfill ancient and interdependent roles.

While Olódùmarè is styled in this ẹsẹ as Odù's male superior, Yoruba cosmogony reveals that Olódùmarè is the progeny of Odù and a product of her immense Womb of Creation. The ẹsẹ, in spite of itself, confirms that Olódùmarè and Odù share objectives, gender, and power. Olódùmarè cannot give Odù that which Olódùmarè does not already possess. Olódùmarè must have Àjẹ́ in order to share it. The ẹsẹ confirms that Olódùmarè gives Odù a bird which is called the "bird of Olódùmarè."[46] This makes Olódùmarè *the* Ẹlẹ́yẹ (The Owner of the Spirit Bird, an oríkì Àjẹ́); this designation is logical because Olódùmarè is an Àjẹ́. Olódùmarè also gives Odù an Igbá (calabash), which is symbolic of the womb that they both possess. The ritual of Olódùmarè giving Odù the Ẹyẹ (Spirit Bird) and Igbá of Àjẹ́ is identical to the ritual of the Ìyálóde of Ọ̀tà giving Ẹyẹ Àjẹ́ and Igbá to the Àjẹ́ of Ọ̀tà.[47] The calabash represents the actual womb and its mysteries which are hidden from view and protected by the clitoris, which appears to be symbolized by the Ẹyẹ. The Ẹyẹ and its calabash home are externalized symbols of biological Àjẹ́, and they are the spiritual-political facilitators of Odù and Àwọn Ìyá Wa.

The fact that the Igbá and Ẹyẹ are externalizations of Olódùmarè and Odù's shared being is evident in the fact that when Olódùmarè asks Odù if she knows the use of the Ẹyẹ on Earth, she reveals that she is aware of how to use the power. Odù states that she will grant children and riches to those who worship her, but if her followers become "impertinent," she will reclaim her gifts.[48] Slights and insults that could be perceived as insolence Odù will answer with warnings in the forms of "headache" and "stomach pain."[49] Odù is also prepared to protect her Àjẹ́: "If she tells someone not to look her in the face, and if he then looks her in the face, she will make him blind."[50] There is no excess or evil here, only adherence to reciprocity and defense and protection of the self.

Odù and Olódùmarè are of one mind in this ẹsẹ of Ọ̀sá Méjì; and because of their oneness, it is easy to spot aberrant patriarchal interjections.

For example, after Odù details how she will use her Àjẹ́, an interesting commentary is included:

> Olodumare says this is good.
> He says, not bad.
> He says, use the power I gave you with reserve.
> *If she were to use it with violence, he would take it back,*
> And of all the men who follow you,
> I will make you their mother.[51]

Line 86, which I have italicized above, is an addition that is not part of the original ẹsẹ. The line not only breaks the continuity between lines 85 and 87, but the speaker is clearly not Olódùmarè: This is evident in the pronouns used. Whoever included line 86, whether it is Verger's informant or Verger himself, includes what he would *like* his patrified God to say.

Line 86 could be the work of the babaláwo; it is not unusual for orature to be edited during transmission. The babaláwo may also have recited the lines exactly as he memorized them; but if that were the case, one wonders why Verger or Drewal and Drewal did not critique this dissonant insertion. Of course, the addition could be Verger's, and that would be especially troubling for obvious reasons. Suffice it to say that line 86 reveals how, from the introduction of gender pronouns to the injection of personal predilection into what is assumed to be sacred, the Gods and their works and powers become twisted.

Patriarchally-authored intrusions and confusions aside, the ẹsẹ is an insightful one because it offers a multidimensional portrait of Odù as a divine entity preparing for life among mortals. Odù's knowledge of her power and glory is so complete and her trust in that knowledge is so firm that she refuses to sacrifice—and to whom would the God who created everything pray? Odù knows that it is to her that mortals and other Gods will pray. It is also intriguing to be privy to her conversation with her ẹnikejì, or second self, Olódùmarè, who is in accord with every one of Odù's pronouncements and actions.

After Odù makes it clear that she will make no offerings, the ẹsẹ shifts to a narrative about Odù owning and controlling Egúngún and Orò. Ọbàtálá is jealous of Odù's dominion and dynamism, so he consults Ifá in hopes of obtaining her power. The ẹsẹ depicts one male, Ọ̀rúnmìlà, who is the diviner, and two patrified Gods, Ọbàtálá and Olódùmarè, covertly conspiring against Odù. Despite Olódùmarè's declaration that Odù "will support the Earth," the ẹsẹ intimates that Olódùmarè encourages Ọbàtálá to "take the world in his hands" and away from Odù.[52] Under Ọ̀rúnmìlà's direction, Ọbàtálá makes a sacrifice that includes snails, a whip, and money. After this sacrifice is discussed, erroneous information is introduced into the ẹsẹ again. It is asserted that Odù will "*àṣejù*," or boast, brag, and exceed the limits of her power, and that she will be forced to "submit herself" to Ọbàtálá and become his "servant."[53] But none of this—overestimation of power and submission and subordination—occurs.

The snails that Ọbàtálá sacrifices play an important role in the ẹsẹ. Snails are known in Yoruba cosmology and pharmacology for cooling and soothing, and they are the signature symbols of Odù, Ọbàtálá, and Egúngún because of their sexual comprehensiveness. Snails are also a culinary treat, and Odù enjoys the snail meat and water so much that she forms a complementary union with Ọbàtálá, and she shares all of her secrets with him. Ọbàtálá, as a true son of the Mother, has no secrets to share, but he partakes freely in every aspect of Odù's life, including her worship of Egúngún. After he conquers his fear and learns the rites of Egúngún, Ọbàtálá goes to the sacred grove covertly and makes changes to the cloth of Egúngún. While the ẹsẹ describes these changes as stunning innovations, it appears to be the case that Ọbàtálá tailors the shroud to enable mortal men to communicate with Gods: Odù does not need to cut holes in the fabric in order to see and then cover the holes with netting to give the appearance of integrity; she does not need to affect a voice to mimic that of the Gods. As the embodiment of Òrò and a God with divine spiritual vision and unlimited communicative powers, Odù does not need to alter or adjust anything. Odù, however, expresses shock and delight at Ọbàtálá's initiative and praises him exactly as a mother would praise her child.

Aware that with Àjẹ́, Ẹyẹ, Òrò, Orò, and Egúngún women hold all power, wisdom, and knowledge, and cognizant that Ọbàtálá and the mortal men "he" represents, here, are yearning for some form of and association with power, Odù, with no prompting, commends Ọbàtálá on his efforts and decrees that men should don the cloth and undertake the rituals of Egúngún and that women shall dance unadorned with Egúngún: Women need no shroud, netting, or simulated voice of power because they are Àjẹ́ and they have Òrò. Women are also embodiments and conduits of Egúngún for they bear the ovum of returning ancestors in their wombs and they carry the histories of the ancestors in their mouths. The immutable authority of Àjẹ́ over Egúngún that is implied in Yoruba culture is made explicit with the acknowledgement that without Àjẹ́'s approval there can be no Egúngún. The Ẹyẹ Àjẹ́ authorizes and oversees Egúngún's arrival and actions, and "[i]n the place where Eégún manifests, there (also) manifests Ẹléiyẹ / All the power used by Eégún, is the power of Ẹléiyẹ."[54]

Rather than overstepping her bounds or sinking into submission, Odù institutes gender balance and social harmony. She massages men's egos while she protects and proliferates Àjẹ́. Mother does not have to deny herself to give. Her pot of gifts, her creativity, and her abundance are ever-renewing, but Mother's bounty must not be taken for granted. In the ẹsẹ, Odù stresses the importance of respecting and revering women, who are the ultimate Creators:

> She says women have more power on earth.
> She says, moreover, [women] brought us into the world.
> She says, all people are born of women.
> She says, anything that people wish to do,
> if they are not assisted by women,
> she says, they will not be able to do it.
> (This is) why men can do nothing on earth,
> unless they obtain it from the hands of women.[55]

The conclusion of the ẹsẹ confirms Odù's pronouncement and adds that "if they [men] pay tribute to women, the earth will be tranquil."[56] This simple statement, which can be interpreted as a fact, a warning, or a threat, is followed by a resonant lyrical demand that seems to come simultaneously from Odù, Olódùmarè, and Ọbàtálá and is issued directly to the listener, reader, and reciter:

> You bend your knee, bend your knee for women.
> Women brought you into the world, this is what makes us human.
> Women are the [wisdom of the world], bend your knee for the women.
> Women brought you into the world, this is what makes us human.[57]

From the final injunction it is clear that all women, as embodiments of Odù, are the literal Creators, Gods, and Mothers of all men—age, status, and title notwithstanding. What is more, directly contradicting the assertion that Odù would submit herself to Ọbàtálá, the ẹsẹ commands men to prostrate before and submit themselves to women.

This ẹsẹ of Ọsá Méjì is a melding of profoundly important and egregiously discordant information that reveals the difficulties that one will encounter when attempting to malign Odù. The "editor(s)" of this ẹsẹ not only fail in their attempts to discredit Odù, but they end up highlighting their own insecurities and obvious anti-Àjẹ́ agenda. What is more, their attempts to make Odù submit cycle back upon the patriarchs who find themselves on their knees before the Mother.

One of the most important attributes of the Ifá spiritual system is the fact that it is grounded in both the logical and the biological. No matter the patriarchal machinations or the ethnocentric alien agendas, the fact that human beings all have their source in the womb, menses, and vagina recurs in Yoruba cosmology as the undeniable truth of which human beings are proof. Ọrúnmìlà is aware of the importance of Odù—the God, the Power, the Womb, the Woman—and the ẹsẹ Ifá describe him as risking his life in order to be as close to Odù and her power as possible.

Verger records an ẹsẹ of Ìrẹ̀tẹ̀ Ogbè that begins with another depiction of the relationship between Olódùmarè, Odù, and Ẹyẹ Ọ̀rọ̀, the Spirit Bird of Àjẹ́, who is named Aragamago. The twinning between Olódùmarè and Odù, which is described in the ẹsẹ of Ọ̀sá Méjì, is evident in the ẹsẹ of Ìrẹ̀tẹ̀ Ogbè which also describes Olódùmarè as the Ẹlẹ́yẹ who gives Aragamago to Odù and tells her that the bird will do whatever she commands it to do.[58] Rather than a patronizing paternal God mollifying an inferior, Olódùmarè emerges, once again, as an Òrìṣà Àjẹ́ sharing power with her ẹnikejì, who is Odù.

It is against the backdrop of Olódùmarè, Odù, and Aragamago forming a trinity of Àjẹ́ that Ọrúnmìlà is introduced into the ẹsẹ. He is desirous of building a life with Odù and Aragamago because they offer incomparable power and complete protection. His diviner tells him he must sacrifice "because the power of this woman was greater than that of Ọrúnmìlà" and to prevent her from killing and eating him "with her power."[59] The reference to "eating" is not literal but refers to a spiritual *cum* physical destruction and infers that Odù's powers are sufficient to not only destroy Ọrúnmìlà, but to demolish his destiny as well. However, the ambiguity of "eating" facilitates the theme of denigration that is employed to undercut Àjẹ́ in many of the ẹsẹ included in "The Rise and Fall." For example, line 56 of the ẹsẹ of Ìrẹ̀tẹ̀ Ogbè avers, "All those whom Odù leads behind her are evil things."[60] However, one cannot malign Odù without maligning Ọrúnmìlà, who struggles desperately to be one of Odù's followers. This is the trap in which the Yoruba man who despises Àjẹ́ finds himself, for in hating the roots of his existence he cannot but loathe himself. The babaláwo who finds Odù and those she leads to be "evil" is in an especially thorny position because not only is he lead by Odù, but he also owes his orí, àṣẹ, ẹmí, as well as his Àjẹ́ to Odù. Every babaláwo is the direct beneficiary of Ọrúnmìlà's trials, humiliations, and struggles to gain access to Odù's Odù, and every babaláwo with his Odù replicates Odù and Ọrúnmìlà's relationship.

The most important information conveyed in the ẹsẹ of Ìrẹ̀tẹ̀ Ogbè is the confirmation that without Odù there can be no Odù Ifá and that there can be no babaláwo without the Iyaláwo because "Odù is the power of the babaláwo."[61] Indeed, the only reason any "father" has knowledge of any mysteries or secrets is because Mother shared her wisdom with her son. The ẹsẹ continues emphasizing the centrality of Odù to Ifá: "[I]f the babaláwo [possesses] Ifá. He says he also has Odù."[62] However, the babaláwo who does not have Odù is not "whole," cannot consult Ifá, and is not actually a babaláwo.[63] This ẹsẹ provides clear confirmation of the centrality and indispensability of Àjẹ́ Odù to the babaláwo, to Ifá, and to the Yoruba ethos.

Odù makes Ọrúnmìlà whole by agreeing to marry him, and she informs him of all of her prohibitions including the fact that no one can gaze upon her. Odù tells Ọrúnmìlà that she has come to lessen his burdens and to "fix everything"; furthermore, whatever he wants destroyed she will obliterate for him.[64] Odù promises to protect and fight for her husband and to go to war against anyone who even wishes to cause him the minutest pain. This ẹsẹ Ifá does not depict an "evil" God who leads "evil" followers; it illustrates the loyalty, devotion, and necessity of Àjẹ́ Odù to Ọrúnmìlà and, through him, all babaláwo. Indeed, the ẹsẹ concludes by stating that once the babaláwo obtains Odù, "[H]e becomes someone that Odù will not allow to suffer."[65] The babaláwo does not become the inheritor of "evil" but of the Mother's perfect protection.

William Bascom's *Sixteen Cowries: Yoruba Divination from Africa to the New World* includes an ẹsẹ that is similar to the verse Ìrẹ̀tẹ̀ Ogbè recorded by Verger, but it has a completely different tone and articulation of Àjẹ́. In an ẹsẹ of Òfún, Ọrúnmìlà struggles, sacrifices, and outwits Ògún, Ọbàluaiyé, and Egúngún to marry Odù, who is recognized as both "difficult" and "important."[66] All Odù asks of Ọrúnmìlà is that he observe her taboos: "No one else may see me. I won't live with anyone else."[67] The couple lives harmoniously, with the husband cooking for and catering to his wife, until a member of Ọrúnmìlà's household steals a glimpse of Odù. When Odù flees the interloper, she unintentionally causes the death of one of Ọrúnmìlà's children.

Ọṣun encounters a distraught Odù, and she greets her with important oríkì including "L'ogbo oje," which means Owner of the Club or Sword of Sacred Metal and is an allusion to Ògbóni's cudgel (*ògbó*) of authority; "Ẹlẹyinju ẹgẹ," which means The One with Protruding and Ensnaring Eyes and refers to Ẹdan, the Òrìṣà of Ògbóni; and "Ajowowo l'awọ," "One who has shining skin."[68] The last oríkì could reflect the fact that Odù's numinosity is so brilliant that she literally glows, which is a characteristic of the Gods.[69] With the first two praisenames, Ọṣun acknowledges Odù's command over Ògbóni, who are the traditional Yoruba guardians and administrators of justice, and she recognizes Odù as being synonymous with Ẹdan, the God of Ògbóni. After Ọṣun praises Odù as the Òrìṣà of justice and divine retribution, Ọṣun takes on the role of Ẹdan and becomes the neutral third-party mediator who resolves conflicts. Ọṣun determines that Odù should return home with a contrite Ọrúnmìlà and revivify the child. In this way, harmony is reestablished.

This ẹsẹ is notable for many reasons, including the fact that it is one of the few verses that portrays Odù as vulnerable, and rather than prey on her vulnerability, Ọṣun assists Odù. While women in general and co-wives in particular are stereotyped as being catty and vicious as they vie for male favors, this ẹsẹ depicts respect, patience, assistance, and love between two Àjẹ́ who were also both wives of Ọrúnmìlà at one time. It is worth noting that the diviner who shares this ẹsẹ of Òfún and the wisdom that constitutes the book *Sixteen Cowries* is Maranoro Salako, Omo Gbonka Igana. Perhaps Salako's name tempers his verses, for, as Bascom notes, Maranoro means "'Don't send spite' (Mà rán oró)."[70] True to his name, the ẹsẹ that Salako shares emphasizes both cause and effect and the ease with which Àjẹ́ institute justice, harmony, and peace after discord.

Igbádù and Àpéré: Storehouses of the Power of the World

Odù's connection with Ọrúnmìlà and babaláwo is reflected in the gifts of communication that she devised for and bestowed upon them. The most well-known communication device bears her name, the Odù Ifá. Yoruba elders state that Odù loved and respected Ọrúnmìlà so much that she "revealed to him the knowledge of divination so that man could communicate with the spirit realm."[71] The Odù Ifá is the systematic codified articulation of Odù's "oracular utterance" which is used to help individuals and societies understand and navigate life. Odù Ifá is Odù's language. It is the whisper of the womb. It is the harmonic vibration of the clitoris. Odù Ifá is the sacred utterance of Àjẹ́. Odù Ifá is the wisdom, knowledge, and understanding of the Cosmos. The reason that Opeola states that a babaláwo must have Àjẹ́ is because the babaláwo is dealing directly with Ọrọ̀ Àjẹ́ and can only act as a conduit for and translate the wisdom of the womb if he is in concord with and possesses his own womb.

Odù Ifá is one of the most obvious sites of patrification. Whether the attempts to bar women from the codified wisdom of their own wombs is accidental and the result of misunderstanding and mistranslation or is an intentional assault, not only do individuals attempt to disassociate Odù the God from Odù Ifá, but it is widely held that women are prohibited from learning and divining Ifá. In *Ifa Divination: Communication between Gods and Men in West Africa*, William Bascom states that "[o]nly men can become babalawo."[72] This commonsense statement has been misinterpreted. But semantic extrapolations aside, it must be noted that a woman comes to Earth with innumerable powers, sources, and forces; furthermore, woman is the embodiment of Odù. She is inherently, from birth, and without expensive rites, rituals, and initiations, iyaláwo. Not only does a woman not need to be a babaláwo because she is the source of the secrets that men seek, but no man—or perhaps only the rarest of men—can become an iyaláwo. The significance of Odù's secrets is evident in her marriages to Ọrúnmìlà and Ọbàtálá and that fact that she shares her mysteries with them whereas they, as sons of the Mother, have no secrets to share. The fact that Odù and her Àjẹ́-born mysteries constitute the source and force of Odù Ifá is evident in Ọrúnmìlà's concerted attempts gain access to Odù's wisdom and in his and all babaláwo's strict adherence to her rules.

Women are not barred from Ifá; they are its source and activator. Females, like males, can devote their lives to the arduous work of memorizing innumerable ẹsẹ Ifá, medicines, and prescriptions of power, for there is no edict preventing any woman from learning Odù Ifá, which is, after all, her birthright. Indeed, ẹsẹ Ifá and ìtàn reveal that Odù, Ọṣun, and Yemọja are all iyaláwo in the sense of mastering and casting Ifá divination. Despite these noteworthy role models, individuals continue to manufacture edicts against women mastering Ifá.

In "The Image of Women in Ifá Literary Corpus," Adefioye Oyesakin states that "[t]here are few, if any, women Ifá priests because women are, like in other traditional Yoruba cults, barred from knowing its secrets."[73] The difficulty of creating a patriarchal law where none exists is apparent in the obvious contradiction: Women cannot be effectively "barred" from an institution if a "few" know the secrets. The erroneous nature of Oyesakin's assertion is further emphasized by the information he includes in a footnote: "I have not been able to find out why there are no women Ifá priests among the Yoruba people. Many Babaláwo (Ifá priests) submitted that nothing bars women from Ifá cult, however, domestic chores cannot allow them to learn about Ifá divination. There is a white American woman currently learning Ifá at Ebute-Meta."[74] The irony of the individual who has secured a room of her own, so to speak, to learn Odù Ifá at the expense of others who are forced to build, furnish, and clean that room and cater to its alien occupant cannot be overlooked, but also significant is the fact that Oyesakin chooses not to include the acknowledgement from the elders in the body of the essay. He gives the space of authority and the appearance of validity to a falsehood.

Women can master Ifá, many have mastered Ifá, and many will master Ifá, but because of the wisdom systems and powers that they are inherently equipped with and their roles in ordering society, women possess a unique set of skills and tools that both encompass the wisdom of Ifá and far transcend it, making mastery of Ifá divination unnecessary. Odù gave men Ifá for the same reason that she gave them Igbádù and Egúngún, because they do not have the Àjẹ́, Ọ̀rọ̀, ọfọ̀ àṣẹ, and àṣẹ that women possess.

Many contemporary high ranking female initiates of Ifá adopt the title *iyánífá*, which means "mother has Ifá." Ìyánífá are accorded great respect, and some may very well divine as do babaláwo.[75] However, the term iyánífá is vague—and the vagueness may be intentional—for anyone can claim to *have* Ifá: It can be held for one's partner; it can decorate one's mantle; it can be an aspect of one's orí or ìwà that one bears and propitiates but does not use to interpret cosmological and ontological forces.

Odù is the God, the Womb, the Àjẹ́: Ifá is a way of living, knowing, and doing that encompasses divination, cosmogony, cosmology, ontology, medicine, and metaphysics. One could say that Ifá is the systematic and holistic articulation of Odù's wisdom. Ifá is the externalization of the cosmic intelligence that is stored in the womb. Consequently, all Africana women inherently *have* Ifá and are Odù. In order to avoid the confusion that the term ìyánífá might cause, I have always used the term iyaláwo, because, to me, it properly represents the depth and breadth of Àjẹ́. I use iyaláwo in both its literal and its idiomatic interpretations to signify a mother of secrets, a mother of the sacred, and a mother of all mysteries and holistic wisdom; and Odù Ifá is merely one aspect of mother's wisdom. Iyaláwo is precisely what Àjẹ́ are, and this is why Ọ̀rúnmìlà does all he can to be near and be accepted by Odù and Àwọn Ìyá Wa. Furthermore, Odù, as *the* Àjẹ́, is the consummate Iyaláwo: The mysteries of the Cosmos swirl in the core of her being.

To better understand the power of iyaláwo *vis-à-vis* babaláwo it is helpful to examine Odù's relationship with Ọ̀rúnmìlà and hence, all babaláwo. Similar to her sharing the power of Egúngún with men, Odù grants to babaláwo, through Ọ̀rúnmìlà, access to her womb-deep wisdom through the Odù Ifá. Consequently, the marriage that is literal for Odù and Ọ̀rúnmìlà becomes a spiritual union between Odù and every babaláwo.[76] All babaláwo must observe Odù's rules, respect her, worship her, and erect in her honor a symbolic womb called Igbádù.

The Igbádù encapsulates several cosmontological representations of Odù, including her complex relationship with Ọbàtálá. In *Orin Òrìṣà: Songs for Selected Heads*, John Mason details the intricacies of Odù's relationship with Ọbàtálá and describes how, together, they bring human and celestial life into existence and how they protect those lives with Igbádù:

> Odùa is reputed to have given birth to all the Ọbàtálás. . . . She is the mother creator of the human species and owner of all heads. Odùdúà and Odùa are called to cure the dying and help women have an easy birth. All of these attributes are also claimed by Ọbàtálá. . . . Odùdúà is represented by two gourds that have been sealed and painted white. The medicine that is contained inside is said to blind you if the gourd is ever opened.[77]

Mason also describes Odù as the Great Grand Mother who gives birth to sixteen Ọbàtálá so that every aspect of her myriad power can be complemented. With Mason's description it is clear that Odù does not merely create existence, she ensures that newborns are safely guided from the womb to the breast and that ancestors have a smooth transition into the womb of the universe after they are reunited with the womb of the Earth.

The ancient rotations and revolutions of the Earth, solar system, innumerable suns, and galaxies through time and space mirror the rotations and revolutions that human beings and Gods experience, and Odù is the Cause of All. She is symbolized by the organs she molds and protects: heads, wombs, the Earth, and the Cosmos. And these globular objects are all symbolized by two power-filled sealed gourds that contain the Àjẹ́ and the àṣẹ of the Earth and the Cosmos. This calabash, which is symbolic of Odùduwà who Crowther describes as representing Ọ̀run's union with Ayé, is the sibling of the Igbádù.

A melding of igbá, "calabash cut into halves"[78] and Odù, the Igbádù is a symbolic representation of the Womb of Àjẹ́ that contains the elements of existence. C. L. Adeoye's seminal book *Ìgbàgbọ́ àti Ẹ̀sìn Yorùbá* includes an ìtàn of Odù that details her existence on Earth, her marriage to Ọ̀rúnmìlà, and the origin of her worship. Adeoye reveals that Odù is called Ìyáalé-Ayé, which reflects that fact that she is the first wife on Earth. The first wife lays out strict rules for her husband to follow: Ọ̀rúnmìlà must not take another wife; Odù will only visit him once every twenty years; and Odù demands privacy and seclusion—probably to prevent mortals from being blinded by her raw power—to the degree that she is called Ìyá Ẹlẹ́hàá, which means the Owner of Confinement.[79] Odù's twenty-year sabbaticals from her husband serve as a clear indication that Odù has greater concerns and responsibilities than homemaking and lovemaking. Odù places her duties to the Earth and Cosmos first, and she is the First Wife in a long line of wives, including Ọya, Orò, and the African women who cyclically found women-only towns, who refuse to sacrifice their divine directives and obligations to fulfill patriarchal desires.[80]

While Odù's rules may seem extraordinarily draconian, to better distinguish the type of mother, God, and wife she is from the images conjured by the words "evil" and "witch," it is helpful to examine Odù's reaction to Ọ̀rúnmìlà marrying another woman during one of her twenty-year absences. Rather than destroy or curse her partner, Odù imposes additional rules:

(i) Odù told Ọ̀rúnmìlà that they would never have intercourse again.
(ii) Ọ̀rúnmìlà must wear a white cloth and hold a live large snail with him to see Odù.
(iii) Odù said that her husband must announce his presence, and he cannot come whenever he wants.
(iv) Ọ̀rúnmìlà should never tell anyone that he is coming to see her.[81]

The rules that Odù establishes for Ọ̀rúnmìlà are the same as those that each babaláwo must observe with his Igbádù, which is his Odù.

Igbádù is Odù's representative, and to "see" and worship Igbádù is a weighty matter. Only initiated men can see Odù, and they must worship her while completely naked. Only male initiates of Ifá can prepare her food.[82] The man with Igbádù finds himself in the position of devoted child who is completely naked, exposed, and open hearted before and can hold no secrets from his Mother. The son must prepare his Mother's foods to her exacting specifications, and even the son cannot gaze casually upon Mother's might. He must have his eyes protected with *omi ẹ̀rọ̀*, which is a preparation of ọ̀dúndún, tẹ̀tẹ̀, and rinrin leaves and shea butter, snails, and other sacred elements, to worship Odù.[83] Given that Odù represents the womb of creation, it may be the case that omi ẹ̀rọ̀ is an approximation of the most sacred and protective waters of all: amniotic fluid.

An ẹsẹ Ifá of Ọsẹ Ọ̀yẹkú recorded in "The Rise and Fall" details how Odù directed the construction of the Àpéré and Igbádù. The beginning of the ẹsẹ describes Odù as holding an "*apèrè*." She is holding an object that, true to its name, is a container overflowing with alternate and interconnected meanings with subtly shifting pronunciations. At the ẹsẹ's beginning, Odù is holding is an *apẹ̀rẹ̀*, a basket or container; however, after it is filled with sacred elements, Àjé, and àṣẹ, it will become both an *apẹrẹ ayé*, an object that represents the Earth, and an Àpéré Ayé, a device that terrestrial entities can use to facilitate cosmic communication and become "rulers" or directors (Àpéré) of earthly (Ayé) events and destinies.[84] Furthermore, Àpẹ̀pẹ̀-Alẹ̀ is another name for the Òrìṣà who is the Mother of the Earth, and Àpẹ̀pẹ̀-Alẹ̀, Ìyá Ayé, and Onílẹ̀ are all manifestations of Odù.[85] To put it another way, the ẹsẹ commences with Odù holding in her hands an *apẹrẹ* (symbol) of Àpẹ̀pẹ̀-Alẹ̀ which represents the Earth and is also a microcosmic reproduction of Odù, herself, and of the Cosmos and of the womb. The diacritical marks of Yoruba are absolutely essential to properly pronouncing, distinguishing, and comprehending the meanings of words, which can be widely divergent. However, apèrè, apẹrẹ ayé, Àpéré Ayé, and Àpẹ̀pẹ̀-Alẹ̀ denote distinct but entwined concepts that reflect, relate to, and represent one another with a richness, subtlety, and complexity that is unique to and emblematic of Yoruba language.

When Odù prepares to return to Ọ̀run, she creates the Àpéré and Igbádù so that her human and divine progeny can contact her. Odù tells four of her children, Ọbàtálá, Ògún, Ọbalúaiyé, and Odùduwà, to fill cut calabashes (igbá) with their signature elements. Ọbàtálá places *efun*, spiritual chalk, which is white in color and represents the power of the ancestors and the spiritual realm, in one igbá. Ọbàtálá says that anything a worshipper asks of the igbá it will do, and Ọbàtálá affirms that he (or she) and Odù "are one single thing."[86] Ọbalúaiyé places in his igbá *osùn*, camwood powder, which is used in casting Ifá. Osùn is also the root word of *irosùn*, which represents menstrual blood, which is also the blood of one's lineage and the blood that is essential not only for directing action and destinies but for creating human beings. Ògún contributes *èèdu igi* (charcoal) which is the bituminous spark that ignites the fires of technology. The Earth holds the ancestors' bodies and provides human beings, flora, fauna, and all other organisms with everything necessary for existence. In addition to being the source of ẹfun, osùn, and èèdu igi, the Earth is literally the foundation of life; consequently, it is fitting that Odùduwà, who is the divine daughter of Odù and the unifier of Ọ̀run and Ayé, contributes herself and places *ẹrẹ̀* or mud in her igbá.

The Igbádù is empowered by the properties of the elements that each God contributes, and even the colors of these elements signify power: Black represents vitality, perfection, pure melanin, and the carbonized building blocks of human existence; red symbolizes the activating and authorizing àṣẹ and Àjẹ́ that flows in veins and turns prayers into realities; white represents the ancestors, and the hue reflects and projects the properties of All. The elements that these hues represent and the colors themselves are powerful independently, but they work most efficaciously together. Because of the powers that they signify, the colors black, red, and white are used to decorate the Àpéré.[87] Within the Igbádù, the black, red, and white elements are unified and vivified by the literal and spiritual power of Ilẹ̀—the home of the ancestors and the unborn—through Odùduwà's mud. These three hues and the Earth can be observed working independently and in combination throughout the Yoruba world, especially in sacrifices to Àjẹ́.

The Àpéré, complete with its Igbádù, is the world in miniature. The ẹsẹ Ifá reveals: "the four corners of the world are in the four calabashes."[88] The Àpéré is also the representative of Odù, and by worshiping the Àpéré one is worshipping Odù. Having Àpéré and following Odù's rules of worship are essential for babaláwo: As the ẹsẹ reveals, if a babaláwo fails to propitiate Odù through the Àpéré "he will accomplish nothing."[89] The conclusion of the ẹsẹ confirms that there can be neither Ifá nor babaláwo without Odù, and it emphasizes the fact that the Odù of Odù Ifá is in fact Àjẹ́ Odù.[90]

The Àpéré is the cornerstone of the Yoruba nation and the throne of Odù. It contains the powers and elemental forces of the four prime Òrìṣà. Given the dynamics of existence on Earth, it is essential that the Àpéré be a holistic and gender-balanced construction. Even more significant is the fact that the Àpéré, like the Igbádù is another representation of the womb. In many Ifá communities there is vigorous debate concerning whether or not women can "have" or "see" Odù in the forms of Àpéré and Igbádù. The discussion overlooks the fact that women *are* Odù. Women are walking, living, breathing, birthing manifestations of the God Odù, of Àjẹ́. While Fatunmbi reveals the significant information that in Ilé-Ifẹ̀ "within the Oni's court there is a council of women who are initiated into a priesthood that is called Odu,"[91] it is not necessary for the Africana woman to be part of an elite political coterie to behold and know Odù. Her inherent divinity and endowments are such that the Africana woman who longs to see Odù need only look within herself into the core of her being and into her womb of power.

The Igbádù is also called Igbá Ìwà, the Calabash or Container of Existence.[92] This terminology offers an even clearer picture of the womb, and it highlights the fact that man has no biological receptacle with which to create, develop, or contain ìwà (existence). Odù created and gave men Igbádù because men do not have vaginas, wombs, and breasts and are incomplete. A babaláwo must have the female power contained in the Igbádù to be a whole entity and to receive Odù's Ifá. And yet, while a babaláwo's Igbádù may be the most stunning on Earth, his Igbádù cannot conceive, birth, or nourish a child. Women do not need not make and consecrate a Container of Existence because each woman owns the original upon which the Igbádù is modeled.

By having Odù, a man is able to have discourse with and access some of the power of Odù. Through the Igbádù, select men have greater opportunities to do what Àjẹ́ have always done: observe, protect, and direct destinies. But while Àjẹ́ have full control over the womb, babaláwo do not command control of the Igbádù. In fact, Odù is so dominant a force that rather than the babaláwo having Odù, it would be more appropriate to say that Odù has the babaláwo. Onadele Epega heralds the Igbádù as a "wonder-working" tool and confirms that its wondrous ways lie forever ensconced in the safety of the womb and forever outside of man's cognition. Epega also warns that the Igbádù "should never be opened except the devotee is exceedingly grieved and therefore anxious to leave this world. Igba Iwa is so made as not to be easily opened."[93]

The same care that babaláwo take with Igbádù, Yoruba men in general take with women, who, as the manifestations of Odù, can guarantee men similarly fatal encounters. The reason Yoruba and other African men fear being slapped with a woman's menstrual cloth or having a woman (especially one's wife or mother) intentionally expose her naked body to them when she is enraged is because the body of a woman is her Àpéré. Her breasts, menses, and vagina are the actual power sources that are replicated in the Igbádù. Many men are cognizant of how close to God they come when they enter the path to heaven and there sample sensual delights. And the same path that offers a man momentary bliss can usher him into eternity.

All Africana women, whether infants or elders, are embodiments of Odù; consequently, the sight of the container of Àjẹ́, which is a woman's intentionally exposed naked body galvanized by her Ọ̀rọ̀-rich curses, is sufficient to destroy a man's destiny. To be slapped with Mother's menstrual cloth is to be slapped and rejected by one's ancestors and unborn *ad infinitum*. The fact that Africana women are power stations of the highest imaginable voltage who are capable of undoing men's destinies is why the lies, hatred, and terrorism against Àjẹ́ were concocted; certain men hoped to disconnect that power. However, man cannot destroy that which created him, and his attempts to destroy his source only confirm his yawning inadequacy and creative impotence.

Onílẹ̀: Mother and Owner of the Earth

Odù's Àjẹ́-filled womb is the source of existence, continuity, and power in Yoruba cosmontology. Whether Àjẹ́ Odù's womb is manifest literally in the bodies of Africana women, symbolically in the Igbádù that babaláwo use to gain wisdom from Odù, or eternally in the infinite perfection of the Cosmos, Odù's power is inconceivably vast. Perhaps the most ubiquitous and overlooked manifestation of Odù's might and magnificence is the Earth, which is yet another Great Mother God.

Ìyá Ayé, the Mother of the Earth, has been the focus of a rather odd attempt at degendering. In "Art and Ethos of the Ijebu," Henry John Drewal asserts quite forcefully and rather peculiarly that not only is the Mother and Owner of Earth a gender-free entity, but also that "[n]owhere in the oral literature, Ifa divinatory verses, or lore about the *orisa* in Yorubaland is there a corpus of praises, prayers, stories, myths, rituals, or images devoted to an 'Earth Goddess.' The concept of an earth divinity has probably never been a central part of Yoruba belief."[94] As Babatunde Lawal reveals in *The Gẹ̀lẹ̀dẹ́ Spectacle: Art, Gender and Social Harmony in an African Culture,* Drewal has overlooked numerous publications that elucidate the centrality and significance of the Earth Mother God.[95]

In *Ìgbàgbọ́ àti Ẹ̀sìn Yorùbá*, C. L. Adeoye reveals that Àpẹ̀pẹ̀-Alẹ̀, in another example of the auto-regenerative power of Àjẹ́, is the Òrìṣà who used her self, the earth, to create her Self, the Earth. As the Earth, Àpẹ̀pẹ̀-Alẹ̀ is the original upon whom the babaláwo's Àpéré is modeled. Àpẹ̀pẹ̀-Alẹ̀—who is also known as Ìyá Ayé (Mother of the Earth), Onílẹ̀ (Owner of the Earth), and Ilẹ̀ (Earth)—is Odù manifest as an eternally rotating and revolving covenant that binds Odù, Ọ̀run (the Cosmos), the Òrìṣà, and humanity. Just as the Earth rotates and revolves, so too do the ancestors become the unborn and the reborn as they continue the cycle of living, learning, evolving, healing and elevating.

Given the obvious significance of the Earth to human existence and divine articulation and manifestation, it is fitting that Àjẹ́ are Àpẹ̀pẹ̀-Alẹ̀'s custodians as well as the bearers of biological Àpéré that they use to ensure the Earth's continuity, harmony, and vitality. The relationship between Àjẹ́ and Àpẹ̀pẹ̀-Alẹ̀ is articulated by Rowland Abiodun who asserts that without the Mothers' authorization, "[N]o healing can take place, rain cannot fall, plants cannot bear fruits and children cannot come into the world."[96] Àjẹ́ and Àpẹ̀pẹ̀-Alẹ̀ are quite literally essential to existence.

Adeoye details the centrality of Àpẹ̀pẹ̀-Alẹ̀, the Earth, in Yoruba cosmontology by divulging that "[t]here is nothing the Yoruba do that they do not pay homage to Ilẹ̀. This is important because all Yoruba know that it is inside of her that they will rest at the end of their lives."[97] Because everyone is the product of and will return to Ilẹ̀, she can be invoked to witness pacts and oaths. That Ilẹ̀ is a vibrant and vigilant living God is emphasized in Adeoye's assertion that "[t]he Yoruba do not use Ilẹ̀ to swear falsely, because they know that anybody who uses the earth to swear falsely will have grievous repercussions."[98] Because of her amalgamated magnitude, anyone who breaks an oath overseen by Onílẹ̀ will find immediate rest in Ilẹ̀.

For the same reasons that Onílẹ̀ is asked to witness sworn oaths, she is used to convey messages of profound importance and urgency, as Adeoye reveals:

> When there is a very knotty issue and a matter that deserves urgent resolution, it is Ilẹ̀ that the Yorùbá use to send a message. A little Ilẹ̀ is put inside a leaf and sent to the person for whom the message is intended. Anyone who receives this kind of message knows it is an urgent message; he must go immediately to the person who has sent the message. This kind of communication is never sent unless the matter is weighty."[99]

The person who sends a missive of Earth is literally sending a message in the care of his Mother, hence the degree of respect and urgency with which the message is treated. What is more, just as most mothers' devotion and labors are so consistent that children often take their mothers' efforts for granted, Ilẹ̀ is so central to existence that she is routinely overlooked as humans walk, eat, cultivate, work, sleep, and perform functions vital to life on and within her. However, when a crisis develops, a bit of the same earth that one previously strolled upon conveys more urgency than a million words. Mother Ilẹ̀ is the perfect embodiment of empowered understatement and profound paradox.

Àpẹ̀pẹ̀-Alẹ̀ is the ultimate message. Unlike other Òrìṣà, she does not have a particular sign because everything constitutes her sign as everything is her product. Furthermore, Adeoye reveals that "Ilẹ̀ does not have a separate place of worship. Anywhere someone is standing is the ojubọ of Ilẹ̀ . . . because Ilẹ̀ is everywhere."[100] Correspondingly, anything can be sacrificed to Ilẹ̀ and any and every day can be used to praise her: "It is every day that people have cause to sacrifice to Ilẹ̀."[101] Ilẹ̀ also does not have or need any specific devotees and priests; all human beings, by virtue of their existence, are all the devotees and priests of Ilẹ̀.

Ilẹ̀ is the promise of Odù manifest. The fact that Onílẹ̀'s revolutions and rotations in Odù's great cosmic womb are eternal is illustrated in an *Oríkì Ilẹ̀* which describes Onílẹ̀ in the following way: "*Òdù yí gbiri gbiri má fòó*" ("Òdù rolls over and over without breaking").[102] The eternally rolling and unbreakable Odù is the Earth. This spinning Pot of Life is replicated in the womb which is carried in the core of every woman's being. No matter what any man decrees, demands, or declaims, only the Mother and Owner of the Pot of Creation can decide when, how, and if she will develop the contents of her Pot.

Because they are divine manifestations of Odù and the living embodiments of Onílẹ̀, Àjẹ́ are the keepers of the covenant extant between Odù and Onílẹ̀ and the Cosmos and the Earth. While C. Osamaro Ibie finds that only the Earth can neutralize or overturn the decisions of Àjẹ́,[103] the relationship between Àjẹ́ and Onílẹ̀ is so intimate that they are indistinguishable; in fact, Àjẹ́ are often simply referred to as Ayé, which means Earth.

Because all of the ancestors reside in her and all unborn will spring from her, Ilẹ̀ is the ultimate judge; this is why she is invoked, sipped, or eaten to seal oaths. Àjẹ́ are Ilẹ̀'s designated enforcers of justice; they ensure balance, harmony, and the potential for evolution and elevation. As Fatunmbi elucidates: "It is through the earth that the concept of justice becomes aligned with the concept of evolution. Those actions that destroy the earth's balance and block the flow of evolution would be unjust from the *Ifá* perspective."[104] It is the job of Àjẹ́ to ensure the "flow of evolution" remains unrestricted, and, in this effort, they stand at the apex of a formidable collective that includes Ilẹ̀, Odù, Ẹdan, and Ògbóni.

The *Oríkì Ilẹ̀* describes the collective's genealogical relationship, stating that "Olódù Ifẹ̀ is the father of Àjẹ́."[105] It is obvious that patrification is at work here, not only because Àjẹ́ has no father, but also because the Owner of Odù who founded Ifẹ̀, the cradle of humanity in Yoruba history, can only be either Odù or her daughter Odùduwà. The oríkì does, however, properly acknowledge the cosmic-biological mother of power in its confirmation that Àjẹ́, Odù, Àbẹ̀ní (The One We Beg to Have, an oríkì of Àjẹ́), and Ẹdan, the God of Ògbóni, are all children of Àpẹ̀pẹ̀-Alẹ̀, who is the Mother of the Earth.[106]

In addition to Odù creating Àpéré so that her progeny could communicate with her after she returned to Ọ̀run, Odù also enlisted Onílẹ̀ to watch over and monitor the actions of her progeny. As a study of endless reciprocity and curvilinear responsibility, Onílẹ̀ nourishes and renews her children, who honor and propitiate the Òrìṣà, who guide and direct humanity, who nourish and nurture Ilẹ̀. Onílẹ̀ appears in the ẹsẹ Ifá as an Earth Mother and as the source who receives (*à la* Iyangbà) sacrifices designed to neutralize negativity, to balance inequality, and to institute harmony. In an ẹsẹ Ifá of Èjì Ogbè, a sacrifice is shared among Ògún, Ọ̀sanyìn, onísẹ̀gun, and Onílẹ̀ to rid the earth of quarrels.[107] In another ẹsẹ Ifá, Òbàrà Méjì sacrifices to "mother earth (Oriole)" and is able to accomplish what too much alcohol talked him into.[108] In another verse, Ìrosùn Méjì sacrifices, and the "ground divinity (Ebora Ile)" reveals to him how he can outwit disease and death.[109]

There are also ẹsẹ Ifá in which Onílẹ̀ is an active agent. In an ẹsẹ Ifá of Ogbè Méjì, Ọ̀rúnmìlà sacrifices to marry Earth, daughter of "the one with the pleasing gown."[110] Earth or Ayé, wears two hundred cloths, much like the multicolored cloth of Àjẹ́, and states that she will marry the man who sees her buttocks. Ọ̀rúnmìlà takes the prescribed sacrifice to the forest, and with the help of Èṣù, he sees the buttocks of Earth and becomes her husband.[111] In a similar ẹsẹ Ifá in *Sixteen Cowries*, Earth is represented by Ọṣun who is said to have "the buttocks of the world."[112] The majority of human beings are conceived through blissful copulation. The genitals are designed to be aesthetically pleasing, highly sensitive, and most delightful. While organized religions often approach sex, sensuality, and the human body—especially the female genitalia—with disgust, shame, and fear, African cosmology heralds the organs and accoutrement that urge us to engage in the celebratory act whose climax is at once a revelation and the possible consecration of a new life.

When one peruses the ruins of Kemet, one finds images of Ausar naked, fully erect, and stimulating science, architecture, astronomy, philosophy, and fertilizing Nwt, whose nude body is the "pleasing gown" of the Cosmos. From depictions of the Gods to those of the God Mothers, the sexually charged and potent aspects of the body are embraced in African cosmology because such exultation is natural and essential. It is for many reasons that Odù is Àbẹ̀ní, The One We Beg To Have.

Rather than a neutered or neutral sphere, Yoruba cosmontology depicts Ilẹ̀ as an active, vital, and vibrant Àjẹ́ Mother God. Whether she is overseeing and sealing oaths or effused in the sensual abundance necessary to create worlds, Onílẹ̀ reveals herself to be a dynamic mother of unpredictable powers and diverse lessons. One of her most celebrated representations is that of the talking skull. It is fitting that, due to both forced and voluntary African migrations, this orature has become a global showpiece and is immortalized in African America in the sculpture of Meta Veaux Warrick Fuller, the orature of Zora Neale Hurston's *Mules and Men*, and the verbal artistry of multitudes.[113]

The Odù Ifá concerning Ilẹ̀'s talking skull reveals that even Ilẹ̀ Ogẹ́rẹ́, Mother Earth, The Slippery One, can breach her own rules of balance and reciprocity and suffer a downfall. Bascom's *Ifa Divination* includes two ẹsẹ of Òtúrá-Bàrà concerning Ilẹ̀'s refusal to sacrifice which leads to her being so poorly interred that her skull is left exposed. In one verse, Ìyá Ayé's skull initiates a cycle of death that leads to the decapitation of a farmer, the members of Ògbóni, and the Ògúngbẹ́ war council.[114] In the second verse, the skull of Ilẹ̀ rests under an Ìrókò tree, and there she teaches her former debtor that the most perplexing puns and riddles are those uttered by Àjẹ́.[115]

Ìyá Ayé's ẹsẹ confirm that anyone can violate the laws of the Earth, even Earth, and that everyone can repair those breaches. However, it is also clear that the supremacy of Àjẹ́ Ìyá Ayé outweighs her perceived violations. In both ẹsẹ Ifá, Ìyá Ayé refuses to sacrifice. Similar to Odù who declares she will not sacrifice before coming to Earth because her destiny is assured, Ilẹ̀ also does not sacrifice: What can the Earth sacrifice to herself? She is Everything, and Everything is Hers. Indeed, rather than destroy her destiny, Ilẹ̀'s refusal to sacrifice grants her additional opportunities to educate—and it is significant that her pupils are men. In both ẹsẹ it is the male rulers and officials who sacrifice to Ìyá Ayé. The sacrifices contain items that are favorites of Àjẹ́ and that boast spiritually significant hues, such as Àjẹ́'s signature dish, àkàrà (deep fried black-eyed bean fritters), which is red in hue; Black Tamarind; and white cloth.[116] The supremacy of the Mother is undeniable, for rather than Ilẹ̀ being forced to submit to anyone or anything, it is the masculine powerbrokers who sacrifice to her, celebrate her, and sing her praises lest they lose their heads.

Òṣùmàrè: Sublime Paradox Divine

Àjẹ́ Odù does not exist in some invisible lair in the Cosmos: She is the Cosmos. Furthermore, Odù and her many manifestations are unlike the Gods of organized religions in that they are at one with the flora, fauna, and the Earth because they *are* the flora, fauna, and the Earth. The curvilinear force of divinity, the eternal covenants of the Gods, and the effortless mutability of Àjẹ́ are richly manifest in Òṣùmàrè.

Òṣùmàrè is associated with either the rainbow or the earthly representative of the rainbow, the Rainbow Boa, which is sacred in many African societies. Òṣùmàrè is also a profoundly important Àjẹ́. Òṣùmàrè reveals that the rainbow is much more than the refraction of water through light providing the eye with a visual spectacle; the rainbow is a living, cyclic, visible reminder of the amalgamated powers and eternal promise of the Womb of Existence. Fatunmbi finds that Òṣùmàrè extends to all life forms the potential to "become transformed and experience rebirth."[117] Òṣùmàrè is the perfect ambassador of the promise of transformative regeneration because that is her hallmark.

A popular African proverb asserts that "the young shall grow," and the second eṣẹ of Èjì Ogbè in *Sixteen Cowries* introduces a diviner whose first name is a nod to the proverb and to Àjẹ́: "Little by little the oka snake becomes thicker."[118] In *Ifa Divination*, Bascom describes Oká as a boa that "does not run away when hunters come to kill it, but rises up and peers out at them to see what is happening"; what is more, Bascom finds that Oká is called "Nana Buruku's snake" (ejo Buku).[119] Nàná Bùrúkù is a manifestation of Àjẹ́ Odù who is recognized throughout Pan-Africa. In *Ìgbàgbọ́ àti Èsìn Yorùbá*, Adeoye describes how Nàná Bùkúù, in a role reminiscent of Odù's creation of the Àpéré, gives Ọbàtálá, Òṣun, Ògún, and Obalúaiyé their signature elements and teaches them how to use them to destroy their enemies.[120] In addition to invoking the power of Nàná Bùrúkù, the diviner of the eṣẹ of Èjì Ogbè has a name that references Òṣùmàrè: "Foolish rainbow in the house, / With his face to the sea, / And his back to the lagoon, / He looks at Olorun on high."[121] While steadily developing like the snake of Àjẹ́, the diviner enjoys the cosmic-terrestrial mobility of Òṣùmàrè who is comfortably ensconced in domesticity but able to unite Olókun with Yemọja while peering into the infinite Pot of Existence that is Olọ́run.

The relationship between Oká and Òṣùmàrè recurs in an eṣẹ of Ìrosùn which compares the ways that the mothers of Oká and Òṣùmàrè solidify their progenies' destinies. The mothers are told to sacrifice a red sash and a black sash. The colors are significant because red and black are the colors that adorn Oká, whose oríkì is "See the world" (*T'ojú b'aiyé*) because of its penchant for observation. Oká's mother sacrifices for her child, who continues to enjoy her view of the world. Òṣùmàrè's mother is confident that nothing can take her child from her, so she does not sacrifice. Ìyá Òṣùmàrè is correct, and while she does not lose her child to death, Òṣùmàrè, as the rainbow, cycles eternally between Òrun and Ayé constantly being reborn from and returning to the Pot of Continuity.

Both Awo Fatunmbi and E. Bolaji Idowu assert that Olódùmarè is a compound word that melds "Owner of Odù" with Òṣùmàrè in recognition of the fact that Olódùmarè is the offspring of Odù and Òṣùmàrè. Fatunmbi finds that Olódùmarè is "[t]he Spirit that maintains all forms that evolve throughout Creation," and that Òṣùmàrè is the manifest promise of Olódùmarè's covenant with creation, including human beings, Òrìṣà, flora and fauna.[122]

An ẹsẹ of Òfún recorded in Bascom's *Sixteen Cowries* elucidates the complex relationship between Olódùmarè, Ọbàtálá, Òṣùmàrè, and Odù. The ẹsẹ reveals that Orishala Osheregbo (Ọbàtálá) marries Erè (Boa) and three children are born of their union: Olódù, Ẹlẹrìn, and Elégunrin. In addition to the ẹsẹ revealing the origin of Olódù, Erè becomes deified after she swallows Ọbàtálá's àṣẹ. Ọbàtálá sees his power illuminating Erè internally. Because he is not able to catch her and reclaim his àṣẹ, Ọbàtálá curses her: "[Y]our arms will disappear; / Your feet will disappear right now / You will walk on your chest."[123] The punishment actually transforms Erè from a woman to a rainbow boa to the God Òṣùmàrè. Her first born child also becomes a God: The ẹsẹ reveals that "Olódù Ọmọ Erè (Olódù, child of Python)" is the meaning of Olódùmarè.[124] The ẹsẹ of Òfún includes no sacrifice or recommendations. The client could interpret this to mean that what appears to be a tragedy will result in triumph; indeed, this pattern of destruction resulting in (re-)creation is a recurring motif in both the ẹsẹ and the actuality of Àjẹ́ Òṣùmàrè.

An ẹsẹ that appears to be the elder of that recorded in *Sixteen Cowries* places Òṣùmàrè, recognized as Erè, at the origin of creation giving birth to Divinity with a fecund odù:

> Erè brought into the world a pot *odù*. She placed four eggs into it. One of them rolls out of the pot and breaks, *Olódù*, this is *Olódù ọmọ Erè*, *Olódù* the child of *Erè*. The second is *Odùdúà* or *Òrìṣàlá*, the third, *Odùà*, and the fourth is *Odù logbo oje ẹlẹ́yinjú ẹgé. . .*, the sole woman among them is àjẹ́; she has more power than the others.[125]

This is the beginning of an ẹsẹ that Verger includes in "The Rise and Fall." He unfortunately, and inexplicably given that Àjẹ́ is the topic of his article, ends the ẹsẹ as indicated above and offers no additional information on the text, or its source, or its Gods.

Despite its truncation, the ìtàn describes Àjẹ́ Erè busily creating with an odù (or a womb) and four ovum. Snakes are often thought to symbolize the penis, but Erè is consistently depicted as a female God. Her gender is important because, as the ẹsẹ confirms, similar to Odù, Erè is a comprehensive God who can create everything, including "male" Òrìṣà, without a "male" complement. Yoruba cosmogony reinforces at every turn that Mother is the consummate creator. Given Mother's completeness, it is important to note that what the orature attempts to describe as male forces are all female Òrìṣà Àjẹ́ who are all obvious manifestations of Odù.

The ẹsẹ recorded by Verger offers especially resonant examples of Àjẹ́'s inherent ability to turn tragedy into triumph. Not only is the egg that rolls out of the pot not abandoned, but it becomes Olódù, the Owner of the

Pot. What is more, rather than its breaking destroying its contents, the egg's crack facilitates the birth of Olódùmarè, the daughter of Odù and Erè.

An ẹsẹ Ifá of Òfún Méjì recorded in C. Osamaro Ibie's *Ifism: The Complete Works of Orunmila* also features the theme of tragedy giving birth to triumph. This ẹsẹ is significant because it documents how the manifestation of Odù who is described in Verger's truncated orature as Àjẹ́—and also as the owner of the sacred club of Ògbóni and the owner of the ensnaring eyeballs of Ẹdan—founds the Ògbóni society. The ẹsẹ features a limbless woman named "Ugbin eenowo eenose, Ejo kodu kodu" (Ugbin Ejo), which means, "Snail without hands and legs, Snake crawling on its abdomen."[126] Ugbin Ejo is the obvious embodiment of Òṣùmàrè, and she is an Àjẹ́ and a true iyaláwo: Ugbin Ejo casts Ifá for Òfún Méjì before he leaves Ọrun for Ayé. Because their destinies are connected, when he returns to Ọrun he casts Ifá for Ugbin Ejo and then carries her on his back to Earth so that she can make the sacrifice that will endow her with limbs and grant her with children.

At the three road junction where Èṣù and Àjẹ́ are known to meet and to change fates, Ugbin Ejo instructs Òfún Méjì to build a windowless and doorless home where she can live in perfect privacy. Ugbin Ejo's needs are similar to those of Odù, who is known as Ìyá Ẹlẹ́hàá because of her demand for seclusion. Ugbin Ejo's home can only be accessed through the "tree of life," and in order to visit Ugbin Ejo, Òfún Méjì must stand with his back to the home under a palm frond and recite the following incantation: "Oro oyin kiimu eyon, eekpa – aikoro lule awo."[127]

As he prepares to make Ugbin Ejo's sacrifices, Òfún Méjì discusses her with his friend Akpena, who expresses an interest in marrying her. Ugbin Ejo agrees to marry Akpena, but first she makes the men swear an oath on "a mysterious wand" that they will not reveal her condition to anyone and that they will blindfold anyone they bring to her home: The only exceptions are Òfún Méjì and babaláwo.[128] Ugbin Ejo's home is called Ilé-Òdì, or Ilédì, which is also the name of the Ògbóni lodge. The wand that Ugbin Ejo uses to seal oaths is Ẹdan, the God of Ògbóni. Ugbin Ejo's husband's name is Apèènà, which is also one of the highest titles in Ògbóni. Mirroring Odù's sixteen children, who are known as the Olódù, Ugbin Ejo and Akpena have sixteen children. The eldest children are twins named Ogbo and Oni, and their fights are so rampant and destructive that Ugbin Ejo takes them to the Ilédì and makes them swear "never to plot or do anything against each other. That was the first initiation ceremony into the Secret fraternity" of Ògbóni.[129]

Just as snails and snakes are closely associated with the Earth with which they are intimately connected, so too is Ugbin Ejo, because of her initial appearance and form of mobility, the most appropriate representative of Ilẹ and her laws. Ugbin Ejo's appearance is also used to test the character of Òfún Méjì. Instead of mocking her or fleeing from her in disgust, Òfún Méjì follows the advice of the Yoruba proverb that directs one to *mọ ìwà fún oníwà*: He respects Ugbin Ejo whose existence was designed by Erè and molded in Odù's Igbá Ìwà. With Òfún Méjì's help, Ugbin Ejo becomes a fully formed woman who literally gives birth to Ògbóni, which is founded and maintained by Àjẹ́ and ensures adherence to the Laws of Onílẹ̀. It is with the ìtàn of Ugbin Ejo that the great versatility and balance of Odù are revealed. Ugbin Ejo seamlessly connects the cosmic and terrestrial forces and figures of Odù, Òṣùmàrè, Odùduwà, Ẹdan, and Onílẹ̀.

Ògbóni's laws and iconography, which are centered on reverence of both Àjẹ́ and the Earth, are central to the Yoruba ethos, but Ògbóni appears to predate the Yoruba people. Ekpo Eyo explains the society's likely origin:

> Ogboni is a secret society connected with earth worship and was possibly in existence before what is now Yorubaland was invaded by the present inhabitants, or at least the kings. Hence, while other Orishas came in with the new people, the Ogboni appears to be the original cult of the autochthonous people, and was adopted by the new comers and used as the main instrument of government, although the Oba is the acknowledged head.[130]

The original inhabitants' system of governance and way of life is known as Imọlẹ̀ or Mọlẹ̀ which is a contraction of Ọmọ Onílẹ̀: Children of the Mother of the Earth.[131] It could very well be the case that the Yoruba who boast unique chromosomal and hemoglobin variances are the direct descendants of the Mọlẹ̀, the original inhabitants of Ilé-Ifẹ̀. What is clear is that the Mọlẹ̀ source of self and architect of existence—which became that of the Yoruba—is Mother, Womb, Àjẹ́.

Mọlẹ̀ and her mother Onílẹ̀ are manifestations of Àjẹ́ Odù who are as integral to Yoruba cosmontology as the Earth is integral to humanity. The oneness between Odù and Onílẹ̀, which recurs in Yoruba philosophy and orature and is evident in Odùduwà's contribution of mud to the Igbádù and in the description of the Earth as a huge pot that rolls eternally without breaking, is also central to the Ògbóni society, as Opeola elucidates: "Odùduwà is known as Onílẹ̀ because the original association before the Ògbóni became Ògbóni was Onímọlẹ̀. So the old Ògbóni cults . . . they have Mọlẹ̀, and they are all sharing the Mother Earth. Mother Earth is the Goddess of Ògbóni and you know Odùduwà contributed the earth [to the Igbádù]."[132] Opeola ends his explication with a telling fact: "Mọlẹ̀ was hated by the colonizers."[133]

. . .

No matter the level of hatred colonizers had for her or the high-tech implements of destruction neocolonials aim at her, Àjẹ́ Odù can never die, and she cannot be killed. Lynch mobs cannot hang or dunk Àjẹ́ to death, and Àjẹ́ cannot be patrified or degendered into oblivion. The study of Odù reveals the intricacy and complexity of Yoruba cosmontology, the foundation of which is Àjẹ́. Not only is Odù fully infused in every single aspect of Yoruba cosmology, ontology, and cosmogony, but she is the Cosmos, and only a fool would seek to destroy that.

CHAPTER TWO

THE VAGINA GIVES BIRTH TO THE WORLD: ÀJẸ́'S SIGNS, SYMBOLS, AND ORDERS OF OPERATION

It is often said that if one seeks to understand a people's culture, one must understand that people's language. This is certainly true of Yoruba culture, and Yoruba language reveals the depth of the culture, for Yoruba is one of the most logical and complex languages in existence. A simple utterance in a Romance language becomes a study of layers, powers, puns, riddles, and interwoven signs and signifiers in Yoruba—and I am referring to *modern* Yoruba. I imagine that esoteric Yoruba is so packed with the power of Mọlẹ̀ that the Ọ̀rọ̀ of each utterance vibrates with soul force.

Yoruba language is not merely a mode of communication; it is a fluid, flexible, organic force, and it is treated as such. Words are linguistic bullets, medicines, and activating agents that come alive and undertake their appointed tasks once invoked. The complexity and power of the linguistic system reflects a profound understanding of the impact and relationship of cosmic forces and signs on flora and fauna, including human beings, and on objects thought to be inanimate like Òkè of Ìbàdàn, water, thoughts, and constellations. Many Yoruba concepts are expressed with words that are what I call *odù kékeré*, little pots of profundity that tuck additional meanings within and underneath standard definitions. In addition to the power contained within actual words, there are many important Yoruba concepts and messages that are conveyed nonverbally through a language of signs and symbols known as *àrokò*.

Yoruba language, similar to Odù, is a force of infinite depths. While one can master the English language and boast complete knowledge of its vocabulary, grammar, and syntax, Yoruba language is constantly growing and evolving, as is Àjẹ́. The language of Àjẹ́, which is the lyrical living wisdom of Odù's womb, is an exploration of Ọ̀rọ̀, àrokò, and operational modes that can only be the beginning of an endless endeavor to better know the infinitude of Our Mothers.

Oríkì Àjẹ́

The flexibility and depth of Yoruba language are brilliantly illustrated in one of the praisenames of Àwọn Ìyá Wa. The term "Ìyàmi" is not a conflation of *ìyá mi* (my mother) and *ìyà mi* (my woe, suffering, wickedness). "Ìyàmi" is an odù kékeré with political, ancestral, and spiritual meanings. Ayo Opefeyitimi confirms that the term Ìyàmi "is deeper than the concept or notion of old age. It is a metaphorical reference to a group of people (the *ìyàmi* in the present usage) who have some powers which ordinary women do not have. These powers have celestial origin."[1] Pierre F. Verger also makes this point in *Ewé: The Use of Plants in Yoruba Society*: "The word *ìyámi*, 'my mother', is normally written with a high tone on the second syllable, but when it's about "powerful mothers, as in this case, the adopted orthography is *ìyàmi*."[2] In cognizance of this linguistic shift, many scholars use "Ìyàmi" when referring to the Mothers, including Wande Abimbola, C. L. Adeoye, Oludare Olajubu, Rowland Abiodun, and the present author.

Babatunde Lawal in *The Gẹ̀lẹ̀dẹ́ Spectacle* includes an *ìwúre*, song of blessing, in which Isola sings praises to "ìyá mi" (my mother) as well as "Ìyà mi ìyá" which Lawal translates as "'My Mother' of mothers."[3] As if to ensure the grandeur of the Mother will not be taken for granted, mistaken, or misconstrued, Isola uses "Ìyà mi ìyá" repeatedly in the closing of the ìwúre as he adorns the Mother of mothers in her oríkì and secures her blessings for the community. Depending upon the linguistic foundation, the orature, the context, and the desired specificity, verbal artists may invoke Àjẹ́ with "Ìyámi," "Ìyàmi," "Ìyáàmi," "Ìyaàmi," "Ìyá ooooo," or a combination of these and other honorifics as necessary to convey their sentiments.

The titles of the Mothers are as encoded, complex, and fluid as their powers. Àjẹ́, itself is a word riddled with complexity. Raymond Prince asserts that Àjẹ́ is a contraction of Ìyá "Mother" and jẹ́ "eat."[4] Every living thing must ingest some form of sustenance, so this is either the most mundane transliteration possible, or, if cannibalism is being inferred, it is a lie. Mothers do not eat their children—if they did, I would not be here writing and you would not be there reading. I have not found Prince's definition reflected in any traditional Yoruba orature, and I have also seen no definitive evidence that Àjẹ́ is a compound word. If it is a compound construction, Àjẹ́ could be composed of *À*, meaning "We" or "Those," signifying a collective, who are bound by *ẹ̀jẹ̀* "blood," or who are bound by *ẹ̀jẹ́* "a vow," or who *jẹ́* "comply," as in with the laws of Odù and Onílẹ̀. Àjẹ́ could be translated as all of this or none of this. Àjẹ́ is untranslatable; it has no foreign language equivalent. I find the best and most appropriate definition and translation of Àjẹ́ to be "Àjẹ́." With this equivalency, no insulting errors can be made, and the Gods of one culture cannot be confused with the fairytales and fictions of another.

Because Àwọn Ìyàmi are masters of riddling, ciphers, and deciphering, the study of Àjẹ́ is an exploration of the most obvious, clear, and irreducible just before it shrouds itself in new mystery, wraps even more ancient enigmas around its power, and splits into sixteen additional divine mothers and daughters. As I state elsewhere, Àjẹ́'s orature are conundrums that *pa ìtàn*, reveal historical and biographical information, and *pa àlọ́*, tell riddles and offer ciphers.[5] This multiplicity and flexibility, this clarity masked by inscrutability, this permanence defined by mutability is the hallmark of Àjẹ́. The powers and the paradoxes of the Gods are apparent in the Mothers' symbols, signs, and orders of operations.

The Vagina—The Source of All Blessings

Whether the search is for human origins, the birth of the Earth, or the conception of the Cosmos, the study of Àjẹ́ leads to the vagina, an organ so important that it is praised as *Ọ̀nà-Ọ̀run*, the Road to the Cosmos.[6] While hypermasculinity, thug profiles, and pimp myths dominate the international mass media and position women in many movies, books, videos, and songs as expendable sexual props whose vaginas are casually bought and sold, splayed and betrayed, in traditional Yoruba culture, men approach the vagina and its attendant Àjẹ́ in a very different manner.

Yoruba hunters are known for their bravery and their mastery of Africana science and technology. Yoruba orature reveals that hunters and Àjẹ́ inspire similar feelings of awe in their communities, and many hunters are necessarily Àjẹ́.[7] But, as a song included in Ulli Beier's *Yoruba Poetry* reveals, the hunter, with all of his wisdom, courage, and spiritual access, pines for *real* power:

> God never did well when he failed to create me a woman:
> I would dance *tadireke*.
> I would open my wrapper and regard my new god
> Who gives birth on the ground and who kills to eat.[8]

Many men may long to feel what a woman does or to have access to her experiences, but few men are confident enough in their manhood to state that desire openly, let alone express it in a moving tribute. The hunter blames the patrified God for granting him the incomplete genetic copy that is the male gender. Rather than admire the undulations of the buttocks of a dancing woman, the hunter longs to know the feelings of she who inspires the dance. He wants his own tender vagina, jutting clitoris, and life-giving womb; in short, the hunter wants to know and be God. Through the hunter's praise, it is clear that many men covet what many women take for granted, including women's fundamental connection to Onílẹ̀ and Ọ̀run, women's ability to create life, and the fact that women are Gods who create Gods.

The hunter's song alludes to a prevalent custom among, largely, established Yoruba women that seems to be an àrokò that signifies the power of their Àpéré. The hunter sings that if he were a woman he would relish opening his wrapper and regarding his new God. The act the hunter describes appears to reference the custom of Yoruba matriarchs who routinely unfurl and retie their wrap skirts. With this simple act, which may occur at a dance, at a market, at a bank, or on a bus stop, not only does the woman secure her garments, but she also alerts the community to the power that is in its midst. In this era, women wear slips underneath their wrappers so that the threat and promise of the àrokò are intimated, but the hunter's song and the women's custom may be referencing an era when a glimpse at the guardian of the eternity and oblivion was always near at hand. This ritual of untying, fanning, and rewrapping one's wrapper can easily be rendered unnecessary with the use of string or knots, but this custom is undertaken so often and with such relaxed flourish that it appears to be an àrokò that indicates, warns, threatens, and promises all while balancing visible and invisible societal forces. It is not surprising that the hunter's desire is to become this power and control the wrapper that constitutes the casual cover of God.

The hunter's resonant ode also offers important information about traditional Yoruba obstetrical practices, and it elucidates the cycle of power existent between Àjẹ́, Onílẹ̀, and Odù. Westernized hospitals have become *en vogue* for many parents, despite the facts that these facilities are breeding grounds for innumerable debilitating pathogens and that contemporary hospitals routinely mandate anti-African and anti-woman practices. However, by kneeling on the ground to give birth, as mothers do in traditional Yoruba society, the mother's labor is aided by gravity, and she is able to work and move with her contractions rather than be immobilized by pain or numbed to her body's and her child's needs. The posture she assumes when giving birth also magnifies her divinity and her Àjẹ́ to the extent that whenever she assumes this posture to utter a curse or make a request after giving birth, the Earth and Cosmos will make her words manifest.

By giving birth on the ground, the mother galvanizes the connection between herself and Onílẹ̀, and she immediately introduces her newborn child to *the* Mother, Onílẹ̀, who is also the magnificent revolving and rotating womb known as Odù. Mother and child consecrate these elemental bonds with the assistance of a collective of Àjẹ́ obstetricians who facilitate the birthing process. The community mothers ensure that the placenta and umbilical cord—which a modern hospital staff will conduct tests on, extract sacred tissues from for nefarious purposes, and then throw away as "waste"—once released from the mother are reunited with the Mother and are buried in the Earth where they extend cosmically and join the grand helix that connects all human beings to Àjẹ́. Indeed, giving birth on the ground is a simple and logical act that resonates with stupendous power.

Onílẹ̀ is one of the most potent and important Gods of Àjẹ́, and she is central to the Yoruba ethos and worldview. It is important that newborns greet Onílẹ̀ because doing so concretizes the celestial and the terrestrial covenants of the child's existence; these are the same covenants kept by the child's elders and ancestors and the child's unborn children as well. As their orature and icons make wondrously clear, children are of paramount importance to such Gods as Onílẹ̀, Yemọja, and Ìyá Màpó and to the Ògbóni society. While Ògbóni is usually associated with elder men, Adeoye's *Ìgbàgbọ́ àti Ẹ̀sìn Yorùbá* describes Ẹdan as originally initiating every resident of Ifẹ̀, all ages and both genders, into Ògbóni.[9] With an early introduction to cosmic and terrestrial laws and lineage, children grow to be responsible adults who are always conscious of the justice of Àjẹ́, the vigilance of Ẹdan, and human beings' obligations to Onílẹ̀.

The hunter's most perplexing reference may be his homage to the God who "kills to eat." Despite what myths would encourage one to believe, the hunter is not praising a witch with a bloodlust. Beier relates the metaphor to the dreaded *mágùn* (literally, "do not mount"), a protective technology that can trap and kill an adulterous male. However, it is more likely that the reference is to the aftermath of sexual climax. The God in question is not actually dining nor is she a cannibal. This God is the Divine Vagina undertaking the work of Iyangbà, the Receiving Mother. After "killing" the penis with pleasure, she receives the sperm and guides it through the womb to the egg and the destiny for which it was made and for which it longs.

"Eating" and "killing" symbolism recurs in songs about and images of Ìyánlá. An oríkì Yemọja intones: "The pot-breasted mother / With much hair on her private part / The owner of a vagina that suffocates like dry yam in the throat."[10] These resonant lines reveal how enticing, perilous, and appropriate a God woman is for man. His desire to please knows no boundary. Even if he perishes while paying homage, the pleasure is worth the pain, for he who suffocates in the Mother is resurrected not only after a period of rest, but also, and more importantly, he is resurrected through conception. It is for reasons like these and many more that Àjẹ́ Yemọja is heralded as "the generous and the dangerous mother."[11]

The Àjẹ́ and the vagina that are the subjects of the hunter's ode and his longing also take the spotlight in the riddle that asks, Who is the small bearded God we must worship while kneeling? The answer is, the Vagina.[12] Ulli Beier recorded this riddle from children who had not been socialized to hate, be ashamed of, or fear their life-giving genitals.[13] When one's mind is in proper alignment with scientific, biological, and cosmological realities, the human body and its relationship to the self, the

Earth, and the Cosmos make sense, and they make love, and they make life.

In kneeling to worship the small bearded God, one can picture man in his rightful position of reverence on his knees before Vagina, praying through and to the God of Life. One can also envision a female on her knees bending forward to gaze at her God of Life. The first thing the beholder sees is the prepuce of the clitoris, the mother of the penis, rich with nerves, sensation, and veins awaiting a rush of blood, engorgement, and ecstasy.

In addition to its role in ancient creation and its ability to provide a woman with independently derived pleasure, the clitoris may be the focal point of Àjẹ́. Rowland Abiodun offers important information about the clitoris and its biological, spiritual, and political power:

> Though very rarely mentioned by field informants, there are indications that the fact of being female contributes to the power of women and perhaps also their entry into and participation in the Eegun cult. For example, the clitoris is traditionally believed to possess some kind of "power", similar to the power possessed by the Eegun, for according to an informant, both are concealed, unseen, and use the power of "our mothers". This is the reason, perhaps, behind the belief that any man, no matter how medicinally skilful or powerful, can be disarmed by a woman.[14]

The connection between the clitoris and Egúngún recalls the fact that Odù brought Egúngún with her from Ọ̀run, and while she gave men the privilege of donning the mask and dancing, Egúngún cannot appear in public without the approval of Àjẹ́, and when it appears, Ẹlẹ́yẹ monitors its every move. John Pemberton finds that Egúngún means "powers concealed,"[15] and this phrase also defines the clitoris, which is the sensual and spiritual stimulator of woman that juts between the labia while being concealed within its prepuce.

The clitoris is many things: a political empowerer, a furtive bird of power, a concentrated "secret of joy," to quote Alice Walker,[16] and an indefinable power source, according to Abiodun. The clitoris is what prompts Àjẹ́ to create woman-only towns and to rid themselves of male excesses and abusers. The clitoris is the eye-shattering Aragamago. The clitoris is the threat to extinguish life and the exultant joy of conception contained in one tiny masterpiece.

Abiodun's findings are important for many reasons, including revealing why the clitoris is the focus of genital excisions: Through its removal, the patriarchy seeks to control and delimit a woman's pleasure while obliterating the capstone of her power. If anything is indicative of "witchery" it is the patriarchal mandate designed to divest women of the ability to find pure bliss in themselves and exert power in the world.

The fact that millions upon millions of women have been robbed of their clitorises and labia minora and majora and subjected to horrific pain, often leading to death, and made to endure a lifetime of unimaginable agony when urinating, menstruating, and childbearing all in the patriarchy's attempt to find the source of Àjẹ́ and extinguish it is chilling. That men would demand the butchering, sealing, and in some cases, customization of the vagina be enacted by mothers on their daughters is the ingenious masterstroke of patriarchal, religious, and gender oppression. However, the excisions of millions of clitorises have not eradicated Àjẹ́; the hackings of millions of labia have not exposed the wisdom of the womb; the sealings of innumerable vaginas have not stopped and will not stop the flow of power.

Vaginal Fluid: Elixir of the Gods

A Yoruba proverb asserts: *Obirin gbọ̀nà; ọkùnrin sá* (Woman takes the road; man runs); man finds it necessary to flee because when woman takes the road, she "takes the road like a river."[17] When a woman has made up her mind there is no swaying her. She moves or alters all in her path like a river in flood or a tidal wave bearing down on a town.

Water, in all of its forms—river, ocean, stream, pond, milk, amnion, blood, lymph—is analogous to Woman because water, like Woman is the foundation of existence. The waters that nourish every human being *in vitro* are spontaneously produced by a biological-spiritual call and response between embryo and mother. From her DNA to her amnion, Mother is complete and transfers that completion to her daughter. While her sons do not receive all of her fully-functioning features, most men grow to develop the nearly all-consuming urge to unite with woman and experience from the outside what they lack within: Even sperm moves courtesy of her waters. While Àjẹ́ is usually associated with blood, it is equally aligned with the water that comprises seventy percent of our bodies, seventy percent of the Earth's surface, and that keeps flora, fauna, and microorganisms thriving.

In "Motherhood as a Source of Empowerment of Women in Yoruba Culture," Taiwo Makinde discusses the dynamic that connects the Òrìṣà to water to power: ". . . *Oya, Olokun, Ogbese, Yemoja* and, *Iyamapo*. . . . All these deities are associated with water, in one way or another. Water in Yoruba culture depicts indispensability."[18] Makinde avers that "the power of these deities is unquantifiable because water is the source of life and, therefore, a necessity. Looking at it from another angle, a woman is a necessity for procreation . . . a woman is a source of life just like water."[19]

The significance of woman and water is evident in Yemọja, the Àjẹ́ who is known as Yewájọbí, Mother of all Òrìṣà and all Living Things.[20] Her waters set Ọ̀ṣun, Ọya, and Olókun, Ìyá Màpó, and countless other Òrìṣà to flowing, and they, in turn, move our mothers and ourselves to flow.

Makinde also discusses the significance of vaginal waters and the vagina in Yoruba cosmontology: "All the deities mentioned above are directly connected with water. Iyamapo, however, refers to the water from the vagina, a part which is considered as the place harboring the secret of a woman's power. The child who exalts the woman to the supreme status of 'precious stone' emerges from the vagina."[21]

In addition to representing vaginal fluid, Ìyá Màpó is also the God of women's professions, crafts, and trades. In "Maternal Goddess in Yoruba Art: A New Aesthetic Acclamation of Yemoja, Osun, and Iya Mapo," Agbo Folarin asserts that Ìyá Màpó "is known in Yoruba culture as the inventor of pottery.[22] Folarin offers a resonant analysis of the God's work:

> Iya Mapo is the potter woman, who embraces the technique of moving round an archetypal hole to mould and shape beautiful potteries. A potter remarked[, Iya Mapo] is many things combined. She is a miner when she digs the clay, she is an artist creating potteries, she is a technologist when firing the pots, and a scientist when glazing the potteries.[23]

The potter's assessment of Ìyá Màpó's work is born of a holistic appreciation of the God and her craft which encompasses the exoteric and the esoteric.

In addition to the obvious similarities to Ọbàtálá who molds human beings in the womb, Ìyá Màpó's powers, iconography, and responsibilities unite her with Onílẹ̀ and Ẹdan. Folarin reveals that Ìyá Màpó's "ancient insignia is an edon (sacred bronze casting) which represents two children close to the goddess. One is held tight to her bosom and the other is strapped with a sash 'Oja' to her back with its head downward."[24] Folarin provides his audience with stunning information and imagery. Carrying infants on her front and back is logical given Mother must accommodate two blessings. However the manner by which she ties the twin to her back connects Ìyá Màpó to Ìyá Ayé, the Mother Earth, who is invoked in a praisesong of Ẹdan as "*Abiyamọ tí í pọn ọmọ rẹ̀ lódì / Òdì, òdì, ni Ìyá-Ayé í pọn ọmọ* (The nursing mother who backs her child usually / Unusually, unusually, Mother of the Earth carries her child)."[25] *Òdì*, which I translate here as "unusually," is actually a very complex concept with meanings and elaborations that are specific to Àjẹ́ and its institutions. The concept of òdì serves to emphasize the fact that in their method of carrying children, their roles in creation, their powerful vaginas, and their Àjẹ́, Ìyá Màpó and Ìyá

Ayé are identical twins and complementary mother-forces born of the womb of Odù.

Under most circumstances, a mother carrying her child upside down would be considered dangerous and abusive, but when the mother is Àjẹ́, her cosmic and terrestrial support are so strong that she has the ability to focus her efforts not only on her children's care, nourishment, and protection, but also on introducing her children to *the* Mother, Onílẹ̀. In *Black Gods and Kings: Yoruba Art at UCLA*, Robert Farris Thompson asserts that the child who is carried òdì boasts an orientation that privileges the perspective of the Earth, Onílẹ̀, and he includes images that depict the ancient custom whereby a mother "greets earth by lifting her child three times, upside-down, over earth."[26] This ritual emphasizes the significance of giving birth on the ground. It is fitting that the child who immediately salutes the Earth when she emerges from the vagina is also carried òdì. With these customs, the child whose existence is the gift, promise, and responsibility of Onílẹ̀ is oriented toward Onílẹ̀.

The child carried òdì provides an arresting articulation of a Pan-African cosmontological concept. Among the BaKongo of Central Africa òdì would be called *kinda*. Ancestors who reside in the spiritual realm, who can see what human eyes cannot, and who can offer direction and wisdom essential for terrestrial existence and manifestation of destiny are kinda and boast divine vision.[27] The infant carried òdì also possesses the vision, wisdom, and divinity of the ancestors.

The child being carried òdì or kinda may also be an allusion to a Yoruba proverb that reveals, "The bat suspends itself upside down but watches the doings of all the birds (Adan dorikodo o nwo iṣe ẹiyẹ gbogbo.)"[28] The bat's superior vision is accentuated by its duality, for while it has some characteristics of birds, it is a mammal. Similar to the bat, Onílẹ̀'s offspring are much more than they appear to be. These children look human, but they are the Gods of God of the Earth, and they thrive in òdì. Consequently, the child who is carried upside down, who appears to be in the most precarious position, and whose view appears to be obscured, is actually monitoring everything, the actions of "all the birds," including those of her siblings and parents and Àwọn Ìyá Wa.

To be upside down and not fall and also to retain one's àṣẹ and Àjẹ́ is a sign of divinity, power, and technology at their apexes. Indeed, the post-menopausal Àjẹ́ is heralded as "the one with the vagina that turns upside down without pouring blood."[29] Not unlike the daughter carried òdì, the post-menopausal elder does not need to die to attain the vision and power of kinda. Her Àjẹ́ and àṣẹ, no longer directed towards giving life, are magnified exponentially within her so that she can focus on guiding her society. The elder woman, whose longevity is augmented by decades of acquired wisdom, knowledge, and understanding, who has seen too much to be astonished, has experienced too much to be fooled, and has felt too much to be irrational, is God. That these elder Àjẹ́ are recognized as emissaries of Ìyá Màpó in particular is illustrated in the following iwi Egúngún:

> *Mo juba okó tó doríkodò tí ò ro.*
> *Mo juba èlẹ̀ tí doríkodò tóò sẹ̀jẹ̀*
> *Ìyámàpó tótó aró nò dákà e kọ kéré abirun lẹ́nu*

> I salute the penis that stands
>   upside down without dripping.
> I salute the vagina that stands
>   inverted without bleeding.
> Iyamapo, please, I beseech you,
>   I do not intend to slight you,
>   you with bearded mouth.[30]

Ìyá Màpó could be properly called the Double-Bearded Deity, for not only does Mother's chin boast a beard, which signifies her spiritual-material mastery and duality,[31] but the Mother's small "mouth," the one that waits between her legs, is also bearded. In this respect, Ìyá Màpó and all of her daughters are the personification of òdì.

Ìyá Màpó is not only associated with water from the vagina, and the secretions that facilitate sex, childbirth, healthy pH balance, and menstrual flow, which Oludare Olajubu asserts is regulated by a "great power," but Ìyá Màpó is also synonymous with and is a euphemism for the vagina.[32] Perhaps the name Màpó signifies a woman's organic purse (*àpo*) of immeasurable and infinite treasures.

The Ifá spiritual system is centered on the biological and the logical; consequently, reverence and celebration of the genitals as sources and forces of existence are everywhere evident. An ẹsẹ Ifá of Ọ̀wọ́nrín Ògùndá discusses Ìṣẹ̀ṣe, a term that signifies both the ancient way of knowing, being, and doing and one's progenitors, the originators of existence, the Gods. The progenitors discussed in the ẹsẹ include Olódùmarè, Orí, Ikin, "Ilẹ̀ Aiyé" ("Mother Earth/Nature"), "One's own Mother" ("Ìyà"), "One's own Father," "Penis," and "Vagina."[33] While the ẹsẹ asserts that these primordial progenitors should be appeased, honored, and understood first and foremost, the vagina, as the source of both Àjẹ́ and of existence, is the subject of even more careful celebration and consideration.

In an analysis that makes the same points that the ẹsẹ of Ọ̀wọ́nrín Ògùndá makes about Ìṣẹ̀ṣe, Olajubu discusses why mother, the vagina, and the womb are the paramount Ìṣẹ̀ṣe:

Three interpretations come to mind when one considers these references to male and female genital organs. It is a salute to their powers of procreation. To the Yoruba, they are great powers to be propitiated and respected. The male and female genitals are mentioned separately because each plays its unique part in the wonderful act of procreation. The Yoruba venerate the "father" and "mother" and particularly the "mother" not only because of the care she gives to her off-spring but also because of her procreative powers. If in the height of anger a mother feels seriously offended by her child she could curse the child in the name of her womb and her breasts. It is believed that nothing could cleanse the effect of such a curse.[34]

Olajubu quotes the lethal curse: "Àfi bí kì í ba í ṣe òbò mi yìí ni mo fí bí ọ./ Àfi bí kì í ba í ṣe ọmú mi méjì yí ni o mu dàgbà, / Òun nìkan ni báyìí o fi ni bá o" ("Except it were not I that gave birth to you from my womb [vagina] / Except it were not I that fed you from my breasts, / That so and so would not befall you").[35] That the Àjẹ́ of motherhood exponentially magnifies Ọ̀rọ̀ is also evident in the supplication, "Mo fi ìkúnlẹ̀ abiyamọ bẹ̀ ọ́!": "I beg you in the name and condition of the woman in childbirth!"[36] Olubayo Oladimeji Adekola, who cites the aforementioned supplication, also reveals that Èṣù, who is routinely patrified, is frequently depicted holding "his" pendulous breasts while kneeling in the pose of a woman giving birth because of the power conferred by motherhood.[37]

Reverence for the life-giving and life-taking power of Mother can be found throughout Pan-Africa. Among the Bambara, a man answers a greeting with "M Ba," acknowledging that he exists because of his mother. The Bambara woman responds to a greeting by saying, "N se," confirming that she is made ever-victorious by virtue of the power of her gender. African American mothers often threaten wayward children by reminding them, "I brought you into this world, and I can take you out!" Similarly, a Kemetic text gives adult children a warning together with its rationale:

> When you were born she (your mother) made herself really your slave; the most menial tasks did not dishearten her to the point of making her say: why do I need to do this? When you went to school for your lessons, she sat near your master, bringing every day the bread and the beer of the household. And now that you are grown up, that you are marrying and founding, in turn, a family, always remember the care your mother devoted to you, so that she has nothing for which she can reproach you and does not raise her arms to God in malediction, for God would answer her prayer.[38]

No matter the circumstances of our lives or those that led to our conceptions and births, it is because we were carried in mother's nurturing waters that we are here breathing the air of this world.

Ìyá Màpó knows the many struggles that await mothers due to the power of their vaginas and their roles as controllers of existence; consequently, she ensures women's autonomy and self-determination by supporting women's use of their inherent talents to produce utilitarian art from clays, dyes, and fibers from the Earth. An oríkì praises Ìyá Màpó's foresight: "You provide for us / better than the market, / you provide for us / better than even the farm."[39] A God of complete womanhood, creativity, economics, and autonomy, Ìyá Màpó gives women "the confidence to protect their craft monopolies," and she safeguards women's creative and industrial dominion for "[n]o Yoruba man is allowed to make pots, dye textiles in indigo or make batik with starch resist."[40]

Ìyá Màpó also guarantees women's control over the creation of odù (pots); this symbolizes her protection of the odù of creation, the womb. Because Ìyá Màpó is, herself, a twin of Odù, the Great Womb of Creation, it is fitting that singers of her oríkì confirm that when standing before the Ancient Mother, human beings, no matter their age, are cherished and open-hearted infants: "Iya Mapo / before you I am completely naked."[41] Ìyá Màpó's children stand before her just as babaláwo stand before Odù, with their honor and intentions gleaming through their melanin. With the calming and creative pool of vaginal waters casting infinite reflections, Ìyá Màpó sees her children, and they see themselves in her: "Iya Mapo / it is your face we are looking at."[42] Ìyá Màpó is at once a God and a celebration of Creation: She is art for life's sake in the making. Ìyá Màpó, as the waters of Woman, as the womb, and as the vagina, constitutes an eternal covenant that reaffirms the sanctity of every manifestation of Àjẹ́.

Àjẹ́ is the most organic, logical, and effortless of powers, and because it is undeniably the Mother of Power and the Power of the Mothers, it has been attacked; indeed, females' power-engorged genitals—as tender and vulnerable as they are—are routinely assaulted by a patriarchy that seeks strength in dismembering, suppression, oppression, and complete avoidance. That hatred of the vagina is alive and well and thriving is evident in the escalating caesarean section rates in modern Western hospitals. In this era, millions of children are forced to enter the world like Macduff of Shakespeare's *Macbeth*—"not of woman born." Women steered into C-sections can suffer long-term or permanent damage to muscles, tissue, and internal organs for the convenience of an obstetrician who does not want to be humbled by kneeling before the Source and patiently coaxing forth new life. Some American obstetricians use any pretext whatsoever to perform C-sections because it is convenient and lucrative for them. Many of these physicians are so morally bankrupt that they will seek court orders to force mothers to have unnecessary C-sections and will attempt to prosecute mothers who refuse unnecessary C-sections.[43]

To facilitate the butchering of women at their and their children's expenses and for the financial gain of the medical establishment, some so-called pre-natal classes do not mention natural birth at all and discuss C-sections as if they are the mother's only option.[44] As a result of obstetrical manipulations, mothers and children are deprived of essential physical and physiological processes and protections. Western obstetrical practices are routinely anti-woman and anti-African; and they are not only barbaric, excruciatingly painful, and unnecessary, but they are also pro-patriarchy and capitalistically-motivated, as doctors get paid for every procedure they perform and every incision they make.[45]

Similar to the woman whose genital excision leaves her with an opening customized for her male partner's member (as is the case in some cultures), with a C-section, the parameters of the vagina are preserved for adult male enjoyment, but the male's desires are sated at the expense of the mother and the child. C-sections also impede the flow of Ìyá Màpó's waters: The production of breast milk may be stymied because oxytocin and other essential hormones that are released during vaginal birth and that facilitate lactation are not stimulated to flow, and it can be agonizing to try and nurse a child after a C-section. To compensate for the damage done by anti-mother and anti-child shortcuts, many hospitals provide new mothers with formula for the newborn's sustenance. With the introduction of formula, not only are the breasts also reserved for adult male play, but capitalism, patriarchy's insatiably greedy child, thrives at the expense of needy children as formula manufacturers grow wealthy.[46] Perhaps the true depth of the depravity of the modern Western world is most apparent in its treatment of mothers and children.

The Great Mothers created nothing by accident. Amniotic fluid is as important to the child as the vaginal fluids, hormones, and antibodies that a mother gives her child during vaginal birth, breastfeeding, and skin-to-skin cuddling. While globalization and capitalism jeopardize the development of mothers and children and the mother-child bond, Ìyá Màpó's water courses around stones, over embankments, and through crevices to offer protection. Rowland Abiodun reveals that even adult children can benefit from the protections and powers of the waters of Mother:

> In the preparation of very powerful Yoruba medicines, the one for curing mental sickness in particular, the patient's mother's breasts are washed into a concoction which is drunk by the patient. Also, if a man experiences a series of inexplicable disasters in his occupation or private life, he is usually advised to perform a ritual

suckling of his mother's breasts to avert a repetition of these undesirable events. This is a means of purifying the source and essence of one's being. It is also believed that through this ritual suckling, a person is once more protected by a mother's powerful influence.[47]

Just as one will always be the child of one's mother, so too can one always access her protection and power. Furthermore, as I examine in chapter five, a mother's sacred protections are not restricted to her biological children: Every Àjẹ́ is a Mother and can mother.

Medicines that are activated by or that approximate women's waters are central to healing and assuaging in Yoruba pharmacology. In "Woman in Yoruba Religious Images," Abiodun explains the relationship between ẹ̀rọ̀, water, and Woman:

> The power of women appears to be similar to that of water, with which most female deities are associated. Water is an active ingredient in the Yoruba preparation of ẹ̀rọ̀ "a softening agent/medicinal preparation" as also is the fluid from a snail and the oil from red palm kernels. All of these are believed able to effect harmony, peace and to eliminate tension and reduce heat through magic powers. Thus, a person's orí "inner spiritual head and destiny" can be improved or "softened" if it is considered "hard" (le).[48]

Preparations of ẹ̀rọ̀ appear to be approximations of Ìyá Màpó's vaginal or amniotic fluid, depending on the context, that are charged with specific pharmacological elements and the type and concentration of Àjẹ́ necessary to attain a particular effect. For example, when the soothing power of snail water is laced with red palm kernel oil, the result is a recreation of blood-tinged waters of vaginal birth—the original and essential baptism. A related preparation, *omi ẹ̀rọ̀* (soothing protecting waters), which is applied to the eyes in order to see Odù and is also used for cleaning and anointing Ẹdan, seems representative of amniotic or vaginal fluid.

Abiodun contends that ẹ̀rọ̀ is "capable of normalising, negating, or rendering impotent any other power, life, or substance. Here, like water, ẹ̀rọ̀ operates noiselessly and unceremoniously. Such is the nature of the power of 'our mothers.'"[49] By comparing ẹ̀rọ̀ Àjẹ́ to water, Abiodun emphasizes the essentiality and centrality of Mother in all her forms and manifestations. He finds that "[w]ith the power of ẹ̀rọ̀, which can be either positive or negative in effect, women are not only feared, but their cooperation is sought in all endeavors. Without their cooperation, nothing would be possible."[50]

The fact that woman is the elemental essential is evident in Abiodun's discussion of the sublime significance of daughters in the pre-patriarchal Yoruba world—the one that existed before men had been encouraged to fear, distrust, and hate women: "It is therefore considered to be good luck if one's first child is female. Such parents are believed to start with ọwọ́ ẹ̀rọ̀ 'the hand of propitiation.'"[51] The newborn girl, as a reincarnation and reproduction of the Mothers, is favored and confers favored status upon her parents. With her tiny vagina, growing womb, and waiting eggs, the infant daughter is a perfect encapsulation of power and glory.

Abiodun offers evidence of not only the genetic transmission of Àjẹ́ and ẹ̀rọ̀ from mother to daughter, but also of the love, honor, and anticipation with which all girls were originally greeted in Yoruba society, for it is the daughter who pleases and appeases Àjẹ́. With a full understanding of the significance of vaginal waters, the image of a woman taking the road like a river is alive with meanings that brilliantly elucidate the multifold significance of vagina's oríkì, Ọ̀nà-Ọ̀run, the road to and from the Cosmos.[52]

The Ovum in the Center of Existence

Every woman is a microcosmic encapsulation of the Cosmos who boasts eggs like the universe boasts galaxies. A woman's eggs are stored in her sacred Igbádù, or ovaries, which frame her internal Àpéré, which is the womb. When Àjẹ́ decide to reinitiate existence, the most perfect ovum—selected to match the destiny and duties of its soul—moves from Igbádù to Àpéré via fallopian tube to await vivification from a sperm. When conception occurs, the womb fills with the holiest of waters to create the optimum protection and optimal conditions to develop a growing fetus, who could very well be a returning God.

With her ovum-bearing ovaries, mother is the literal storehouse of existence, and she has phenomenal defenses to guard her delicate eggs. The ovaries are tucked into the core of a woman's being and while her cycle may be altered by stress or trauma, her eggs do not break. She can run, jump, roll; she may be beaten, raped, and suffer a lifetime of abuse, but her eggs will not break. Mother's eggs are protected in a manner identical to the protection the Cosmos guarantees planets, which, as the oríkì of Ilẹ̀ reveals, roll and roll without breaking.[53] To further emphasize the biological and cosmic protections of the Mothers, a Yoruba funeral song compares mother's eggs to others' eggs:

> An egg falls to reveal a messy secret.
> My mother went and carried her secret along.

She has gone far –
We look for her in vain.[54]

Unlike a hen's egg which when dropped exposes its truths and loses its sanctity and power, one can never exhaust the wisdom of one's mother. When mother stops menstruating, her Àjẹ́ is magnified. When mother returns to the Mother, she leaves her daughters a divine endowment that reinforces their cosmic obligations. No one has or knows more secrets and keeps them better than Mother. She is the Guardian of the Sealed Calabash in which shimmer the eggs who have and will become us. With life cycling in the core of her being, Mother is Eternity.

Eggs, especially fertilized eggs, are a staple of many Pan-African spiritual technologies, sacrifices, and medicines. Eggs are often offered to the Òrìṣà with the prayer that the Gods carry the supplicant's destiny or request as gently as one carries an egg. Women of childbearing age are encouraged to keep eggs in their homes to ensure their fertility and abundance. There are Africana love prescriptions that involve eggs and the crossroads. Eggs can be used to cleanse one's body and clear one's Orí, and eggs can also be used to cure an infant's herniated navel. Verger's *Ewé*, a rich compendium on Yoruba flora, fauna, and pharmacopeia, includes a "Medicine to have a healthy body" which includes an empty egg shell and the confirmation that a hen calmly lays and broods her eggs and the "shell is always found empty," referring to holistic health, completion and perfection.[55]

Eggs can also communicate messages and signal an irreparable breach. In the Yoruba judiciary, if the Ọ̀yọ́ Mèsì and Ògbóni are severely displeased with the Aláàfin,

> [t]hey could not depose the Alafin, but could ask him to commit suicide (if his rule was not in the interest of the empire) by sending the Bashorum to present an empty calabash or a dish of parrot's eggs to and pass a sentence of rejection on the Alafin in the following words
> *The gods reject you;*
> *The people reject you;*
> *The earth rejects you.*
> By tradition such Alafin must take poison and die.[56]

As further evidence of the Mother's complete power over existence and continuity, Alfred Burdon Ellis describes how, upon receiving a calabash of parrot's eggs, a "king forthwith retired to his apartments, as if to sleep, and then gave directions to his women to strangle him, which they accordingly did."⁵⁷

Because of the richness, intricacy, and vastness of Yoruba language and semiology, objects thought to be mundane or irrelevant in other lands are stunning missives in Yoruba culture. Messages that are conveyed through objects and symbols are called àrokò.⁵⁸ Patrick J. Ebewo describes àrokò as "a visible sign of something invisible."⁵⁹ The two àrokò for dethroning a Yoruba sovereign bring to mind the elements of Àjẹ́: the vagina, the clitoris, the blinding Igbádù, and Odù, the Womb of Eternity.

While in many cases the calabash is symbolic of the womb and its fecundity, the àrokò of an empty calabash seems indicative of barrenness: The empty calabash appears to represent a ruler who is bereft of destiny, who has reached the end of existence, and who must sojourn in oblivion.

Parrot eggs constitute a richly riddled àrokò. The ruler, like all human beings, has his source in the egg of the womb of his mother; however, he can only be made a king by the Mothers, Àjẹ́, who are the literal kingmakers, as I detail in chapter four. The eggs used in the àrokò are those of the African Grey Parrot, a bird that is a favorite of Àjẹ́. The parrot egg àrokò seems to signify to the sovereign that those who made him king have now unmade him and that his next journey will find him assuming the shape of an egg and returning to his essence.⁶⁰

In a salient elucidation, Rowland Abiodun describes the ìkó oódẹ, the crimson tail feather of the African Grey Parrot, as the transformative catalyst of the parrot egg àrokò:

> About the offering of parrot's eggs to Yoruba sovereigns as an àrokò that they must go to sleep, my understanding of that visual metaphor is connected to my interpretation of the use of the grey parrot's red tail feathers (ìkó oódẹ)—a most potent visual symbol of the power of our mothers. As I have pointed out in a couple of my publications, ìkó oódẹ is forbidden in blacksmith's forge or workshop since it is strongly believed that they can change the chemical property of metals. From this premise, we must consider grey parrot's eggs as even more powerful than its tail feathers. The message sent would seem to imply more than just "change" or "abdication" but "death" because the parrot's egg alludes to the very beginning of life itself.⁶¹

Abiodun's explanation emphasizes the paradoxical poetics of Àjẹ́, in that the eggs simultaneously represent "death" and the "beginning of life." When a ruler opens a calabash and finds whole and pristine eggs glowing therein, he is literally and spiritually being shown the door of existence through the àrokò of the womb (calabash) and egg (ovum). The pure and emergent power of the ìkó oódẹ is the embodiment of what Abiodun describes as "hidden power." When used as an àrokò for sovereigns, the ìkó oódẹ acts in the same manner as its twin, menstrual fluid, as both are covert-overt silent forces that are capable of nurturing ovum to existence and also devolving destinies.

The power of the parrot egg àrokò is also that which women harness when they remove their clothing and curse a man. By showing a wayward man her Àpéré, which is his source, she is introducing him to the spiritual realm. And just as the ìkó oódẹ and albumin remain hidden in their shell, so too does woman's nakedness both conceal and project the immense Àjẹ́ of her Odù and that of the millions of eggs she carries: When a mother has been moved to make of her body the ultimate àrokò, she need not utter a word or lift a finger to obliterate her violator.

The Powers in the Blood

Blood is a central element of African spiritual systems, rituals, medicines, and technologies because it carries the unique and personal biological and spiritual code of its bearer. This is why certain medicines, curses, or technologies only affect the persons for whom they were intended and why blood sacrifice of certain animals is required for certain Òrìṣà. Ògún demands dogs for sacrifice because the àṣẹ of their blood magnifies and stimulates his àṣẹ. The sacrificed dog does not "die" in the Western sense; it embarks on its appointed cosmic-terrestrial mission as a messenger, facilitator, or activator. The recognition and harnessing of spiritual DNA in blood reflects interdependence between fauna and the Gods.

Blood is arguably the most prevalent and powerful component of Africana spiritual works, and the mother of all blood is menstrual blood. The menstrual fluid that makes a girl a woman, a mother, and a God swirls with unimaginable power. According to Ulli Beier:

> Potentially every woman is "aje", because the "mothers" control the blood of menstruation. The mothers can cause menstruation to cease, or they can cause an excessive flow of blood. They can also stop the child in the womb, which can then only be born after special sacrifices to the mothers. Thus the "mothers" control all women through these mystic powers. One dancer told me: "All women are united through the flow of blood."[62]

Every human being begins life as an ovum embedded in the uterus and nourished on the blood and nutrients that would otherwise have been released menses. Motherblood is the literal foundation of human existence.

This sacred fluid is what makes the human family matrilineal whether societies choose to acknowledge this fact or not.

It is mother's blood, water, womb, nutrients, and choice that provide every human being with life. While some may argue that men are essential for life, they are not. Sperm is necessary for creation, and sperm can survive without its ejaculator; this is why sperm banks have exploded in popularity (although they are, ironically, hastening man's obsolescence). The Ancients also understood semen's portability. In his classic poem *Idanre* Wole Soyinka describes Ògún as carrying

> seven gourdlets to war. One for gunpowder,
> One for charms, two for palm wine and three
> Air-sealed in polished bronze make
> Storage for his sperms[63]

Ògún knows that his semen can thrive for hours after ejaculation and can perform its duty even if he is otherwise occupied or unable to rise to the occasion. By contrast, mother is indispensable; her womb is essential; her blood is the foundation of all human existence. Without mother, there is no life.

The power of Motherblood is evident in the fact that when a woman begins to menstruate, her body is sending a clear sign that she is capable of conceiving and bearing life. A woman's monthly flow of blood is the àrokò that gives life and meaning to all other àrokò. Her menses is the promise of infinite life waiting in millions of eggs, and it is the reason for sperms' restless motility. When a woman's blood ceases its flow for nine months, her body is sending another sign: Odùà and Ọbàtálá are busy turning mother's blood into a child. When mother's menstrual blood ceases flowing permanently, she is in the process of evolving into another manifestation of divinity—that of Àgbà, the grand elder Àjẹ́.

Because all human beings find their source in the womb and in their mothers' blood, Àjẹ́ control the movement of blood through veins, and they know when that flow must cease.[64] Menses, in particular, is symbolic of Àjẹ́ because that blood represents the sanctity of life, whether it is the blood that nurtured the eggs that our mothers brought to term, or the blood that will enrich the eggs that our daughters will coax into existence, or the blood that is being used to introduce a pedophile to oblivion. Menstrual blood is liquid Àjẹ́, and it and can do and undo, as necessary, simply with its presence. Because of its power, menstrual blood is carefully harnessed and highly revered in traditional African societies.

The traditional African worldview revolves around the celebration of life and the fortification existence; consequently, in traditional African philosophy, ontology, and culture, menstrual fluid, semen, and the human genitals are not considered dirty, polluting, or accursed. Indeed, such a belief constitutes a condemnation of humanity, for if semen and menstrual blood are foul then so too are the lives they create. Unlike the African worldview, the Judeo-Christian social order is firmly rooted in and is dependent on the condemnation of the genitals and their by-products, including human beings and especially menstrual fluid.

While biblical scriptures of Leviticus and Ezekiel abound with assertions that menses is impure and polluting, Yoruba ontology, grounded in biological and scientific facts, espouses no such views. However, rather than attempt to learn from the Yoruba biologists, scientists, and geneticists they encountered, Caucasian missionary colonizers indoctrinated Africans with Judeo-Christian ignorance, superstition, and, most of all, their abhorrence for the "way of women," also known as menstruation.

Caucasian Christian colonizers taught Africans to feel what every "civilized" Caucasian feels when he looks at his body: shame and disgust. Africans who relished the sun kissing every part of their melanin-rich bodies were made to cover up. The organic, balanced, logical understanding of the genitals displayed in songs, riddles, and art was branded evil, nasty, uncivilized, and shameful. Caucasian missionary colonizers bombarded Africans with their hatred and distrust of menses and women. The Caucasian colonial misogynist mandate went beyond associating sex, menstruation, and childbirth with sin; they labeled individuals and entire societies who did not hate their bodies, origins, and mothers as accursed and did everything they could to destroy them. One of the most significant targets in the Yoruba world was Ògbóni—with its reverence of Mọlẹ̀, the Great Mother who binds all women with her blood and who nourishes all children with the sweet milk of her breasts—and Mọlẹ̀'s breathing reproductions, Àwọn Ìyá Wa. Although Mọlẹ̀, Ògbóni, and Àjẹ́ survived colonial assaults, they emerged with scars and with a self-consciousness that only systematic terrorism can induce.

Racism, religious terrorism, colonialism, and indoctrination have impacted people the world over, and these forces routinely warp discussions about Àjẹ́—no matter the ethnicity of the informant. However, it is both possible and necessary to distinguish Àjẹ́'s truth from destroyers' lies. An extraordinarily fruitful site for reclamation and revelation is the acclaimed Gẹ̀lẹ̀dẹ́ festival. The word *ẹlẹ̀* is a euphemism for vagina and, while it may be coincidental, ẹlẹ̀'s appearance in the heart of the word Gẹ̀lẹ̀dẹ́ is telling, for Gẹ̀lẹ̀dẹ́ remains one of the few places were frank celebrations and elaborations about the genitals, copulation, conception, and creation can occur in the neocolonial patrified Yoruba world.[65] It is not surprising that Gẹ̀lẹ̀dẹ́ became an important battleground for religious and academic colonization.

The Caucasian patriarchy's desire to condemn "the way of women" even while discussing a festival held in honor of women and their ways, is evident in the analyses of Gẹ̀lẹ̀dẹ́ that are couched in pseudo-scientific Eurocentric doublespeak about the hue white's supposed cleanliness as differentiated from the filth and malignancy of menstrual blood. The following passage from Drewal and Drewal's *Gẹlẹdẹ* is illustrative:

> Mother masks are whitewashed. In the realm of the "white deities" (orișa funfun), whiteness is synonymous with outer composure (tutu) and covert action—two supremely feminine attributes. White may also suggest the state of purity or cleanliness ascribed to elderly women past menopause, for it is said that "Ososomu is clean. She doesn't like anything that is dirty. . . . When women are passing blood, it is a bad thing." Yoruba males who regard menstrual blood as polluting explain that its purpose is to "wash out all that has been happening between a man and a woman." More important, menses, which by definition contains aṣẹ, can bring misfortune to a man . . .[66]

The running dogs of racist imperialism have done their job well, as it seems Drewal and Drewal stepped into an African society that is eager to affirm the myths of "whiteness" that Caucasians have desperately sought to associate with themselves. According to Drewal and Drewal's informant(s), the hue white has gone from symbolizing death, the ancestors, and myriad possibilities to signifying "purity" and "cleanliness," concepts that Caucasians oddly associate with both "godliness" and themselves by linking their ethnic groups to a color that does not reflect their appearance and by relating that color to values that do not reflect their morals or ethics. (An area that deserves serious academic and psychoanalytical examination is why the concepts of the purity and cleanliness preoccupy the minds of a people who raped, lynched, colonized, slaughtered, and debased entire continents of people the world over.)

While earlier in their book Drewal and Drewal come closer to understanding the multiplicity of Àjẹ́'s power when they assert, "The Great Mother herself is the epitome of patience; that is, her inner head is composed. She is in control. She does not become visibly angered, but she exacts revenge covertly,"[67] Drewal and Drewal's discussion about menstruation and "whiteness" seems to come from the Caucasian ethos and its racially skewed color valuation. The researchers' ethnocentrism is apparent in their assertion that post-menopausal women exist in a state of purity and cleanliness. This association makes no sense unless the blood that is necessary for existence and that flows in all human veins does not flow in these elders' bodies. While Drewal and Drewal also note that elder Yoruba women are heralded as having vaginas that turn upside down without pouring blood,[68] through the Caucocentric lens, these women would not embody white's alleged "purity" and cleanliness"; these women would be containers of pollutants.

What I find most intriguing about Drewal and Drewal's analysis of menstrual blood is the way that European and African misogyny flow together seamlessly—or are made to appear to. Drewal and Drewal include an undocumented unauthenticated statement ostensibly from a Yoruba man who argues that the Great Mother is "clean" and does not like anything "dirty" and that menstruation is "bad." The Great Mother would not only be revolted by the reflections of her Self who are born of her very own menstrual blood and womb, but she would also have to be disgusted by herself. Also of note is the informant's assertion that the purpose of menstruation is the "clean" a woman of her sexual relations with a man. This assertion ignores the fact that virgins and abstinent women menstruate.

The statements of the unidentified informant(s) do not make sense scientifically, biologically, or cosmontologically, and these contentions are not found in Yoruba science, philosophy, ontology, or cosmology. However, Drewal and Drewal choose to privilege erroneous anonymous voices and views and bypass informative published studies such as Ulli Beier's "Gelede Masks," which expounds on the connection between menstrual blood, the Great Mother, Àjẹ́, and existence. What is even odder is that Drewal and Drewal follow the obtuse misinformation of their informant(s) with their own blanket assertion that menses can "bring misfortune to a man." Drewal and Drewal cite Raymond Prince's article "The Yoruba Image of the Witch" to validate their claim, but they take Prince's findings out of context. It is not menstruation that brings misfortune to men. Menstrual fluid is the literal foundation of the life of every human being (including squeamish men and misogynists). As I discuss in detail in chapter five of this book, Prince specifically refers to women using their menstrual cloths to defend themselves as they fight against oppression and tyranny.[69] Drewal and Drewal take a powerful spiritual-political tool that is used in emergencies and make of it a general indictment against menstrual blood and women, especially Africana women.

It is important to analyze the concept of menstrual and vaginal filth. A common assertion is that the menstrual cycle is a form of "cleaning." What dirt is in the uterus, fallopian tubes, and ovaries that needs cleaning? What dirt is in the vagina that needs cleaning? How can menses, which is defined as polluting, also clean? Since blood is essential to existence, how can it be considered dirty? More specifically, if menstrual fluid exists to clean a woman of her sexual relationship with a man, would it not also be "cleaning" away their attempts at conception and a successful conception? That a woman's vagina and blood are polluting or need cleaning makes no sense—except in a worldview that sees a woman's body as the source of sin and that asserts that human beings are all sinners who are conceived in sin.

This myth of the dirty genitals can be found wherever patriarchy and the tools of ideological, religious, and economic oppression reign. Ironically, while in the Western world it is the touch of a man that defiles a woman, that "makes a virgin into a whore,"[70] men have successfully projected their self-loathing onto women and directly into the womb, menses, and vagina. Consequently, mothers around the world promote genital excision to their daughters by telling them that the procedure is a "purification" rite that will make them "clean" and marriageable.

Christianity, Judaism, and many other religions erect a special tier of loathing for the blood of menstruation. Women in various cultures are quarantined when menstruating and considered extra foul and filthy. It is not possible for the genitals to be polluted and issue a clean product, so self-hating patriarchs decreed themselves to be inherent sinners conceived in sin. The cure for "original sin" is baptism as overseen and administered by a man. Even the desire to be covered in the blood of Jesus has its genesis in the disgust of the genitals, the hatred of the mother, and the biological reality that every human being's conception, *in vitro* development, and birth originates in, is animated by, and is dependent on the blood of a line of mothers that extends all the way back to Odù and her Womb of Origins.

The menstrual cycle has nothing to do with cleanliness or dirt. It has nothing to do with sin or a curse: It is a signal that a woman is able to create life. The absence of the blood is a sign that she is creating life. It is helpful to recall the hunter's lament, for his song elucidates the Yoruba man's original reverence for Woman. Despite his intimate knowledge of his mother's womb and of his wife's vagina, the hunter's ultimate desire is to possess the embryonic, menstrual, vaginal, and clitoral power of Woman and feel as well as behold from above the God who gives life to all. The hunter seeks to possess the undulating hips that frame and feel the blood flow from the God who can create and destroy.

Despite the fact that modernity and capitalistic objectives entice women to delay or forgo motherhood, one could argue that woman's prime directive is to create life. The fact that the woman who has never given birth to or breastfed a child is more susceptible to ovarian, uterine, and breast cancers offers staggering evidence of the significance of life-bearing to women. From this perspective, menstrual blood offers reminders to women that it is Life, and every month this divine living blood seeks justification.

As it relates to the God of all Òrìṣà funfun, Ulli Beier found that the Nago Yoruba herald Odúà as "the mother of all," the "pure one," and "the mother who turns blood into children."[71] The Great Mother loves the blood of life, and she revels in its richness because the infinite power and possibilities of her white cloth can only become human realities shining with the melanin of cosmic perfection through fecund menstrual blood.

Not only is menses not shunned as a polluting element in traditional Yoruba culture, but the dynamic properties of menstrual fluid and Àjẹ́ are widely heralded, harvested, and harnessed in Yoruba spiritwork. The importance of menstruation is evident in certain flora and fauna which are prized because of their menses-related characteristics and properties. Babaláwo harness the power of the blood of life through irosùn, which is symbolic of menstrual blood and used to cast Odù Ifá.[72] Verger's *Ewé* includes a "medicine to stop a haemorrhage after delivery" that includes "Èso àkàrà Àjẹ́" (cnestis ferruginea), which are blood red fruits that symbolize àkàrà, a favorite food of Àjẹ́.[73] A "medicine to help a woman become pregnant" includes *ewé fèsoṣèjè* and the invocation, "fèsoṣèjè, change the menses into a child."[74] In addition to being rich in nutrients, red palm oil is a staple in ritual sacrifices of atonement called ètùtù because the lubricant cools and soothes and represents menses and fecundity.[75] The African Grey Parrot holds a place of indisputable significance in Yoruba science and iconography because its tail feathers resemble and boast the same properties as menses. The crimson feathers are collected and used to adorn the heads of initiates and rulers so that they appear to be steeped and crowned in the Motherblood of Àjẹ́.

Menstrual blood and Àjẹ́ are often discussed in juxtaposition to àṣẹ, with the former being pegged as malevolent and the latter as benevolent. However, àṣẹ coexists harmoniously with Àjẹ́. One of the things that makes women so powerful is that while men have to slash themselves to access the àṣẹ of their blood and animals are sacrificed to access their blood and àṣẹ, women's blood comes every month, and they are endowed with both àṣẹ and Àjẹ́. As Oyeronke Igbinola chants in the *Ìtàn-Oríkì Ìyàmi Òṣòròngà*, "Àwọn Ìyàmi, herself, gives me àṣẹ!"[76] What is more, while everything has àṣẹ, Àjẹ́ is restricted to select Gods, human beings, and flora and fauna.

While Àjẹ́ and àṣẹ have distinct compositions and roles, they are similar and work most efficaciously together. It is important to reiterate that, because they are endowed with both àṣẹ and Àjẹ́, Africana women also command Òrò, Power of the Word. This is an important dynamic for, as Awo Fatunmbi explains,

It is the polarity between Àjẹ́ and Òrọ̀ that makes effective prayer possible. The ability to pray effectively is called ọfọ ạṣẹ. Ifá scripture suggests that women have ọfọ ạṣẹ as a consequence of menstruation. Men receive ọfọ ạṣẹ as a consequence of initiation. Because the power of the word is a natural birthright of women, this power has been erroneously associated with "witchcraft" by those who have tried to give it a negative connotation. The power of the word for both men and women is an ethically neutral phenomena that relies on character development to insure that it is used for elevated spiritual purposes.[77]

The catalyst of Àjẹ́ and such forces as àṣẹ, Òrọ̀, and ọfọ̀ àṣẹ and the fluid that transmits and transfers them intergenerationally is menstrual blood. It is the fear of and dependence on that which is woman-owned and mother-controlled that gives rise to accusations of "witchcraft" and nonsense about dirty genitals and polluting blood.

The differences in the Caucasian and Yoruba ethoi become most apparent in these cultures' interpretations of colors and menstrual fluid. To facilitate their attempt to dominate the world, Caucasian pseudo-scientists constructed a hierarchy of colors that they associated with both arbitrary values and human beings. Caucasians placed themselves and their lack of melanin at the top of their racial hierarchy so as to create a construct of "white" supremacy. By plugging peoples of various ethnicities in descending order into their racist scale, not only could Caucasian ideologues justify the concept of "white" supremacy globally, but they could also rationalize their oppression and destruction of millions of people. The power of the Caucasian hierarchy of dehumanization is evident in the fact that most people of this world—consciously and/or unconsciously—associate themselves with colors and the Caucasian values associated with those colors despite the fact that those values, and, often, those colors, have no relationship to their cultural, genotypic, or phenotypic makeup. Caucasians are not white, and they are not pure, holy, without stain or blemish. Native Americans are neither red nor are they savage or bloodthirsty. Asians are not yellow, and they are not cowardly, sneaky or sly. Being endowed with undiluted melanin does not make one devoid of light, dirty, evil, wicked, or calamitous—quite the opposite.

As I discuss in chapter one of this book and in *Our Mothers, Our Powers, Our Texts*,[78] the colors black (*dúdú*), red (*pupa*), and white (*funfun*) are the signature hues of Àjẹ́ because these three hues represent elements that comprise the fundamentals of existence. Black is the perfection and totality of the Cosmos; consequently, Odù and Odùduwà both signify and embody the infinite magnificence of Blackness through their names, their cosmic origins, and their creative dynamism. The Kemetic God Ausar is honored as the Lord of Perfect Blackness because, like Odù and Odùduwà, he constitutes the power of the Cosmos genetically, spiritually, and phenotypically.

The desire of human beings to be bestowed with the undiluted divinity that Blackness signifies is evident in a human soul's request to Ọbàtálá:

> Make me black,
> Do not make me yellow
> Make me black,
> Do not make me white
> Dye me with my ìwà first
> At the dawn of creation.[79]

This is a demand for aesthetic perfection, cosmic completion, and spiritual supremacy. The soul is not condemning yellow or white, but, cognizant of the power of the undiluted and original state of existence (ìwà), the soul wants phenotypic excellence to complement and magnify its genetic and spiritual perfection. What is more, by requesting, while in the womb (odù), pure Blackness (Dúdú) to complement its existence and character (ìwà), the human soul is asking to be fashioned with the flawlessness of Odùduwà.

Red represents the menstrual blood of life and the Àjẹ́ and àṣẹ that comprise the literal foundation of human existence. Mother's blood is the nutritional and biological base of humanity. Whether it is released as menses or retained to nourish an egg, Motherblood is the liquid of life. Òrìṣà Àjẹ́ funfun, such as Ìyánlá, Ọbàtálá, and Odúà, funnel the blood of existence through the reflective properties and scientific principles of the hue white to imbue each person with a signature blend of ìwà, Orí, and àṣẹ. So perfect are these Gods' labors that each person they create is wholly unique and uniquely empowered.

The Yoruba determinations of dúdú, pupa, and funfun reveal a profound understanding of these hues' scientific, esoteric, and exoteric properties that has nothing to do with Western valuations of "good," "bad," "dirty," "evil," or "pure." Yoruba science, cosmogony, epistemology, and cosmontology reveal these valuations to be irrelevant. Because of the forces they signify and their roles in creation, protection, defense, and retribution, these three colors are used in myriad ways by Òrìṣà Àjẹ́, on totems of Àjẹ́, and in sacrifices for Àjẹ́. Empowered red objects that signify the blood, presence, and protection of the Mothers, abound on shrines, in sacrifices, and in ritual ceremonies for Àjẹ́ in particular and Yoruba culture in general, because Motherblood is life; and life is power; and power is Divinity.

The Many Odù of Odù

Yoruba cosmology likens Ayé and Ọ̀run to both the copulatory creative melding of Odù and Ọbàtálá and to calabashes that have been filled with power, sealed, and set to revolve and rotate eternally in the Cosmos. The Igbádù is a symbolic womb, and both the womb and the Igbádù are considered to be Igbá Ìwà, the Calabash of Existence. The vagina's oríkì, the path to Ọ̀run, signifies its role as the unifier of the cosmic and terrestrial calabashes. Given the recurrent use of the calabash in representing the world, the Cosmos, the womb, and Odù, herself, it is logical that it is one of the most resonant symbols of Àjẹ́.

In addition to the biological odù that is her womb and the àpéré of her body, the Africana woman can also possess an external material Odù in the form of Igbá Ẹyẹ, the Calabash and the Spirit Bird of Àjẹ́. The bird enclosed in the calabash represents the genitalia of women which boast coverings that protect, signify, and lead to power: The prepuce shielding the clitoris, the labia majora and minora protecting the vaginal chamber, and the vagina guarding the uterus all serve as examples. In the light of Aragamago's fierce defense of Odù and Abiodun's assertions about the concentrated power of the clitoris, Ẹyẹ Àjẹ́ appears to be the clitoris' ẹnikejì, its second self. The Igbá Ẹyẹ is a replica of that which Olódùmarè shares with Odù, and while it is similar in form to the Igbádù of the babaláwo, the Igbá Ẹyẹ is a decidedly political extension and facilitator of Àjẹ́. Although the Igbá Ẹyẹ is kept in a sacred secret space known only to its owner, it grants its bearer sociopolitical dominion. Another àrokò-at-work, the Igbá Ẹyẹ is unseen yet omnipresent and omniscient.

Because of the significance and centrality of the odù of Odù in Yoruba cosmontology, it is necessary and logical that both odù and Odù are well-protected and well-armed. An ẹsẹ Ifá of Írẹ̀tẹ̀ Ogbè reveals that Aragamago's defense of Odù is identical to the Igbádù's method of self-defense. If Odù's enemies are so bold as to look at her bird, "[S]he would shatter their eyes (she would make them blind), / with the power of this bird, she would shatter their eyes."[80] It is because Odù and Aragamago offer complete power and protection that Ọ̀rúnmìlà risks his eyesight and life to unite with them. He does not seek to subjugate Odù, steal her odù, or denude her of power; he seeks to be as close to her as he can in all possible ways. After Ọ̀rúnmìlà proves he is worthy of being Odù's partner, Aragamago and Odù become warriors on Ọ̀rúnmìlà's behalf and offer him their perfect protection. Together, Odù and Aragamago symbolize the symbiosis between the hidden womb and the jutting protecting clitoris and the immaculate sanctuary that they offer.

The calabash that protects, houses, and empowers Aragamago is Onílẹ̀'s natural container and server, and it has a sibling in Ìyá Màpó's clay pot. Calabashes and pots serve innumerable spiritual, domestic, and symbolic purposes and are essential to familial, ritual, and industrial productivity. These containers also act as symbolic representatives of the womb and vagina which are the loci of conception and creation and the home of Àjẹ́. Indeed, to prepare ètùtù, an offering of appeasement, and place it in a pot or calabash and set it at the crossroads is to present a most efficacious offering to Àwọn Ìyá Wa, for that sacrifice replicates the Mother's work of conceiving, nurturing, nourishing, and birthing eternally in the Odù that rolls and rolls and will never break.

Yoruba cosmontology reveals that lives are cyclically saved, granted, reclaimed, and reconstituted in the odù of Odù which include biological wombs, pots and calabashes, the Cosmos, and the Earth. The curvilinear power of the Pot of Existence—manifest as the Earth that holds the souls, àṣẹ, and bones of the ancestors and that forms the foundation for the reconstitution of existence through newborns—rotates and revolves eternally in the thriving womb of Àjẹ́. Just as Àjẹ́ determine the conception and destiny of each human being, so too do they determine when each human being is to enter the womb of the Earth. Rowland Abiodun avers that Àjẹ́'s control over life, death, and rebirth is essential to civilization: "Whatever enables 'our mothers' to extinguish life in this matter, that is, without any visible or materially attributable force, presupposes their foreknowledge of the metaphysical principles of life, especially its source. . . . This belief makes 'our mothers' and all women indispensable to normalcy, orderliness, increase, and progress in traditional society."[81]

The roles of odù Àjẹ́ (containers of Àjẹ́) in the solidification of continuity and immortality resonate with power in Yoruba ancestor rituals that seamlessly combine domestic, spiritual, terrestrial, and cosmic forces. In *Egúngún among the Ọ̀yọ́ Yoruba*, S. O. Babayemi reveals that at the funeral ceremonies of Egúngún members, the pots of the deceased are ritually broken.[82] This custom signals to the departed the end of their terrestrial mission and provides them the impetus to enter Ọ̀run and commence their next mission in peace. The broken pots serve the additional purpose of keeping the deceased from lingering at the crossroads of the terrestrial and spiritual realms and summoning relatives to join them on the other side. This important ritual also helps the survivors to properly process the transition and continue manifesting their destiny in the terrestrial realm.

While pots from the past life are broken, Babayemi describes a ritual called "*aaro oku*" (Ààrò Òkú) that uses new pots and calabashes to ensure that the ancestor has all she needs for her sojourn in Ọ̀run. Babayemi reveals that Ààrò Òkú is performed by and for female members of

Egúngún guilds and that the ritual is fittingly centered around *ààrò*, the hearth. Ààrò is another odù kékeré that offers multiple and multiply encoded meanings, including *arò*, which means "lamentation, sadness, sorrow," and has clear significance to Ààrò Òkú; *aaró*, which signifies "the system of working for each other by turns"; and *àró*, "a title of honour among civil authorities."[83] The ritual of Ààrò Òkú connects all of these seemingly disparate concepts because the ancestors are, indeed, on rotational missions to assist in the development of the world and the Cosmos, and those individuals who have distinguished themselves by manifesting their divinity and immortality during their lives would be those whose return is eagerly awaited and actively facilitated.

Òkú also boasts intriguing linguistic relations. *Òkú* means "corpse," but *o kú* is defined as "a salutation to wish one a long life."[84] O kú is one of the most common Yoruba expressions, and it precedes any of many states, acts, and activities: *O kú ààrò*, for example, means "good morning." While at the outset a corpse and a salutation appear to have little to do with one another, the confluence of these terms is clear with the expression *òkú-áyamọ*, which is defined as a "salutation to the bereaved" that "the dead will be reborn."[85] The term Ààrò Òkú, then, not only honors a departed mother, but it also salutes her eternal spirit as she sojourns with the ancestors prior to returning to her progeny as her progeny.

It is significant that the hearth is central to the aptly titled ritual of Ààrò Òkú. Perhaps as a show of appreciation for the sustenance that the deceased supplied as well as to provide her with what she will need in the spiritual realm, the departed is given "a new small cooking pot, a new calabash with its cover, a new plate, spoon, small bag with some cowries" and soup ingredients.[86] The utilitarian, spiritual, domestic, culinary, and economic become one in this ritual which emphasizes the all-important roles of the Odù Ìwà, the Calabash and the Pot of Existence. Ààrò Òkú also facilitates the reanimation of the ancestor's terrestrial existence through a ritual to honor the deceased's Orí: "A small goat is killed[;] the head of the goat is also put inside the calabash. The calabash is then covered and the blood of the goat dripped over the calabash."[87] This preparation is wrapped in a white cloth and carried to a sacred grove or placed alongside a stream by either a member of the lineage Egúngún or a woman who wants children because "[i]t is believed that whoever carried such a ritual 'aaro oku' would later be blessed with children."[88] It is fitting that honoring the Orí, the Divine and Directing Head and Destiny, of the departed facilitates her immaculate rebirth complete with Orí Pípé, a Perfect and Complete Head, that emerges from the womb filled with ancient wisdom and anxious to gain new knowledge.

While men may have the most obvious places of regard in Egúngún rituals and festivals, it is the female Egúngún members, bearing humble pots and calabashes that contain the forces of immortality, who enact Ààrò Òkú for members of their ẹgbẹ́ and ensure continuity, immortality, and the development of Àjẹ́ intergenerationally.

Àjẹ́'s Sylvan Sentinels

It is customary to find pots of sacrificial items for Àjẹ́ placed at trees because trees are avatars and portals of power. The living energy, medicinal power, and àṣẹ of trees are expertly harnessed by Àjẹ́.

An ẹsẹ of Ogbè Ọ̀sá that is included in Verger's "The Rise and Fall" describes specific trees that empower Àjẹ́ and that assist them in their terrestrial missions. The ẹsẹ recounts Àwọn Ìyá Wa's arrival from Ọ̀run and their alighting on the "seven pillars of the earth," which are seven sacred trees. Each tree has unique ìwà, àṣẹ, and Àjẹ́. The Íwọ tree will bring people longevity, prosperity, and good luck.[89] Orógbó, the bitter kola nut tree, is described as the "chief of the trees of the [forest]," which implies domination in terrestrial endeavors.[90] The Arère tree will result in the destruction of pleasing things whereas Oṣé ensures pleasing things will be acquired. The Ìrókò tree is where hardheartedness results in accidents. The Òbọbọ tree helps one who has committed a violation be pardoned. Alighting on the Iyá tree makes it possible to "rapidly take someone to the sky."[91] While Verger associates the journey to the sky with death, and that may be what is intended, examples of individuals using trees as portals to travel to the spiritual realm abound in Pan-African cosmology, literature, and orature.[92] Terrestrial-cosmic mobility and accessibility are also granted by Ìyàmí's preferred home and power base—the Àṣúrín tree.

Àṣúrín is a formidable tree, and in *African Philosophy, Culture, and Traditional Medicine* Moses Akin Makinde discusses its unique attributes: "Wherever it grows, no other tree grows near it. It kills other trees if their roots touch it."[93] Because of its inherent protective qualities, the bark of Àṣúrín is used to make powerful medicines, but such medicines are rare and dear for, as Makinde reveals, because of its lethality, babaláwo and oníṣègun "rarely touch" the "mysterious" Àṣúrín tree.[94] That Àwọn Ìyàmí Ọṣòròngà make their primary residence in the tree that obliterates anything that touches it reveals their complete control over all flora and fauna—even the most lethal—and illustrates their command over life, the most powerful medicines and technologies, and death.

The ẹsẹ of Ogbè Ọ̀sá avers that the individual with the temerity to climb and the wherewithal to survive perching on the Àṣúrín tree will be the recipient of wonders: "Anything that you would like to set in motion will be realized."[95] One can journey to the sea, to the lagoon, across the Earth, and to Ọ̀run by climbing the Àṣúrín tree and chanting, "All the ẹlẹ́iyẹ climb the àsùrìn tree" three times.[96] The difficulty, of course, is in individuals being able to survive touching, let alone mounting, the tree. With a powerful understatement, the ẹsẹ warns, "Not anyone can stay" on the Àṣúrín tree: However, Àjẹ́ are not just "anyone"—the "àsùrìn tree is the place where the ẹlẹ́iyẹ obtain their power."[97]

Samuel M. Opeola reveals that there are seven different kinds of Àjẹ́,[98] and the ẹsẹ of Ogbè Ọ̀sá may very well be describing their arboreal counterparts. The seven trees of Àjẹ́ and seven types of Àjẹ́ also appear to correspond to the primary emotions, needs, and predicaments that human beings will experience in the course of existence. The ẹsẹ reveals these trees' organic endowments of àṣẹ and Àjẹ́ and the technologies, protections, and forms of retribution and empowerment that Àjẹ́ have thoughtfully distributed throughout nature for the benefit of humanity. Through the ẹsẹ of Ogbè Ọ̀sá, human beings learn not only how to access the power and wisdom of Àjẹ́ in flora but they also obtain a better appreciation of the scope of Àjẹ́. In the realm of arboreal avatars alone, the Mother's influence is unrivaled and can be as exalting as it can be lethal.

The information regarding Àjẹ́'s relationship to trees as detailed in the ẹsẹ of Ogbè Ọ̀sá is important, but it is not exhaustive. The trees that are associated with Àjẹ́ are not limited to seven, and some of the seven trees discussed boast additional relevant attributes.

Ìrókò may be the tree most closely associated with Àjẹ́. In many ẹsẹ, Ìrókò is described as the "brother" of Àjẹ́, and when in distress, Àwọn Ìyá Wa readily seek solace with Brother Ìrókò. The Ìrókò is also significant because its wood used to create the mask of the Ìyánlá, and when Ìrókò becomes Ìyánlá, its power is magnified, as a Gẹ̀lẹ̀dẹ́ song reveals:

> Only three trees we recognize on earth
> "Apa" is without class
> But "ìrókò" is the authority
> But when trees are to be compared to one another
> The mask is supreme.[99]

Apá, the Mahogany Bean Tree, which is favored for carvings, is eclipsed in prominence by Ìrókò, the "sylvan primate."[100] However, when Ìrókò is transformed into the Àjẹ́-filled mask of Ìyánlá, it becomes a unique spiritual specie.

Ìyá Màpó is a mother of many manifestations: In addition to the vagina and vaginal waters, Ìyá Màpó is symbolized by the tree of life which is represented by the uber utilitarian palm tree. As Awo Fatunmbi explains, "The palm tree is one of the symbols of Ìyá Moopo. She is the Ifá symbol for the cosmic tree of life. . . . The palm tree is a symbolic representation of the idea that invisible forms give structure to visible reality."[101]

Ìyá Màpó is a profoundly diverse and ancient Deity, and Ibie's *Ifism* includes an ìtàn that reveals her seniority. The orature describes the Òrìṣà arriving on Earth and finding that everything is covered in water with one exception: "There was only one palm-tree which stood in the middle of the water with its roots in heaven, which was the gateway from heaven."[102] All of the Gods cling to the branches of the palm tree to survive: "That is why the palm-tree, the first creation . . . which had its roots from heaven, is respected by all the divinities. It is the root of their genealogy. All the divinities spread out from the palm-tree to establish their various abodes in different parts of the earth."[103] The palm tree that Ibie describes is the same one that Ugbin Ejo uses as a portal to enter her Ilédì.[104] What is more, the image of an inundated Earth that boasts only the Tree of Life which acts as the "gateway from heaven" evokes the image of Ìyá Màpó's powerful and soothing vaginal waters being eternally protected and empowered by a sylvan clitoris.

Another tree that is associated with Àjẹ́ is Croton Zambesicus, which is known as Àjẹ́ kòbàlé or Àjẹ́ òfòlé. In addition to its aromatic and culinary uses, the leaves can be used to cure diarrhea, dysentery, pain, and convulsions; the root shoots help with menstrual complications, and the root is an effective laxative.[105] Because of the tree's name, it is thought to provide protection against Àjẹ́. However, given the dynamic of Àjẹ́ and its authorship and ownership of the world and its flora and fauna, it is not the case that Àjẹ́ can be vanquished by a tree (or a mineral, like salt; or scattered grains; or newsprint, for that matter).

Oyeronke Igbinola has an Àjẹ́ kòbàlé thriving in her courtyard because the tree is a facilitator of Àjẹ́. In fact, the name Àjẹ́ kòbàlé, which is often translated as "Àjẹ́ do not alight," may constitute a warning for the uninitiated, which could be translated as "Àjẹ́: Kòbàlé," meaning do not molest or attempt to mount the tree of Àjẹ́. Verger's *Ewé* reveals that Àjẹ́ kòbàlé is used in various ways. *Ewé* includes a medicinal preparation "To become [Àjẹ́]" ("*Ìmú ni di Ìyàmi tàbí Àjẹ́*"), and one of the ingredients is Àjẹ́ òfòlé.[106] *Ewé* also includes a prescription for protection from Àjẹ́ that uses Àjẹ́ òfòlé and a preparation to find favor with Àjẹ́ that is activated by Àjẹ́ kòbàlé.[107] The only caveat concerning Àjẹ́ kòbàlé that Igbinola made known to me is that one must not pluck the living leaves from the branches; one must harvest only the leaves that have fallen of their own accord. With this practice, Àjẹ́ ensure the life of Àjẹ́ kòbàlé, and the tree reciprocates.

Aragamago and Her Offspring

While trees are the homes of infinite spiritual and medicinal forces and entities, their most visible residents are birds, and birds are synonymous with Àjẹ́. Doves, pigeons, parrots, owls, vultures, and buzzards—the latter two being birds of divine judgment and discernment that facilitate transformation and the transportation of messages to the Gods—are some of the many birds that are symbolic of Àjẹ́. But the Mothers are most often linked with birds of cosmic origin. Ìyánlá is associated with and depicted as Aragamago, who is also known as Ẹyẹ Òrò, the Spirit Bird.

Aragamago and her innumerable offspring dominate Yoruba ritual and spiritual totems. The *adénlá* (great crowns) of Yoruba rulers boast flocks of Ẹyẹ whose total vision is often greater than 720°. The Ẹyẹ on adénlá, similar to the Ẹyẹ arranged in the pot of Òsanyìn, provide resonant echoes of the womb and clitoris. Òsanyìn is the Òrìṣà of healing, and he boasts a necessarily intimate association with Àjẹ́ because he owes all of his medicinal wisdom to Àwọn Ìyá Wa, who are the owners of the Earth and its flora and fauna. Rulers with their crowns, Òsanyìn and oníṣẹ̀gun with their pots and birds, Òrúnmìlà and babaláwo with their Igbádù, and Egúngún with its Ẹyẹ all offer clear evidence that empowered males must have Àjẹ́ and that they must obtain the approval and guidance of the Mothers to undertake their work. Aragamago represents the fact that without Àjẹ́ there can be no Egúngún, Ọ̀ọ̀ni, Aláàfin, oníṣẹ̀gun, or babaláwo. There can be no Yoruba culture or society of any kind without the Mothers and their empowering Àjẹ́.

While Aragamago is associated with sacred icons, she is not restricted to them. Aragamago loves festivals and appears at the Gẹ̀lẹ̀dẹ́ as Ẹyẹ Òrò, who is described as a large white bird with a blood-reddened beak,[108] and these two colors, red and white, appear to symbolize the Mothers' ability to behold and judge all actions and exact justice for violations against Onílẹ̀. Ẹyẹ Òrò's work is so important that she takes a position of prominence in the Orò secret society and is depicted on bronze Ògbóni rings devouring the severed heads of violators.[109] Manifest as Ẹyẹ Òrò, it is clear that the Great Mother is not at all disgusted by blood of any kind. What is more, the blood on her beak symbolizes her maintenance of social harmony and social hygiene, as well.

Ẹyẹ Òrò, with her tell-tale red beak, is also not shunned by the community or considered foul or polluted. She is honored and revered as the manifestation of Odù, the Mother of All:

> Spirit Bird is coming
> Spirit Bird is coming
> Ososobi o, Spirit Bird is coming
> The one who brings the festival today
> Tomorrow is the day when devotees of the gods will worship
> You are the one who brought us to this place

It is your influence that we are using
Ososobi o, Spirit Bird is coming[110]

While Ẹyẹ Ọrọ takes center stage at festivals, her work is extraordinarily diverse, and her sphere of influence is boundless.

Àjẹ́ are *abáàra méjì*, the ones with two bodies, and one of those bodies is Ẹyẹ Ọrọ. The Mothers sing of their duality and power with pride and with a warning:

Ìyàmi Àbẹ̀ní
Mo lẹyẹ nílé
Mo lẹyẹ níta
....
Mo rìnde òru
Mo rìnde ọ̀sán
Ti mo bá lọ sóde
Ẹ fọ̀wọ̀ mi wọ̀ mí o

[My Mysterious Mother Àbẹ̀ní
I have a bird in the house
I have a bird outside
....
I walk in the night
I walk in the afternoon
When I go on outings
Give me my proper respect][111]

The respect that Ẹyẹ Ọrọ enjoys is also evident in the oríkì "Iyami Ajubaba" which Ayo Opefeyitimi translates as "my mysterious flying beings" and "my passion the-flying-beings."[112] These praisenames indicate that Ẹyẹ Ọrọ is more than a bird, more than a woman: "She" is a collective of individuals who functions as a unit, and their presence is ubiquitous, their power is overwhelming, and their blessings are greatly desired for they hold the destinies of all human beings in their hands.[113]

Ẹyẹ Ọrọ is an exceptional entity, but Àjẹ́ can take wing in any of many birds, including the most common. Many ẹsẹ Ifá that appear to be ecologically-based explications of the habits of certain birds, upon deeper inspection, offer insight into Àjẹ́'s manifestations and methodologies. An ẹsẹ Ifá of Ìwòrì Ogbè begins with Ọṣun telling her husband Ọ̀rúnmìlà to request a sacrifice of two pots, a switch, five yams, 105 ears of corn, and a knife from his next client because there is "not a pot in the house."[114] The clients who come for divination are Pigeon: Elemele of the house, and Dove: Elemele of the farm. Ọ̀rúnmìlà prescribes Ọṣun's recommended sacrifice to stop the sisters' train of àbíkú births. Both sisters had overheard Ọṣun's directive, and Elemele of the farm refuses to sacrifice.

Dove's refusal to make the sacrifice seems logical, because Ọṣun appears to be using sacrifices to replenish her domestic supplies. But Dove also asks, "How is it that if Ọrunmila knows so much about Ifa, his wife is teaching him what sacrifice to prescribe?"[115] This saucy query is similar to what many people would say if placed in the same situation. While the idea of using spirit work to restock supplies is duplicitous at best, the bigger affront seems to be that a woman is advising a man. Dove is unaware of the fact that Ọṣun has command over Mẹ́rìndilogun (Sixteen Cowrie) divination and that she is also an iyaláwo, proper, who works in tandem with Ọ̀rúnmìlà to teach Ifá divination to the world.

Ọṣun's relationship with Ifá divination is elucidated in Ifayemi Eleburuibon's *The Adventures of Obatala*. Eleburuibon discusses an ẹsẹ Ifá of Ọ̀kànrànsodè that concerns the acquisition of "wisdom and knowledge of the divine," which is Odù Ifá. Ọṣun, like many Òrìṣà, has divination cast so that she can find the coveted item. However, she is so confident because of her knowledge and status and close ties with other Òrìṣà that she refuses to make the prescribed sacrifice. Ọṣun finds tangible wisdom and knowledge and puts it in her pocket, but she loses it because she did not sacrifice. Ọ̀rúnmìlà finds the object and becomes the head of Ifá divination; however, "Osun got her share from Orunmila, and *the rest of them received theirs through her*."[116] The central, elemental, and indispensable roles of such Àjẹ́ as Odù, Yemọja, and Ọṣun to Ifá are routinely ignored by practitioners of both genders. What is more, rather than develop their own unique skills and powers, some women, like Dove, spew venom on their sisters who manifest wisdom and knowledge of the divine.

To make tangible the relevance of Ọṣun's prescription, Èṣù sends a lesson-teaching storm to Dove and Pigeon. Dove's children, whom she raises in the Araba or Silk Cotton tree, which is the home of Egúngún, perish in the storm and become an immediate sacrifice for the ancestral spirits dwelling therein.[117] By contrast, Pigeon places herself and her children into the pot of protection that she sacrificed, and they survive. In addition to a covert message regarding the need for solidarity among women and the obvious moral to sacrifice no matter who you think will benefit, the ẹsẹ offers a gentle reminder that the safest home anyone will ever know is the Pot or Womb of Odù. Elemele of the house affirms, "My child touches the pot with its head; it will never die."[118] The child's head touching the pot provides a visceral reminder of the protections afforded the child who enters the world naturally and touches the birth canal and vaginal "pot" with her head.

Wande Abimbola asserts that the pigeon "stands for honour and prosperity," and, revealing a clear connection between birds, humans, and

Gods, Abimbola reveals that "the pigeon is said to have become a domestic bird after it had been helped to have twin children by Èjì Ogbè."[119] Following the birth of her children, Pigeon decides to build her nest near Èjì Ogbè's home. In honor of their bond, Èjì Ogbè decrees that any time Pigeon gives birth, she will have twins. As an additional link connecting Àjẹ́ and pigeons, it is interesting to note that Nigerian women have the highest twin birth rate in the world, that "[t]he òrìṣà of Gẹ̀lẹ̀dẹ́ and twins are same," and that Gẹ̀lẹ̀dẹ́ maskers dance in pairs in homage to Ìyá's dual birthing womb and to affirm that they "are born by the same mother."[120]

While Dove and Pigeon have different Orí and ìwà, they both enjoy honor and respect in Yoruba culture. A Gẹ̀lẹ̀dẹ́ song makes it clear: "The domesticated pigeon will always be prosperous / The dove will always find tranquility."[121] Pigeon's favored status results in pigeons being one of the signature sacrificial items of Àjẹ́ because "*Léyẹ, léyẹ là á bá ẹyẹlé.* (The pigeon always commands respect and honor.)"[122] Dove's refusal to sacrifice does not condemn her. Doves enjoy great respect in Yoruba culture and are considered symbolic of Àjẹ́. Displaying the duality of the Mothers, Dove is abáàra méjì, the one with two bodies. She is praised for her tranquility, but she can transform into Ìyánlá Ẹyẹ Ọ̀rọ̀ when necessary:

> My Mother Osoronga, famous dove that eats in the town
> Famous bird that eats in a cleared farm who kills an animal
>   without sharing with anyone
> One who makes noise in the midnight
> Who eats from the head to the arm, who eats from the liver to the
>   heart[123]

In many respects, Pigeon and Dove could be considered ẹnikejì: Pigeon is the domesticated and faithful companion of Àjẹ́; Dove is the protecting Àjẹ́ of covert and divine retribution. It would be ludicrous to assert that Dove is "evil" and Pigeon is "holy": Both birds are respected for their specific Orí and ìwà and for their distinct contributions to and roles in society.

The power of Ẹyẹ Àjẹ́ is found in various birds, places, and spaces. The termite hill is the geographical symbol of Àjẹ́'s of clitoral power, and an ẹsẹ Ifá of Ọ̀ṣẹ́ Méjì describes three different types of Ẹyẹ Àjẹ́, including those who "flew to the earth from inside the termite hill," helping Ọ̀rúnmìlà attain immortality.[124] In this confluence of symbols, the powers of the clitoris, the prepuce, and the womb are reformulated as the Ẹyẹ Ọ̀rọ̀, the termite hill, and the Earth, respectively.

A Sixteen Cowries ẹsẹ of Èjì Ogbè also intimates a link between Ẹyẹ Ọ̀rọ̀, the clitoris, and the termite hill. "Fresh is how we meet Orisha's worshipers / Who have red feathers on their heads" is the diviner for

"Queen Ant of the Termite Hill" whose presence signifies a "blessing of children."[125] The red feathers that adorn the heads of Òrìṣà worshippers are those of the African Grey Parrot, Odídẹrẹ́, whose brilliant ikóódẹ represent Àjẹ́ and the mighty menses. Odídẹrẹ́'s oríkì is "*ọmọ à fidí ṣ'òwò èjè* (offspring of the one with the menses)."[126] From the freshness of the Olórìṣa to the praise of Odídẹrẹ́, menstrual blood is not considered filthy or polluting in Yoruba cosmontology: Gods, initiates, rulers, and worshippers bedeck themselves in the symbol of the Mother's rich raw power.

The menses-red feathers signify the power of Ẹyẹ Àjẹ́, spiritual rebirth, and anointing in Àjẹ́ through Motherblood. Rowland Abiodun describes this convergence of force in his analysis of the Àjẹ́-at-work during the Igógó festival of Òwò:

> . . . [C]ult members of Yeye Olorisha in Owo spend hours and sometimes days doing their hair elaborately for the annual Igogo festival to honour Oronsen (Òrọnṣẹn), a female deity. The hairdo is not considered complete without the insertion of ornate brass and, of recent, plastic combs which hold up bright red parrot feathers. Dressed thus, these women at the peak of their performance in the Igogo festival create their own aesthetic atmosphere, magically charging it with their "bird (ẹyẹ) power". This "bird power" like aṣẹ, "a form of prophetic power", enables women to accomplish anything that they wish. It is probably because of this power also that men fear to move too close to these cult members as they believe that they may lose their sexual potency. It is interesting that the red parrot feather which is on this occasion believed to possess the magical power to alter the nature of persons and objects, is also prohibited in the blacksmith's premises lest his metals change their chemical properties.[127]

The act of styling and beautifying hair for a festival becomes an exhibition of power once the electrifying ikóódẹ crown the heads of Àjẹ́; and as the song warns, when Àjẹ́ and Ẹyẹ go on outings, they must be given their proper respect—or else. That ikóódẹ is not merely a symbol of Àjẹ́ but that it *is* Àjẹ́ is evident in the fact that the feather and menstrual blood have the same impact on the metals of Ògún and the properties of masculinity: One misstep of any male—human or God—will result in a short-circuiting or electrocution through Àjẹ́.

Abiodun further elucidates Àjẹ́'s social-political influence in Òwò:

> In Owo's most important festival to honour Oronshen the favourite wife of a past Olowo (Ọlọ́wọ̀) "the ruler of Owo town", Yeye Olorisha, a powerful women's cult plays a leading role. It would

appear that the overall welfare and prosperity of the town rest with them. All visual evidence points to the influence and power of women. Male chiefs including the Olowo plait their hair to respect and acknowledge the authority of the goddess Oronshen. Depending on the status of a chief, one, two or three red parrot feathers are stuck in the hair with or without the brass comb. The Olowo in addition, wears two long white egret feathers to distinguish him as the Oba (Ọba) "ruler" of Owo. Is it reasonable to assume that wearing these egret feathers is also a kind of acknowledgement of the "bird power" mentioned earlier in this paper?[128]

When man finds his power with and within woman, his respect for her rolls in waves from his pages, appearance, pen, plaits, and powers.

The town of Ọ̀wọ̀ is named after the word ọ̀wọ̀, which means respect.[129] Perhaps respect in Ọ̀wọ̀ is represented by the colors red and white, for these colors, which are highly symbolic of Àjẹ́, dominate the Igógó festival in Ọ̀wọ̀. The hue white magnifies the rich melanin of the citizens and catalyzes the brilliance of the ìkóódẹ that adorn the heads of select men and women and signify the power of Àjẹ́.[130]

At the Igógó festival, the Ọlọ́wọ̀ becomes Ọ̀rọnṣẹ̀n, and his long white egret feathers mark him as the emissary of the Ẹlẹ́yẹ of Ọ̀wọ̀. It could be the case that his complete immersion in the magnificent menstrual power of Ọ̀rọnṣẹ̀n's Àjẹ́ is signified by his wearing of the *pàkatò*, an elaborate smock constructed of brilliant tubular red beads that is made more stunning by the voluminous white skirt he wears called *àbòlúkùn*.[131] The Ọlọ́wọ̀ is joined by high-ranking males who also dress as divinely empowered mothers who boast the dynamism of Ẹyẹ. These males' appearance signifies that, despite their gender, Àjẹ́ has made them whole. It seems that the men of Ọ̀wọ̀ understand that the most powerful force in the world is Woman, and that the most privileged man is he who is made complete by her and is worthy of wielding and displaying her totems of power.

Eternal Ties of Àjẹ́

The bond between mother and child is remarkable and readily apparent, especially in Africa. In addition to the union that is formed through gestation in the womb and that continues after birth with years of breastfeeding, the mother-child bond is also evident in African mothers tying their children to their backs with at least one wide panel of cloth. Because of the nature of the society, African children, especially prior to the destructive modernization that came with globalization, often go with mother to work, which further strengthens their connection. With such closeness, mother and child learn one another's rhythms, moods, and melodies, and the child watches, learns from, and respects mother's often ceaseless labors. With the child being privy to all that the mother witnesses, says, hears, and feels, fundamental pedagogical, emotional, spiritual, and psychological ties are formed. It is not surprising that the bonds connecting mother to child are eternal and that the genetic, biological, and material objects that strengthen and signify these bonds are powerful symbols of Àjẹ́.

There are many things that symbolize Àjẹ́; indeed, as the Mothers of the World, everything can symbolize them, but the ọ̀kẹ́ (amnion), ìwọ́ (umbilical cord), gèlè (head tie), ọ̀já (cloth used for tying child to one's back), breast milk, and liver are key symbols. The ìwọ́ and ọ̀kẹ́ are essential to existence, but the bonds established by these organs foster a spiritual connection that far outlives their physical roles. The ìwọ́ and ọ̀kẹ́ not only provide every human being with her or his only method to exist *in vitro*, but they also endow the fetus with the genetic material that will become his identity and assist in the manifestation of his destiny and, perhaps, divinity. The ìwọ́ and ọ̀kẹ́ transmit the powers of the Egúngún and Òrìṣà to the child along with chromosomes, blood, lymph, tissues, and nutrients. When the child emerges from the womb, the presiding mothers read the ọ̀kẹ́ and ìwọ́ to determine his spiritual lineage. Following this, the internal implements of existence become externalized in the breasts and their milk, which is rich in essential antibodies, proteins, and amino acids. Breast milk is a perfect and complete food upon which a child can live exclusively for at least a year. A mother breastfeeding her child is a powerful organic exhibition of sufficiency, autonomy, and divinity.

Another essential external implement of existence is the ọ̀já. This simple strip of cloth makes it possible for mother to undertake important tasks and maintain her independence and power while keeping her progeny ever near the Source. The ọ̀já literally ties the child to her mother, providing another effortless exhibition of divinity. When she is not carrying a child, a mother may transform the ọ̀já into a gèlè. Used in this manner, the ọ̀já signifies a woman's status as a mother by literally crowning both her orí and her Orí. Ọ̀já and gèlè can be voluminous, and in the superficial sense, this signifies material wealth; esoterically, the long gèlè represents the magnanimity of motherhood. Not only does abundant cloth ensure the security of the child, but the cloth expands symbolically to represent the fact that one mother is all mothers, and they give birth to, nourish, and wrap the world in their eternal protection and control.

The bond that connects the Mothers to their children does not end when the child becomes responsible for his actions; Àjẹ́'s administration of existence simply becomes more cosmically inclined. The *Ìtàn-Oríkì Ìyàmi Òṣòròngà* reveals that Àjẹ́ can be found at the crossroads of sixteen roads holding sixteen long livers.¹³² With those livers, Àjẹ́ control human existence. The liver is not the obvious choice to express cosmic-terrestrial control, but for that reason and many others it is a most appropriate one. The liver is the largest internal organ in the human body and one of the most important. The liver creates bile to facilitate the digestion of food, it changes food into energy, and it cleans alcohol and toxins from the blood.¹³³ The liver is a vital organ; not only can human beings not live without it, but its affliction will cause debilitating diseases that will directly affect the blood, heart, kidneys, and intestines. Conversely, a strong healthy liver will result in an energized body that boasts effective circulatory, digestive, and excretory systems.

With their control of the liver, the Mothers ensure that human actions and activities have direct physiological impacts. Even slight pressure on or imbalance of the liver can be enough to inspire change, and the warnings that Àjẹ́ send through the liver can be easily reversed. The liver is large in size, but it functions silently, making it a perfect organ to symbolize the Mothers. While the liver may be overshadowed by other organs like the heart and lungs, it quietly monitors what human beings put into their bodies just as Àjẹ́ monitor the actions of human beings on Earth. It is important to note that while the Mothers hold the livers of humanity, human beings are the directors of their own destinies. The Mothers simply register and respond to human stimuli.

In addition to holding sixteen long livers, the *Ìtàn-Oríkì Ìyàmi Òṣòròngà* describes Àjẹ́ standing at the sixteen crossroads that connect Ọ̀run and Ayé and holding sixteen long Ẹdan.¹³⁴ Thus the Mothers and Ẹdan seamlessly unite and control both biological and cosmological spheres of existence.

The image of Àwọn Ìyá Wa standing at the crossroads of continuity and holding sixteen Ẹdan that stretch from Ọ̀run to Ayé is resonant for many reasons including the fact that male members of Ògbóni are most often depicted carrying Ẹdan, bearing Ẹdan around their necks, and/or employing Ẹdan for judicial purposes. However, when Àwọn Ìyàmi Òṣòròngà stand at the crossroads of all being holding sixteen terrestrial-cosmic Ẹdan, no man stands beside them.

Orders of Operation

Yoruba language in general and its spiritual linguistics in particular are extraordinarily intricate. The complexity, poetry, rhythm, riddling, and deciphering of Yoruba offer ample evidence of a culture steeped in Power of the Word. The phrases that describe Àjẹ́ are no exception. When uttering the oríkì of the Mothers, the tongue skips and struggles not to trip as it curls around fire. Some oríkì depict a gargantuan mother: Afọkọ́yẹrí, One Who

Uses a Hoe to Style Her Hair. Others signify Mother Earth's necessary lesson-teaching obstacles: Ilẹ̀ Ọgẹ́rẹ́, The Slippery or Precarious One. In some instances, the power of Àjẹ́ is grotesque, shocking: "They are the eaters of human liver without vomiting"; "She drinks bile from the belly, Ògàlàntà."[135] These oríkì indicate a Mother whose powers are unimaginably vast and whose responsibilities are extraordinarily complex.

Àjẹ́'s multiplicity, immensity, and impenetrability reflect the fact that they are the owners and controllers of both the terrestrial and cosmic realms. Furthermore, as the Ìtàn-Oríkì Ìyàmi Òṣòròngà reveals, Àjẹ́ are the "Ambassadors of the sun / Ambassadors of the afternoon / Ambassadors of the night"; they "bring sunrise and sunset" and are essential to revolutions and rotations of the Earth.[136] It is fitting that those who created existence would also control it and the concept of time that textures and orders existence as well. As Àjẹ́ structure time and space and direct destinies, they do so in full accord with Àjẹ́ Ọlọ́run. The Mothers revel in the depth of their divine lineage, and when coming from and embarking on outings, they greet Ọlọ́run chanting: "Aláàfunfun, aláàfunfun, aláàfunfun," which means "immaculate white."[137] With this greeting, Àjẹ́ herald Ọbàtálá, Odùa, Ẹyẹ Òrò, and all other Òrìṣà funfun who are all also aláàwọ méjì, the ones with two colors. The two colors may be any combination of the cosmic force of black, and the retributive and regenerative power of red, and the reflective power of white: With the Mothers, two colors become three. Seeing the inside and the outside, front and back, Àjẹ́ are also olóju méjì, the ones with two faces. Moving as if by osmosis to and from the material and spiritual realms, the Mothers are abáàra méjì, the ones with two bodies. The duality of Àjẹ́ which gives birth to infinite and unfathomable multiplicity is essential to the monumental work they undertake.

Ensuring Justice

Àjẹ́'s control over life and death might very well inspire fear in the hearts of those who do not have this power and whose existences are determined by it, and such power may cause trembling in the souls of those who are inclined toward wickedness. But it is important to note that the Mothers' work is not influenced by jealousy, greed, hatred, vindictiveness, revenge, or any such human emotions. Ìyàmi Òṣòròngà is praised as "One who kills without motivation of inheritance."[138] She does not seek to profit from death; she does not seek a profit from life; the Western concept of profit is irrelevant. Furthermore, as Yoruba orature makes clear, Àjẹ́ òngbìjà ènìyàn ni ó di kòkó délé wi (Àjẹ́ attends the meeting and fights on your behalf, but when she sees you, she doesn't say a word).[139] Àjẹ́ does not seek recompense for her assistance any more than the mother who breastfeeds her child, because it is Àjẹ́'s responsibility to ensure the elemental balance and harmony of the Earth as dictated by the laws of Onílẹ̀. While the oríkì of Àjẹ́ have been used by manipulators to rationalize the erroneous definition of "witch" and to justify gruesome "witch hunts," these oríkì also swaddle the Mothers in lyrical and spiritual protection by making it clear that these are not Gods to play with because the justice they administer comes from the ultimate authority.

Because Àwọn Ìyá Wa are literally Our Mothers, they do not wish to see our bodies ravaged by disease and death—no matter our offenses. Consequently, when a person has been found to be in violation of the Law, the ẹgbẹ́ Àjẹ́ visits the offender, warns him, and tells him to seek help. The violator has seventeen days to make amends for his trespasses, and he is encouraged by Àjẹ́ to seek help from Àjẹ́ because they are best suited to assist him in making reparations: Ìyàmi is the one who devastates, and she is the one who delivers the devastated from destruction.[140]

An ẹsẹ of Òdí Méjì reveals that babaláwo teach human beings who are seeking help to beseech Ìyàmi with a plaintive tone: "Little mother, you know my voice. / Ìyámi Òṣòròngà, you know my voice. / Ìyámi Òṣòròngà you know everything I say."[141] Because Àjẹ́ are bound by the same laws as everyone else and are subject to the same astral enforcements, the tender voice in which they teach human beings to plead is that which has worked for them as well. Àjẹ́ are so conscious of their responsibilities and the fact that justice is distributed equitably that they pray that everything that they do—the steps they make, the words they speak, the actions they undertake[142]—is in accordance with Onílẹ̀, who can also simply be referred to as Òfin, Law. Rather than be accorded preferential treatment or diplomatic immunity from Òfin because of their status, Àjẹ́ are held to the same standards as the general population. Ibie argues that Àjẹ́ "probably operate the most equitable system of justice. They do not condemn without a proper and fair trials. If anybody approaches them with an indictment against anyone, they will consider all sides before reaching a decision."[143] Adebayo Faleti confirms Ibie's findings and asserts that Àjẹ́ is "the most disciplined cult in the world."[144]

It is often said that Àjẹ́ is a power that women can use malevolently or benevolently, for good or for evil. This argument reveals the mores, dichotomy, and parochialism of a worldview that originates outside of Africa as well as a complete misunderstanding of Àjẹ́. At the outset, I must state the obvious: *Any* individual or group—ethnicity, spiritual affiliation, occupation, and motivation notwithstanding—can intimidate, threaten, harass, or kill others. However, the ẹgbẹ́ Àjẹ́ cannot undertake actions based on personal vendettas, and it cannot select people to antagonize. Àjẹ́'s enforcement of justice corresponds directly to the actions, violations, and trespasses committed by an individual or a group—and that violating individual or group could easily be Àjẹ́. The system of checks and balances in the Mọlẹ̀ judiciary is such that if an Àjẹ́ or an ẹgbẹ́ decided to kill an innocent person or a group of innocent people, that Àjẹ́ or ẹgbẹ́ would find themselves standing before Ẹdan's captivating eyes and bottomless stomach awaiting the ultimate dispensation of justice.

As I assert in the introduction of this book, a bifurcated equivocation that asserts that things or people can be both "good" and "bad" is meaningless. "Good" and "bad" are relative and highly subjective concepts: *Any* person, place, or thing—a religion, a color, foods, a gun, genitals, liquor, knowledge—can be described as being or be used for "good" or "evil." While this dichotomized détente may have been offered by Africans to help Caucasians understand phenomenal forces or to persuade Caucasians that certain forces were not "evil," this type of compromise does not represent the depth, complexity, and discernment of Àjẹ́. Furthermore, Àjẹ́ and forces and organizations like Ògbóni, Orò, Ọ̀rọ̀, àṣẹ, and Ẹdan are not concerned with reductive alien definitions and concepts or the Western proclivity to bifurcate, separate, and, deprecate. The Mothers focus on ensuring their progeny's ability to grow, evolve, and elevate and on dispensing justice equitably.

The Laws of the Law

It is not difficult to live a life that is in harmony with Àjẹ́; general conduct is guided by common sense. While the most egregious violations are the most obvious—murder, theft, abuse, and dishonesty—Opeola reveals three lesser known but profoundly important laws of Àjẹ́:

1. Do not dabble in herbalism (do not use herbs without thorough knowledge of their nature and use).
2. Do not display wealth.
3. Share everything.[145]

The edict against dabbling in herbalism is designed to prevent individuals from unwittingly harming or killing themselves or others. The wisdom of *ewé* (flora) is placed in the hands of those who know ewé best, Àjẹ́. Opeola describes Àjẹ́ as "empiricists" with a knowledge and command of flora and fauna that makes them general medical practitioners *par excellence*. As the Mothers raise children, monitor pregnant women, oversee births, and care for newborns, they share essential knowledge of pharmacopeia with one another and with their children so that wisdom flows cyclically, organically, and intergenerationally. In addition to the medicines and technologies of the Mothers, oníṣẹ̀gun and babaláwo, both of whom must have Àjẹ́, are also repositories of medicinal and technological information.

The second and third laws of Àjẹ́ reflect an ethos structured on holistic communal interdependence as opposed to capitalism. Everything that every human being will ever need exists on the Earth. There is no thing that a human being needs that the Earth does not have. There is no Bank of the Earth that one must access to plant, hunt, fish, harvest, weave, build, manufacture, or create. Trees do not have price tags embedded in their trunks; fish do not have values etched in their scales; land does not rise from the Earth's crust in ready-to-purchase parcels; and no child is emerges from the womb clutching a cache of bullion or banknotes. However, in the midst of infinite abundance, greedy, lazy, spiritually bankrupt individuals created the myths of currency and capitalism and then reified those myths with a World Bank and an International Monetary Fund. In addition to burying billions of people in fictional debts loaded with palpable consequences, global capitalists have turned entire countries and continents into factories and have forced multitudes to spend their lives raping their lands of natural resources to make endless generations of robber barons wealthy.

Capitalism is as dependent on usurpation as it is on gaudy displays of what has been usurped. Without show-offs and advertisements, haters do not know what to envy and neighbors do not know what to covet. Capitalism creates societies in which individuals focus on money-making schemes as opposed to developing their unique innate endowments. Rather than creating innovative necessary products that boast longevity, companies churn out flashy gadgets that will be rendered obsolete in mere weeks by a new wave of soon-to-be-defunct devices: The goal is to keep the masses on a treadmill of material acquisition that creates unimaginable wealth for a few and psychological, social, and spiritual destruction for the many. Capitalism also foments greed and selfishness. At one time, American schoolchildren were enjoined to "share and share alike" so that no one was left out or without. In the 21st century, sharing is anathema in America and is attacked as "socialism" and "communism," two economic systems that are considered "evil" because their principles are rooted in the equitable distribution of the Earth's bounty among all earthlings.

Societies that are structured on capitalism create fragmented, isolationist, crippled communities: The rich are inundated in mind-numbing and soul-addling decadence; the poor live in destitution-soaked hovels. Drugs become the answer for everyone, and Western physicians, pharmacists, and drug manufactures reap billions of dollars and dig billions of graves by dabbling in herbalism. The three laws of Àjẹ́ seem simple, but in nations filled with people who are dazzled by gewgaws, consumed with quick fixes, and addicted to addiction, these laws are extraordinarily difficult to uphold. Other laws of the Earth, which are elemental, are readily broken once the three stones upholding society have been smashed.

Appeasement

When the laws of the Mothers are breached, whether through ignorance or willful wickedness, reparations must be made. The root word of reparation is repair. Repairing or replacing what has been damaged, broken, depleted, or destroyed ensures holism, which is the cornerstone of the African ethos. One of the ways that reparations can be made for violations against Àjẹ́ is through a sacrifice of appeasement called ètùtù. Ètùtù varies from region to region, as different communities have different customs and offer different items, but the purpose is the same: to offer elements that correct a breach or an imbalance. In *Ifism*, ètùtù usually consists of, among other items, eggs, a rabbit, palm oil, and white cloth. These items are all of symbolic and literal importance to Àjẹ́.

In *Ifism*, Ibie credits Ọrúnmìlà with making the first ètùtù, which contained "rabbit, eggs, plenty of oil and other eatable items."[146] Later, when Ọrúnmìlà sacrificed to Àjẹ́ in order to marry, he offered a feast of àkàrà, ẹ̀kọ, other edible items, and a rabbit. Rabbits are included in the majority of the ètùtù that Ibie describes. Àjẹ́'s fondness for rabbit meat may reflect that fact that rabbit is Ọlọ́run's "favourite" companion.[147] The àṣẹ and Àjẹ́ of the rabbits sacrificed to Àwọn Ìyá Wa in the terrestrial realm cycle to Ọ̀run where they empower Ọlọ́run, who is a profoundly important Àjẹ́ herself.

The rabbit's intelligence and cunning made it a favorite in Ọ̀run and a revered icon of Pan-African orature;[148] rabbits are also known for their fertility. Fecundity and facilitators of abundance are logically important symbols of Àjẹ́; consequently, ètùtù often contain rabbit and/or eggs. Eggs are a staple of ètùtù because they embody the mystery, reality, and fragility of life and birth. The egg is also an elegant symbol of the world and the Cosmos. The power contained in the egg is microcosmically and infinitely manifest in woman and her life-bearing eggs. It is fitting that the egg, the object that symbolizes the creative forces of the world and of existence, should be given as a gesture of respect to those who own the world and control existence, and the one who offers an egg for sacrifice must carry it as gently as the she who accepts that sacrifice.

Palm oil is essential in West African culinary, cultural, and spiritual arts, and it is also used to soothe and cool both burns and tempers. Palm oil's medicinal and restorative properties are identical to those of mothers. Indeed, Ibie finds a direct correlation between "the length of time Ifa stays in palm oil before being brought to life" and "the gestation period we spend in the womb."[149] Odù's womb, with its blood-rich walls encased in the perfect Blackness of the Cosmos and creation, is replicated in the pot filled with palm oil in which Ifá incubates and absorbs the symbolic blood of being and the rich amniotic fluid of life. Rather than avoiding palm oil because of its relationship to Motherblood, Ifá is dependent upon it, and ètùtù is routinely drenched in it.[150]

The oil of ètùtù not only cools and soothes Àjẹ́, but, in its approximation of the blood of the womb, palm oil also places the supplicant in the position of vulnerable embryo dependent on the elemental sustenance, protection, and guidance that only Mother can grant. Here, again, is evidence of the reverence for menses and menses-related elements in Yoruba semiotics and culture.

Given its literal and symbolic significance, it is no surprise that Ìyánlá, is so fond of palm oil that her oríkì describes her as "'My Mother' of mothers / The famous one of the night, / Who has water in the house but uses palm oil for her laundry."[151] Lawal argues that these lines are indicative of "Àjẹ́'s lust for human blood."[152] However, given the number of miscreants on Earth and Àjẹ́'s clichéd misrepresentation as bloodthirsty "witches," if the Mother wanted to wash her clothes with blood, she certainly could and would be vividly described as doing so. But by using palm oil to wash her clothes, Ìyánlá is able to swaddle herself in calming, enriching, womb-reminiscent power. When she appears as a palm oil palliative before her community, Ìyàmi not only reveals her acceptance of all of the community's ètùtù but she also becomes an embodied ètùtù for her community. The image of Ìyàmi covered in palm oil-reddened cloths is reminiscent of the Olọ́wọ̀ appearing at the Igógó festival bedecked in a beaded crimson pàkatò. The emergence of both figures signifies immeasurable wealth, healthful regeneration, and, most important, peace.

Ètùtù often include a white cloth, which may relate to the Olọ́wọ̀'s expansive àbòlúkùn. The white cloth symbolizes the terrestrial Àjẹ́'s tie to Ìyánlá, the Great Mother, who is signified by her white beard, whose mask is shrouded in a white cloth, and who dances Gẹ̀lẹ̀dẹ́ with her long white cloth trailing on the ground.[153] The white hue of the cloth reflects Ìyánlá's dominion over all lives and destinies. The cloth that crowns the head, that binds the child to his mother, and that ties the human Àjẹ́ to Ìyánlá extends to envelop Olọ́run as well as Obàtálá and Odúà who reside in the womb where they turn blood into babies. The seemingly simple offering of white cloth reflects all of the ìwà, Orí, and àṣẹ of the universe that Àjẹ́ command.

The eṣẹ Ifá describe sacrifices of ètùtù comprised of specific items and elements—often of specific hues—being offered to balance social, terrestrial, and cosmic imbalances. Èjì Ogbè serves the Orí of his wife with white cloth and a white goat.[154] In one verse of Òtúrá-Bàrà, Ayé (Earth) receives an ètùtù of a bundle of white cloth and a ewe, and in another verse of Òtúrá-Bàrà, Ayé's ètùtù contains a powerful melding of red, white, and black items, including a ewe, white cloth, Black Tamarind, palm wine, and àkàrà.[155] Òrúnmìlà takes white kola to white birds inside of the termite hill, red kola to white spotted birds on the left side of the termite hill, and Guinea pepper to the birds who flew to the Earth from the inside of the termite hill.[156] These three sets of birds combine their requested elements with a tortoise and a snail—the favorites of Òsanyìn, the healer—to make Òrúnmìlà a medicine for immortality.[157]

As the ẹsẹ Ifá reveal, offerings to Àjẹ́ boast both diversity and contextual specificity. To avoid death, Òsá Méjì sacrifices a goat, a hen, a rabbit, and a stem of plantain prepared as a coffin; on another occasion, to determine the cause of his problems, Òsá Méjì sacrifices eight eggs and a castrated he-goat to "the elders of the night."[158] Iyaláwo Ugbin Ejo tells Òfún Méjì that he must sacrifice sixteen snails to soften his aggressiveness.[159] When He-Goat, Snake, and Pigeon are terrorizing the sixteen principal Yoruba towns, Òbàrà Méjì takes a sacrifice of a cock, a rabbit, and mashed yam to the crossroads along with a he-goat for Èṣù in his successful efforts to secure the safety of the towns.[160] Òkànràn Méjì offers a sacrifice that includes a rabbit to Àjẹ́, and he becomes the "Head Chief of the Town."[161]

Ògúndá Méjì's relationship with sacrifices is as interesting as his exploits, and both merit a detailed discussion. *Ifism* reveals that Ògúndá Méjì is known as Eji-Oko in Òrun, and when Eji-Oko leaves Òrun and travels to Earth, he takes another person's large flag instead of the small flag that is meant for him. While the flag leads him to prosper immensely on Earth, because the flag is stolen, Eji-Oko's success is confounded by calamity. Also indicative of his paradoxical existence is that fact that Eji-Oko does not enter Earth through the womb like the majority of entities. He crosses time and space with his pilfered flag until he arrives on Earth and meets Oyi, who, despite several marriages, has no children. Eji-Oko casts Ifá for her and Oyi sacrifices, among other items, a pigeon, a cock, and a hen: "The eggs found in the bowels of the hen were used to prepare medicine for her."[162] Eji-Oko's assistance to Oyi is impacted by the filched flag in such a way that Oyi's blessing overwhelms her. She gives birth to so many sets of twins, twenty-two, that she cannot settle with one husband.

Eji-Oko goes on to become a master hunter who is called Alamiyo, and while he is able to kill destructive birds and deer that are ravaging various towns, Èṣù turns the citizens of the towns against Alamiyo because of his refusal to sacrifice to Èṣù, Àjẹ́, Òrúnmìlà, Ògún, and his Orí. When Alamiyo settles in Iléṣà, he is told to sacrifice or end up burying himself alive. His response is exceptional: "Alamiyo then in tears said that he had done so much favour to humanity, and had been paid with so much ingratitude, that he did not consider himself to be under any obligation to continue to be charitable to anyone."[163]

That the Mothers will be moved by the anguish of their children and will assist them is a recurrent theme in Yoruba ontology and orature. As I discuss above, the *Ìtàn-Oríkì Ìyàmi Òṣòròngà* describes the ẹgbẹ́ Àjẹ́ as feeling pity for violators who are being punished and encouraging them to pray to Àjẹ́ for deliverance,[164] and an ẹsẹ Ifá of Òdí Méjì instructs human beings to sacrifice to Àjẹ́ and invoke the Mothers with a sad voice.[165] These examples reveal how deeply the Mothers are touched and how quickly they move to assist their children. Àjẹ́ are not thirsting for blood and tricking their children to death: When they hear a cry of distress, Àjẹ́ fly into action to assist their children. As a case in point, when Alamiyo's tears fall, the mothers of Iléṣà comfort him and make the necessary sacrifices on his behalf.[166]

Alamiyo's steadfast refusal to sacrifice teaches an important lesson that recurs in the Odù Ifá: One's Orí, fittingly, determines one's destiny. Sacrifice can help one manifest one's destiny, but refusing to sacrifice will not necessarily result in destruction. Indeed, numerous ẹsẹ Ifá describe entities whose ìwà, àṣẹ, and divinity are augmented *because* of their refusal to sacrifice. Alamiyo is one such entity. Not even a pilfered flag derails his destiny. It is also important to note that the Mothers are not his antagonists; in fact, the mothers of Iléṣà aid Alamiyo. While Èṣù consistently sends adversity to Alamiyo because he does not sacrifice, Èṣù also provides him with the tools and opportunities to solidify his legacy. The diversity and flexibility of both Àjẹ́ and the Yoruba worldview are evident in the exploits of Ògúndá Méjì a.k.a. Alamiyo a.k.a. Eji-Oko.

Enlisting Àjẹ́'s Assistance

Àjẹ́'s forces, figures, and forms can take any of all shapes and states. The fact that Àjẹ́ do not have shrines, as do the Òrìṣà, lends even more flexibility and ubiquity to these Gods and this power. While the closest equivalent to a shrine of Àjẹ́ is the womb, Àjẹ́ are said to congregate at crossroads, incinerators, rubbish heaps, and any number of spiritually significant trees. One can place ètùtù at these locations for the purposes of reparations. One can also initiate actions and gain assistance by making certain offerings to Àjẹ́.[167]

Oyeronke Igbinola reveals that for attracting money and keeping secrets, every month one should sacrifice a pigeon to Àjẹ́. A sacrifice for peace and prosperity consists of *èkuru funfun*, ground white beans that are seasoned with salt but cooked without oil and offered on a clay plate. Palm oil is not used in certain sacrifices for Àjẹ́ funfun; the red hue would limit the reflective ability of whiteness.

To ask Àjẹ́ to adjudicate a matter, one can take five small balls of àkàrà to a three-road junction, and state the offender's name or the situation. For a blissful life one can make a sacrifice of six or eight àkàrà covered in honey. It is important to note the use of salt in these offerings; in addition to seasoning èkuru with salt, àkàrà is also seasoned with salt and other condiments before being cooked in rich palm oil. Àjẹ́ enjoy well-seasoned food in both the spiritual and material realms. This fact reveals the fallacy of the assertion that salt—or any other mundane item—can stymie Àjẹ́. There is no force capable of destroying Creation.

Àjẹ́: The Foundation of the Yoruba Nation

The womb rests within the core of Woman which reflects the fact that the womb is the center of the center of life; correspondingly, Àjẹ́ is the womb of the Yoruba nation and the foundation of its judicial, spiritual, and cultural societies; its political system; and its entire ethos. Because of its ubiquity, centrality, and organic biological composition, Àjẹ́ neither have nor need any special regalia, clothes, jewelry, canes, pots, or rocks. And while there are rituals that one can undertake to magnify some or obtain other spiritual abilities,[168] Àjẹ́ is not a force that one can be initiated into, and it cannot be acquired like a title of chieftaincy. Àjẹ́ cannot be bought or sold. It is either dominant or latent in one's spiritual DNA or it is not.

While there have been attempts to depict Àjẹ́ as a furtive fringe element cloaked in secrecy and shame, Àjẹ́ is the core, mantle, and crust of Yoruba culture, ontology, epistemology, and cosmology. In a series of interviews that he generously granted me while I was a doctoral candidate at Obafemi Awolowo University, Dr. Samuel M. Opeola revealed profound information about how Àjẹ́ structured and maintains Yoruba society.

Opeola asserts that the compound system, in which a multigenerational family lives as a sprawling interconnected interdependent network, was created by Àjẹ́.[169] This structure not only ensures that the Mothers are cognizant of and available to address the family's social, medical, culinary, and spiritual needs, but it also encourages dynamic interactivity among members of the compound, the community, and the town.

Opeola credits Àjẹ́ with the institution of polygamy and reveals that polygamy insures the proliferation of Àjẹ́ in many ways. Polygamy guarantees the autonomy of the elder woman who is "free to do as she pleases."[170] Rather than sinking into obsolescence or pining for "lost youth," post-menopausal Yoruba women are the masters of their own and directors of others' destinies. Polygamy is also essential for expecting and breastfeeding mothers who must ensure the sanctity of their bodies, their progeny, and their breast milk by abstaining from sex. In a polygamous home, the expecting or nursing mother is not badgered by a sexually frustrated husband; consequently, she can focus on herself and her child, and the mother-child dyad is of paramount importance to the proliferation of Àjẹ́ and to the health and evolution of the Yoruba family and nation.

The compound system with its bevy of mothers, wives, aunts, and grandmothers—all of whom are regarded and respected equally as mothers by all children—provides exceptional support for women who have difficulty conceiving or breastfeeding and those who need or want to breastfeed for more than three years. The injunctions forbidding sex for pregnant and nursing mothers works in concert with polygamy to ensure that mothers' bodies are completely healed before they conceive again, and polygamy provides parents with the ability to space the births of their children to reduce maternal stress and, most important, reduce maternal and infant mortality. At every step, from conception to puberty and from birth to breastfeeding, Àwọn Ìyá Wa are present, guiding, and directing because their work ensures the vitality and continuity of the nation.

Opeola contends that the compound system, polygamy, injunctions forbidding sex with expecting and nursing mothers, and all other institutions founded by Àjẹ́ are rooted in one objective: "The focus of Àjẹ́ is on protection."[171] In addition to being the protectors of the community, Opeola asserts that Àjẹ́ also necessarily "control everything" in the community.[172] Àwọn Ìyá Wa are the heads of the compound and the mediators of conflicts. They teach their progeny ìtàn, oríkì, and other orature that contain the lineage, history, and destiny of the family. Àjẹ́ are also central to the spiritual health of the community, as they propitiate the Gods and maintain their shrines.

Àjẹ́ monitor and guide members of the community from conception to resurrection, literally. They ensure the physical, spiritual, cultural, intellectual, and social continuity of the family, and the dissemination of wisdom and knowledge is not relegated to certain hours, days, or events, but occurs at all times. Under the tutelage of Àjẹ́, every moment is a didactic one. While Opeola finds that the most important discussions take place at the shrines, which Àjẹ́ maintain, he also contends that the work of the Mothers occurs when the elder women gather in the room of a bride to comfort and educate her, when women are cultivating land and harvesting crops, when women oversee funeral ceremonies during which they will "sleep for seven days with relatives of the deceased" and console and support them, when fetching water, when trading at the market—at all times—Àjẹ́ are busy educating, guiding, and correcting community members and resolving knotty political, spiritual, and social issues.[173]

Opeola avers that Àjẹ́'s most important work concerns children, and their support of children begins before conception. The Mothers ensure the solidity of the family's foundation not only by preparing girls for womanhood but also by grooming brides for marriage. Opeola reveals that

Àjẹ́ "receive the wife and they have to initiate the wife, the new bride, as *ojuto*. They have to undress and give her a proper bath so that she washes way things from the parents' womb and takes a new life with a new people."[174] When the wife receives the seed, conceives, and prepares to bring new life into the world, Àjẹ́—the world's most trusted obstetricians—attend the birth. Ushering life into the world is of such importance that Àjẹ́ "are always present at the birth of every child," and following delivery, Àjẹ́ prepare sacred and essential baths and meals for mother and child.[175] The support and attention given newborns continues as the child ages. Opeola reveals that, traditionally, the elder women of the community would go to each home every morning to inquire as to the health of everyone, especially the children: "That is why they are called alágbuọmọ because they are the old and wise caregivers of the children."[176]

In addition to birthing, healing, and guiding children, Àwọn Ìyá Wa begin the holistic spiritual training that is essential to the actualization and evolution of Àjẹ́ "right from infancy" through the use of symbols. Opeola explains the process:

> That is what many people have not understood about the Àjẹ́. They thought it was like Ògbóni where you get some people, initiate them, and so on. No! Right from the beginning, old and experienced women would train children by giving them symbols. And you know how the Yoruba are very specific in giving symbols. So they give symbols and administer certain aims and objectives with the symbols. And they will be measuring whether [the child] is active and if he is accepting the symbols. So if he's not accepting the symbols . . . they will abandon [the training]. And those who are training well will go on to be Àjẹ́. So that's it. . . .
>
> I'm very close with the function of [Àjẹ́] through my paternal grandmother. I can from my reminiscence understand why this old woman was doing [what she was doing]. I was the only boy. I can see now the treatment of a few of us as opposed to the others. The few of us who received the training have become successful, whereas the others have nothing to write home about.[177]

From àrokò to ààlè to Àjẹ́; from oríkì to Ògbóni to Odù Ifá, every aspect of Yoruba wisdom transmission and knowledge acquisition reveals a mastery of semiotics. As Opeola elucidates, some of the most powerful information is transmitted not through words but via symbols which are silent save for the information that they convey to the soul of the recipient of the knowledge. It is the ability to respond to communication on this level that reveals an individual's innate Àjẹ́ or lack thereof. The fact that its wisdom is conveyed via holistic esoteric communication is precisely why Àjẹ́ can never be fully explicated and why it can never be eradicated.

With the foundation provided by Opeola, one is better able to appreciate the experiences of Yoruba artist Moyo Okediji who was made whole by Àjẹ́. In an interview published in *Know*, Okediji reveals that children in traditional Yoruba society are considered gender-neutral—which further emphasizes the significance of the "ó" pronoun—and that the society and the child's interactions therein determine "whether the child will be male or female."[178] Okediji goes on to divulge that "[i]f you are fortunate enough that these females decide that you can be one of them, they will take you through the process of becoming female."[179] Okediji became female in this way.[180] Okediji, who often creates art as his female persona, Orisagbemi, makes it clear that to be female is to be supreme, and his revelations elucidate how and why certain men, such as priests of Òkè and Ọ̀sun, chiefs of Ọ̀wọ̀ and the Ọlọ́wọ̀, and certain manifestations of Èṣù and Ṣàngó, appear as women: They are entities with male genitalia and/or gender who have necessarily been made whole through Àjẹ́.

Okediji's testimony is important for many reasons, including the fact that he confirms, once again, that Yoruba culture is created, undergirded, and cyclically reinvigorated by a multidimensional network of terrestrial and cosmic Mother Creators. Okediji affirms the fact that, while the male anatomy is inherently limited and limiting, men can be born with Àjẹ́, can have their latent Àjẹ́ developed, can be made women, and can be made whole in myriad ways. I stress here, again, that becoming female and being made whole in these contexts has nothing to do with bisexuality, cross-dressing, hermaphroditism, queering, homosexuality, transgenderism, or any other Western concepts or categorizations. The dynamic being articulated cannot be defined by any Western paradigm, term, experience, or theory, especially not those rooted in the social constructs of gender or in the politicization of sexual orientation, because the dynamic being manifest does not concern sexual orientation or the politics of division: The dynamic at work is that of cosmontologic completion.

The need for certain men to be complete and the celebration of male completeness are ubiquitous in Yoruba society, from the longings of hunters, to Gẹ̀lẹ̀dẹ́ maskers, to depictions of certain Gods, to the rulers and priests of Ọ̀wọ̀, and completion in no way compromises or alters masculinity. As I detail in subsequent chapters, Yoruba culture is also rich with women who house or embody male ancestors or Gods, and these women may be honored as Bàbá. But unlike the man who is made female, or given a synthetic womb, or depicted with ample breasts, Àjẹ́ need not alter anything to be Bàbá. Àjẹ́ is complete. She boasts chromosomal completion, Odù Ìwà, the pathway to Ọ̀run, breasts of bounty, and a catalyzing clitoris. With these organs, she creates, births, raises, and encompasses both "male" and "female." When mother's life-producing era has ended, her estrogen decreases and she develops the classic beard of Àjẹ́. Mother's beard does not signify masculinity but a woman who is fully suffused with divinity: an entity with two bodies, two faces, vast wisdom, and all power. The beard of the elder woman signifies a Divinity fully manifest on Earth.

The traditional Yoruba articulation of gender establishes a firm and fertile foundation for the development of the "harmonious dualism" that Cheikh Anta Diop finds is the cornerstone of traditional African matriarchy. As Diop's research reveals, African matriarchy is a profoundly important social system because it makes it possible for all members of a society to develop and excel according to their skills and abilities, their ìwà and Orí—not their gender.[181] This holistic and open approach to identity provides room for Àjẹ́ to develop despite both the absence of a womb and the presence restrictive male genitalia. Because of its biological manner ofacquisition, its organic method of development in infants and children, its maturation and actualization throughout life, and its centrality to spiritual, social, and cultural cohesion, Àjẹ́ is the eternal essential. Opeola describes the significance of Àjẹ́ in succinct and stunning terms: He avers that without Àjẹ́, "the civilization of the Yorubas is impossible."[182]

. . .

Every sign, symbol, Òrìṣà, and oríkì emphasizes the fact that Woman is All. She is the treasure, and she is the treasure's safest storehouse. She is the Creator; she is creativity. She is a Divinity, and she is divination. Any endeavor undertaken without her authorization, balance, and assistance will fail.[183] The symbols of Àjẹ́—calabash, pot, womb, Ẹyẹ, womb-marinated ikin, menses-evoking irosùn—abound in Ifá divination and its verses. Odù and her Àjẹ́-rich signs must be present for it is, after all, her Ifá. That Odù is the container and maintainer of Ifá is logical; because, when seeking solutions to life's dilemmas, who better to consult than Odù who is Life? Where better than Odù's womb to store what is precious or to imbue something that is sacred with cosmic energy and life? What safer, more secure, more sterile container can one find than the Womb of Existence or as close an approximation of Odù Ìwà as possible?

With perception augmented by òdì orientation it becomes clear that Mother is everything, and she is everywhere. Indeed, the venue that seems completely bereft of her could easily be where her influence is strongest. The power, symbols, and totems of Àjẹ́ are so deeply steeped in divinity that they do not merely represent the Mothers; they are the Mothers' representatives, and they are alive and thriving.

CHAPTER THREE

ÀWỌN ÌYÁ WA IN THE ẸSẸ IFÁ

Evidence of Àjẹ́'s monumental impact on and influence in Yoruba culture is found in various ìtàn, oríkì, and ẹsẹ Ifá whether or not the works are dedicated exclusively to Àwọn Ìyá Wa. The impact of Àjẹ́ in Yoruba orature and literature mirrors its influence on society, for the majority of Yoruba people of all ages, affiliations, and religions know oríkì Àjẹ́ and proverbs about the might of the Mothers or are familiar with Ìyàmi's exploits, whether or not they make mention of their knowledge. As further evidence of the Mothers' cultural significance, while Yoruba men and male Gods are valiant, handsome, intelligent, and boast undisputed historical, spiritual, and cultural importance, there is no extensive body of orature devoted specifically to the exploits and intrigues of Àwọn Bàbá Wa.

In addition to appearing to be quite comfortable in the privileged position of sons of the Great Mother, Yoruba men play key roles in the dissemination of information about the ways and wisdom of Àjẹ́. While mothers and grandmothers chanting ancient oríkì, dispensing wisdom, and concocting cures contribute immensely to the dissemination of knowledge about Àjẹ́, it is largely through the recorded recitations of Yoruba men, which are often filtered through Caucasian researchers, that the remarkable depth and breadth of Ìyàmi's wisdom, wonders, and wiles are available for international appreciation. The roles that Ìyàmi's sons—especially oníṣègun and babaláwo—play in transmitting knowledge about Àjẹ́ are profoundly important. However, the training that the sons receive, the indoctrination that they may have been subjected to, and the manipulations to which their recitations are subjected after they have been uttered can alter perceptions of Àjẹ́.

While the fact is often ignored, academic publications about Africana spiritual systems in general and Àjẹ́ in particular are routinely framed by and interspersed with racist, anti-Àjẹ́, Christocentric, misogynistic rhetoric masquerading as universal truth. References to "lower" and "higher" Divinities; "black" (bad) and "white" (good) spirits; imagined demarcations of "nether regions" of the universe; the use of such loaded words as "evil," "pagan," "heathen," "holy," "polluting," and "clean"; and default reverence of a male Caucasoid God—including capitalizing only

Caucasian Deities and religious constructs—are some of the many signs that alert the reader to the fact that an Africana spiritual system is being filtered and refracted through and distorted by an alien lens. Rather than crushing the infinitude of Àjẹ́ into a straitjacket of pseudo-academic conformity, my goal with this chapter, and this entire book, is to use a Mother's perspective to examine the Mothers' phenomena.

This chapter consists of two interrelated parts. In the first part, I examine the complications born of both Yoruba and Caucasian patriarchal misdirection, with close examinations of the works and words of Pierre Fatumbi Verger, Wande Abimbola, and C. Osamaro Ibie. The second part of this chapter analyzes the diverse portraits of Àjẹ́ in the ẹsẹ Ifá. My analyses focus largely on the verses included in Verger's "The Rise and Fall of the Worship of Ìyámi Òṣòròngà (My Mother the Sorceress) Among the Yorùbá" and Ibie's *Ifism: The Complete Works of Orunmila*, but I also reference other verses in my effort to elucidate the multidimensionality, versatility, and ubiquity of Àjẹ́. With a close reading of the ẹsẹ Ifá, it becomes clear that not only have centuries of racist misogynistic assaults left Àjẹ́ unbowed but also that it is the Mothers' detractors who eventually find themselves, in spite of their best efforts, prostrate before her power.

The Mothers in the Mouths of Men

Pierre F. Verger is one of the most lauded scholar-practitioners of Ifá. I was first introduced to his work through *Ewé: The Use of Plants in Yoruba Society*. Meticulously translated and dutifully rendered with the assistance of a team of Yoruba linguists "who spent many long hours correcting the Yoruba and translating some of the more metaphysical texts received [from] the *babaláwo* and *onisegun* and others within the Yoruba culture," *Ewé* is an extensive catalogue of Yoruba medicinal preparations and incantations that exhibits no ambivalence toward women.[1] *Ewé's* neutrality could result from the fact that ewé (literally, "leaves" or "flora"; idiomatically, "medicine") is often compartmentalized as the domain of predominantly male babaláwo and oníṣẹ̀gun despite the fact that the Mothers oversee and authorize the use of all of the ewé and ẹran (fauna) of Earth. The book's largely gender-neutral stance could be attributed to the fact that it is a pharmacopeia and does not include Verger's analyses. The Yoruba linguistic team could also have ensured the text's balance and propriety. Suffice it to say that *Ewé* is an important study that offers information in a culturally appropriate manner. The work for which Verger is most known, however, is not *Ewé* but "The Rise and Fall of the Worship of Ìyámi Òṣòròngà (My Mother the Sorceress) Among the Yorùbá" ("The Rise and Fall"), and this article is marred by the very ethnocentrism and condemnation of which *Ewé* is free.[2]

For his exposition on Àjẹ́, Verger chooses a title that gives the impression that Àjẹ́ is an organized religion that was founded one day and fell on another; however, the concept of Àjẹ́'s worship rising and falling is problematic for many obvious reasons: Àjẹ́ is an organic aspect of the Cosmos, creation, and Yoruba culture. There is no church, temple, cult, or shrine of Ìyàmi Òṣòròngà other than the womb, motherhood, and existence. Consequently, there is no established ritual worship to rise or fall. There are, however, customs and signs of respect, and, ironically, given his title, Verger, mentions various ways in which Àjẹ́ are heralded and revered. Even in Verger's closest approximation to a fall he depicts Àjẹ́ as resolute and standing as firm as the Earth while protecting the Gods: "In families converted to Christianity or Islam, the guard of the family temple and cult practice [is] left to the care of a select few elderly women, who are often the target of sects of prophet healers and witch hunters."[3] In addition to the fact that Verger echoes Opeola's findings about the centrality of Àwọn Ìyá Wa to Yoruba culture, it is important to note that being targeted does not equal eradication. The evidence of the effectiveness of the Mothers' safekeeping of divine continuity is found in the fact that Onílẹ̀'s progeny are today, as they were in ancient times, perfectly positioned around the Earth.[4] Whether or not his title is designed to act as a comforting code to his neocolonizing peers is unknown, but Verger's title does indicate the perspective with which he chooses to view the Mother of All Gods.

"The Rise and Fall" consists of two parts. The first part is Verger's analysis of ten specific ẹsẹ about Àjẹ́. The second part is titled "Texts and Translations," and it contains the Yoruba transcription and French or English translations of the ten ẹsẹ that Verger analyzes in his article and an oríkì Àjẹ́. Verger does not name the Yoruba babaláwo who recited the orature for him. The only way the reader can ascertain the provenance of the ẹsẹ Ifá is by reading a brief concluding note in which Verger states that the verses "were recorded on tape in 1963 and 1964 in Oshogbo, Nigeria," and after being transcribed and translated on site, they were "submitted for review to those that gave them."[5] It is extraordinary that Verger casually consigns to anonymity the Yoruba wisdom keepers, whose contributions are absolutely essential to this text. While communal ownership is often customary in Africana societies, as spiritual and technological arts are created and shared for social enrichment and elevation as opposed to individual profit, for a Caucasian to omit acknowledgement of the sources of an academic study that would not exist without said sources is problematic for a number of reasons, chief among them being that Verger gives the impression that he does not consider his African informants worthy of naming. From an academic standpoint, by not crediting his sources, Verger makes it impossible to verify or confirm the integrity of or obtain clarification on the data he presents.

Having banished his sources to the realm of irrelevance, Verger positions himself as the sole analyst, the chief interpreter, the master of definitions. He is the authority with the intellectual mastery to decode the mumblings of anonymous Africans. More important, Verger can prove to his Caucasian colleagues that, despite their worship of "witches," the Yoruba actually are "human."[6] From the stance he assumes, and with Caucasian "experts" and fables as his most trusted sources, it would be difficult for Verger to offer a balanced discussion of Àjẹ́.

Because of the complexity of Yoruba language, mistranslations are not at all uncommon, and I know this all too well. However, in some instances words and concepts are intentionally contorted: such is the case with "Àjẹ́" and also "Èṣù," whom obtuse Christians misnamed "the devil." Linguistic twisting is not restricted to the misinterpretation of Gods; any word can be mistranslated and used to further an alien agenda. For example, after he discusses the honorific titles of Àjẹ́, Verger describes to his audience a ritual:

> When these names arise in conversation, it is considered wise to touch the Earth lightly with one's fingers; *bí a bá peri akọni, a fi ọwọ́ làlẹ̀* (If we mention someone of a violent character, we make a mark on the ground); people seated stand up for a brief moment as a sign of respect and humility."[7]

Verger translates *akọni* as "someone of a violent character"; however, *A Dictionary of the Yoruba Language* translates akọni as "a brave, bold or strong person, a hero."[8] Akọni is so esteemed that it is a popular personal name and is routinely used to praise both humans and Òrìṣà. Indeed, the ritual Verger describes is also used to honor both Òrìṣà and remarkable human beings.[9] Verger's erroneous translation of akọni literally makes all of the difference in the world, as lies and stereotypes take on the appearance of truth through misuse of language. Because Verger did not stoop to discuss the involvement of his informants in his analysis, the reader must credit the author with this translation and wonder if Verger gave akọni a negative definition to reify his denigration of Àjẹ́ and to justify what he proclaims is Àjẹ́'s "fall."

The correct translation of akọni reveals the ritual that Verger mentions to be a powerful demonstration of the bond that unites Odù, Ilẹ̀, Àjẹ́ and their progeny. The mention of Àjẹ́ inspires the speaker and listeners to rise in respect for Odù, the Womb of the Cosmos, and to greet Onílẹ̀, the Womb of the Earth. In paying homage to Odù and Ilẹ̀, the human being becomes both the divine product of and the conduit linking these Great Mother Gods: The human being also becomes at one with the akọni. With a full understanding of Odù, Ilẹ̀, Àjẹ́, and akọni, a ritual that is portrayed as a dubious superstition to ward off "evil" takes on a completely different character and meaning. Ironically, especially given the fact that participants in the ritual ascend and descend, the custom that Verger, himself, describes debunks his assertion that Ìyàmi's worship has fallen.

Verger's misreading of the ritual and his mistranslation of akọni work together to serve an important purpose in his essay: They buttress his premise that Ìyàmi is a monstrous sadistic destroyer. In a passage subtitled "Ìyàmi Still Remains Angry," Verger offers a character assessment of the "akọni" of his imagination:

> Ìyámi remains forever angry and is constantly ready to unleash her anger on humans. She is always irritated, whether treated poorly or not, whether in abundant company or entirely alone, whether she is praised or condemned, or whether she is never spoken of at all, consigned to oblivion without glory. All and everything may serve as a pretext for Ìyámi to become offended. . . . Ìyámi grows offended if someone leads too virtuous a life, if any person is too happy in their affairs or amasses an honest fortune, if a person is too beautiful or pleasant, is too well supported or has numerous children, and if this person does not think to assuage these feelings of jealousy by making secret offerings.[10]

If such an irascible, miserable, vicious entity as Verger describes were to actually exist, let alone be reproduced in all African mothers, she—and we all—would have withered to extinction because she is too hate-filled to give life and no one would or could build a life with her. Indeed, the entity that Verger describes is antilife.

Not only does the figure that Verger describes not exist in Yoruba cosmontology but Verger actually includes ẹsẹ that he himself subtitles "How Ọrúnmìlà Calmed the Ìyámi's Anger" and "How Ọrúnmìlà Calmed the Ìyámi" that contradict his assertion that Ìyámi is the embodiment of senseless ceaseless rage. Rather than analyze the orature he collected and explore their nuances, Verger concludes his analysis with a clumsy attempt at rationalizing "the anger of Ìyàmi" by using examples that range from Greek "hubris" to Navaho "witchcraft" to "original sin."[11]

Verger asserts that the savage mercurial rage that he attributes to Ìyàmi "touches upon the subject of the jealousy of the gods, discussed in a book by Tournier, as well as the subject of 'feelings of jealousy and frustration of an elderly person before the apparent happiness of another person as motives that may drive them to revert to sorcery for relief,' which is discussed by Lucy P. Mair."[12] While the postulations of Mair and Tournier reveal nothing about Àjẹ́ they do shed light on why the African phenomena they write about so closely resemble Caucasian phenomena.

It seems Caucasians retained and evolved their childhood fears for adult use. As they travelled the world and began exploring and exploiting others, with all of the solipsism and ethnocentrism they could muster, they butchered and discarded the philosophical, cosmological, and ontological intricacies of other cultures that their minds could not comprehend and forced the minutia that was left into childish Caucasian categories. If Verger's description of Ìyàmi reminds the reader of the wicked old witch of the *Wizard of Oz* or the hag who builds a gingerbread house to lure, bake, and eat Hansel and Gretel, it is because these fairytale creatures are the entities about whom Verger, Tournier, and Mair are writing.

Generation gaps, oedipal passions, and assumptions that elders hate the exuberance of youth are Western myths, preoccupations, and hatreds. The concepts of grandmothers hating their own grandchildren and elders despising neighborhood children only make sense in a Western culture where such feelings are commonplace because elders are often abandoned and pushed to the fringes of society where they become objects of fear and ridicule. The concept of African elders hating the happiness of others, especially their own progeny, is absurd in the extreme and is not a part of the African ethos. In traditional African societies and in many modern African societies as well, elders are indispensable caregivers for their grandchildren. Their support is essential to the existence of the child, the family, the society. The significance of such bonds is elucidated by Opeola in his discussion of Àjẹ́, and the indelible impact of elders on their progeny is on grand display in such memoirs as Maya Angelou's *I Know Why the Caged Bird Sings*, Malidoma Somé's *of Water and the Spirit*, and Wole Soyinka's *Aké: The Childhood Years*.

Verger does not limit himself to creating false cultural equivalents; he also organizes a masquerade in his efforts to defame Ìyàmi. In chapter one of this book I discuss the erroneous additions to an ẹsẹ Ifá of Òsá Méjì in "The Rise and Fall." While the logical assumption is that the babaláwo reciting the verses made the interjections and insinuations, the additions could be the words and work of Verger. Just as Verger offers an inaccurate translation of akọni in such a way that it appears that he is merely quoting his informants, in his analysis of an ẹsẹ Ifá of Òsá Méjì, Verger adopts a babaláwo's language, cadence, and tone to exclaim: "Ha! Àgbà the elder exaggerated. . . She refuses to make the offerings prescribed by Ifá, refuses to listen to Olódùmarè's suggestions, and refuses to act with calm and patience."[13] The ẹsẹ to which Verger refers and that he includes in "Texts and Translations," reveals that Àgbà Odù does not go to extremes, exaggerate, or refuse council. But what is more troubling than deliberately misrepresenting the ẹsẹ's events is the casual manner in which Verger dons the persona of a Yoruba wisdom keeper in order to authenticate his misrepresentation.

It appears to be the case that because the African witch that Verger wants to write about does not exist, he creates her by twisting the ẹsẹ and weaving the mythology of his imagination around Àjẹ́. Verger is so invested in his "witch" creation that when he is confronted with positive information about Àjẹ́ he undermines it, as the following illustrates:

> In 1885, the abbé Pierre Bouche published a book on the Slave Coast, where he was from 1866 onwards. In it he speaks fondly of the belief in Ìyágbà "this goddess who so resembles the Holy Virgin. Like the Virgin, she holds a child in her arms; she is called the maternal savior, the savior of men."
>
> The author was probably unaware that Ìyá àgbà, who he praised so highly, was none other than *iyámi*, the witch.[14]

The "Holy Virgin" that Verger is desperate to disassociate from Ìyàmi is a Caucasian misrepresentation of Ast, the ancient African God who, identical to Odù, is heralded as the source of existence: Ast is "The Goddess from whom all becoming arose."[15] Ast (erroneously known as Isis) is the founder of both agricultural and biological fertility. She is often depicted breastfeeding her divinely conceived son, Heru. And like Ìyàmi, Idemili, Ani, my own mother, and me, Ast is prepared to kill anyone who would hurt her progeny. Anyone. Such defense is not "witchcraft"; it is a Mother's duty; it is her passion.

The air of condescension and arrogance with which Verger carefully distinguishes Ìyàmi from Mary and then denigrates Ìyàmi is most telling because it is most unnecessary. Verger could have let Bouche's findings stand and resonate in the reader's mind. But it seems Verger cannot allow the African God to be showered with the same respect as the African God who has been co-opted by Caucasians. Verger's compulsion to distance his Virgin from the Mother is so pathological that he cannot even allow Ìyàmi to share space with Mary in the same paragraph. But more than saving Mary from contamination, by placing his derogatory disclaimer in a separate paragraph, Verger is able to drive home to his audience his completely unsubstantiated assertion that "ìyámi [is] the witch." Indeed, Verger returns to and further stresses his allegations about the wickedness of Ìyàmi a few pages later. Now speaking on behalf of "Òrìṣà Priest[s]," Verger expounds: "[I]f for the abbé Bouche Ìyá àgbà was a goddess such as the Holy Virgin, the Mother Savior, for the Òrìṣà Priest this was the fear-inspiring and powerful Mother, the Mother forever in anger."[16]

When Verger is not able to undercut sources that speak positively about Àjẹ́, he falls silent. Verger quotes from an article by Dapo Fafiade published in the *Sunday Express* in which Fafiade avers, "No force on earth can conquer the forces of the *àgbà* (witches) derived from the superhuman powers directed by God."[17] A Yoruba informant tells Fafiade that Atinga, the "witch hunters," have "no power" and are impotent before Àjẹ́.[18] The informant also reveals, "Witches are not bad people, like part of the public is led to believe, because they hold the powers of life. . . (But he says no more than this, unfortunately)."[19] However, Verger could have said more. He could have related the points made in Fafiade's article to the ẹsẹ that he collected that highlight Àjẹ́'s proclivity to educate and their diverse creative powers, but he does not. Verger does not discuss Ìyàmi's gifts or Àjẹ́'s tricksterian nature; he affords the Mothers little analytical depth and no genuine consideration. Verger even attributes Ìyàmi's role in curbing excesses and assuring just division of wealth to society's response to being terrorized and terrified by "the constant anger of Ìyámi."[20]

What I find most troubling about "The Rise and Fall" is not what Verger posits, but that he wrote as if he knew that his assertions no matter how erroneous, insulting, or skewed, would be accepted as truth. Sadly, for the most part, he was correct in his assumption.

Because Western religious and cultural terrorism and indoctrination are global phenomena, they have affected nearly every human being on this planet. Wande Abimbola is one of the most revered Ifá scholars and practitioners, and his work has included some of the most damning statements about Àjẹ́. In *Sixteen Great Poems of Ifá* Abimbola asserts that "[t]he Àjẹ́ represent the negation of all that human beings cherish"; and that "Àjẹ́ (witches) are believed to be the avowed enemies of man who have no other business in life apart from the ruination of man's handiwork."[21]

However, in "The Image of Women in the Ifá Literary Corpus," published twenty-two years after *Sixteen Great Poems of Ifá*, Abimbola offers a different perspective. He undertakes an insightful analysis of the diverse roles of women and Àjẹ́ in the ẹsẹ Ifá and Yoruba iconography and the impact of women and Àjẹ́ on Yoruba culture. He also offers a compelling and highly plausible theory to explain why certain ẹsẹ, proverbs, and folktales are riddled with misogyny:

> It is only women who experience *ikúnlẹ̀ abiyamọ* because it is only a woman who can carry a fetus in her womb and bring it forth as a child. What a woman experiences during labor, can never be shared by a man. Furthermore, *ikúnlẹ̀ abiyamọ* is an act of creation which a woman shares with our creator during labor.[22]

In this thoughtful analysis, Abimbola not only heralds the divinity and creative power of literal mothers, thus emphasizing the organic force of

Àjẹ́, but he also, perhaps unconsciously, acknowledges the Àjẹ́, vagina, and womb of "our creator."

Rather than reveling in their positions as sons and protecting the divine mother-child dyad, some men have given in to jealousy, short-sightedness, and slander and use the ẹsẹ Ifá to reify and amplify their misogyny. In "The Image of Women in the Ifá Literary Corpus," Abimbola includes an ẹsẹ Ifá that begins with a complete condemnation of women: "Women are deceitful. / Women are liars. / Let no man open his mind for a woman to see."[23] The verse describes Olójòngbòdú, Death's wife, revealing all of her husband's taboos and weaknesses to his enemies so that they can disable Death and become immortal. Death's enemies who work with Olójòngbòdú include not only babaláwo, who become the direct recipients of her knowledge, but also the individuals for whom this verse is cast, for they will be advised to use Olójòngbòdú's information to attain immortality. The fact that Olójòngbòdú is a clear advocate for babaláwo and human beings is overshadowed by the synecdochical and incongruous attack on all womanhood.

Abimbola offers an important rationale for the existence of such discriminatory orature as that concerning Olójòngbòdú. He proposes that Yoruba men may "secretly fear and envy their women because of the possibility that any woman may be an Àjẹ́, but no king, no noble man, no chief or village head can hold a successful council without authentic representatives of women, in order to sustain a balance in the universe and to maintain the all-important connection with the supernatural."[24] As evidence of Àjẹ́'s vast sphere of influence, Abimbola points to Yoruba women's domination of commerce as well as the ubiquitous presence of Ẹyẹ Àjẹ́ on the crowns of Yoruba sovereigns, the Òsùn staff of the babaláwo, and the staffs of Òsanyìn. Abimbola's analyses offer evidence of the wisdom to which one becomes privy when one has liberated one's mind from one's oppressor's lies.

Africans who have been subjected to Christianization and/or Europeanization can find it especially difficult to respect let alone enter African culture in general and African wisdom-systems and the sphere of the Mothers of Power in particular. In *Ifism: The Complete Works of Orunmila*, C. Osamaro Ibie reveals his life-long struggle to remove the tentacles of Caucasian mental and religious indoctrination from his mind so that he can embrace his divine inheritance. As evidence of the tenacity of mental colonization, Ibie's book is filled with tell-tale Caucocentric and Christocentric rhetoric. Ibie, however, is honest and forthcoming about his perspective, his entrée into Ifá, and his objective.

He begins the first book in his multivolume exposition of Ifá by discussing his father's relationship with Ifá:

> My father retired as a civil servant at the age of 48 in 1951 after which he took to farming and politics. But the Ifa pull became so strong that he eventually gave up farming for an [in-depth] study of the Ifa religious corpus. At eighty three today, he is a practising Ifa priest. I had always argued with him that it bordered on laziness for him to take to such "fetish [idolatry]". He would always respond by ridiculing me with the remark that in time I would change my mind.[25]

Ibie's relationship with Ifá would come to mirror his father's. Ibie found that he, a Bini man who did not speak Yoruba and who was born in a Christian household, had come to Earth with Ifá.

After Ibie retired from practicing law, he encountered Chief Obalola who asked him if he had learned Yoruba language yet. Ibie remarked that not only had he not learned Yoruba despite being married to a Yoruba woman and living in Lagos and Ibadan for many years, but that he also did not consider it important for him to learn the language. Obalola, a babaláwo, informed Ibie that Òrúnmìlà revealed at Ibie's naming ceremony that he would do "great things through" Ibie when he learned Yoruba. This revelation emphasizes the importance of understanding Yoruba language if one is to understand Yoruba culture, philosophy, technology, and cosmology, let alone attempt to cast and interpret Ifá. Ibie's retort was typical of a Christianized individual: "I asked what in this world would Orunmila hope to do through me when I did not even believe in him."[26]

"Belief" is irrelevant to African Gods, technologies, and wisdom systems which are all grounded in empirical knowledge acquisition. Consequently, the Gods did not alter Ibie's beliefs; they continued drawing him with their magnetic pull until Ibie was so overawed by Òrúnmìlà's power that he "could not think of any other thing except how to make other people know about the secrets of the Ifa religion."[27] Before Ibie reached this point, he spent his entire life resisting Ifá and, consequently, suffering many hardships, including inexplicable illness, impotence, and depression. An elder told Ibie that "Orunmila was not given to punishing or blackmailing those who refused to follow him."[28] Ibie's was suffering because he was refusing the protection afforded him by his Orí, Òrúnmìlà, Ifá, and Àjẹ́. While one would expect Ibie to attribute his trials and tribulations to Àjẹ́, as his crises fit their stereotypical *modus operandi*, Ibie never mentions "witchcraft," "angry mothers," or "evil Àjẹ́." The reader comes to the same realization as Ibie: The only entity to whom Ibie can ascribe his misfortune is himself.

Knowing defiance of one's Orí is detrimental, and it is customary for an individual who is chosen but refuses to become a babaláwo to suffer an avalanche of tragedies. Individuals run from Ifá not only because the initiations are expensive, but also because the original super computer that is the brain is fully utilized and committed to the memorization of the innumerable figures, rituals, medicines, verses, and sacrifices of Odù Ifá. The study is beyond arduous: Becoming a babaláwo requires a lifetime of service and sacrifice.[29] Another possible deterrent, one expressed by the character Badua in Ama Ata Aidoo's play *Anowa*, is that inherent divinity takes precedence over humanity in wisdom workers, and they necessarily become one with "the gods they interpret."[30] Another important disincentive is that originally there was no financial benefit in being a babaláwo; in fact, a well-known expression asserts that "no one becomes a babaláwo to make money."[31]

In historical and in conscientious modern Africana societies, charges for divination, healing, and other forms of spiritwork are minimal because capitalism and commerce are antithetical and destructive to spirit. In *Olódùmarè: God in Yorùbá Belief*, Idowu confirms that wealth and luxury are at odds with the work and "worth" of the babaláwo:

> It is laid down that a *baba'láwo* must not abuse his office in any way: if he does, he will never be received into heaven. Therefore, no *baba'láwo* should use his position to enrich himself in any way; he must not refuse anybody his service on account of money—if the person is too poor to pay the customary pittance for divination, the *baba'láwo* must divine for him free of charge; or if the person cannot afford the prescribed sacrifice, the *baba'láwo* must take whatever he can afford and translate the will for the deed. It seems, in fact, that the *baba'láwo* is under a vow of poverty, *to spend himself in the service of the community, making just enough to keep himself, his real reward being in the service of Òrúnmìlà*. Now that materialism is the order of the day, however, this sacred injunction is largely disregarded, and there are many who appear not to know it at all. Charlatans abound.[32]

Idowu's use of language is genius: In "spend[ing] himself in the service of his community" the babaláwo is a spiritual repository whose funds can never been depleted, overdrawn, exhausted, misappropriated, or embezzled because they continuously cycle from the Cosmos to the Earth through the babaláwo to the needy community. However, as Idowu notes, capitalism and the exoticization of the "other" are so rampant in this era that actual babaláwo are rare. Not only do some individuals purchase initiation to become babaláwo strictly to make money, but these "charlatans," to use Idowu's term, are some of the greediest individuals in their communities: Perhaps they endeavor to be like religious leaders of Judeo-Christian faiths who are some of the wealthiest and most selfish people in the world.

Although Ibie consented to follow Ọrúnmìlà and spend himself in service to his community he did so with a lifetime of Christian indoctrination polluting his mind. The poison of that parochial and oppressive worldview often infects Ibie's writing, and it is so obviously incongruous with the truth of Ifá that Ibie finds himself reinterpreting and reconsidering definitions given him by racist oppressors even as he is writing. For example, early in *Ifism*, Ibie refers to Èṣù as "the Evil divinity,"[33] and chapter eight, "The Place of Esu in the Planetary System," begins with an all-out assault on Èṣù, comparing him to Satan and equating him with wickedness and evil. However, Ibie sweeps aside his Christian indoctrination and admits that "Esu can be helpful if one does not underestimate or undermine him."[34] Ibie goes on to acknowledge that Èṣù is "the divinity of reason" who operates in "a variety of ways."[35] A culture war of this type occurring in the text may seem inconsistent, but it is healthy, as it shows honesty, integrity, and the desire to grow. Most of all, it moves the reader to follow the writer's lead and think more deeply about and challenge certain issues and assumptions.

Ibie's attitude about Àjẹ́ can only be described as refreshing. After detailing the myth that the Mothers are evil, wicked, and in league with the devil, Ibie asserts that the opposite is true:

> I have come to discover that they belong to a cosmogonic sphere, which has earned them the name of the elders and owners of the night. . . . I have also come to discover that they are not as evil as they are often painted to be. . . . They probably operate the most equitable system of justice. They do not condemn without a proper and fair trial. If anybody approaches them with an indictment against anyone, they will consider all sides before reaching a decision. . . . Orunmila tells us why he does not kill anybody unless the person has traversed the oath taken between Orisa-Nla, Orunmila, and witches. The witches do not kill any man who truly operates according to the ethos and taboos proclaimed by the Almighty God.[36]

Ibie's elaboration on Àjẹ́ echoes Fafiade's article as quoted by Verger. Most significant, Ibie describes Àjẹ́ with the tone and tenor befitting a Mother's son, and he endeavors to maintain this holistic perspective and discernment as he discusses the myriad forms, faces, and forces of Àjẹ́.

Àjẹ́ in Ẹsẹ Ifá

When one compares ẹsẹ about Àjẹ́ from various compilations, the impact that a diviner's training has on the verses he knows and his recitation and interpretation of those verses is evident. For example, a study of William Bascom's *Sixteen Cowries* reveals that Salako, whose wisdom is preserved in the book's pages, makes reference to "Àjẹ́" only once. This is not because he is ignorant of the concept: Many of his verses deal with singular aspects and Òrìṣà of Àjẹ́. However, an overt articulation of Àjẹ́ is simply not part of his divinatory repertoire.

By contrast, Samuel Elufisoye and the babaláwo who contribute verses to Bascom's *Ifa Divination* offer several ẹsẹ in which Àjẹ́ boast diverse roles, powers, and capacities. Àjẹ́ is so intrinsic an element in certain verses recorded in *Ifa Divination* that the names of the mythistorical diviners, which are often given at the beginning of an ẹsẹ, often serve dual purposes: They signify the diviner's manifestation of Àjẹ́, and they introduce a protagonist who is an Àjẹ́. For example, a diviner of an ẹsẹ Ifá of Ogbè-wòrì is named "An elder [àgbà] who sits without leaning back gives the appearance of a person standing," and he divines for an Àjẹ́ of unparalleled strength whose character-reflective oríkì is "Wherever honor turns she finds wealth."[37] This verse reveals that Orò, the sacred and secret enforcement arm of Ògbóni, is a woman and an Òrìṣà Àjẹ́.[38]

In a verse of Òfún Méjì, recorded in *Ifa Divination*, Ọ̀rúnmìlà consults a diviner named "Death kindles a fire of ipin wood; disease kindles a fire of ita wood; Witches and Eshu kindle a fire of munrun-munrun wood" to save his sick child.[39] By divorcing Ikú (Death), Èṣù, and Àjẹ́ from Western fairytales and pejorative connotations it becomes clear that these forces, similar to Olójòngbòdú, are best qualified to provide the cure and eternal protection for Ọ̀rúnmìlà's child because they know what can reverse their effects or alter their paths. An ẹsẹ Ifá of Òfún-wòrì also focuses on the protection of one's offspring, and one of the three diviners of the ẹsẹ is "A cloth of many colors is the cloth of a witch [Mọṣamọṣa laṣo ajẹ]."[40] This ẹsẹ details how Alákàra (sellers of àkàrà, known as Alákàra, are widely revered as Àjẹ́) sacrifices to save her child, who, similar to the Àjẹ́ featured in the ẹsẹ of Ogbè-wòrì, is named "Honor."

The ẹsẹ in *Ifa Divination* reveal the diversity of Àwọn Ìyá Wa and their similarities to both the Gods and to human beings: Àjẹ́ sacrifice to save their children, as do others; individual Àjẹ́ harass people, as do mortals;[41] and Àjẹ́ accept sacrifices to empower and save lives, as do other Gods.

While it is necessary to carefully sift through most Odù Ifá compilations to find ẹsẹ concerning Àjẹ́, Verger's "The Rise and Fall" includes ten ẹsẹ that are exclusively devoted to Àjẹ́ and the issues, symbols, and Òrìṣà important to them, such as Ọ̀rúnmìlà.

Adeoye's oríkì Ọbàtálá states that those who call the God an Àjẹ́ are not wrong:[42] The same could be said of Ọ̀rúnmìlà, for every ẹsẹ recorded in "The Rise and Fall" that includes Ọ̀rúnmìlà finds one of the most respected figures in Ifá doing everything he can—from making signature sacrifices, to mediating, to marrying—to be as close to Àjẹ́ as possible. Ọrúnmìlà's quest to be at one with Àjẹ́ is logical in that Odù is the author of his existence and the creator and administrator of Ifá, which is his way of life. In the verses that concern Àjẹ́'s interactions with human beings, Ọrúnmìlà is featured as both questing initiate and mediator who translates the Mother's confounding wisdom for human appreciation and education.

The primary focus of the ẹsẹ of "The Rise and Fall" is one of Odù's most important manifestations: Àwọn Ìyàmi Òṣòròngà, who could be considered Odù's representative for human affairs, especially in regards to jurisprudence. Ìyàmi Òṣòròngà is the tutelary Deity of Àwọn Ìyá Wa, and her role is to protect, guide, and empower terrestrial Àjẹ́ and to facilitate social harmony, gender balance, and political and spiritual elevation and evolution.

While the majority of ẹsẹ involving Ìyàmi concern Àjẹ́'s interactions on Earth with human beings, Ìyàmi also occupies a unique position and undertakes essential duties in Ọ̀run. According to Ibie, Àwọn Ìyàmi Òṣòròngà are the only Gods that a patrified Ọlọ́run trusts to guard Ọ̀run while he is bathing, and they are the only Òrìṣà who are allowed to see him nude. This intimacy is not only reminiscent of Odù's demand that babaláwo approach her only when they are completely naked, but it also implies that Àjẹ́ are the Mothers of the patrified Ọlọ́run. Ìyàmi's authority is such that, following Ọlọ́run's bath, she often signals the cock to crow to awaken the world.[43] With these responsibilities, Ìyàmi shows herself to be the ambassador of time and of the revolutions of the Earth, just as Oyeronke Igbinola asserts in the *Ìtàn-Oríkì Ìyàmi Òṣòròngà*.[44]

Odù and Ìyàmi Òṣòròngà appear to be two divine aspects of the same God. With their division of divinity they boast command over Ọ̀run and Ayé: Odù controls Ọ̀run, and her interactions on Earth are relatively few although profoundly important; Ìyàmi Òṣòròngà's exploits in Ọ̀run are few in comparison to the treasure trove of ẹsẹ about her and Àwọn Ìyá Wa on Ayé. Ọrúnmìlà's relationships with these Gods also boast similarities: Just as he struggles and sacrifices to marry and secure the protection and power of Odù, he must also struggle and sacrifice—and match wits, wiles, and wills, as well—with Ìyàmi Òṣòròngà and the terrestrial ẹgbẹ́ Àjẹ́ to secure their infinite blessings and protection. It is also interesting to note that while both Odù and Ìyàmi have been assaulted by the patriarchy, Ìyàmi is the subject of much more negative orature and myth than Odù; this may be due to Ìyàmi Òṣòròngà's terrestrial prominence and dominance.

Àwọn Ìyàmi Òṣòròngà: The Trickster Mothers

The ẹsẹ included in Verger's "The Rise and Fall" offer rich meticulously layered portraits of Àwọn Ìyàmi Òṣòròngà, who is both a God and a divine collective. Even though laced with numerous patriarchal distractors, these verses shed much needed light on the motivations and methodology of Àjẹ́. Unlike the classic format of most divination verses, the ẹsẹ included in "The Rise and Fall" are ìtàn that explain the historical origin and methodology of Àjẹ́ and divulge important affiliations and orders of operation. The verses recount Àwọn Ìyàmi Òṣòròngà coming to and settling on Earth, consolidating and introducing the world to their power, and establishing the manner in which they will be worshipped.

An ẹsẹ of Ìrẹtẹ̀ Méjì describes the arrival of Àjẹ́ to Òtà, a Yoruba town that is regarded as the stronghold of Àjẹ́. The Ìyálóde presides over Òtà, and she is clearly the embodiment of Ìyàmi Òṣòròngà. Ìyálóde is an influential position in Yorubaland. Ìyálóde literally means, "Mother of the Outside," indicating that she is the leader of women's social, political, and economic affairs. The reference to "outside" is important, because Àjẹ́, like women's genitalia, is concealed, covered, and protected. When Àjẹ́ make public appearances, fates change. The power that Àjẹ́ commands, once externalized, is the power of the woman who shows her naked body and the gateway to oblivion to a reprehensible male. The external power of Àjẹ́ is that about which Oyeronke Igbinola sings when she warns that in addition to having "a bird in the house," she has "a bird outside" and must be given her proper respect.[45]

The Ìyálóde, as the civic and political leader of Àjẹ́, is the unabashed Ẹyẹ glorying in her power, and she does not set herself apart from her community: In the ẹsẹ of Ìrẹtẹ̀ Méjì, the Ìyálóde grants her sisters the same power she enjoys. In a reenactment of Ìyánlá Olódùmarè giving Odù her Igbá and Ẹyẹ, the Ìyálóde gives the 201 Àjẹ́ of Òtà calabashes of power that were prepared, most tellingly, at the request of babaláwo.[46] These calabashes of Àjẹ́ are identical to Odù's Igbá Ẹyẹ, and just as Odù can accomplish whatever she wants with her calabash and Aragamago, so too can her earthly representatives, Our Mothers.

The energy and responsibility that wait inside the prepuce, that remain tucked between the legs, and that rest concealed in the core of woman's being are manifest in the powerfully charged symbol of the bird in a calabash. Àwọn Ìyá Wa, constituting the most just and organized society in the world, are the real power of the Yoruba nation. These women, with their biological and political calabashes and birds, are the architects of existence. Just as a tree will die if its roots are exposed, so too will the womb disintegrate if it is removed from its life source; consequently, once the Ìyálóde distributes tangible political power to the Àjẹ́, they do what babaláwo do with the Igbádù; they do what the clitoris does when at rest; they tuck their Igbá Ẹyẹ into secret and sacred places of which only they have knowledge.

The ẹsẹ reveals that Àjẹ́ use their Ẹyẹ Òrò (Spirit Birds) to enforce justice at home and abroad. While the mention of London, England alerts the reader to the influence of modernity on this orature, the reference also serves to inform the reader that Ẹyẹ's sphere of influence is unlimited. The missions of Àjẹ́ and their Ẹyẹ are judicial in nature and reflect their eternal efforts to balance, restructure, and harmonize society. If the Mothers need to support a pregnancy or end one, facilitate a death or help a struggling person elevate, they can undertake this work and much more anywhere on the Earth around which they are expertly positioned. By stating that "[t]hey do not fight alone, unless they do not wish to enter the (àjẹ́) society," the ẹsẹ confirms that the majority of the judicial work is undertaken by the ẹgbẹ́ Àjẹ́.[47] But whether acting as a group or individually, all Àjẹ́ are held to the same standards and subject to the exacting laws of Onílẹ̀.

The ẹsẹ reveals that while some individuals may have technology to shield them from astral justice, the laws of Onílẹ̀, Ẹdan, and Àjẹ́ demand that imbalance be corrected. Consequently, after the ẹgbẹ́ Àjẹ́ reaches a verdict, they send the Ẹyẹ Àjẹ́ to warn the violator. The Ẹyẹ can shift shapes and take the appearance of an Òrìṣà or an ancestor and can arm herself with a club, whip, or knife. The majority of Òrìṣà must be or have Àjẹ́, so it is logical for Ẹyẹ and Òrìṣà to work together and share forms. Ẹyẹ is the overseer and authorizing agent of Egúngún, so it is natural that Ẹyẹ would take the form of Egúngún or the appearance of the violator's ancestor and use Egúngún's whip in its work. The fact that Ẹyẹ can become an ancestor or an Òrìṣà could indicate that the offender's ancestors and Òrìṣà are part of the ẹgbẹ́ and are enlisted to send warnings and offer advice to their progeny; this would be in accordance with the Yoruba ethos and its ethics.

References to Ẹyẹ wielding a knife could refer to an association with Ògún, the God of weaponry and war; however, the reference is most likely an allusion to Ògbóni. With the mention of Ẹyẹ using a club, the affiliation with Ògbóni is unmistakable. "Ògbóni" has been described as a compound word that melds the words *oni*, "one who possesses," and *ogbó*, "old age or a sword with two edges" and/or *ògbó* "a wooden club."[48] One could surmise that Ògbóni members use the wisdom gained from age along with their signature weaponry to adjudicate and mete out justice. Ògbóni and Àjẹ́ are sibling organizations, and they work in concert to enforce Ẹdan and Onílẹ̀'s laws. Many members of Ògbóni necessarily have Àjẹ́, and the ẹgbẹ́ Àjẹ́ is integral to Ògbóni. The fact that these organizations share greetings, weapons, methodologies, and symbols reveals their consonance. The political, social, spiritual, and judicial unity of Ògbóni and Àjẹ́ is also expressed in familial terms, for Ògbóni members refer to themselves as Ọmọ Ìyá, Children of the (Same) Mother, and that Mother is Àjẹ́ Onílẹ̀.

In chapter one I detail the similarities between Odù and Onílẹ̀, and the oneness of these Gods is further emphasized in the oríkì of Odù that connect her with Ògbóni. Odù is called Ẹlẹ́yinjú Ẹgẹ́, which means "The One with Protruding and Ensnaring Eyes." This title refers to Ẹdan, the Mother and administrator of Ògbóni. Odù is also called L'ogbé Òjé which means, "Owner of the Sword or Club of Òjé."[49] While *oje* means tree sap and *òjé* means lead and the two appear to be completely different materials, they are related.[50] In a divination verse recorded in Ulli Beier's *Yoruba Myths*, Ọbàtálá turns an Ìrókò tree into "*oje*, the sacred white metal."[51] Oje is transformed into òjé, and a cudgel of this divine element is sacred to Ògbóni and wielded by Odù, who is the owner of the sacred club and of the budging and ensnaring eyes of Ẹdan.[52]

Boasting a variety of forms and wielding immense powers, Ẹyẹ can reach offenders in any number of ways and can choose the most efficacious form to convey their messages. The ẹsẹ of Ìrẹtẹ̀ Méjì also emphasizes a profoundly important point: Àjẹ́ are not merely at one with Egúngún, Ògbóni, and the Òrìṣà—Àjẹ́ *are* Egúngún, Ògbóni, and the Òrìṣà. Despite the fact that Àjẹ́ is rarely openly associated with these intuitions, as I detail in chapter four, Àwọn Ìyá Wa oversee every judicial institution and political society in Yorubaland from Ògbóni to Orò.

It is because of Àjẹ́'s essentiality to every aspect of Yoruba society that Ọrúnmìlà risks his life to enter the Mothers' circle of power. An ẹsẹ of Ìrẹtẹ̀ Ọ̀wànrin describes Ọrúnmìlà as traveling to Ọ̀tà, the "village of the ẹlẹ́iyẹ," to determine if he is "capable of knowing its secret" and "bringing back its good."[53] However, rather than gird himself in honesty, Ọrúnmìlà arrives in Ọ̀tà bearing a white sack that contains the head of an Ọká snake, a white pigeon, white and red kola nuts, palm oil, ẹfun, iyerosùn and a calabash. While his bag contains signature elements of Àjẹ́ as well as important red, white, and black signifiers, his items are not empowered with àṣẹ or Àjẹ́. Ọrúnmìlà's sack is a decoy that he hopes to use to trick the Ẹyẹ into thinking he is an Àjẹ́.

When Ọrúnmìlà's ruse is revealed, the Àjẹ́ prepare to kill him. In a fascinating development, Ọrúnmìlà's original diviner, Owúyẹ̀wuyẹ̀, who lives with Ọrúnmìlà and who advised him to undertake this scam, refuses to divine for him again; furthermore, Èṣù, who bragged to Àjẹ́ about Ọrúnmìlà's bird, also abandons him. Ọrúnmìlà is stranded in Ọ̀tà, the stronghold of Ẹlẹ́yẹ, with an impotent sack and a mundane bird. Whether Èṣù and Owúyẹ̀wuyẹ̀ are assisting the Àjẹ́ or testing Ọrúnmìlà's mettle is unknown, but they leave him in a stunning predicament.

The significance of interdependence, which is a recurrent theme in orature about Àjẹ́, is evident in the fact that Ọrúnmìlà does not pull out his tools and cast Ifá for himself. He has to find a diviner to assist him. He may be the "God of Wisdom," but his sagacity is only as great as the diviners whom he and Òṣun have trained. In this, Òrúnmìlà is not unlike Olódùmarè whose omniscience is the result of her ability to listen to and behold the perspectives of all of her creations.[54] After a consultation with Tẹ̀máyẹ̀, Òrúnmìlà sacrifices "ekujẹbu (a hard grain)" and an "òpìpì chicken (one with frizzy feathers)."[55] The use of ekujẹbu gives rise to such rituals as placing newspapers, grains of rice, sand, and other elements around one's home in hopes of distracting Àjẹ́ and thwarting an attack. In Òrúnmìlà's case, ekujẹbu represents him: Àjẹ́ cannot eat the hard grain, and they will not be able to eat Òrúnmìlà. The frizzled rooster is well known in Africana communities, particularly those of the Ìtànkálẹ̀, for its ability to peck out roots that have been planted to control or harm someone. However, in this orature, the òpìpì chicken represents Àjẹ́ because, just as òpìpì are unable to fly, Àwọn Ìyá Wa will be unable to fly and land on Òrúnmìlà. This ẹsẹ is significant because it includes defensive strategies known throughout Pan-Africa; however, these distractions cannot stop Àjẹ́, and they do not help Òrúnmìlà discover the secrets of the Ẹléyẹ.[56] Indeed, he is almost killed for his effrontery and deceit.

As Òrúnmìlà's quest to learn the *awo* (mysteries) of the Mothers continues, it becomes clear that Àjẹ́ are not interested in killing or eating Òrúnmìlà in any sense. They seek to gauge his intellectual depth and determine his worthiness for the weighty role of mediator between Mothers and mortals. It is essential to Ifá and Yoruba civilization for Òrúnmìlà and Àjẹ́ to work together, and this can only occur if Òrúnmìlà develops and masters the wisdom of the Divine. Consequently, Àwọn Ìyá Wa educate Òrúnmìlà in the arts of profundity, paradox, and power.

The tricksterian nature of Àwọn Ìyàmi Òṣòròngà, which is intimated in Ìrẹ̀tẹ̀ Òwànrin, is made explicit in an ẹsẹ of Ogbè Ògúndá or Ogbè Yónú. The ẹsẹ's introduction alerts the audience to the fact that ojú inú will be necessary to understand this verse. The ẹsẹ begins, "What you do to me, I will do to you," which is a promise or threat of reciprocity; the second line reveals, "The tree of the fields has a crown on its head," which reflects the supremacy of Àjẹ́'s arboreal avatars; the third line, "Cotton is not a heavy burden (but a heavy load is not as thick)," infers that appearances can be deceptive—what seems simplistic may actually be inscrutable and vice versa.[57]

The ẹsẹ concerns Àjẹ́ establishing rules that are impossible for human beings not to break. These violations will provide Àjẹ́ with an excuse to seek vengeance and wreak havoc. The ẹsẹ brings to mind the scarecrow's classic lament in the film *The Wiz*: "You can't win / You can't break even / And you can't get out of the game."[58] However, the diviner reveals that Àwọn Ìyàmi are actually giving the people of the world a riddle that they must solve.[59] Òrúnmìlà deciphers the riddle by simply confirming to the

Mothers that everything he owns—his home, his fields, and his crops, his road, his self—actually belongs to them.[60]

Àjẹ́ use injunctions that are impossible to know or follow to remind human beings that the Mothers are Ayé, the source of all existence, the "ground of all being."[61] Most important, given Verger's decision to portray Ìyàmi as "forever in anger," after Ọ̀rúnmìlà has solved the riddle by offering recognition, the Mothers state that "*if* they were angry before, they are no longer angry."[62] What is perceived as rage and intractability is Ìyàmi's ruse to determine how well people will respond to adversity and if they have the mental acuity to solve complicated ciphers.[63] In this ẹsẹ, and many others included in "The Rise and Fall," Àwọn Ìyàmi Òṣòròngà act as classic and prototypical Africana tricksters who, by making requests that are seemingly impossible to fulfill and by making magnificent threats, are actually motivating their communities to move to higher states of elevation and evolution.

The tricksterian ways of Àjẹ́ are comparable to those of Èṣù Ẹlẹ́gbára who, orature reveals, found the house and veranda too small to accommodate him but was able to stretch out and relax inside of a nut.[64] His oríkì describes Èṣù as the embodiment of a riddle:

> Lying down, his head hits the roof.
> Standing up, he cannot look into a cooking pot.
> He throws a stone today
> And kills a bird yesterday.[65]

As a strolling cipher, Èṣù "[t]urns right into wrong, wrong into right," and, by doing so, he, who boasts the completion of Àjẹ́ and is very much a she, nullifies all dichotomies. When dichotomized distinctions and juvenile judgments have been dismissed, preparation and perspicacity are left.

While African orature is designed to be entertaining and memorable, the primary purpose of riddles, proverbs, ẹsẹ, oríkì, ìtàn, and the like is to deepen and expand the mind. Awo Fatunmbi shares the riddling power of Yoruba wisdom with his audience in *Ìwa-pẹ̀lẹ́: Ifá Quest* with the query, "What are you willing to do to receive enlightenment?"[66] The essentiality of tricksterian wisdom is also showcased in African American orature, especially the folktales and revised divination verses that feature culture heroes John, Jack, and, arguably the most important trickster in African America, Devil, who is indispensable to knowledge acquisition and intellectual expansion and has nothing in common with the Judeo-Christian devil.

Rather than an "evil" entity who is shunned, Devil is a community favorite because he keeps everyone—protagonists, verbal artists, and audience—perpetually sharp, and he forces members of his community to be unique and masterful problem solvers.[67] When Devil tells Jack to perform impossible feats, like pluck a goose and retain every single feather, he wants to know what skills Jack has in his repertoire.[68] Devil challenges John to a contest of strength for the same reason.[69] When Devil tells God that he can make a turtle but ends up making a tortoise, Devil reveals his own power to create, name, and claim.[70] When comparing orature featuring African American tricksters and the formidable riddles and actions of Àwọn Ìyàmi Òṣòròngà, it is clear that in both cases the narrow alien constructs of "witch" and "devil" are used as shields to protect and promote the complexity, diversity, and indispensability of African wisdom workers and wisdom systems.

In the African worldview, in order to acquire wisdom, reading books is irrelevant. One must be able to read àrokò, paradox, and ìlà (markings). One must not only be able to understand divine paradox and profundity, one must be able to manipulate, create, and become paradox. Wisdom and its accompanying tricksterian skill set can manifest themselves in the ability to know that a riddle is being asked as well as being able to answer a riddle with one's extensive knowledge of flora and fauna, with a wad of cotton, or by invoking sufficient humility to cry.

Tricksterian wisdom suffuses the ẹsẹ Ifá and is present in the diviners' names, the protagonists' defining actions, and the sacrifices necessary for healing, evolution, and self-actualization. The second ẹsẹ of Ogbè Yọ́nú also begins, "What you do to me, I will do to you. / The tree of the fields had a crown on its head. / Cotton is not a heavy burden (but a heavy load is not as thick)." The ẹsẹ concerns human beings, who are called "the people's children," who have committed serious violations. The Mothers ask Olódù Ogbè Yọ́nú to judge human beings' case. This ẹsẹ provides insight into the procedures that Àjẹ́ follow. Àwọn Ìyàmi do not suffer a slight and start slaughtering. They monitor a situation and when misdeeds multiply, the issue is brought before a neutral party. In this case, the neutral party is the verse's Olódù, who finds "the people's children" guilty; Ọrúnmìlà is also found guilty of violations.[71]

That disagreements must be settled by a neutral party is a central tenet of the Ògbóni society; two members must always seek an unbiased third party to mediate a conflict. That third party represents Onílẹ̀, who is the Earth and its wisdom, and Ẹdan, Onílẹ̀'s ever vigilant daughter. The eyes of true justice cannot be blindfolded or gouged out: They must see everything to adjudicate fairly. Consequently, Ẹdan is heralded as Ẹlẹ́yinjú Ẹgẹ́, The One with Bulging and Entrapping Eyes. Ẹgẹ́, which means "trap, snare," has been routinely confused with ẹlẹgẹ́, which means "delicate" and "dainty," despite the fact that these two words have completely different spellings, pronunciations, and meanings.[72] If Ẹdan had dainty eyes, those sensitive orbs would be constantly squinted or shut. Not only is Ẹdan's vision unencumbered, but her eyes never close. The antithesis of delicate, the bulging yellowed eyes of Ẹdan behold *everything*. Indeed, in the case of the ẹsẹ of Ogbè Yọ́nú, Ẹdan, Onílẹ̀, and Olódù Ogbè Yọ́nú have all seen the violations of "the people's children" and Ọ̀rúnmìlà.

In order to reify the myth of Àjẹ́ being evil enemies of humanity, the ẹsẹ establishes a false dichotomy by attempting to distinguish "the people's children" from "the children of ẹlẹ́iyẹ." However, Ìyàmi are the literal and figurative mothers of "the people's children": The Mothers cannot kill their children without destroying themselves. It becomes evident that not only do the Mothers have no desire to destroy their progeny but also that they seek to provide Ọ̀rúnmìlà with a stage upon which to showcase the wisdom he has acquired from his previous encounters with Àjẹ́.

Ọ̀rúnmìlà makes a sacrifice that includes a bowl, an egg, an African Grey Parrot's red feather, honey, *ojúṣàjú*, *ọ̀yọ́yọ́* leaves, *àànu* leaves, and *agògo ògún* leaves. The sacrifice is filled with spiritual-medicinal power as each element inspires particular sentiments: "Ọ̀yọ́yọ́ means you are happy with me"; ojúṣàjú "is telling you to respect him with all kindness"; àànu means, "your whole society would take pity (ṣ'àànu)"; agògo ògún indicates that Àjẹ́ will guide and protect Ọ̀rúnmìlà wherever he goes.[73] Honey sweetens the dispositions of all parties. Ẹfun is used to bring Ọ̀rúnmìlà luck, and osún brings luck to Àjẹ́.[74] The parrot's feather, Àjẹ́'s signature symbol, unifies and galvanizes all of these powerful elements.

It is not sufficient for Ọ̀rúnmìlà to simply offer these items; at this stage in his development, he must be able to decipher and specify the spiritual-medicinal oríkì, codes, ìwà, and application of each item and amalgamate their collective power. Ọ̀rúnmìlà must prove that he has grown in wisdom since his ruse with the impotent sack. Ọ̀rúnmìlà must be able to *pàlọ́* (tell riddles) and *ladi àlọ́* (solve riddles) with the same verbal grace, mental acuity, and spiritual-physical dexterity as Àjẹ́. After he offers the harmonizing items, the Mothers ask Ọ̀rúnmìlà a riddle, and he must not only answer the riddle; he must *be* the answer to the riddle. When Àwọn Ìyá Wa say "throw" ("dẹ̀ṣọ") seven times, Ọ̀rúnmìlà responds by saying "catch" ("dẹ̀hán") seven times.[75] Ọ̀rúnmìlà must also physically catch a hen's egg. To perform this feat, Ọ̀rúnmìlà turns the Olódù's metaphorical name into his literal tool of preservation and power, as he catches the egg seven times with a wad of cotton. This ritual, which shows and proves Ọ̀rúnmìlà's worthiness, indicates that he is able and willing to value, support, and protect life with the same dedication as Àjẹ́. The Mothers welcome their son into their circle of power by blessing in-advance everything he will ever dream to attempt.[76]

It is absolutely essential for Ọ̀rúnmìlà to become one with Àjẹ́. Ọ̀rúnmìlà is the father of the fathers of secrets and mysteries; his name indicates that he is the master of interpreting Odù's writing or Òrun's *ìlà* Òrúnmìlà must have Àjẹ́ in order to understand and decode the cosmological and ontological intricacies of Odù Ifá, and his encounters with Àjẹ́ seem designed to catalyze and magnify his Àjẹ́ to its highest degree so that he can be whole. While Òrúnmìlà is often glossed as the adversary of Àjẹ́ who avenges humanity, the fact is that not only is his relationship with Àjẹ́ one in which he consistently seeks them out to gain from their wisdom and share in their power, but also that Òrúnmìlà, like Ọbàtálá, Ògún, oníṣègun, babaláwo, and other empowered males, *must* have Àjẹ́ to undertake his work and *be* Òrúnmìlà.

The ẹsẹ of Ogbè Ògúndá illustrates the significance of the symbols and symbolic training that Opeola asserts is an essential part of identifying and galvanizing Àjẹ́ in children and adults. This ẹsẹ also stresses the interconnectedness between Yoruba language and culture. For one to simply have various items of power is insufficient; also irrelevant are the often Caucasian-affiliated so-called "scientific" names of flora and fauna. To unlock an item's àṣẹ one must not only know Yoruba, one must *understand* (*yé*) Yoruba.

The nexus of òye (understanding), Òrọ̀, and àṣẹ is central to an ẹsẹ of Òdí Méjì recorded in "The Rise and Fall"; in fact, the introduction of the ẹsẹ discloses that Àwọn Ìyàmi Òṣòròngà "want to hear the voice of the ọmọ awo [children of the diviners]."[77] The ẹsẹ begins with the recurring theme of Ìyàmi coming to Earth to kill, ravage, and destroy. Once the Àjẹ́ commence their work of destruction, the community seeks help from babaláwo who teach them to sacrifice specific items that "speak" to Àjẹ́, to the people's needs, to the ecology, and to the Cosmos. The ability to use one's understanding of Yoruba to activate the àṣẹ of an item is made explicit, for the people learn that by sacrificing *ọgbọ́* leaf, Àjẹ́ are "sure to understand" them.[78] Here, *gbọ́*, which means "to hear"—and relates to the ọgbọ́ leaf and also intimates *ọgbọ́n* (wisdom)—is equated with understanding. Òrọ̀ becomes a tangible and transferrable force carried in the calabash (igbá) used for sacrifice which signifies that Àjẹ́ will bring (*gbà*) the answers to prayers.[79] Most significant is the fact that the babaláwo teach the people to cry in a plaintive voice, identical to that a child would use to plead with her mother, to secure Àjẹ́'s assistance.[80] Clearly, it is reverence and acknowledgement, not murder and mayhem, that Àjẹ́ seek.

The methodology employed by Àjẹ́ in this verse is identical to that used by Àjẹ́ Òṣun who is described in an ẹsẹ of Òṣẹ as inflicting the children of Òṣogbo with fever as a reminder to the citizens that they must honor and praise Òṣun, who gave them children. The theme of the ẹsẹ of Òṣẹ is that a person's kindness should not cause them sorrow. Àwọn Ìyàmi and Òṣun, hurt at having been overlooked and taken for granted, reprimand their constituents to ensure that neither Àjẹ́ nor its life-bringing gifts will be overlooked again.

The ẹsẹ from "The Rise and Fall" confirm the fact that the Ìyàmi are literal and Divine mothers who must be invoked, respected, and honored as such and that babaláwo and Àjẹ́ work together along with Ọlọ́run and Ọ̀rúnmìlà to achieve balance and harmony.[81] It is important to note that when Àjẹ́ receive their specific ritual praise and sacrifice, they are instantly forgiving of any and every trespass. The threats to devour and destroy in these ẹsẹ are revealed to be ontological, botanical, and existential riddles that human beings and Ọ̀rúnmìlà must solve. Likewise, the unbelievable rules and veneer of rage initially displayed by Àwọn Ìyá Wa serve as stimuli to move people to be respectful of Àwọn Ìyá Wa, and women in general, and to remind human beings that the Gods are much closer and more powerful than they might think.

The Many Images of Ìyàmi

While the objective of "The Rise and Fall" is to document the roles and impacts of Àjẹ́ in Yoruba life and orature, the focus of Ibie's *Ifism: The Complete Works of Orunmila* is on sharing the wisdom of Ifá with the world. It appears to be the case that the ẹgbẹ́ Àjẹ́ chose Ibie as a vehicle to tell their truths as well because Àjẹ́ emerge as a force of diverse and undeniable presence and power throughout his book.

In addition to its many rich and intricate portraits of Àjẹ́, *Ifism* also offers a different way to appreciate the ẹsẹ Ifá. Odù Ifá, like the children of Imọlẹ̀, spans the globe; consequently, it must be able to communicate across time and space to address any and all circumstances. The verses of *Ifism* demonstrate how the flexibility and malleability of the divination verses facilitate customization, for the ẹsẹ of *Ifism* appear as narratives and biographies, and this style may have been conducive for Ibie, who began learning Yoruba later in life, to memorize the ẹsẹ. Because of the style in which they are rendered, the ẹsẹ in *Ifism* blur the Western constructs and demarcations of spiritual, historical, and material even more than traditional ẹsẹ; in this, *Ifism* reflects the convergence existent in reality. With ancient diviners (and their wonderfully relevant names and attributes), the Òrìṣà, the Olódù, and flora and fauna all appearing as characters, *Ifism's* verses may be best described as "biomythographies," a neologism created by Audre Lorde to describe the textualization of her art, life, and spirit.[82]

While the rhythm, rhyme, riddling, and other forms of word play that classic ẹsẹ Ifá boast are reduced in the verses Ibie offers, his contributions resonate with unique perspectives and perceptions. Ibie's *Ifism* reveals the ability of the Odù Ifá to adapt to diverse forms of discourse and changes in time, culture, and geography. Because *Ifism's* ìtàn personalize the exploits and offer multidimensional portraits of the protagonists of the orature, Ibie provides his audience with a unique entrée into the traditional Yoruba world. Ibie's narratives depict the Olódù as divine human beings who, similar to the Òrìṣà and diviners, lead rich and full lives in Ọ̀run as well as on Ayé. Most significant to this discussion, the narratives provide an excellent showcase for the myriad manifestations of Àjẹ́ in Ayé and Ọ̀run.

Ifism includes an ẹsẹ about Àjẹ́ that turns on its head the myth that Àjẹ́ are bloodthirsty cannibals lusting for human blood. The verse describes Ìyàmi Òṣòròngà leaving her only child in the care of her human sister Ogbori, who has ten children. Instead of Ogbori's children caring for their cousin, who traditionally would be considered a sibling, in their mother's absence, they eat the child. A devastated Ìyàmi seeks solace with her brother Ìrókò, and the siblings decide to obtain retribution by killing Ogbori's children one by one.[83] Ọ̀rúnmìlà, Ìyàmi's faithful mediator, appeals to Ìyàmi Òṣòròngà and Ìrókò, and they agree to accept an ètùtù of "rabbit, eggs, plenty of oil and other eatable items" and to end the conflict.[84] Ìyàmi suffers an unjustifiable outrage that she rightly avenges before accepting an especially modest sacrifice in recompense. This ẹsẹ recalls the ẹsẹ of Ogbè Yọ́nú in "The Rise and Fall" in which the people's children along with Ọ̀rúnmìlà are found guilty of violations. In both ẹsẹ, human beings are the guilty parties, but Àjẹ́ readily grant pardons after sacrifices and ritual atonement are made.

Conflicts and their resolutions are central to Odù Ifá, and *Ifism* recounts one of the most storied of wars which is a battle of the sexes. After suffering chronic abuses from the men of Ifẹ̀, all of the women, who are all Àjẹ́, leave Ifẹ̀ and establish a town known as both "Ilu Omuo" (The Town of Breasts) and "Ilu Eleye" (The Town of Spirit Birds). The women wage war on Ifẹ̀, and they successfully defend Ìlú Ọmú against all adversaries. The men enlist Ọ̀rúnmìlà to help them conquer the women, but, instead of heading off to war, he has Ifá cast. After making the required sacrifice, he enters Ìlú Ẹlẹ́yẹ with a procession of singers and dancers. The Ẹlẹ́yẹ join the festival, and they all dance back to Ifẹ̀ where gender balance is restored.[85]

While another version of this orature features Òṣun as the dancing unifier,[86] it is significant that Ọ̀rúnmìlà is the one who dances for and pacifies the women because his presence emphasizes the importance of gender balance; indeed, with his dance and song, Ọ̀rúnmìlà is not unlike a Gẹ̀lẹ̀dẹ́ masker performing and transforming in honor of the Gods of Society. This ìtàn also reminds men to bend their knees before the power of the Mothers. If men refuse to respect and revere their Source, Àjẹ́ need not kill or maim anyone: They can simply leave and establish another Ìlú Ọmú, or they can found a town where women live harmoniously and marry one another as is described in Amos Tutuola's *My Life in the Bush of Ghosts*,[87] or they may apply for citizenship in the all-woman town of Umoja, Kenya which was founded in 1990.[88]

While Ọrúnmìlà is a central figure in the realm of Àjẹ́, *Ifism* elucidates the lives of the Olódù. The Olódù are the figures of Ifá that signify specific sets of divination verses. In addition to their roles as cosmic signs, the Olódù are the celestial progeny, the sons, of Odù; and, similar to their mother, the Olódù are Divinities who enjoy both cosmic and terrestrial lives. Ibie chronicles the diverse exploits in the Olódù in *Ifism*, and, in the process, he reveals the organic suffusion of Àjẹ́ in the cosmic and terrestrial worlds. Ibie's work reveals that many Olódù are Àjẹ́, and, in many cases, their terrestrial wives, parents, and children are Àjẹ́ as well. *Ifism* also confirms that even with their abundant power, Odù's divine emissaries and their Àjẹ́-rich relatives go through the same struggles, heartache, celebrations, and revelations as the general populace: These vicissitudes are essential to the Gods' growth.

Rather than be locked in dichotomous opposition or be rendered stagnant by hierarchy, in the African ethos, the spiritual and terrestrial realms flow seamlessly into one another just as divinity flows into and is the rightful inheritance of select human beings. Gods live human lives so that their divinity can be further magnified by the experiential and empirical wisdom gained from terrestrial existence. Accessing the divine and developing wisdom are not pursuits restricted to human beings and Gods, either. The Odù Ifá offers innumerable examples of flora, fauna, hills, lakes, and oceans overcoming obstacles, fully self-actualizing, and manifesting their divinity and immortality. Indeed, the ẹsẹ Ifá could be considered a manual for the holistic development of divinity. Even when entities refuse to sacrifice or when their plans are thwarted, they still acquire knowledge and most experience self-actualization. That manifest numinosity is the ultimate goal of existence is expressed in the Yoruba proverb, *àikú pariwà*: immortality is the ultimate manifestation a perfect of existence.[89]

Èjì Ogbè's ìtàn confirms Àjẹ́'s ability to recognize and catalyze divinity. Èjì Ogbè is known as one of the wisest Olódù, and this is logical for he embodies Orí, the Spiritual Head and Divinity of Destiny that guides human beings. His ìtàn reveals that Èjì Ogbè owes both his wisdom and station in the Odù Ifá to Odù. When Òrìṣànlá is tasked with determining who should be the head of the Olódù, as part of his selection process he prepares food for the Olódù. In each instance, Èjì Ogbè, the youngest Olódù, is given the head of the quarry to eat, and he accepts the proffered heads without comment and in complete understanding.

Before the selections of divine order begin, Èjì Ogbè goes for divination and is told to give a goat to Èṣù. With Èṣù's assistance, Èjì Ogbè meets an elder, and he helps her with her burden. The woman informs Èjì Ogbè that he will be selected the king of the Olódù. This elder, who Ibie describes in incongruous Christocentric terminology as "the mother of God the son,"[90] is Àjẹ́ Odù. The Great Mother herself wraps Èjì Ogbè in a white cloth, crowns his head with a red parrot feather, and places ẹfun in his right palm. Odù directs Èjì Ogbè to stand on a white stone in the middle and at the apex of 1460 stones. When Òrìṣànlá and the other Olódù see Èjì Ogbè swathed in royalty and crowned with divinity, they prostrate before the obvious king of the Olódù.[91]

While living on Earth, Èjì Ogbè must struggle to rise from destitution to success, just as he did in Ọ̀run. After his first wife leaves him, Èjì Ogbè's marries Iwere were who is an Àjẹ́ and whose earthly plight mirrors Èjì Ogbè's trials in Ọ̀run. Because Èjì Ogbè's objective is to see his community fully self-actualize, he spends himself in service to his community, to use Idowu's phrase, and rarely charges for divinations. As a result of his integrity, honesty, and community focus, Èjì Ogbè and Iwere were live on the edge of survival. However, Èjì Ogbè always gives Iwere were the head of whatever quarry he brings home to eat, no matter how small or unappetizing. With this gesture of respect, Èjì Ogbè gives honor to the personification of his Orí, Àjẹ́ Iwere were.

When their family grows prosperous, thanks in part to his mother, Olayori, who has Ifá cast and sacrifices to open the path to prosperity for her son, Èjì Ogbè decides to celebrate his success with the slaughter and feast of a cow, Iwere were expects to be given the head as usual, but she is rebuked by male priests who charge that "the head was not the right part of a cow to give a woman."[92] Èjì Ogbè does not counter the priests, and, for the first time in their marriage, Iwere were is denied her rightful portion.

Iwere were leaves Èjì Ogbè and moves in with her brother Ìrókò like Ìyàmi Ọṣọ̀rọ̀ngà before her. When Èjì Ogbè finds her and asks her why she left, Iwere were presents him with a verbal àrokò that describes the relationship of her head to his own:

> Who can claim to be bigger than the buffalo?
> Who can boast of being more influential than the king?
> No head-tie can be wider than those used by the elders of the
>   night!
> No rope can be as long as the one used by the witches!
> No hat can be more famous than a crown;
> In width or in breadth, the hand cannot be taller than the head.
> The palm frond is often taller than the palm leaves on the head
>   of a palm tree;
> Wherever there is a musical performance it is the sound of
>   the bell that sounds louder than all other instruments; and

> The palm tree is more influential than all other trees in the forest.[93]

With an exquisite cipher, Iwere were marries logic and ecology to cosmology. The references to Àjẹ́ are obvious in the gèlè and rope mentioned in lines three and four. But Àjẹ́'s force undergirds the entire orature. Line one refers to Òrìṣà Ọya, whose totem animal is the buffalo, and the references to the palm tree invoke the power of Ìyá Màpó. When Iwere were asks, "Who can boast of being more influential than the king?" the answer is "mother." Every ruler, whether he reigns in Nigeria, France, Kenya, Spain, or the Kongo owes his existence to both his mother and *the* Mother.

The actions of Iwere were are not those of a "witch." When she is offended, Iwere were first lets her absence speak for her. When she verbalizes, she offers her husband an àlọ́ that he must ladi to determine both his missteps and his way forward. Her encoded message is also a praisesong of herself. Iwere were's exhortation or *ijúbà* (chant of praise) is the perfect expression of her powers of Ọ̀rọ̀ and ọfọ̀ àṣẹ. With a mélange of history, proverbs, and invocation, Iwere were makes Èjì Ogbè aware of the fact that his status is dependent on hers because she is the personification of his Orí. The head of an animal is not always considered the most succulent portion; but, for Èjì Ogbè in Ọ̀run and for Iwere were on Ayé, these proffered heads represent their destinies and identities, and they magnify their powers.

Èjì Ogbè is constantly surrounded and strengthened by Àjẹ́. Odù leads him to his destiny and crowns him with the feather of Àjẹ́ and, hence, the leadership of Olódù. His first wife, Eji Alo, whose name may symbolize the riddles that add texture and complexity to Èjì Ogbè's life, leaves him alone to raise their child, and, by doing so, she impresses upon him the importance of sacrifice and teaches him the rigors of childrearing: Eji Alo's decision also reveals that free will and diversity in womanhood are very much a part of the ancient Yoruba world. Èjì Ogbè's mother, Olayori, a name that means the Honor of the Superior Head, works to ensure her son will prevail in spite of his hardships. Iwere were, whose name may signify the thoughtlessness that led her to chant her riddled oríkì, teaches Èjì Ogbè that true power can teach monumental lessons through absence and through orature. Àjẹ́ is central and essential to all phases of Èjì Ogbè's life, destiny, and empowerment; also crucial is Èjì Ogbè's infinite capacity to learn from all of these powerful women and circumstances.

The influence of Àwọn Ìyá Wa is also apparent in Ọ̀yèkú Méjì's lives and his lineage. As Ibie reveals: "The father of Oyeku Meji was as patient as the rubbish dump . . . while his mother was as strong as the three road junction."[94] Rubbish dumps and three road junctions (oríta mẹ́tà) are both considered gathering places of Àjẹ́, and their sacrifices are often made at these locations.[95] Ọ̀yẹ̀kú Méjì's parents complement one another perfectly; however, Ibie reveals, "When the powers of the wife became too overbearing for [Ọ̀yẹ̀kú Méjì's father], he went for divination and was told to make sacrifice with a boa."[96] As if recasting Ọ̀ṣùmàrè giving birth to Olódùmarè, following the sacrifice the boa, Ọ̀yẹ̀kú Méjì's mother becomes pregnant with him, and nine months later, when his mother is frightened by a boa, she runs to a three-road junction, the signature of her power, and gives birth to her son. Because he is conceived and swaddled in the Àjẹ́ of his parents and Ọ̀ṣùmàrè, Ọ̀yẹ̀kú Méjì, is celebrated as the "king of the Night."

The fact that Àjẹ́ establishes the foundation of this Odù, its characters, and the client for whom this Odù is cast is clear in Ibie's assertion that when Ọ̀yẹ̀kú Méjì is cast for a woman seeking a child, "[S]he should be told that she is responsible for her barrenness because *she is not only stronger but also sees farther than the husband*. She should be advised to submit to the authority of the husband if she truly wants to have a child."[97] However, the ìwà of Ọ̀yẹ̀kú Méjì's mother, and any woman for whom this figure is cast, is identical to the ìwà of Odù, which is to be "as strong as the three road junction." Odù tells Olódùmarè that she will not sacrifice or submit to anyone: She knows her power. Ọ̀yẹ̀kú Méjì's mother does not submit either; it is her husband who patiently waits, sacrifices, and receives assistance from boa who acts as a phallus facilitator. The Àjẹ́ of Odù and Ìyá Ọ̀yẹ̀kú Méjì is beneficial to them, to their partners, and to their biological and spiritual progeny. Rather than attempting to delimit and reposition women or have them weaken, bind, and blind themselves to conform to an alien mandate rooted in patriarchal inadequacy, perhaps the women for whom this ẹsẹ is cast should simply continue to be themselves as did Odù and Ìyá Ọ̀yẹ̀kú Méjì. This prescription is logical in the light of the fact that if this Odù is cast for a man, he is advised to follow the path of Ọ̀yẹ̀kú Méjì's father: patience and sacrifice—and perhaps submission to his wife's strength and far-ranging vision.

Throughout *Ifism* the mothers of the Olódù are revealed to be storehouses of power for their sons. Ọ̀bàrà Méjì's mother is especially noteworthy for she repeatedly extricates her son from conflicts that he becomes enmeshed in as a result of drinking too much. While intoxicated on palmwine, Ọ̀bàrà Méjì declares he will reveal who has been killing the king's children. The king's court decides to kill Ọ̀bàrà Méjì if he fails, and the murderers also plan to kill him. Ọ̀bàrà Méjì's mother consults a babaláwo, and while setting the required sacrifice of yams and soup at a riverside, she see a group of men and invites them to eat the soup. The men reveal that they have been murdering the king's children. Thanks to his mother's efforts, Ọ̀bàrà Méjì reveals the identity of the culprits, who are sacrificed to Èṣù, the town forefathers, and Onílẹ̀.

Because Ọ̀bàrà Méjì's father misinterprets the town's thunderous cheers and thinks his son has been killed, he commits suicide. Ìyá Ọ̀bàrà Méjì is also preparing to hang herself, but when she realizes that her son is being celebrated, "she removed her head from the rope into which she had hung her head preparatory to suicide. She then used the rope (Oja or Oza) to thank her own mother. That is the rope that people use to tie the shrine of their departed mothers in parts of Yorubaland and Benin to this day."[98] Ibie recognizes the rope as ọ̀já, the cloth that mothers use to tie their children to their backs. Ìyá Ọ̀bàrà Méjì's ọ̀já also represents the rope and head-tie that Iwere were herald in her oríkì. The ọ̀já also clearly symbolizes the ìwọ́, the literal umbilical cord that binds a mother to her child and the figurative umbilical cords that give Àjẹ́ knowledge of and power over all lives.[99]

Ọ̀bàrà Méjì's mother uses the rope that would have carried her to Ọ̀run to celebrate the wisdom of the Mothers, to further strengthen her and her son's bond with Àjẹ́, and to reinforce the eternal connection that all children have with their mothers. Ìyá Ọ̀bàrà Méjì's actions become a ritual that anyone can undertake to honor and access the power of his Ìyá in Ọ̀run. As further indication of the intricacy of this ìtàn, Ọbara means cord or rope. With the masterful word-play that is the ẹsẹ Ifá's trademark, Ìyá Ọ̀bàrà Méjì's name, actions, and symbols become an amalgamated signifying force for her son and for any individual for whom this verse is cast.

Ibie informs his audience that it is forbidden for Ọ̀bàrà Méjì's biological and spiritual progeny to drink alcohol: They may begin boasting like their progenitor and not have an Àjẹ́ to assist them. In a precedent-setting incident, a drunken Ọ̀bàrà Méjì claims that he can do the impossible: "wash a black cloth to become white"; and do what is forbidden: "serve the Olofen's [Aláàfin's] head."[100] The Aláàfin invites Ọ̀bàrà Méjì to perform these feats or face death. To assist her son, Ọ̀bàrà Méjì's Ìyá befriends Aro, a fish. While Ọ̀bàrà Méjì is washing a black cloth in a river during his trial, Aro exchanges the black cloth for a white one. Ìyá Ọ̀bàrà Méjì also sacrifices to Èṣù who teaches Ọ̀bàrà Méjì the incantations and rituals necessary to serve the Aláàfin's head. When Ewú Òkété (a large rodent) is unable to serve the Aláàfin's head because he neglected Èṣù, Ọ̀bàrà Méjì is summoned and successfully does what had been forbidden.

Ìyá Ọ̀bàrà Méjì is the force who can turn her son's braggadocios into realities.[101] However, following the remarkable assistance that his mother provides him, Ọ̀bàrà Méjì accuses her of "being a flirt."[102] Ìyá Ọ̀bàrà Méjì does not curse or kill her son or commit suicide. She decides to take leave of the Earth and sojourn in Ọ̀run. Before her departure, she decrees that the hand that Ewú Òkété used to serve the Aláàfin would be used to dig the earth and that the white cloth produced by Aro should be used to wrap human corpses. Ibie avers that the force of Ìyá Ọ̀bàrà Méjì's proclamation is such that it "is used to cause havoc at the shrine of Esu when there is justification for it."[103] It could be the case that Ìyá Ọ̀bàrà Méjì's decrees are an encoded warning that those who dishonor their Mothers are literally digging their own graves and preparing their own winding sheets. While Ìyá Ọ̀bàrà Méjì only punishes her son with her absence, leaving him to struggle to solve his own impossible dilemmas, she establishes an Ọ̀rọ̀ that will make the Earth heave if Àjẹ́ are disrespected.

Unlike Èjì Ogbè, Ọ̀yẹ̀kú Méjì, Ọ̀bàrà Méjì, and other Olódù, Ọ̀kànràn Méjì's interactions with Àjẹ́ reveal a dissonance that may be the result of his initial association with and disassociation from Àjẹ́. When leaving Ọ̀run for Earth, Ọ̀kànràn Méjì was originally going to travel with a gourd and a clay pot—two of the signature symbols of Àjẹ́. However, his diviner advised him "to travel alone by a different route."[104] Had Ọ̀kànràn Méjì continued his journey with those avatars of Àjẹ́, his destiny may have been similar to that of Ọ̀sá Méjì whose interactions with Àwọn Ìyàmi Òṣòròngà are legendary. Ọ̀kànràn Méjì's diviner ensures that Ọ̀kànràn Méjì follows his own path, and it is one with little appreciation for Àjẹ́.

While married and living on Earth, Ọ̀kànràn Méjì and his wife are unable to have children. After being spurred by a dream of success, Ọ̀kànràn Méjì's wife sacrifices so that she can "turn her hard luck to good fortune," but the couple remains childless.[105] Ọ̀kànràn Méjì's Orí informs him that his wife is "a destructive and ruthless witch" and that he prevented Ọ̀kànràn Méjì from impregnating her.[106] His Orí provides his rationale in a poem:

> A snake begets a snake
> Like a witch begets a witch
> From its mother's womb
> The snake inherits the venom sac
> Just as the witch sucks
> Witchcraft from the mother's bowels.[107]

If Ọ̀kànràn Méjì's wife had undertaken any destructive acts at all such condemnation and banishment would be understandable, but her brief depiction shows her to be a committed and helpful partner. It is also interesting to note that Ibie's interpretation of this ẹsẹ does not include a denunciation of Àjẹ́; he simply states that the marriage was "not sanctioned by [Ọ̀kànràn Méjì's or the client's] guardian angel [Orí]."[108] Because the first line of poem recited by Ọ̀kànràn Méjì's Orí is a popular saying in contemporary African orature; it could be the case that the poem was expanded and grafted into the ẹsẹ in the contemporary era to reify the "African witch" construct. The facts that Ọ̀kànràn Méjì's wife's sacrifice for success and the comparison of Àjẹ́ to a snake provide the springboard for Ọ̀kànràn Méjì's ascension further emphasize the dissonance of this ẹsẹ.

Ọ̀kànràn Méjì begins life anew as a hunter, and while on an expedition, he kills a sacred boa. Such an act is usually taboo because the boa is the embodiment of Òṣùmàrè; however, because the boa had been killing people Ọ̀kànràn Méjì is hailed as a hero. Ọ̀kànràn Méjì acquires imí Òṣùmàrè and the oil of the boa, and, true to Idowu's assertions, Ọ̀kànràn Méjì becomes the most powerful diviner in town. Ọ̀kànràn Méjì also effectively harnesses other Àjẹ́-related symbols and elements: By using iyerosùn and Òrò̩ he causes rain to fall and ends a drought. After sacrificing a "he-goat for Esu, a goat for Ifa, a Rabbit for the night, and a cock for his head," Ọ̀kànràn Méjì becomes the Head Chief of the Town.[109] The fact that Ọ̀kànràn Méjì attains—with assistance from the Àjẹ́ of Òṣùmàrè, the Àjẹ́ of iyerosùn, and the Àjẹ́ of "the night"—the heights that his wife dreamed about and sacrificed for makes her condemnation especially incongruous.

Ibie concludes his discussion of Ọ̀kànràn Méjì with a verse that is unrelated to Ọ̀kànràn Méjì, the person but that continues the exploration of Àjẹ́'s multifaceted intricacies. The ẹsẹ's events center on Adeguoye, who is preparing to assume the throne and is told to sacrifice to Èṣù and Àjẹ́ to ensure that he will live through the coronation. Because he is a young man, Adeguoye scoffs at the prophecy and refuses to sacrifice. Ibie reveals that Àjẹ́, who "will not normally strike without giving their prospective victim advance warning, visited him and rubbed his body with their hands."[110] Ibie provides important information confirming the methodology of the ẹgbẹ́ Àjẹ́. Perhaps because Adeguoye has not committed a violation but is simply nearing the end of his earthly existence, rather than Egúngún's whip or Ògbóni's club, Àjẹ́ use the power of touch, perhaps simulating the way that mourners wash and anoint corpses for burial, to encourage him to sacrifice to extend his life. However, Adeguoye ignores Àwọn Ìyá Wa's warnings, and while he sojourns in Ọ̀run, his infant son is crowned king.[111]

One of the elements that provides richness, layers of complexity, and depth to the ẹsẹ Ifá is the fact that its divine protagonists are journeying towards self-actualization, and during their journeys they can stumble, be misled, and suffer setbacks. These events do not in any way diminish their divinity; they act as roadmaps, sacred counsel, and essential lessons for the Gods of the ẹsẹ and for the human beings for whom these verses are cast. The ìtàn of Ọ̀wọ́nrín Méjì, for example, offers evidence of the fact that the Gods must experience and learn how to resolve domestic conflicts.

When discord among Ọ̀wọ́nrín Méjì and his mother and his wives leads to a scuffle during which Ọ̀wọ́nrín Méjì pushes his mother, Ìyá Ọ̀wọ́nrín

Méjì asks the ẹgbẹ́ Àjẹ́ to adjudicate the matter. Ibie reveals that the elders to whom Ọ̀wọ́nrín Méjì's mother confides

> were some of Owanrinmeji's deadliest enemies who also belonged to the witch cult. They had previously sought in vain to find fault with him as an excuse for condemning him in the witch club. Normally, the rule of the club is that no victim is punished without the benefit of a fair trial and conviction. In fact it is well known that no matter however much witches may hate a person, they do not strike until the person has been tried and found guilty.[112]

Without revealing the reason why, Ibie states that Ọ̀wọ́nrín Méjì's wives had "long teamed up with his enemies in the witch-club to destroy him," but they were unsuccessful in convicting him until Ọ̀wọ́nrín Méjì's "own mother provided a prima facie case against him."[113] Ibie warns that people should resist the urge to air family grievances publicly because the case may find its way to the court of the ẹgbẹ́ Àjẹ́, but Ibie overlooks the most important injunction: A child should never hit his mother. It is because he hits his mother that Ọ̀wọ́nrín Méjì is convicted "in absentia" and sentenced to death.

The ẹsẹ of Ìrẹtẹ̀ Méjì in "The Rise and Fall" asserts that some individuals will use various means to attempt to escape the judgment of Àjẹ́. Ọ̀wọ́nrín Méjì has numerous forms of such assistance. His Orí reveals to him in a dream his trial and conviction, and he consults Ifá and escapes execution. When the ẹgbẹ́ uses initiation into Orò as a ruse to execute Ọ̀wọ́nrín Méjì, he consults Ifá again. Èṣù protects him with ọfẹ, a device that immediately transports its bearer away from imminent death.[114] When Ọ̀wọ́nrín Méjì is walking toward the altar on which he is to be executed, he trips on an "invisible obstacle" placed by Èṣù to activate ọfẹ, and Ọ̀wọ́nrín Méjì "disappear[s] into invisibility. He miraculously [finds] himself in his house."[115]

Ọ̀wọ́nrín Méjì's temporary reprieves are made permanent by his mother. Because she placed the issue before the ẹgbẹ́ Àjẹ́, only she can repeal it. To save her son, Ìyá Òwánrín Méjì assumes the most powerful pose: that of ìkúnlẹ̀ abiyamọ.[116] Kneeling on both knees, the same posture she assumed while giving birth to her son, Ìyá Ọ̀wọ́nrín Méjì obtains a reversal of the death sentence. Ọ̀wọ́nrín Méjì is spared, and he gives Àjẹ́ a goat as a sacrifice. The ẹgbẹ́ Àjẹ́ takes the life of one of Ọ̀wọ́nrín Méjì's wives who dies in her sleep: Perhaps she was the initial instigator. Ọ̀wọ́nrín Méjì divorces the other wife.

In *Ifá: An Exposition of Ifá Literary Corpus,* Wande Abimbola asserts that the only force that can save one from Àjẹ́ is one's Orí, which is one's personal God and destiny director.[117] Whether they need saving or not, the lives of the Olódù bear out Abimbola's assertion because Orí faithfully assists its human counterpart. The Orí of the Olódù may be even more in tune with and helpful to them because the Olódù are doubled-doubles. The actual signs that signify the Olódù appear as doubles (which is why all of their names include "Èjì" or "Méjì," both of which mean two), and the Olódù are at once Divinities and human beings. While some individuals, like the Olódù, have intimate knowledge and communication with their Orí, most people are not consciously connected to their spiritual double. Yoruba cosmontology holds that while the soul chooses its Orí in Òrun, when human beings enter Ayé and learn to communicate and navigate in this world, they forget their destiny and purpose.

Human beings' struggle to determine and manifest their destinies can be traced to Ìrosùn Méjì who refused to sacrifice to Èṣù and Yèyé Múwọ̀ when he was coming to Earth. Ibie's *Ifism* does not include tone marks, so the exact meaning of "Muwo" is left open to interpretation; this flexibility is important because Muwo is a concept and a Mother of multiple meanings. Ibie describes Muwo as "the keeper of the Divine chamber," which would yield Yèyé Múwọ̀ (Mother Who Lodges or Houses) and intimates that Yèyé Múwọ̀ is yet another manifestation of Odù. Ibie also refers to her as "the Mother of obstacles," which would be pronounced Yèyé Múwọ́ (Mother Who Makes Things Crooked): This is a Mother who is adding depth, texture, and intricacy to existence—another Trickster Mother. Ibie also describes her as "Elenini" and "the misfortune divinity."[118] With the latter two terms, Ìrosùn Méjì's refusal to sacrifice, which is the source of discord, becomes secondary to the emergence of the stereotype of the evil woman/"witch" who is the cause of all ills. However, the term "Elenini" may point to an alternate reading of Yèyé Múwọ̀. Elénìnì is literally translated as "backbiter."[119] But rather than the negative connotation, in the context of this ẹsẹ, the term may be a reference to the fact that Yèyé Múwọ̀ literally marks every human being's back with a spinal indentation.

Yèyé Múwọ̀ is yet another prismatic mother of power who defies definition. In *Ifism*, Yèyé Múwọ̀ is clearly the patrified God's equal, if not his superior. The "Almighty Father," as Ibie's Christian training leads him to refer to Olódùmarè, fulfills all of the requests and wishes asked of him. But Yèyé Múwọ̀ adds the *múwọ́* to existence that makes Odù Ifá, sacrifice, and júbà necessary: Ibie asserts that the spinal indentation that all humans have serves "to constantly remind us that the only way we can escape the long hand of misfortune is by making sacrifice."[120] In addition to reminding humans to ensure continuity, reciprocity, and balance through sacrifice, the mark also obfuscates cosmic memory so that human beings must struggle to determine their orí (destiny).[121]

It is the search for identity, purpose, and meaning and the struggle for full self-actualization that gives life its dimensionality. If all of life's questions were answered and all obstacles removed, our existence would be without purpose and significance. Indeed, the reason that the Olódù and Òrìṣà find themselves struggling, confused, and engulfed in problems during their sojourns on Earth is so that they can become complete and more complex entities by overcoming impediments. Furthermore, the lessons that the Gods learn become humanity's teaching tools, for they are immortalized in the Odù Ifá. Given her role in imparting the meaning of life and infusing life with meaning, Yèyé Múwọ̀ could be considered the Mother of Necessary Complexity.

Yèyé Múwọ̀ has effectively inscribed her own Odù on all of humanity, and her mark connects conception to the Cosmos to the *ikin* (divination palm nuts) of Ifá. Ibie describes the significance and symbolism of Yèyé Múwọ̀'s first inscription, which was performed on Ìrosùn Méjì's back:

> The pain of the injury [caused by Yèyé Múwọ̀] made Irosun-meji unconscious and he lapsed into a trance of utter darkness. When he woke up, he found himself on his bed in earth. He had forgotten everything that happened before then. He however went about his business and prospered long afterwards.
>
> The state of darkness is symbolized by the length of time that Ifa stays in palm oil before being brought to life. It also symbolizes the gestation period we spend in the womb, during which we lose all recollections of what we plan to do on earth.[122]

Ifá is not a mere tool or instrument. When one has Ifá, one has the sentient manifestation of the God of Divination; consequently, Ifá must be conceived and born and fed. The sacred palm nuts are implanted and gestate inside of the Divine Chamber, or the Odù, of Yèyé Múwọ̀. The ikin come to term in a warm womb of palm oil and are anointed and fed with palm oil throughout their lives. In addition to palm oil approximating the menses of existence, it is not coincidental that Ìrosùn, the name of the Olódù, is similar to the name of the tree (Irosùn) that produces the iyerosùn that is used to cast Ifá and that is symbolic of menses.

Ibie's *Ifism*, even with its occasional Christocentric references and sometimes questionable depiction of Àjẹ́, provides the reader with insight as to the far-reaching influence and import of Àjẹ́ as well as the force's diverse wielders, manifestations, textures, natures, and proclivities. Not only does each Àjẹ́ portrayed in *Ifism* boast a unique iwà, as do all human beings and Òrìṣà, but also, just as the Òrìṣà and babaláwo have to have Àjẹ́ to some degree, so too are the Olódù necessarily empowered by Àjẹ́. The Olódù "have" Odù, as the title signifies, not only because they are babaláwo who have Àpéré and Igbádù but also because they are the offspring of Odù. In addition to their divine inheritance and status, some Olódù inherit Àjẹ́ from their terrestrial mothers, as does Ọ̀yẹ̀kú Méjì. Those who do not inherit Àjẹ́ biologically surround themselves with Àjẹ́, as do Ọ̀bàrà Méjì and Èjì Ogbè; or they harness the Àjẹ́ of empowered animals and objects, as does Ọ̀kànràn Méjì. *Ifism's* portraits of Àjẹ́ are significant because they confirm that the power is interwoven throughout the Yoruba ethos and worldview.

Ifism is groundbreaking in revealing the lesser-known, rich, and diverse intimacies between the Olódù and Àwọn Ìyá Wa, and it also includes an in-depth elaboration of the Olódù most often associated with Àjẹ́: Ọ̀sá Méjì. Ibie begins the ìtàn of Ọ̀sá Méjì with a popular ẹsẹ that is also included, with Ọ̀rúnmìlà featured as the protagonist, in Abimbola's *Sixteen Great Poems of Ifá*.[123] During divination to determine his path on Earth, Ọ̀sá Méjì is told to sacrifice "because he was going to practice his Ifa art in the midst of witches."[124] He is so anxious to get to Earth that he does not sacrifice, and because he neglects Èṣù, his Ífá, and his Orí, he gets lost. When he arrives at the river that divides Ọ̀run and Ayé, he meets Ìyàmi Òṣòròngà who convinces him to swallow her so that she can cross while inside of him. Once inside, Ìyàmi refuses to leave Ọ̀sá Méjì's belly. When he threatens to starve her out, Ìyàmi replies that she will simply dine on his liver, heart and intestines.[125]

Ọ̀sá Méjì consults Ifá about his gastrointestinal dilemma and is directed to sacrifice a goat, palm oil, and Àjẹ́'s signature white cloth: Abimbola calls this sacrifice *èèsè*.[126] Ọ̀sá Méjì cooks the sacrifice, and Ìyàmi leaves his stomach to enjoy the feast. John S. Mbiti finds that, in many regions, the divine nature of African kings makes it taboo for anyone to see them eat;[127] similarly, no one can watch Ìyàmi dine. Ọ̀sá Méjì makes her a privacy tent with the sacrificial white cloth, and while she is eating he runs away and enters a womb. It is logical, given his orí and the manner by which he left Ọ̀run, that Ọ̀sá Méjì enters the womb of a woman who is an Àjẹ́.[128]

As a human, Ọ̀sá Méjì's relationship with Àjẹ́ is especially intimate. Ibie reveals that Ọ̀sá Méjì's "mother touched his head with the wand that made it possible for him to accompany her to the meeting of witches."[129] However, Ibie notes that Ọ̀sá Méjì is not able to eat with the ẹgbẹ́ Àjẹ́ because "he was not formally initiated."[130] Ibie goes on to state that "[t]o this day, it is possible with the aid of similar preparations, for a novice to hold meetings with witches, without being formally initiated into their cult."[131] The ability of Àjẹ́ to fight alone or with the group, as is observed in "The Rise and Fall's" ẹsẹ Ìrẹ̀tẹ̀ Méjì, and the ability of select lay people to attend meetings without sharing in the feasts shows, again, the diversity, flexibility, and egalitarian nature of the ẹgbẹ́ Àjẹ́.

It is important that Ọ̀sá Méjì can attend Àjẹ́'s meetings because his first task on Earth is to save his father who the ẹgbẹ́ has sentenced to die. Ọ̀sá Méjì is able to save his father because of his association with Àjẹ́. While the ẹgbẹ́ is deliberating, he cries out "Iyami Osoronga" which alerts his mother who leaves the group to tend to her son.[123] Ọ̀sá Méjì instructs his father to serve his Orí with a goat in order to save his life. Ọ̀sá Méjì places part of the sacrifice in a pot with lots of oil, salt, and sand, the equivalent of the iyerosùn used for marking Ifá, and he places this offering at an incinerator. Ibie asserts that this sacrifice "was the first offering by any human being to the elders of the night and is also how offerings are made to them to this day."[133] The ẹsẹ intimates that Ìyá Ọ̀sá Méjì had been misdirecting her Àjẹ́ because after the ètùtù is made she dies.

Throughout his life, Ọ̀sá Méjì finds himself surrounded by Àjẹ́: "As soon as he grew up to be a man, he got married to a young, beautiful girl who was also a witch. The house he lived in was also inhabited by witches. The entire town in which he lived was a witch-infested place. Esu pushed him to the place as a punishment for stubbornly refusing to give him a he-goat."[134] The wheel of reciprocity does not cease spinning whether it is correcting imbalance in Ọ̀run or Ayé. But more than Èṣù's punishment, Ọ̀sá Méjì resides in Ọ̀tà, or a similar community, because that is his orí.

Ọ̀sá Méjì's first task in the land of Àjẹ́ recalls ẹsẹ Ogbè Yọ́nú from "The Rise and Fall" in which Ọ̀rúnmìlà offers a riddle-solving sacrifice and then shows with cotton that he can catch an egg and protect the life therein: Ọ̀sá Méjì's must successfully deliver a pregnant woman's child, which he does. But as he searches the house for food, Ọ̀sá Méjì accidentally breaks a spiritually empowered egg. This incident highlights Ọ̀sá Méjì's duality: He ensures some lives and manners of existence, and he imperils and destroys others. The reflective properties of the egg, once released, find their way to the hands of the responsible party, and Ọ̀sá Méjì's hands lose their pigment. The melanin is not restored to Ọ̀sá Méjì's hands until he gives Èṣù his long-awaited he-goat. With the assistance of Èṣù, and by regularly making required sacrifices, Ọ̀sá Méjì is able to routinely outwit death and death sentences.

Because of his close association with Àjẹ́, Ọ̀sá Méjì often finds himself and his clientele in situations where they must perform the ètùtù to Àwọn Ìyá Wa. The ètùtù is usually a rabbit, eggs, palm oil and a castrated he-goat. Had the sixteen sovereigns for whom Ọ̀sá Méjì cast Ifá listened to his pronouncement, they would have made the ètùtù, as he did, and avoided death. After killing the sixteen kings, the Elders of the Night go to Ọ̀sá Méjì's home. There, they feast on the ètùtù he made for them, and they perform a symbolic burial, which seems to represent the end of their conflict with Ọ̀sá Méjì. Despite the détente, Olódù Òràngún Méjì accuses Ọ̀sá Méjì of being a "witch."

To say that Òsá Méjì has a complex relationship with Àjẹ́ is the apex in understatement. However, despite Òràngún Méjì's accusation, Òsá Méjì is not considered an Àjẹ́; this may be the result of efforts to denigrate Àjẹ́ and conflate it with both women and "evil" while celebrating patriarchs and styling them heroes. However, Òsá Méjì's body was the temporary home of Àjẹ́, he lives a life surrounded by Àjẹ́, and he is welcome at their meetings. Ibie asserts that Òsá Méjì is intimately connected with Àjẹ́ because he is "the one who brought [Àjẹ́] to the world and he was the one who saved them from total extinction from the face of the earth."[135] Because of their bond, Òsá Méjì routinely begs others to forgive Àjẹ́ who have committed infractions. He also readily forgives Àjẹ́ for violations. For example, when Òsá Méjì discovers that his Àjẹ́ wife has been engineering all of his problems, he does not banish her as Òkànràn Méjì did his wife; Òsá Méjì forgives his wife and the couple lives in harmony.

The most well-known interaction between Òsá Méjì and Àjẹ́ concerns a battle over fresh water during the dry season. Given that nearly every version of this conflict is predicated on the alien concept of "ownership" of water, which is an essential community resource, and in the light of Àjẹ́'s edict to "share everything," the entire clash appears to be contrived to further an anti-Àjẹ́ agenda. However, it is important to compare various versions of the water war because by doing so one gains insight into the subtle shifts, covert concerns, idiosyncrasies, and machinations of various patriarchs.

In the version included in "The Rise and Fall," Àjẹ́ are the owners of a river that never goes dry, and Ọbàtálá "steals" ("*jí*") their water to make human beings—again, the concept of someone stealing water, especially from an inexhaustible source, is absurd in the traditional African worldview. Absurdities aside, when the Àjẹ́ confront Ọbàtálá, he seeks refuge with Egúngún, and the Mothers threaten to swallow Egúngún's cloths. Ọbàtálá runs to Ògún, and the Àjẹ́ counter that they will devour his weapons and tools. Ọbàtálá runs to Òrúnmìlà, and Àjẹ́ threaten to eat the ọ̀pẹ̀lẹ̀ and ikin of Ifá. Òrúnmìlà welcomes them anyway and prepares a feast of *èkuru* and a mixture of sheep, goat, chicken, and bull blood. This feast satisfies the Àjẹ́ and peace is restored.[136]

As I have detailed in earlier passages of this book, Àjẹ́ is the source of Egúngún and its cloths, Ògún and his weaponry, and Òrúnmìlà and Ifá. Àjẹ́'s threats to devour the signature implements of Egúngún, Ògún, and Òrúnmìlà, seems to infer that the Mothers are capable of reclaiming not only the gifts they gave these Òrìṣà but also those Òrìṣà. Thanks to Òrúnmìlà's perspicacity, no reclamation is necessary in this humane account of the water battle. Other versions, however, approach Àjẹ́ with weapons in hand, erroneous definitions in mouth, and Exodus 22:18 in mind.

In "The Òrìṣà and the Àjẹ́ Conflict," which is included in Wande Abimbola's *Sixteen Great Poems of Ifá*, the lake is also described as belonging to Àjẹ́. This ẹsẹ attributes the source of discord to Yemòó, Ọbàtálá's wife, who not only pilfers water from the lake, but also bathes in the lake and leaves it red with menstrual blood. With its sly attempt at likening menses to a pollutant, the ẹsẹ attacks both womanhood in general and female Gods in particular. The authors of this ẹsẹ have taken a page from the Bible and determined that the "way of women" trumps and, thereby, nullifies any divinity that a female God might have.

When Àjẹ́ find their lake bloody and discover the cause, they swallow Yemòó, and later they devour Ọbàtálá, Eégún, and Orò. Ọ̀rúnmìlà prepares a feast for the Àjẹ́, and using a methodology similar to that described in an ẹsẹ of Ọ̀ṣẹ́ Ogbè that is recorded in Bascom's *Ifa Divination*,[137] he captures and beats them to death and then dances with glee.[138] But in celebrating the death of Àjẹ́, Ọ̀rúnmìlà and the ẹsẹ also celebrate the deaths of Yemòó, Ọbàtálá, Eégún, and Orò, four of the most important Yoruba Gods and forces, who all just so happen to also be Àjẹ́.

It is important to remember that Àjẹ́ is Àjẹ́, and it cannot be hierarchically scaled or dichotomized. The Àjẹ́ that Yemòó uses to mold ovum and strengthen umbilical cords works in concert with the menstrual blood that Odùà and Ọbàtálá use to create children. The Ẹyẹ of Odù that will blind the eyes of a violator is the same Ẹyẹ who authorizes the festival of Egúngún and oversees its actions, and this simultaneously overt and covert force is concentrated in the elegant clitoris. However, in many ẹsẹ and ìtàn, Àwọn Ìyàmi Òṣòròngà are not described as being part of the very continuum that they created and that is dependent upon them. Àjẹ́ are often set apart so that they can be made to appear deviant and so that constructs that did not exist in the Yoruba ethos prior to colonization—such as inherent evil, misogyny, polluting menses, and original sin—can be made to appear as if they are naturally occurring.

The viciousness and shortsightedness of "The Òrìṣà and the Àjẹ́ Conflict" is better appreciated when that text is compared to "A Mysterious Friend of Ọ̀rúnmìlà Threatened His Home in His Absence," which also appears in *Sixteen Great Poems of Ifá*. The mysterious entity is Ọ̀rọ̀. Abimbola and *A Dictionary of the Yoruba Language* both define Ọ̀rọ̀ similarly as a "fairy" that is part of a class of "lesser supernatural forces or spirits who are believed to dwell in rivers, trees (for example the Ìrókò tree), rocks, caves, hills and mountains."[139] The use of Western and Christocentric terminology and dichotomy skews the meaning and significance of Ọ̀rọ̀. As Rowland Abiodun reveals in "Verbal and Visual Metaphors: Mythical Allusions in Yoruba Ritualistic Art of Orí," Ọ̀rọ̀ is a word that has many definitions: *ọ̀rọ̀* is, in a mundane sense, simply "word";

in the divine sense, Ọ̀rọ̀ is Power of the Word, which is an aspect of Àjẹ́.[140] Ọ̀rọ̀ is also described as a Divinity which may be the physical embodiment of Power of the Word.[141]

Ọ̀rọ̀ is a profoundly important power, and, as Abiodun's research elucidates, Ọ̀rọ̀ has its own rich origins, ìtàn, and multitudinous manifestations.[142] It is also important to recall Fatunmbi's observation that "[b]oth Àjẹ́ and Ọ̀rọ̀ are found at the iroko tree. Ọ̀rọ̀ is the manifestation of power of the word. Àjẹ́ is the force that gives the power of the word the intensity needed to effect change. It is the polarity between Àjẹ́ and Ọ̀rọ̀ that makes effective prayer possible."[143] Ọ̀rọ̀ can take many forms, and no matter the shape it takes, Ọ̀rọ̀ is central to Ifá cosmology, a key aspect of Àjẹ́, and an exhibition of pure power.

In the orature recorded by Abimbola, Ọ̀rọ̀ appears to have come fresh from the womb of Odù, and Ọ̀rọ̀ is tellingly referred to as Mọlẹ̀. This is the same Mọlẹ̀ who is the daughter of Imọlẹ̀, the Mother of the Earth. Mọlẹ̀ is also the Òrìṣà of Àjẹ́ who is known as Ẹdan who cleansed Ifẹ̀, founded Ògbóni, and left Àjẹ́ to ensure adherence to Onílẹ̀'s Law.[144] Mọlẹ̀'s influence in Yoruba cosmontology is as well distributed as her earth: Indeed, she is both the actual foundation of the Earth and the foundation of Yoruba cosmontology. The term Ìrúnmọlẹ̀ has its root in the word Mọlẹ̀, as the term literally means the race, species, or offspring (irú) of Mọlẹ̀. The Ìrúnmọlẹ̀ are innumerable Gods, spiritual forces, and energies, and Mọlẹ̀ is their progenitor. According to Olawole Francis Famule, Mọlẹ̀ is "considered the mouthpiece of all other spiritual beings";[145] in other words she is the Mother and administrator of her Irú. Because of Ọ̀rọ̀'s tremendous importance, which is coupled with the God's womb-fresh fragility and celestial profundity, Ọ̀rúnmìlà is entrusted with the care of this precious God and "told to take care of Mọlẹ̀."[146]

Every aspect and facet of Mọlẹ̀'s being is rooted in Àjẹ́, but because Abimbola in *Sixteen Great Poems of Ifá* defines Àjẹ́ as an evil aberration and not a holistic aspect of Yoruba cosmontology, Ọ̀rọ̀'s lineage and deeper relationships are not acknowledged and this tremendous entity of amalgamated and compounded power is not only patrified but is also reduced to the form of an anomalous anonymous "fairy."

Perhaps because it is a fusion of immense cosmic powers, Ọ̀rọ̀'s human form bears what humans would consider profuse oddities and deformities. But Ọ̀rọ̀ is not alone in this; the diviner of this verse is "The cripple with short arms, / The cripple with short legs."[147] The diviner's condition echoes the original state of Ugbin Ejo, the limbless iyaláwo who is credited with founding Ògbóni society in *Ifìsm*. The ẹsẹ recorded by Abimbola helps one comprehend Ugbin Ejo's initial desire to be hidden from view, for when the residents of Ọ̀rúnmìlà's home see Ọ̀rọ̀, they burst into laughter. Proving that he is no mere "fairy" or "lesser" spiritual force who can be casually mocked and ridiculed, Òrò retaliates by inflicting his antagonists with diseases.

After being alerted to the disaster, Òrúnmìlà literally turns into wind and flies home. When he encounters Òrò, Òrúnmìlà does not attack the God; he weeps and begins a heartfelt chant called *iyèrò*. He admits to Òrò, "If they abused you, I am the cause. . . ." to which Òrò responds, "Nobody has ever abused me like that. / If they abused me, you are the cause."[148] Òrúnmìlà takes full responsibility for all of the abuse Òrò suffered not merely because Òrúnmìlà did not sacrifice in a timely manner but because Òrúnmìlà *is* the responsible party; Òrò's protection, comfort, and care are his responsibility. It is clear that Òrúnmìlà respects and cherishes Òrò; indeed, Òrúnmìlà is more worried about Òrò's hurt feelings than he is about his disease-stricken family. However, one must wonder how this ẹsẹ would have been changed if Òrò's identity as an Àjẹ́ were elucidated and if Òrò had not been patrified.

In contrast to the consideration that Òrúnmìlà showers on Òrò, in many ẹsẹ, even when Àwọn Ìyá Wa have been unjustifiably wronged by other parties, they are savagely attacked and butchered, as if their existence alone merits murder. The blood of Àjẹ́ runs in rivers in *Ifism's* version of the war over water. In this version, Ọbàtálá's wives are featured as instigators, but Èṣù plays an interesting role in that after he assists the Àjẹ́, he helps Ọbàtálá and Òsá Méjì capture the Àjẹ́. Èṣù's actions are not duplicitous; they are uniquely Ẹlẹ́gbárian: He is, after all, the Trickster. Èṣù explains his methodology and motivations in this way: "[M]y friend is the one who respects and feeds me, while my enemies are those who despise and starve me. I have neither farm nor a trade of my own. My farm is the entire universe and my wares are the creatures of God."[149] Èṣù's multiplicity creates a playing field that is always level—depending on your perspective.

With Èṣù's help, Ọbàtálá and Òsá Méjì kill all of the Àjẹ́ except for one pregnant Àjẹ́ who has taken refuge under Ọbàtálá's shrine to Òrúnmìlà. Òsá Méjì insists that, just as Ọbàtálá's life was spared when he sought refuge under Òrúnmìlà's shrine, so too must the Àjẹ́ be spared. In order to institute balance and harmony, Òsá Méjì turns to Mọlẹ̀'s Mother, Onílẹ̀. Harnessing the supremacy of the Earth and her power to seal oaths, Òsá Méjì digs a hole in the ground, fills it with food, and crowns it with a kola nut.[150] Ọbàtálá and Òsá Méjì make the surviving Àjẹ́ swear on this sacrifice to never kill any of "God's or Orunmila's children without just cause."[151] Ibie asserts that the tradition of offering a scapegoat originates with this pledge and that if Àjẹ́ find the blood of an animal in front of a home, "That is a signal that the offender has atoned to them for the offense committed."[152]

Ọ̀sá Méjì goes on to decree that Àjẹ́ should recognize that

> any food prepared in a pot and deposited at a road junction, by the wayside or on top of an incinerator. . . is from Orunmila's child and she should accept the food and leave the offerer alone. This is the Etutu . . . that Orunmila often advises his followers to make to the night when they are in trouble with the witches. That is why the Iyerosun markings of Osameji are often marked on the divination tray when offerings are being made to the night. [153]

What is most intriguing about this concordat is that two "men"—Ọbàtálá, a patrified Mother, and Ọ̀sá Méjì, the equivalent of an honorary Àjẹ́—seek to impose the patriarchy's laws, rules, and orders upon the Mother of Power. While *Ifism's* conclusion is more balanced than the ẹsẹ that Abimbola records, the driving force behind both of these verses is the domination and delimitation of Àjẹ́. Rather than an attempt to kill all of the Àjẹ́, which would mean the obliteration of existence, perhaps the ẹsẹ that revel in massacring Àjẹ́ are really hoping to kill women's knowledge of and ability to access and activate their powers.

. . .

The diverse portraits of Àwọn Ìyá Wa drawn in various collections of ẹsẹ Ifá make one thing clear: Àjẹ́ boast the same range of diversity, power, humility, jealousy, passion, and devotion as other Gods and human beings. Àjẹ́ is not a monolith that can be narrowly defined and dismissed. And they are not "witches." Perhaps one of the most overlooked character traits of the Mothers is their patience, for they have withstood a plethora of attacks and insults from multitudinous entities, and yet they continue to support, educate, trick, challenge, and ensure the existence of humanity.

An ẹsẹ Ifá of Ogbè Alara included in Solagbade Popoola's *Practical Ifa Divination* offers another window into the world of Àjẹ́. In the ẹsẹ, Ọ̀rúnmìlà consults Ifá so that he can understand "the secrets of the world."[154] He makes a sacrifice of a goat and waits nearby and watches as a naked woman comes and feasts on the sacrifice. After dining, the woman tells Ọ̀rúnmìlà that "women are the secrets of the world."[155] She tells him that women control the success and failure, honor and disgrace, love and hatred, and joy and sorrow of humanity. She warns him to never underestimate a woman.[156] This is most excellent advice, even if the men and women who are in a position to offer it do not always remember to take it.

CHAPTER FOUR

"THE LEFT IS FOR THE GODS": ÀJẸ́ IN SECRET SOCIETIES AND SACRED INSTITUTIONS

Discussions concerning sacred Yoruba societies are often framed with pat declarations that women are barred from knowing the mysteries, attending the meetings, or belonging to such organizations as Ògbóni, Orò, Egúngún, and Gẹlẹdẹ́. The fact that each of these societies has already been mentioned in this book should serve as an indication that these assertions are no more than patriarchal posturing. While it is the case that women have been historically banned from certain Islamic and Judeo-Christian sanctuaries and institutions and prohibited from participating in certain rituals, this is not the case for women in the traditional Yoruba world. Women founded and continue to play crucial roles in the administration and proliferation of Ògbóni, Orò, Egúngún, Gẹlẹdẹ́, and the Yoruba polity. And the women who are the active and activating agents of these institutions are Àjẹ́.

"Women are behind the secrets of Ògbóni"

In order to fully understand the impact of Àjẹ́ in Yoruba secret and sacred societies, one must understand the role of Àjẹ́ in Ògbóni. In order to understand Ògbóni, one must know Imọlẹ̀, the Mother of All and the Mother of Mothers. To know the Mother of All, one must know her progeny: Mọlẹ̀ and the Onímọlẹ̀. I refer to the original inhabitants of Ifẹ̀, whom the Yoruba met upon their arrival, as the Onímọlẹ̀ because the term means One Who Has Mọlẹ̀, and because Imọlẹ̀ signifies their way of life.[1] The term Onímọlẹ̀ also serves as a powerful articulation of inherent divinity, because the Onímọlẹ̀ are at once the devotees of Mọlẹ̀ and they, themselves, are the ọmọ of Imọlẹ̀, better known as Mọlẹ̀.

After political wrangling and social struggles, the Yoruba and the Onímọlẹ̀ successfully melded their cultures, languages, and worldviews, and, according to Biodun Adediran, "all powerful groups in the town were brought together in the imole cult which was reorganized into an effective governmental organ."[2] As a holistic and organic administrative force that, like Mother, encompasses all aspects of existence, including the social, political, judicial, spiritual, and biological, Imọlẹ̀ emerged as the logical method of social organization and governance and a fitting unifier of both peoples.

Ìmọlẹ̀ has been mentioned in various capacities in previous chapters of this book because Ìmọlẹ̀ is Àjẹ́. E. Bolaji Idowu translates Ìmọlẹ̀ as "*Iye 'malẹ̀ (Iya Imalẹ̀)*—'The Mother of the divinities' or 'Mother-Divinity'."[3] Ìmọlẹ̀'s daughter, Mọlẹ̀, is also an Àjẹ́ who is a central and essential figure in Yoruba culture, and Mọlẹ̀ is also known as Ẹdan. As C. L. Adeoye explains, "Ẹdan is what this Ìrúnmọlẹ̀ is called in ọ̀run. The reason she is called Mọlẹ̀ is because Ilẹ̀ is the mother who gave birth to Ẹdan in ọ̀run. The child Ilẹ̀ gave birth to is 'Ọmọ-Ilẹ̀,' which is shortened to 'Mọlẹ̀.'"[4] However, the child, Mọlẹ̀, who is also Ẹdan, represents her mother, Onílẹ̀, who is also Ìmọlẹ̀. Just as the Cosmos is a womb that creates a womb that gives birth to a womb, so too is the Earth held together by a complex matrix of Motherpower.[5]

Adeoye reveals that the Mother and Owner of the Earth, Onílẹ̀, who is also known as Ilẹ̀, Ìyá Ayé, Àpẹ̀pẹ̀-Alẹ̀, and Ìmọlẹ̀, gave birth to both Ẹdan and Àjẹ́ in Ọ̀run.[6] Adeoye describes Ẹdan's arrival as being prompted by social upheaval; the turmoil may be a reference to the conflicts that arose when the Yoruba immigrants began settling in the lands of the Onímọlẹ̀.

Although it was agreed that Ọ̀rúnmìlà was the appropriate person to ask Ẹdan for help, he did not want to seek her assistance because a request for aid would indicate that he had failed to complete the task assigned him by Olódùmarè.[7] Ọ̀rúnmìlà put his feelings of inadequacy aside and turned to Ifá. An ẹsẹ Ifá of Àtẹpa-Ìwòrì recalls the event:

> Ha, I caught it!
> Before the others could
> Divined for Ọ̀rúnmìlà
> Ifá was going to ọ̀run
> To go and call Mọlẹ̀
> Who was going to carry out repairs in Olú-Ifẹ̀
> As someone repairing a broken calabash
> They repaired the earth, repaired the earth
> The earth was no longer harmonious
> They washed the earth
> As if washing a calabash for sacrifice[8]

Àtẹpa-Ìwòrì reveals the might and size of Mọlẹ̀; she is capable of washing and repairing the Earth as a human would clean and mend a calabash. Another indication of her immensity is revealed by Adeoye who reveals, "'One who is expertly placed around the earth' is the oríkì of the mother of Ẹdan."[9] This oríkì refers to the perfect positioning of the land of this Earth on which we live: the ilẹ̀ of Onílẹ̀. Fittingly, Ẹdan's oríkì is "Child who is expertly placed around the earth."[10]

With Adeoye's explication not only is there riddling within revelation—which is the hallmark of Àjẹ́, to offer an àrokò that conceals while it reveals—but the image of multitudinous mothers creating life biologically and cosmically resurfaces. Imọlẹ̀, Ẹdan, and Ìyá Ayé are not associated with male partners because males are not necessary for creation. The insignificance of the male principle to cosmic and divine creation highlights both the inherent completeness of Mother and the inadequacies of her sons which are evident in Ọ̀rúnmìlà's prideful reluctance to admit that he needs help. Adeoye's research also offers another view of the special relationship between Ọ̀rúnmìlà and Mọlẹ̀, which is featured in "A Mysterious Friend of Ọ̀rúnmìlà Threatened His Home in His Absence." In the orature recorded by both Abimbola and Adeoye, Ọ̀rúnmìlà and Mọlẹ̀'s relationship is framed by misunderstandings and violations that are eventually rectified. It is also important to note the obvious: Adeoye's research buttresses my assertion that Mọlẹ̀ is not a "fairy" or entity of negligible significance but a Mother of unfathomable power.

The process by which Mọlẹ̀ repairs Ifẹ̀ involves ritual cleansing which returns all inhabitants to the amniocentesis of their origins. Following the purification, everyone agrees to adhere to the social and judicial system of Imọlẹ̀. To unite and bond all of the citizens of Ifẹ̀—male and female, young and old—make a sacrifice of three rats, three fish, and three pigeons and proclaim that anyone who lies, steals, or is disloyal or deceitful will die. With Ọ̀rúnmìlà leading the citizens in the ritual swearing of the oath of loyalty before Mọlẹ̀, every member of the community is initiated into Ògbóni and becomes Onímọlẹ̀.[11]

Rather than a secret society comprised only of male elders that meets and acts clandestinely, Ògbóni is revealed to be a holistic tool for community cohesion and elevation. Nathaniel A. Fadipe confirms that, before colonization and Christianization, Ògbóni was a society in which "every freeborn male and female in the community was supposed to belong from a fairly young age. . . . Admission was by initiation."[12] Initiation into Imọlẹ̀ would logically occur during childhood so that children would be knowledgeable of their obligations to the Earth from the earliest formation of their consciousnesses. These children, who greet the Earth immediately upon birth and who are placed perfectly around the Earth, literally and figuratively, use reverence of the Mother as a unifying principle because they are, in fact, Ọmọ Ilẹ̀, the Children of the Earth or Imọlẹ̀. Similar to the curvilinear power of Àjẹ́ that has its source in Odù and is continuously regenerated in Africana women, those who take the oath of Mọlẹ̀ become like Mọlẹ̀—loyal, upright, and conscientious.

Mọlẹ̀'s work did not end with cleansing and bonding; to ensure the development and prosperity of Ifẹ̀, Mọlẹ̀ created two interconnected organs and charged them with the administration of justice. As Adeoye reveals: "The babaláwo agree that when Ẹdan came to Ifẹ̀ she gave birth to Àjẹ́, and all the people who know the 'àṣírí' [mystery] of Ẹdan are elders called 'Ògbóni.'"[13] This terrestrial birth of Àjẹ́ could be a reference to the ẹgbẹ́ Àjẹ́ which specializes in the enforcement of justice and the institution of balance. Adeoye makes it clear that rather than Àjẹ́ being evil cannibalistic "witches," Àjẹ́ is the progeny, brainchild, and braintrust of Ẹdan. And rather than being at odds with and working in opposition to Ògbóni, Àjẹ́ is the sacred force that animates and directs Ògbóni.

The assertion that Ògbóni is the child of Ẹdan does not refer to a solely figurative or cosmic relationship but to a literal one. In "Art And Spirituality: The Ijumu Northeastern-Yoruba Egúngún," Olawole Francis Famule, echoing the *Oríkì Ilẹ̀* recorded by Adeoye, finds that Ògbóni was originally a resident of Ifẹ̀, and she was the daughter of two mothers: Àbẹ̀ní, The One We Beg to Have and Àdẹ̀, The One Who Sets Traps.[14] Àbẹ̀ní is an oríkì of Ìyàmi Òṣòròngà, and Àdẹ̀ is an oríkì of Ẹdan who also known as Ẹlẹ́yinjú Ẹgẹ́, The Owner of Bulging and Ensnaring Eyes. Given her provenance, Ògbóni was destined to be a powerful woman.

According to Famule, Ògbóni

> had virtually all the earth's attributes . . . while she was alive. For instance, it is held that she was so knowledgeable . . . that the then *Ooni* (King of Ile-Ife or *Ife Oore*) made her the head of the judicial arm of government, where she became a celebrity for her effective and efficient way of delivering judgments. She determined quickly and accurately whether or not accused people brought into her court were guilty or innocent of the charge(s) against them by a mere look into their eyes—no lie detector could be more effective. Thus, whoever is involved in any antisocial behaviors cannot escape [being] caught and punished—inasmuch as the person walks, dwells, or lives on the earth or land (*Ile*).[15]

Ògbóni is indistinguishable from her mother, Ẹdan, who has all-seeing eyes and a bottomless stomach, which is the Earth or Ilẹ̀, which is capable of swallowing deceitful people whole. When Ògbóni's terrestrial life ended and she returned to the bosom of Onílẹ̀, her power was magnified exponentially and dispersed throughout the Earth. Consequently, Ògbóni is manifest as the ilẹ̀ upon which humans live, the ilẹ̀ where their bodies are and will be interred, the ilẹ̀ the Yoruba use to swear oaths, and as Ilẹ̀ who watches every action and infraction committed on the Earth. Ògbóni is also, logically, present in the Ògbóni sacred society, whose members are her progeny and the enforcers of her Law.[16]

Àjẹ́ is Ògbóni and Ògbóni is Àjẹ́: The two cannot be separated. Because they are holistic, Earth-born, all-encompassing powers, Ògbóni and Àjẹ́ are appropriate for any and every community. Famule reveals that in Èkìtì and Ìjùmú Yoruba communities, women dominate Imọlẹ̀ rituals and rites, and the devotees of Imọlẹ̀, who are called Onímọlẹ̀, are primarily women.[17] Famule also finds that the Ookun-Yoruba use the term Imọlẹ̀ to refer to female Gods.[18] By contrast, in some parts of Yorubaland, such as Ọ̀yọ́, Ifẹ̀, and Ìjẹ̀bú, Ògbóni is largely associated with men. However, these men all identify themselves as Ọmọ Ìyá, the Children of the Mother; what is more, as Opeola explains, certain male members of Ògbóni must have Àjẹ́ or be Àjẹ́ to hold particular titles and undertake certain duties. Imọlẹ̀'s profusion and diffusion, her diversity and flexibility underscore her relevance, ubiquity, and indispensability. Imọlẹ̀'s omnipresence is also logical given that she is perfectly positioned upon the Earth and that her daughters are the literal mothers of the Yoruba people and the world.

Babatunde Lawal opens "*À Yà Gbó, À Yà Tó*: New Perspectives on Edan Ògbóni" with an Ògbóni chant and elucidates the objectives of the organization and the irreducible influence of Àjẹ́ therein:

Call:	**Response:**
Ògbóni	*Ògbóràn*
The old ones	Increase with age
Erelú	*Àbíyè*
Titled female elders	May children be born to live
Eríwo yà!	*À Yà Gbó, À Yà Tó*
The Lord of secrets, descend!	For longevity and prosperity![19]

This chant confirms that unity, harmony, and cooperative work bind the males and females and adults and children of Ògbóni, and all parties are heralded for their roles in community evolution and elevation.

It is important to note the reference to Erelú in the invocation above. These titled women are honored with the encomium Ìyá Àbíyè and Erelú Àbíyè, which mean Mothers of Thriving Children and Titled Elders of Thriving Children, respectively.[20] Just as mothers who birth and raise thriving children are absolutely essential to existence, the titled women of Ògbóni are the blood and milk upon which the Ògbóni organization thrives. Indeed, a Yoruba saying reveals that "'*bi ko si Erelu, Osugbo ko le da awo se*' (without the *Erelu*, the *Osugbo* cult cannot perform its rituals)."[21]

The close relationship between Ògbóni and Àjẹ́ is highlighted in numerous passages of the *Ìtàn-Oríkì Ìyàmi Òṣòròngà*. The text describes Ìyàmi Òṣòròngà situated at the crossroads of sixteen roads holding "sixteen long Ẹdan" that unite Ọ̀run and Ayé; the Àjẹ́ collective is revealed to undertake their work of enforcement with a grand ẹgbẹ́ that includes Ògún, Ọbàtálá, and Ògbóni; Àjẹ́ regularly herald one another with the call, "Ògbóni" (The Elders); and the response, "Ògborọ̀" (Elders Proliferate).[22] The *Ìtàn-Oríkì Ìyàmi Òṣòròngà* also includes the following information:

Tá a bá fẹ́ bọwọ́ Ògbóni
Ọwọ́ òsì la á nà
Á nàkan síwájú
Á nàkan sádárin

[If we want to shake hands with Ògbóni
We use the left hand to shake
We extend one forward
We extend one in the middle][23]

Samuel M. Opeola and A. P. Anyebe confirm that the sacred handshake of Ògbóni symbolizes the fact that the members all nursed at the breast of the Mother.[24] The Great God and Mother of Life and Power—whether she be honored as Odù, Ẹdan, Onílẹ̀, or Mọlẹ̀—is Àjẹ́.

References to Ògbóni in the *Ìtàn-Oríkì Ìyàmi Òṣòròngà* are significant because they emphasize an important point: The ẹgbẹ́ Àjẹ́ use the greetings, signs, and methodology of Ògbóni because they *are* Ògbóni. In fact, one could call Àjẹ́ the mothers of Ògbóni. The impact of Àjẹ́ is also apparent in fact that Ògbóni is known as Ẹdan Ògbóni. The organization is also known as Ògbóni Ìbílẹ̀: Ìbílẹ̀ means "aboriginal," but the word is constructed of *ibí* (progeny) and Ilẹ̀ (the Earth). Ògbóni Ìbílẹ̀ can be translated as the Wise Elders Who are the Offspring of the Mother of the Earth. No matter the title her children use, Àjẹ́'s presence and impact are wondrously clear.

The supremacy of Mother, as both biological progenitor and as God, is evident in the fact that Ògbóni members call themselves Ọmọ Ìyá. The specificity of and emphasis on Mother is intentional. Rather than straining to make room for a father, motherhood, as the indisputable source of life, bounty, and continuity, signifies divinity, and mother's milk is the elixir of the Gods. The importance of the bond forged by breast milk is symbolized in the sacred Ògbóni handshake and in the mantra: "*Omú Ìyá dùn ún mu; gbogbo wa la jo nmu ú*" (Mother's milk is sweet to drink; we all drink it).[25] Lawal reveals that this maxim is chanted three times "by members when greeting each other or touching *edan* with the tongue."²⁶ All Ògbóni members, especially men, are positioned as contented children before the Mother. Rather than being confounded by an oedipal conflict or motivated by a desire to "cut the apron strings," Ògbóni society eternally recreates and celebrates the safety, security, scent, embraces, protection, and perfection of Mother. The bounty derived from the breasts is so important in Yoruba culture that an Ifá divination verse warns: "*Ọmọ tí kò bá tí ì f'ẹnu kan lára ìyáa rè/Kò ní í ṣe ànfààní láéláé* ('Any child who has not tasted of his mother/Will never become useful in life')."²⁷ It is not surprising, then, that Ògbóni males of all ages eagerly assume the most privileged of positions—that of cherished ọmọ who lingers and learns at the breast.

The act of tasting the mother is rich in ambiguity: While the reader may assume the reference is to breast milk, the taste of mother could be that which the child experiences when he makes his miraculous journey into the world and passes through his mother's vagina. The protections—physical and physiological—that the mother and child derive from vaginal birth are symbolized by Elemele of the House whose sacrificial pot represents the birth canal and vagina which assures her child's life and immortality: "My child touches the pot with its head; it will never die."²⁸ The protections that Elemele of the House grants her offspring are reproduced in vaginal birth. The mother's labors foment the release of oxytocin which dilates the cervix to accommodate the head of glory.²⁹ When the child touches his head to the vaginal pot and he tastes his mother, hormones that are essential to both mother and child flow, and the child receives antibodies and microbes that are vital to his health.³⁰ The touching of the head to the vaginal "pot" and the tasting of the mother's protective secretions—from the vagina and breasts—are normal and natural fundamentals of a healthy existence.

When a child tastes his mother, he is receiving the literal taste of life, and it is not coincidental that many men spend their adult lives yearning for and relishing the taste of mother through their wives. When the wife takes on the role of Iyangbà, the Receiving Mother, and successfully guides the husband's sperm to her waiting ovum, wife becomes Mother. Furthermore, the physical odù (womb) that the wife uses to create life and become a mother is also the one that she can wield as an àrokò against an abusive husband.³¹ One could say that man's fertilizing semen magnifies the numinosity of woman by endowing her with motherhood which confers upon her the ultimate power and glory. Consequently, Iyangbà is not merely a mother who receives; by transforming reception into conception, she creates divinity, and men—cognizant of the Mother's painstaking efforts to guide them, via their sperm, to immortality—taste, hold, and behold her with awe.

Tasting the mother also has a ritual equivalent, as bonds are established and oaths are sworn with the literal tasting of the Mother Earth, Onílẹ̀. When the Yoruba use Onílẹ̀ to establish sacred bonds, they do so before every one of their ancestors and every yet-unborn child. What is more, every oath is sworn before the ever-present third party who witnesses everything, whose eyes never go blind, and who created a system of justice to ensnare prevaricators, traitors, and miscreants.

In "The Communicative and Semiotic Contexts of Àrokò among Yoruba Symbol-Communication Systems," Philip Ogundeji reveals the spiritual-utilitarian power of the soil of Onílẹ̀:

> The inclusion of some sand or soil in an àrokò usually signifies that the sender is a very close friend of the receiver. Such a serious friendship usually implies a sort of oath-taking referred to in ọ̀rẹ́ imùlẹ̀, which literally translates as friendship based on an oath taken by drinking water mixed with some soil. What the soil symbolizes may vary in detail from context to context but there is usually a common denominator expressed by the epithet "... ilẹ̀ tí n ó wọ̀ sùn ...", "... the ground/soil in which I will have my final rest ...". With this, reference is being made directly or indirectly to death. So in the case of the two friends sending the soil to one another as a pointer to their friendship, they are also referring indirectly to the oath taken as the bond of friendship. It is believed that any of the two who breaks the bond of friendship shall die: Ẹni tí ó bá dalẹ̀ ọ̀rẹ́ á bálẹ̀ lọ, "He who betrays the bond of friendship shall die".[32]

Opeola offers a similar articulation of the power of Ilẹ̀ to seal oaths: "When a group of people take an oath, or *mulẹ̀*, they do so in the name of Onílẹ̀. When a person says, 'Ilẹ̀ yio mu oooo,' he is saying that 'Onílẹ̀ will punish you if you do wrong.'"[33] The expression "Ilẹ̀ yio mu oooo" speaks on overt and covert levels, for *mú* signifies "take," whereas *mu* means "taste." The expression seems to imply that Mother Earth will taste the blood of the traitor when she takes him into her tomb of retribution.

Onílẹ̀ Àjẹ́ is the ever-giving womb and all-receiving tomb. With the verbal and physical act of mulẹ̀, participants place the Earth of the ancestors, unborn, and all Ìṣẹ̀ṣe and Ìrúnmọlẹ̀ in their mouths. By doing so, they literally taste the Mother Earth and *mu* (drink or suck) Ilẹ̀ or mulẹ̀. With this taste of the Mother, every contributor to one's existence bears witness to the oath and handles violators accordingly. Mulẹ̀ gives deeper meaning to the concept of "son of the soil," for the son ingests the living soil that he touched when he emerged from the womb. That same earth gives him sustenance throughout his life, will provide him with progeny, and will grant his bones rest—or restlessness, as they case may be. As surely as soil gives life to flora and fauna, the soil is living, watching, fertilizing,and facilitating. Onílẹ̀ is elegant evidence that Àjẹ́ is All. To kneel and taste Her is to suckle eternity.

The Orientation of the Gods

With the entire Mọlẹ̀ nation reborn and bonded, Ẹdan left Àjẹ́ and Ògbóni to ensure adherence to Onílẹ̀'s laws. Peter Morton-Williams finds that the association between Àjẹ́, Ògbóni, and Onílẹ̀ forms the foundation of the organization and the Yoruba ethos:

> The secret of the Ogboni, which has been closely guarded from other, uninitiated Yoruba as well as from outside inquiry, is that they worship and control the sanctions of the Earth as a spirit. Earth, they hold, existed before the gods, and the Ogboni cult before kingship. Earth is the mother to whom the dead return. Earth and the ancestors, not the gods (*oviṣa*) [*sic*], are the sources of the moral law.[34]

The fact that Onílẹ̀ is the Earth and God Mother whose power is reconstituted in biological mothers is confirmed by both Adeoye and Opeola, the latter of whom affirms: "Women are behind the secrets of Ògbóni."[35] This is the same point made by Kolawole Ositola who confirms, "The foundation of [Ògbóni] is Àwọn Ìyàmi Òṣòròngà."[36]

Ògbóni and Àjẹ́ are Ẹdan-Onílẹ̀'s guardians and administrators of moral law. Given the seriousness of their duties, Ògbóni have their own laws, the foremost being, "That the eyes should see / That the ears should hear / That the mouth should be silent."[37] Ògbóni's respect for the oaths made by and with the Earth is apparent in a simple but powerful maxim: "The mouth of an initiate does not leak."[38] There is, rightfully, great mystery surrounding Ògbóni, and even the organization's external symbols, icons, and signs are storehouses of esoteric profundity.

Ògbóni's mystery and power can be traced directly to Àjẹ́, Onílẹ̀, Ẹdan, Ìyá Màpó and the elemental powers of motherhood which are often misunderstood, especially when they appear in òdì orientation. An oríkì of Ẹdan describes Ìyá Ayé as carrying her child "òdì."[39] While the dictionary definition of òdì is "contrariness, perversity, wrong side of anything," in our analyses of the *Oríkì Ẹdan*, I translate òdì as "unusually," and Babatunde Lawal translates it as "in an unconventional manner."[40] It is clear to Lawal and me, at least, that Ìyá Ayé is not a contrary or perverse Mother. But while the words "unusual" and "unconventional" are not brimming with judgmental ignorance, they are not exact translations for òdì in this context either. Furthermore, because Ìyá Ayé is literally carrying her child upside down, the term doríkodò (upside down) could be used, but it is not. It appears to be the case that in the context of Àjẹ́, the term òdì constitutes an odù kékeré with a meaning that is unique and specific to Ìyá Ayé, the Mother of the Earth.

In *Black Gods and Kings*, Robert Farris Thompson analyzes the concept of òdì in Ògbóni speech and symbolism. Thompson asserts that the word òdì may be concealing meaning and infusing depth within the phrase "Ogboni meji, o di eta," which is translated as "two [Ògbóni] members, it becomes three" and is uttered by two people swearing an oath.[41] Thompson finds that the phrase "o di" signifies both the dictionary definition of "òdì," wrong contrary, and perverse, as well as "the foe" and "the mother."[42] Thompson conflates these definitions and concludes that the mother in question, Onílẹ̀, constitutes "a horrific maternal force."[43] While Thompson's depiction of Onílẹ̀ is identical to Verger's (and their descriptions seem to elucidate not only the inadequacy that Caucasian men feel before this Great African God, but also the source of the myths and lies about Àjẹ́), it does not represent the Mother who cradles and suckles every inhabitant of Ifẹ̀ and the Mother whose care and covenant are so sure that they are recalled in greetings, maxims, handshakes, and hand signs. The Mother who offers her progeny an eternal pot of protection and projection, the Mother who provides the farm and then betters her provision, the Mother We Beg to Have is not a force of horror: How could She be? She is the farm and the farmer. She is the Mother and every African mother. She is the Ultimate Mediator and she is every neutral person who is asked to mediate. She is also every Ògbóni member and she is Ògbóni.

Thompson's macabre description of Onílẹ̀ appears to be rooted in his Caucocentric worldview and his reliance on the layperson's definition of òdì as perverse, wrong, and an enemy. While these translations of òdì are valid in mundane discourse, these definitions are not at all relevant to Onílẹ̀, because Onílẹ̀ is a God and she is the planet Earth. Although Caucocentric cartographers racially skew maps and globes to make Caucasian-affiliated lands appear to be at the top of the world,[44] the Earth is a sphere, and a sphere can be viewed from any position. There is no upside down, inside out, perversity, or incorrectness as far as the Earth, cosmogony, and cosmology are concerned: There is Earth. And just as there is no wrong way to gaze upon one's self, Onílẹ̀'s orientation and the manner by which she chooses to examine her creation can never be aberrant, perverse, or contrary. It is especially incongruous for human beings to assert Onílẹ̀'s orientation is incorrect because Onílẹ̀ is the reason human beings have any orientation at all.

Onílẹ̀ is the God of the Earth, and, given her terrestrial and cosmic dominion, her perspective necessarily differs from that of mortals. What is more, Onílẹ̀'s progeny and inheritors of her power also manifest the intricacy of òdì orientation. Òdì is the multidimensional vision of Ìyá Ayé as well as that of her child, Mọlẹ̀, who is described as being perfectly positioned all around the Earth in some orature and is depicted as a baby tied òdì to Onílẹ̀ in other orature. Òdì orientation is also evident in women giving "birth on the ground" and killing to eat. The vagina that stands upside down but pours no blood is standing òdì. Ọ̀rúnmìlà's "unusual" friend Ọ̀rọ̀, who is also known as Mọlẹ̀, wears clothes that are "òdì" and so do the members of Ògbóni.[45]

In *Black Gods and Kings*, Thompson offers an analysis of the symbolism of the Ògbóni sash called *ṣàkì Ẹdan*:

> The ruler of Iperu-Remo told me in the summer of 1963 that the special tasseled cloth worn as a badge of Ogboni office, the shaki, itself puns upon a word for guts, *shaki* (lit. "tripe") in this sense: the wearer upon the investment is told that earth and the minions of the earth will see into his guts forever, that nothing can possibly be concealed from their gaze. To become Ogboni is to become transparent. The Ogboni member is the man turned inside-out, revealing the odd, left, inner side to his existence.[46]

The "minions" to whom Thompson refers are not random or anonymous spirits, but one's ancestors. The all-seeing Earth to whom Thompson refers is Ẹdan, who "never goes blind" and who beholds the actions of all individuals—including and especially Àjẹ́ and Ògbóni—and dispenses justice equitably to all violators.[47] The ṣàkì Ẹdan, then, works in at least two ways: The Ògbóni elder who appears before his community bedecked in the ṣàkì Ẹdan constitutes a visceral reminder to the general populace that everything that they do is being observed by Ìyá Ayé; at the same time, the ṣàkì Ẹdan signifies that everything that the Ògbóni elder does is also being scrutinized by his ancestors and Ẹdan. The circle of divine continuity and responsibility is readily apparent to all.

An important characteristic of the Ògbóni society that has generated great debate is its orientation to the left. In certain parts of the world, the left hand is used to clean one's waste. Consequently, in general Yoruba society, individuals avoid giving, taking, and touching items and waving to or pointing at parties with only the left hand because of what those gestures signify. However, using both hands to offer a gift or to wave at a party indicates tremendous respect in Yoruba culture. Clearly, in certain contexts the left does not pollute or diminish; it exponentially magnifies respect and power.

As is the case with òdì and numerous other sacred aspects of Yoruba culture, the left is a signifier of potent profundity. Ògbóni members use the left hand for their highly symbolic handshakes; the left hand takes the dominant position in Ògbóni hand signs; and ritual Ògbóni dances are oriented to the left as well.[48] An Ògbóni elder offers a succinct explication of the significance of the left that sheds even more light on the powerful forces of òdì and Àjẹ́: "[T]he right is used by humans; the left is for the gods."[49]

While Africana cosmology describes the spiritual realm as being similar in many respects to the terrestrial realm, the spiritual realm is characterized by various fittingly "otherworldly" attributes, such as òdì and other forms of inversion.[50] The natural way of knowing, being, and doing of the Gods and of the spiritual realm is considered òdì on the Earth, and òdì expressions, icons, and actions are confounding to mortals simply because they do not have divine vision and orientation. However, individuals who are identified by òdì actions, icons, and regalia are Gods living on Earth, and if "the left is for the gods," then Àjẹ́ are, not surprisingly, the Gods of the Gods.

In "*À Yà Gbó, À Yà Tó*," Lawal reveals the myriad ways in which left represents woman in Yoruba cosmontology, including the Odù Ifá, the human big left toe, and the left hand signifying èrọ̀ and being considered "owó àlááfíà ('the hand of tranquility')."[51] As Lawal continues his elucidation of the sacred nature of the left in the Yoruba ethos, the force of Àjẹ́ emerges as the undeniable source of all signs, symbols, and signifiers:

> . . . [B]ecause of its infrequent use, the left hand is *owó isúra* or *owó ipamó* ("reserved hand"); keeping something in mind is "hiding it in the left hand." In the realm of the occult, the left connotes concealment; hence it is *owó awo* ("hand of secrecy"), and the left handshake affirms cultic knowledge and solidarity (*ìmùlè*). Thus, in Ògbóni iconography the left signifies the female and the bond between mother and child and among the "children of the same mother" (Omo Ìyá), the mystique and ambivalence of the earth deity, and the spirit of togetherness and self-discipline expected of initiates.[52]

In every conceivable way, the left signifies the overt-covert supremacy of Àjẹ́ and the understated dynamism of the Mother and of all mothers.

The Ògbóni society and its icons, maxims, and rituals constitute an overt exhibition of the covert profundity of òdì. The ṣàkì's inversion displays one's loyalty, honor, honesty, and integrity. The left-hand handshakes reveal reverence to Onílẹ̀ but conceal the source of the bond which is reaffirmed by covered fingers. The Ògbóni hand sign in which the left fist sits atop the right with both thumbs concealed is a brilliant overt-covert display of òdì empowerment. Morton-Williams states that this gesture implies that no secret can be hidden from Ògbóni "any more than hiding the thumb prevents their knowing it is there."[53] The hand sign could also symbolize life in the form of a penis inside a vagina, or a mouth embracing a milk-giving nipple. Twins are sacred to Ògbóni and the thumbs could represent twins in a womb. Given the significance of thumbs to human life, the hidden thumbs could indicate the obvious but invisible presence of sublime and understated power—not unlike the clitoris. With this multiply encoded sign, the thumbs become, like Onílẹ̀, the hidden third element that unites the two fists into one force of myriad covert meanings.

Lawal's "À Yà Gbó, À Yà Tó," includes a stunning image of an Onílé (Owner of the House) altar figure.[54] The Mother makes the Ògbóni sign as she kneels and assumes what is arguably a woman's most vulnerable and powerful pose. This God, who appears as a paradoxically defenseless-fearsome entity, is protected by her jutting clitoris which stimulates and charges the air and Earth while it simultaneously titillates, prepares, and protects her concealed vaginal cavity and womb. Onílé kneels as if she is giving birth, but because there is no visible pregnancy, she must be giving birth to unfathomable power. Mother's genitals, with their jutting concealment and internal-external displays of power, offer stunning evidence of the elegant perfection of òdì.

Because of the nature of their divinity, it is fitting that òdì orientation pervades nearly every aspect of Àjẹ́ and Ògbóni. Indeed, Àjẹ́ and Ògbóni are able to successfully undertake their judicial duties because they view the world through òdì orientation and they can therefore rínú rode (see the inside and the outside). What is more, when Àjẹ́ and Ògbóni gather to deliberate on issues, they do so in the lodge that is called Ilédì, which is a compound word constructed of Ilé and Òdì: The Ògbóni lodge is the literal Home of Òdì.

In "À Yà Gbó, À Yà Tó," Lawal discusses the significance of concealment and òdì orientation to Ilẹ̀ and Ògbóni:

> It is Edan who, on behalf of Ilẹ̀, passes judgment in the Ògbóni lodge. Small wonder that the brass figures bear her name. Edan's mediatory role between Ògbóni and Ilẹ̀ may explain why Ilẹ̀ is rarely personified in sculpture but is frequently symbolized by sacred substances concealed in the ground beneath an altar displaying the large male and female brass figures (Onílé or Onílẹ̀). It is probably because of this concealment that the Ògbóni lodge is known as Ilédì, that is, "the house of secrets" (Ilé odì) or "the house of concealment" (Ilé tí a di nnkan sé).[55]

The paradoxical melding of the obvious and the unseen, òdì is the handshake that conceals an ancient bond; òdì is the mother whose prayer for forgiveness is a curse; òdì is the wife whose naked body teaches her husband about his origin and end; òdì is the calabash that contains an egg that contains a tail feather that is yet to be formed but is capable of devolving destinies; òdì is the child-carrying technique that appears to be a grievous error but is actually the highest honor. Òdì is truly the orientation of Àjẹ́, the orientation of the Gods.

That òdì orientation, Àjẹ́, Ẹdan, and Ògbóni are not meant to be understood or accessed by mortals is emphasized by Adeoye in the following pronouncement: "*Ẹdan kì í jade sí ògbẹ̀rì. Àwọn ẹlẹ́sìn rẹ̀ àti mọlẹ́bí wọn ni Ẹdan máa ń jade sí*" (Ẹdan does not appear to the uninitiated. Ẹdan only appears to her true devotees and mọlẹ́bí)."[56] This information is important not only for confirming the exclusivity between Ẹdan and her progeny in an age in which it seems money can buy anything but also for its elucidation of the ways by which her progeny are identified. The word *mọlẹ́bí* is yet another odù kékeré. Mọlẹ́bí is translated as "relatives," but it is more than that, for in addition to *ẹbí*, which means "family," the word mọlẹ́bí also intimates recognition of Mọlẹ̀, who is the source of cosmic-terrestrial relatives and also the creator of *ọlẹ̀*, embryos, which are stored in *ilé ọlẹ̀*, the "house of embryos," which is the womb.[57] In the context of Ẹdan, then, mọlẹ́bí could be translated as the children who are born of Ẹdan's embryos: This would be an appropriate title and reminder for the progeny of the Mother of All.

It is important to remember that all inhabitants of Ifẹ̀ Oòye were initiated into Mọlẹ̀; there were no gender restrictions. The only gender-based restriction given by Adeoye in regards to Ẹdan Ògbóni is that women of childbearing age should not see the image of Ẹdan that is swaddled in cloth and kept inside a sacred container called ọpọ́n ọlọ́mọrí. This object with a seemingly mundane translation, tray with a lid, contains multifold power, for the visual of Ẹdan enveloped in cloth and waiting in the ọpọ́n ọlọ́mọrí invokes the image of a child ensconced in the womb. The ọpọ́n ọlọ́mọrí emerges as yet another odù (container, womb) of Odù where creation and power are eternally reborn and stored.

It is said that if women of childbearing age see the image of Ẹdan in the ọpọ́n ọlọ́mọrí, they will no longer menstruate and will be unable to bear children.[58] Perhaps seeing the image of Ẹdan swaddled òdì in the womb would immediately catapult women into òdì orientation where they, similar to Ẹdan, become àgbàláàgbà whose Àjẹ́ is so magnified that their vaginas, even when turned upside down, do not pour blood. While certain women are exempt from sex and childbearing because of the spiritual duties they must perform, the caveat that Adeoye details is designed to protect the ọlẹ̀ within the ilé ọlẹ̀ of Ẹdan's mọlẹ́bí. While this injunction appears to restrict access to Ẹdan to a largely male coterie, it actually ensures gender balance for, as the embodiments of Odù and Onílẹ̀, women bear their own biological ọpọ́n ọlọ́mọrí from whence the future mọlẹ́bí of Ẹdan will spring.

As the guardians of ilé ọlẹ̀ who give life to infinite mọlẹ́bí, Mothers are Gods. Mothers giving birth, breastfeeding, and backing children are the most effortless, powerful, and logical displays of Divinity in this world. Àjẹ́'s inherent numinosity is such that they need no cloaks, signs, or jewelry to signify their powers. By contrast, because men lack organic attributes of Divinity, they display their relationship to and custodianship of the Earth with various icons including Ẹdan brass staves.

Sue Picton finds that the staves "are used in Ogboni ritual and every member of the Ogboni society has a pair of these figures made for his initiation into the society."[59] Ẹdan can take many forms including two simple rods linked by a chain, a male and a female connected by a chain, or two figures that are a melding of genders. Lawal observes that some Onílé figures, which are large freestanding representations of a man and a woman, "are joined back to back to emphasize the oneness of the pair."[60]

The theme of unity that pervades Ògbóni iconography reflects the organization's work. Ògbóni members use Ẹdan to swear oaths, solidify the community, and establish new communities because "it has the most àṣẹ because it is the thing that combines all of them [community members and forces] together. It is a symbol of unity."[61] Margaret Thompson-Drewal finds that Ògbóni's emphasis on unity and gender balance reflects that of the larger society:

> The male and female figures reflect the make-up the traditional judiciary; which includes both men and women, although males are in the majority. The paired brass figures signify the union of men and women, the founding of the community, which represents their progeny, and the oaths of truth and secrecy sworn by the members of the town's judiciary in the witnessing presence of earth, the abode of the spirits and ancestors.[62]

Gender balance is the cornerstone of Ògbóni because it is essential for a thriving heterogeneous society.

Lawal explores the significance of gender harmony in his article, "Ejiwapo: The Dialectics of Twoness in Yoruba Art and Culture." Lawal's title is inspired by the Yoruba expression *takọ tabo, eéjì wà po*: male and female, the two exist as complements; however, one member of the pair is the elder and empowerer, and she can exist independently. When Ẹdan images clearly represent a female, she often boasts a beard which is symbolic of *Ogbọ́n Ayé*, the Wisdom of the World, which only Àjẹ́ can attain. That beard also signifies a being who is not only a fully evolved woman but is also an entity who encompasses and, therefore, eclipses man and, as a result, attains a third dimension of identity and divinity. As Lawal elucidates, the Ẹdan icon is an exhibition of the inclusivity and supremacy of Mother:

> That the pair does not represent two different characters is evident in the fact that both the AOF [Aboriginal Ògbóni Fraternity] and ROF [Reformed Ògbóni Fraternity] factions refer to the two figures as Iya ("mother"), treating them as one unit. Besides, all members of the society metaphorically regard themselves as Omo Iya ("Children of Mother Earth"), not as children of two parents, a father and a mother.[63]

The Yoruba cosmontological purview stresses the fact that Mother is the source, foundation, and cause of existence. Man is dependent on the vagina, womb, and breasts of his mother for existence; he is dependent on the vagina, womb, and breasts of his partners and daughters for continuity. Rather than seek to subjugate, delimit, or destroy ascendant Àjẹ́, the men of Ògbóni position themselves as reverential children before the generous Mother who is also every mother. As the Ògbóni hand sign and mantra illustrate, from conception to breastfeeding, the Ẹdan icon is a reflection of life and a study of òdì orientation, for what appears to be two or even three, with the swearing of an oath and the insemination of ọlẹ̀, is actually one—the all-encompassing dynamic force of Mother.

In the light of the autonomy and power that women enjoy as a result of their clitoral completion, it could be the case that takọ tabo, eéjì wà po is a plea for woman to bond with man and include him in the development of existence and not undertake the rigors of creation independently: Genetic endowments of the past and scientific developments of the present certainly facilitate women's ability to do everything they need and want to do without men. The repeated references in Yoruba history, orature, and literature to towns peopled solely by Àjẹ́ and the contemporary existence of the female-exclusive town of Umoja, Kenya make it clear that because women are complete, they can flourish in a gender-exclusive society. However, the inhabitants of an exclusively male town can only look forward to extinction. This is why men, when threatened with exclusivity, will martial all of the forces in Ọ̀run and Ayé in hopes of facilitating a reunification with women.

Ògbóni icons also boast furtive manifestations of the power of òdì and the preservative and regenerative force of woman. Ẹdan Ògbóni brasses—including freestanding Onílé/Onílẹ̀, portable Ẹdan, swords, rings, and other symbols—have hidden in their cores a kernel of iron that is discernable through x-ray.[64] That each Ògbóni icon has hidden within a minute iron spirit brings to mind the concealed and powerful clitoris. But unlike the clitoris which can, like the Spirit Bird, experience the world at will, the iron implement is ever-ensconced within Mother. This iron fragment seems more representative of man's strength and his fragility, his power and his limitations, for his existence is dependent upon protection within and projection through the womb of woman. As a symbol of masculinity, the tiny iron filing could represent a single sperm eternally fertilizing and vivifying the ovum of existence. It could represent a male fetus, complete with sperm-filled testes, ever-protected in the womb. It could represent the creation of Òrìṣà Ògún within the Womb of Odù.

In the most obvious sense, the hidden force of iron, which could, perhaps, be considered the center and stabilizing heart or *ọkàn* of Ògbóni, represents Ògún, the Òrìṣà of iron, technology, and raw masculinity. While Ògún is not overtly associated with Ògbóni, he is intimately connected with Onílẹ̀, and she and Ògún are united on Ògún's shrine. Awo Fatunmbi elucidates these Gods' intimate relationship, symbiosis, and symbolism:

> *Onilẹ* is represented on *Ogun's* altar by an iron pot. The pot is trimmed by a metal chain and a red strip of cloth. It is a symbol of the primal womb bleeding at birth as it passes the grain of genetic memory. The pot is sprinkled with *irosun*. The *irosun* is a red power that comes from the camwood tree. In Yoruba *irosun* means . . . "menstrual blood". Inside the pot are spikes, symbols of *Ogun's* virility and sperm. Just as the snail is the *Ifá* symbol for androgynous procreation, *Ogun's* pot is the Ifá symbol for heterogeneous procreation.[65]

The Onílẹ̀-Ògún dynamic reflects both the delicate gender and biochemical balance that is essential for human existence and the scientific knowledge that undergirds the spiritual system of Ifá. Ògún's iron is a key component of the blood that the Mothers control, and the procreative powers of Ògún and Onílẹ̀ are even evident in the spikes of the pot, which could represent Onílẹ̀'s clitoris as easily as Ògún's penis: Since there are several spikes, both organs could be represented.

The intimacy of Onílẹ̀ and Ògún is logical because Ògún's iron tools are instrumental to martial, architectural, agricultural, and culinary arts and sciences. Without Ògún's iron implements, agriculture, which is the mainstay of African economies and the world's oldest profession, becomes exceedingly difficult. The fact that Onílẹ̀ is heralded as Afọkóyẹrí, She Who Styles Her Hair with a Hoe, indicates the importance of her bond with Ògún, for, in the process of accentuating Onílẹ̀'s stupendous beauty, Ògún's tools provide humanity with sustenance and with civilizations.

Ògún is clearly a son of the Mother, and this is reflected in the fact that one of his roads, or divine manifestations, is Ògún Onílẹ̀. Ògún's relationship with Onílẹ̀ also confirms Opeola's statement that Ògún has Àjẹ́ and that he has to have it to create, defend, build, plant, and harvest.[66] Ògún must also have the approval and cooperation of the Mothers in order to build plant, defend, protect, and harvest. For, as Abiodun reveals, with all of Ògún's masculine might and power, he can be rendered impotent with one ìkó oódẹ. Àjẹ́ and Ògún must establish a perfect balance lest their attempts at creation result in chaos. Onílẹ̀'s Àjẹ́-drenched pot on Ògún's shrine reveals how effectively this pair works together, and humanity is the proof of the success of the union of these Gods, their organs, and their vocations.

Ògún's connection to Ògbóni may not be the most obvious—it could even be described as existing in òdì—but it is fundamental. Ògbóni icons articulate the supremacy and expansiveness of the Mothers through brass and the dependence and fidelity of their sons through Ògún's iron. A similar correlation is expressed in a proverb that compares the brilliance and permanence of mother to the fragility of father: *Ìyá ni wúrà: Bàbá ní dígi* (Mother is gold: Father is glass). Despite iron's strength and usefulness, when exposed to the elements, iron will rust, disintegrate, and readily return to dust. Similarly, with all of man's physical strength and might, he is genetically incomplete, and the Y chromosome is evidence of his fragility and instability. By contrast, brass, which is symbolic of woman and the dominant X chromosome, has a composition that does not allow for easy degradation and disintegration.

The obvious differences in the strength and integrity of brass and iron are readily apparent on any number of Ẹdan staves because, in addition to bearing the hidden iron filing, the staves are mounted on iron rods. The Ẹdan, which members may wear around their necks, is usually placed horizontally on the ground for rituals; however, in some instances the Ẹdan is positioned upright "by sticking the prongs into the ground."[67] When lodged in the Earth, Ògún's iron galvanizes Ẹdan's connection with Onílẹ̀ and catalyzes their elemental forces. The inability of Ògún and iron to conduct pure Àjẹ́ for extended amounts of time is evident in the fact that the external iron prongs of Ẹdan readily rust and disintegrate while the brass remains whole and often glows like gold. Ògbóni members are cognizant that man's protection and the source of his continuity is literally, figuratively, spiritually, and sexually with and within woman; indeed, while the external prong degrades over time, the tiny iron filing, empowered by òdì, remains intact.

Samuel M. Opeola avers that Àjẹ́ epitomizes protection, and this is evident in Ẹdan's òdì-oriented signs, symbols, and functions and in the characteristics and manifestations that may be more easily understood by the general populace. In "Ejiwapo," Lawal describes additional aspects of Ẹdan's intricate and layered character:

[S]ince the Yoruba often associate femaleness with softness and coolness and maleness with hardness or harshness, the female figures of the Onile/edan pair evidently refers to the motherly disposition of the goddess, and the male figures to her punitive or potentially dangerous tendencies. That is why the chained edan Ogboni brass figures may be detached for sending coded messages. A male figure connotes bad news and may be used to summon those who have committed serious offences to appear before a special court. The female figure, on the other hand, hints at good news, such as being cleared by the court of a crime or selected to receive a chieftaincy title. However, the significance of each figure varies from one context to another. Some edan Ogboni are specially made for healing purposes. When worn like a pendant, the male figure is expected to energize the body, facilitating speedy recovery from illness. The female figure, on the other hand, may be prescribed for relieving muscular pain and high blood pressure. Above all, the juxtaposition of the male and female figures sends clear signals about the interconnectedness of the opposite sex in the perpetuation of life and preservation of the social order. Needless to say, when worn in public, the edan Ogboni denotes the male/female membership of the society.[68]

Rather than unprovoked rage, casual murders, and free-flowing evil, the female aspect of Ẹdan reflects the qualities manifest in and symbolized by Yoruba mothers generally—qualities that could be described as being as precious and as permanent as gold. The male aspect can, depending on the context, represent the danger of a broken mirror that need be immediately repaired or removed before its shards draw blood. However, it is not the case that the male figure symbolizes evil and the female signifies good: The Ẹdan Ògbóni icons represent Ẹdan's comprehensiveness and her ability to address any situation and to represent all community members. This is especially evident in the use of Ẹdan icons to heal, invigorate, and regulate the human body.

While Ẹdan's response to forces that seek to hurt, betray, or destroy her progeny and her creation may be considered masculine, her ferocity can just as easily and perhaps even more accurately be described as logical and maternal. Ẹdan is truly a complete and holistic God, but the fact that Lawal and Yoruba elders celebrate what are considered to be her feminine attributes further elucidates Àjẹ́'s truth. Àwọn Ìyá Wa are given the same adoration as biological mothers and are heralded as "compassionate," doting, and empowering healers whose presence is begged for, whose love is as enduring as gold, and whose vaginas contain the soothing waters of èrò. Àjẹ́ are the Gods who protect with vengeance, who educate with Òrò, whose elaborate hairstyles mirror the bounty of Mother Earth, and whose support is complete and eternal.[69]

Ẹdan Ògbóni: The Synthesis of the Political and the Spiritual

One of the most long-standing myths about Àjẹ́ gave birth to one of the most protracted lies about Àjẹ́. As I discuss in *Our Mothers, Our Powers, Our Texts*,[70] as a result of religious oppression and racism, Àjẹ́ were not only denigrated as "witches" but they were also categorized in a racist hierarchy. Àjẹ́ is often discussed as having three classes. Àjẹ́ funfun is at the top of the hierarchy because "white" in a racist worldview is associated with good, holy, and, bizarrely, Caucasian. Àjẹ́ funfun are styled as "good witches." Reflecting the racist belief that the more melanin a person has the more degenerate he is, Àjẹ́ pupa (red) are classed as savage and bloodthirsty. The irredeemably nefarious, evil, and malevolent Àjẹ́ are, in this scheme, Àjẹ́ dúdú (black).

That this color-coded hierarchy is the product of alien racist indoctrination becomes clear when one compares myths about Àjẹ́ pupa to the work of Ògbóni. Àjẹ́ pupa are described as relishing blood so much that they will do anything to make it flow. Àjẹ́ pupa will allegedly trick cooks into cutting their fingers while dicing meat and vegetables; they will engineer auto accidents; they will foment domestic and social brawls, wars—whatever it takes to generate calamity and bloodshed. These fantasies run counter to the work of Àjẹ́ and Ògbóni. In his article, "The Yoruba Ògbóni Cult," Peter Morton-Williams reveals that in the Yoruba ethos, "To shed human blood upon the ground, whether the wound is slight or grave, except in sacrifice is to profane the Earth."[71] Because they are the guardians and custodians of the Earth and the enforcers of moral, terrestrial, and cosmic law, Àjẹ́ and Ògbóni are responsible for adjudicating any case involving bloodshed.

The myths of Àjẹ́ funfun, pupa, and dúdú are rooted in ignorance of the laws of Àjẹ́, Ẹdan, and Ògbóni. These laws are the foundation of the Yoruba nation and cannot be contravened by any entity or ẹgbẹ́ without just cause. Aside from the socio-political facts, simple logic is sufficient for demystification, for what mothers create and rejoice in accidents that injure or kill their children? What mothers erect stumbling blocks and dig pitfalls to destroy the evidence of their divinity? If causing bloodshed in general is to profane the Earth, how does one interpret the actions of the "African witch" who butchers, cooks, and serves her progeny, who are also Onílẹ̀'s children, known as Ọmọ Ìyá, for dinner? In order for Àjẹ́ to meet the criteria of the "African witch" and the "Àjẹ́ pupa" and "Àjẹ́ dúdú" myths, the Mothers would have to successfully and routinely contravene the laws of Onílẹ̀ and Ẹdan and the laws of self-preservation, community elevation, and holistic immortalization. The myths about Àjẹ́ pupa, funfun, and dúdú simply have no place in Yoruba history, politics, or cosmontology.

Tremendous powers are invested in Àjẹ́ and Ògbóni, and those powers are used with the utmost seriousness and discernment. Anyebe's *Ògbóni: The Birth and Growth of the Reformed Ògbóni Fraternity* describes how judiciously the Apèènà, one of the highest ranking Ògbóni officials, fulfills his obligations:

> Apena is said to be in charge of the Edon. He offers sacrifices to it from time to time, and it is believed that he can employ the Edon through magical means to kill an enemy. But it is the rule of the society that he must not use it capriciously, without the sanction of the society. Else, he may bring danger on himself. . . . This shows that the Apena can only employ the Edon for the collective action of the society.[72]

That Apèènà must conduct himself righteously and act only with group consensus is consistent with Ibie's and Faleti's findings that Àwọn Ìyá Wa administer the world's most disciplined and equitable judicial system.

Whereas Western systems of justice are compromised by capitalism, greed, racism, and power, every member of Yoruba society, including Ògbóni officials and Àjẹ́, must defer to Ẹdan Onílẹ̀, The Mother With All-Seeing and Ensnaring Eyes. In America, people get the amount of "justice" that they can afford or they get a "justice" that is influenced by racism and/or ethnic identity. However, Àjẹ́ have no profit motive, and Ẹdan's eyes see *all* actions, whether they are committed by an ẹlẹ́sìn (initiate) or an ògbẹ̀rì (commoner). Because Mọlẹ̀ is the Earth on which we live, she is ubiquitous as well as omniscient. She is the entity who witnesses the pact between two friends that is sealed with earth and water, and she provides the grave for the body of the betrayer of a trust. Ẹdan is also completely neutral: her reactions, like those of Àjẹ́ correspond directly to human actions.

Ògbóni, also known in some regions as Òṣugbó, was the signature judicial system of precolonial Yorubaland and the highest tribunal of the land. Given its rootedness in and reverence for the Earth and its responsibility for ensuring human continuity, Ògbóni's power goes beyond "the maintenance of law and order, and dispensation of justice" and extends "to the power of life and death."[73] In the contemporary era, Ògbóni exercises varying degrees of power in different regions but the same element of awe. While the fabrications about "African witchcraft" come straight from the mind of the Caucasian ideologues, justice as dispensed by

Ògbóni is real, absolute, and stunning. In the light of Morton-Williams' findings and the ritual rings thought to depict the executions carried out by Ògbóni's enforcement arm, Orò, it is clear that Àjẹ́, Ògbóni, and Orò are rightly feared and revered.

Ògbóni rings depict a male official, perhaps the Olúwo or the Apèènà, presiding over decapitated bodies. The victims' arms and mouths are bound, and Ẹyẹ Ọ̀rọ̀ Aragamegun is feasting on their heads.[74] These phenomenal icons not only reveal the seriousness with which violations of Onílẹ̀ are dealt but they also subtly emphasize the curvilinear development and continuity that Ògbóni ensure. The circular motif of the ring is indicative of the evolution that takes place in the midst of what the Western mind considers to be death. The individual who is beheaded returns to Odù's pot only with the help of the Ẹyẹ Ọ̀rọ̀, who in this case takes the form of a vulture. While vultures and buzzards are often shunned by Westerners because of their work, Pan-African cosmology regards them as birds of divine judgment that are absolutely essential to terrestrial hygiene, fecundity, evolution. The depiction of Ẹyẹ Ọ̀rọ̀ and the circular layout of the Ògbóni rings help elucidate why the term "sleep" in regards to dethroned rulers is so appropriate: Everyone will ultimately be restored to Onílẹ̀'s womb; whether they return to the Earth or not and how they return is dictated by the lessons they have learned in Ayé and Ọ̀run.

The curvilinear scope of Ògbóni, which finds them presiding over death in order to ensure the sanctity of life is symbolized by spiral and circular designs that often appear on Ògbóni brasses and connote "increase, dynamic motion."[75] Another symbol that is indicative of how Àjẹ́ orders and empowers Ògbóni is the crescent moon that often graces Ẹdan Ògbóni implements. Lawal reveals that the crescent moon is

> a symbol of newness and regeneration. The Yoruba refer to menses as a "sign of the moon" *(nkan osù)* because the women use the waxing and waning of the moon as a calendar for the menstrual cycle. Moreover, during its waxing phase, maidens and newly married women pray to the moon to make them fertile and give them the strength with which to carry a baby on the back. Apart from its menstrual and fertility associations, the crescent motif, according to an elder of the Ògbóni society, empowers a special ritual called *àjídèwe* ("Wake up and feel like a youth") performed in ancient times to ensure longevity, making an individual look and feel younger with the waxing of the moon.[76]

Menstrual blood flows freely and elegantly through Yoruba ontology with neither trace of disgust nor fear of pollution. The "sign of the moon" confirms to women their fertility, and women ask the moon justify that fertility with new life. Rulers and initiates bedeck themselves in ìkóódẹ to signify having been crowned in the Motherblood of Àjẹ́. Elders harness the life and vitality promised by the Moon and, by extension, menses to restore their vigor. Nkan oṣù, the sign of menses, is truly the sign of life, making it the perfect symbol for Ògbóni.

Orò: Woman Takes the Road—Man Runs!

Àjẹ́ and Ògbóni ensure that the laws of Onílẹ̀ are followed, and when those laws are broken, they see that reparations are made. When violations that are so outlandish that they cannot be mended occur, Orò is summoned. In *Ògbóni* Anyebe defines Orò as the "most secret of Yoruba institutions" and the "executive arm" of Ògbóni.[77] Anyebe describes the sound of Orò's approach, which is produced by bullroarers as, "the wailing spirit of the ancestors."[78] The whirring of Orò signifies the coming of justice, for "[a]ny evil doer condemned by Ogboni was taken to the sacred grove in the bush and there executed by Oro."[79] As a magnificent pun, the wailing of the ancestors often indicates that new souls will join their ranks. The Ògbóni rings depict part of what occurs after balance has been restored; however, no one knows what happens after this because, as a popular saying contends, *A kí ì ri àjẹkù Orò*: No one ever sees the remains of Oro's meal.

The prevailing consensus on women and Orò is "Bobinrin foju kan Oro, Oro yo gbee": "If a woman sees Orò, it will carry her away."[80] This statement is qualified by social strictures that demand the confinement of women when Orò is invoked. However, it would be more accurate to say that if the uninitiated see Orò they will be carried away, because anyone— male or female—who is not a member of Orò who violates the curfew or enters the sacred grove will be consumed by Orò.[81] Debunking the myth of gender exclusivity outright is a maxim that states, "A woman's knowledge of Oro is kept to herself (*Mo sinu l'obinrin nmo Oro*)."[82] This adage is more realistic, especially given that women are central to Ògbóni which directs the actions of Orò; however the statement is misleading because men must also keep their knowledge of Orò to themselves: Orò is, after all, a secret society.

It is likely the case that the maxims of Orò, like those of Ògbóni, were originally gender-neutral. Gender-specific injunctions may have developed in response to colonization as Yoruba men began to mimic Caucasian patriarchal oppressors in their attempt to carve out a realm of authority in the midst of social, political, and cultural upheaval. My theory that gender-specific rules in Orò, and Egúngún as well, are not organic aspects of the Yoruba ethos is supported by many facts, including the fact that Yoruba cosmontology heralds women as the storehouses of the most sacred.

Reticence is one of the cornerstones of Àjẹ́. Yoruba men interviewed by Drewal and Drewal assert that "women are more secretive than we" and that "we men usually open our secret to anybody"; however, "Women have many secrets that they will never tell . . . except [to] their mothers."[83] As I discuss above, woman is identified with the left, and both woman and the left signify silence and reserve. Ìyánlá is heralded as the "All powerful mother, mother of the night bird / . . . / My mother kills quickly without a cry."[84] Gẹ̀lẹ̀dẹ́ orature confides: "Something secret was buried in the mother's house / A secret pact with a wizard."[85] A popular saying about the Mothers confirms, "An Àjẹ́ attends the meeting and fights on your behalf, but when she sees you, she doesn't say a word."[86] Rather than admonish women for casually spewing secrets, Yoruba wisdom keepers and orature confirm that the people who are best able to protect what is sacred are the Mothers.

While proverbs and aphorisms offer important inferences, the roles of women in Orò do not have to be extrapolated from orature. J. R. O. Ojo finds that in northeastern Yorubaland, "Women past childbearing age are initiated into the Oro cult. The initiated members share the same room as the young male initiates."[87] In the light of the fact that Ẹdan appointed Àjẹ́ to oversee Ògbóni, and given that the dispensation of justice must be in accord with the Earth and her appointed guardians, the legitimacy of Orò would be questioned if women were *not* a part of it. Ojo further illuminates the bond between Àjẹ́ and Orò: "It is also interesting to be told that the ancestors' visit to the earth, a part of the ceremony [of Orò initiation], is called *Eye ni a'ye*, 'the mothers visit the earth.'"[88] Rather than being excluded from Orò, Àjẹ́ is essential to every aspect of the force, its work, and its proliferation.

Àjẹ́'s connection to Orò is also revealed in numerous divination verses. A sixteen cowries divination verse of Ọ̀wọ́rín recounts the origin of Orò, and reveals that it is men who flee in terror from the force of Woman. In the ẹsẹ, Orò bears the oríkì "Something Scarce." Something Scarce's true force is revealed when her father, the king of Ọyọ Ajorí, marries her to the chief of Ejigbó against the will of her Orí. When Something Scarce and her retinue go to meet the chief, they are armed with the tools of Ògún and the cudgel of Ògbóni. Something Scarce destroys a house, all the wares of the market, and the Chief of Ejigbó's sacred tree because whenever she encounters an obstacle she sings: "If you destroy this house [or these goods or this tree], / I will cook lots of ogunmo / For the chief of Ejigbo, my husband; / Destroy this house [or market or tree]."[89] When the chief emerges from his home to greet his bride, Something Scarce sings, "Chop this person down, / and I will cook lots of ogunmo / For the chief of Ejigbo, my husband,"[90] and he is also chopped down—just like everything else that had been in her path. When the king of Ọyọ Ajorí decides to marry

Something Scarce to the chief of Ejigbó's younger brother, her new groom "went into the house and hid" upon her arrival.[91]

Something Scarce's actions led to an important custom: "A Yoruba husband should not be present to receive his bride when she arrives at his house with her wedding party."[92] With every marriage, Yoruba men run and hide from the mythistorical Orò of Something Scarce that accompanies their brides. That men must flee their betrothed also serves as a reminder to men that they can only experience continuity and immortality with the agreement of women because Woman is Mother is God. Indeed, after their union produces children, her new husband asks Something Scarce what she wants and she replies, "Everything you have."[93] This exchange is reminiscent of that between Òrúnmìlà and Àwọn Ìyàmi Òṣòròngà in Ogbè Ògúndá, when after testing the community with riddles and catch-22s, Òrúnmìlà reaches a *détente* with Ìyàmi after he admits that "all the things he owns, are to become hers."[94] Indeed, what does one give to the woman who has and is everything? Recognition.

The ìtàn of Something Scarce resonates on many levels; in addition to revealing that Something Scarce is, in fact, Orò, she is clearly an Àjẹ́ whose destiny is to elevate without a male partner. Because her father contravenes divine law—perhaps to consolidate his terrestrial and political power—the chief of Ejigbó, along with everything in Something Scarce's path, becomes the sacrifice necessary for her to alter the development of her divinity. The chief of Ejigbó becomes the first victim of Orò whose remains are not seen.

Rather than women being terrorized by a masculine Orò, Orò is revealed to be pure raw Àjẹ́. Orò uses her Àjẹ́ in concert with her Ọ̀rọ̀ (Power of the Word) to reshape her destiny and that of everyone and everything in her vicinity. Orò exercises her linguistic skills masterfully and uses Ọ̀rọ̀ to conceal complete devastation in a song that promises domestic bliss. Orò's Ọ̀rọ̀ is so effective that she never has to cook ogunmọ for the chief of Ejigbó or do anything else for him. The chief of Ejigbó's male counterparts learn from his encounter and cater as carefully to Orò as babaláwo do to Odù and the coveted Igbádù. It is also important to note that, similar to Odù and Ìyàmi Òṣòròngà, Something Scarce does not sacrifice: She is the dominant force who owns "everything you have"— from trees to markets to men's lives. Bascom notes that in another ẹsẹ concerning Something Scarce, the chief of Ejigbó is synonymous with Egúngún.[95] Odù gave men Egúngún as a gift, but Àjẹ́ remain the owners and overseers of the force. Perhaps the ìtàn of Something Scarce are Odù's reminders to a power-hungry patriarchy: Remember and respect the source of your power, because she is also the controller of your destiny.

My assertion that Orò is a melding of undiluted Àjẹ́ and Ọ̀rọ̀ is brilliantly confirmed in the ìtàn of Olùfọn. Olùfọn and Ọbalùfọn, which both mean "Law-giver," are oríkì for Ọbàtálá, but they can refer to terrestrial rulers as well. In a sixteen cowries ẹsẹ of Òsá, Olùfọn is told that he must buy a slave and make her his wife in order to have children. Olùfọn buys Orò, but when he brings her home, all she says is "What is Olufon? Olufon Bah!"[96] One of the most obvious issues of importance in this ẹsẹ is the inappropriateness of the term "slavery" to define certain interpersonal relationships among the Yoruba. Orò not only defies the definition of "slave" but she also views the institution of marriage with contempt. Her unions with the chief of Ejigbó and Olùfọn are by force, not by choice, so she expresses her outrage through Òrò. Her rebuff of Olùfọn is so resonant that it is memorialized in the sound of the groaning bullroarers. While Orò may have come to be largely associated with patriarchs, "Olufon Bah!" constitutes a complete rejection of patriarchal power. With her denunciation, Orò informs the "Law Giver" of his significance *vis-à-vis* The Law. Orò's Òrò may also serve as a reminder that Orò's justice does not discriminate, and its enforcers must be mindful of their actions lest the bullroarer whir for them.

Ẹsẹ Ogbè-wòrì in Bascom's *Ifa Divination* reveals that Orò, Ọbalùfọn, and Àjẹ́ share an intimate bond. In this verse, Àjẹ́ is honored with the oríkì Wherever Honor Turns She Finds Wealth.[97] In addition to boasting a power that is unsurpassed on Earth—and she sacrifices to ensure her dominion— Wherever Honor Turns She Finds Wealth is the child of "Those Who Make Oro and Who Make Obalufon" ("A ṣ(e)-Oro ṣ(e)-Obalufon").[98] Although Bascom translates *ṣe* as "worship," ṣe means, "to do, to act, to make, to cause, to be."[99] The difference between worshipping a God and making or causing a God to be is important to comprehending the connection between Wherever Honor Turns She Finds Wealth's mother and Orò. Wherever Honor Turns She Finds Wealth is Àjẹ́. The progenitors of Àjẹ́, in this context, are Mọlẹ̀, also known as Ẹdan, and her mother, Imọlẹ̀, which is also the name of the ancient Yoruba system of governance. As Adeoye's research confirms, when Ẹdan cleansed Ifẹ̀ and initiated everyone into Ògbóni, she created Àjẹ́ so that the Mothers could ensure human beings' compliance with Imọlẹ̀'s Law. This is the lineage to which the ẹsẹ refers.

Orò and Ọbalùfọn often appear together in orature because they work as a team in reality. Orò is the ultimate manifestation of judgment in action or Law. The Ọbalùfọn is the terrestrial administrator of law or the "law giver"; as it relates to divinity, the title signifies the "god of peace of the kingdom."[100] A society can enjoy peace only when the Law prevails, and the ẹsẹ of Ogbè-wòrì confirms that Àjẹ́ is the central hub of administrative power around which Orò and Ọbalùfọn, and Ògbóni and Egúngún, as well, revolve. Rather than a human woman worshipping Orò, which implies hierarchy and subservience, the ẹsẹ of Ogbè-wòrì is describing Àjẹ́'s centrality and indispensability to the Mọlẹ̀ judiciary. What is more, rather than an evil aberration or a rouge force, Àjẹ́ is so esteemed and essential that it is heralded the literal embodiment of Honor (Ọlá) upon whom Wealth (Ọlà) is showered.

Some scholars may assert that these ẹsẹ are merely metaphors for Orò's spiritual force or for bullroarer technology; however the historical, gendered, and ontological significance of Orò is evident in the conclusion of the ẹsẹ featuring Olùfọn and Orò, which states that the man for whom the verse is cast must sacrifice "so that his wife may not surpass him."[101] This is the same fear of the phenomenal wife that surfaces in *Ifism* in regards to Ọ̀yẹ̀kú Méjì's mother and that taints ẹsẹ Ọ̀sá Méjì of "The Rise and Fall." That this issue recurs in Yoruba orature reveals the immutable power of Àjẹ́ and its natural inclination for elevation. The fear that some men have of fully self-actualized women and the efforts to which they will go to subordinate those women are evidence of a patriarchal insecurity that may be rooted in the antagonism, nihilism, and self-hatred fomented by colonial and neocolonial oppression. The concerns expressed in these ẹsẹ smack of defeated men parroting alien, oppressive, colonial mores rather than sons glorying in the holistically enriching powers of their Mothers.

The compulsion to shutter a woman's horizon of possibilities is not an aspect of the traditional Yoruba ethos, and every Òrìṣà, Àjẹ́, and institution that I discuss in this book offers ample evidence of that. However, the fact that elements of the Yoruba patriarchy have employed Ifá to justify and facilitate the suppression of Àjẹ́ and women is significant. It reveals the rapidity and ease with which spiritual systems can become organized religions that foment oppression. The desire of men to delimit women's power is a misogynistic egomaniacal preoccupation that completely ignores the fact that a wife's success directly benefits her children, her partner, their family, the community, the nation, and the world. Relationships are not constructed in such a way that only one member of a family can enjoy success or only one partner in a relationship can exercise power. Women's successes do not come at the expense of men's. However, it is the case that individuals who invest their energies in oppressing others do not have the means or time to develop their own gifts or enjoy self-actualization.

Attempts to restrict the roles of women in Yoruba society will be as fruitless as attempts to ignore women's relationship with Orò. In addition to the influence of Ìyá Orò, who represents women in the Orò society,[102] Ulli Beier in "Gelede Masks" reveals that Orò society is governed by the Ìyáláṣẹ̀: "Even the dreaded Oro society must ask permission from her, before they can come out to perform their ceremonies, or before they can proceed to execute a death sentence, which is their special prerogative."[103] Beier finds that Orò's subordination to Ìyáláṣẹ̀ "applies only to the male

Orò. In this particular part of Yoruba country [Beier does not specify the region] there is also a female Orò, which is not known elsewhere. The female Oro do not have to ask permission from Iyalashe before they come out."[104] Despite assertions to the contrary, Àjẹ́'s relationship with Orò is as undeniable as it is fundamental.

Àjẹ́, The Power of the Throne

The Àjẹ́ that undergirds Orò, Ògbóni, Ẹdan, and the existence of every human being also controls the creation and revocation of Yoruba rulers. Samuel M. Opeola asserts that the Yoruba Ọba system, the literal making of kings, was created and is maintained by Àjẹ́.[105] Àjẹ́'s role in king-making and king-termination likely stems from their acknowledged position as the creators and maintainers of existence. Given the significance of Àwọn Ìyá Wa to Yoruba cosmology, ontology, and social stability, it is logical that women would rule and be central to the administration of nations. Indeed, by many accounts, the first rulers of the Yoruba world were women. In "Women, Rituals, and Politics in Pre-colonial Yorubaland," Biodun Adediran offers a list of female rulers that includes Olokun, Yemoo, Aje, Osara, Moremi, Luwo and, possibly, Ajiboyede and Orompoto.[106] With the names Olokun, Yemoo, and Aje (most likely Àjẹ́, the God of Wealth) the line between Gods and humans is blurred, and this speaks to the inherent divinity of Africana people in general and Àjẹ́ in particular.

Although female rulers saw a sharp decline after the 16th century when the patriarchal shift was in full swing, the Mothers used òdì orientation to submerge their powers and direct destinies covertly. A Yoruba adage asserts that "*Àpọ́nlé ò si f'ọba tí kò l'ólorì*": "An ọba without a wife in his domain (palace) is neither respected nor honoured by his subjects."[107] Yoruba palaces are filled with women, and while they are often labeled "wives" few of them are. The majority of the women who surround Yoruba rulers are royal officials who constitute an Àjẹ́ conglomerate from whom the sovereign obtains wisdom, advice, authority, and power. Some would even argue that the Palace Women are the power controlling the throne. What is more, it is not only the ruler who is empowered by Àjẹ́; Adediran reveals that all male palace officials have authorizing female agents known as "official mothers."[108]

The importance of official mothers to Yoruba rulers is evident in Peter Morton-Williams' recollections of the court of the Aláàfin of Ọ̀yọ́: "[N]o man was ever alone with the king, and whatever other men might be there, at least one *Ayaba* would always be in attendance, and she would rank senior to the man received in audience and command his deference."[109] Marveling at the wall of Woman surrounding the sovereign, Adediran exclaims, "It was as if men could not be trusted with the safety of the *Alaafin*!"[110] The ruler cannot be trusted with men whose ambitions may be as dangerous as glass shards, so like the iron kernel safely tucked into the core of Ẹdan, the ruler is surrounded by the protecting gold of Royal Mothers.

The protection of Àjẹ́ is a perfect protection; consequently, there is a Palace Woman to attend to every and any need the ruler will have. The Ààrẹ Orí Ìtẹ́, which means the Chief Overseer of the Sovereign, ensures the ruler's "domestic comfort" and is "constantly by his side" during public appearances.[111] The ruler's chief physician and pharmacist is Ìyá Ilé Àgbo, which means Mother of the Home of Medicines.[112] The Ààrẹ Orí Ìtẹ́ and Ìyá Ilé Àgbo together comprise a sealed Igbá of protection, health, and power that fortifies the king's body and mind.

One of the most notable Palace Women is Ìyá Ọba, the King's Mother. Because of the powerful biological, spiritual, and emotional bonds they share, a birth mother can easily influence her son; consequently, "If his mother happens to be living when he is called to the throne, she is asked to 'go to sleep,' and is decently buried in the house of a relative in the city."[113] This custom emphasizes the impact of curvilinear time in Yoruba society. "Sleep" is not a euphemism, and death is not the end. The womb is the literal and spiritual pathway to and from Ọ̀run and Ayé, and the journeys it facilitates are timeless; consequently, those who "go to sleep" awaken in the spiritual realm and can eventually be reborn in the material realm.

With the biological mother in the spiritual realm, Ìyá Ọba performs essential duties for the king. According to Adediran, Ìyá Ọba "was the only other person present with the *Alaafin* when the *Basorun* divined the king's spiritual condition to determine whether or not the *Alaafin* was fit to continue as king."[114] Ìyá Ọba is present when Ifá determines that an empty calabash or one filled with parrot's eggs must be prepared for the ruler. She may be the individual who prepares those calabashes: This would be appropriate because Ìyá Ọba represents the ruler's literal and figurative doorway to and from existence from the moment he is crowned.

In addition to his Official Mother, the ruler has an Ìyá Kékeré, which means "Little Mother." The diminutive title actually belies a formidable power, as Adediran's research reveals:

> [Ìyá Kékeré] was head of the scores of officials (both male and female) called *ilari*, for it was in her apartment that each *ilari* was created and the guardian spirit was kept. In this capacity, apart from ensuring the safety of the *Alaafin*, the *Iya Kekere* had a restraining influence on most palace officials including the *osi ofa*, the most influential palace official. In addition, the *Iya Kekere*

wielded immense power because she was in charge of the king's treasures, the royal regalia including the crown and other state paraphernalia. These latter duties put her in a position that gave her approval for all state receptions.[115]

Perhaps to properly galvanize and magnify her Àjẹ́ and to focus her mind fully on the spiritual-political duties of her station, Ìyá Kékeré is celibate for the duration of her term. As the person who maintains the spirits of the royals and the state's religious icons, Ìyá Kékeré is the Mother of sovereign and state. Her power is so complete that she could prevent "the holding of any state reception" if displeased with the king.[116] It is crucial that Ìyá Kékeré's mind is properly and completely focused.

The Yoruba political system is fully and inextricably entwined with its spiritual system. Àjẹ́, who are essential to the functions of every Yoruba spiritual society, are logically the center of the Yoruba polity. Adediran finds that the rites for "two major cults—those of *Orun* and *Sango*" are controlled by "*Iya Oba, Iya Naso, Iya Monari,* and *Iya Afin Iku*."[117] Given that women are the owners of the road to Ọ̀run, it is appropriate that they control the propitiation and worship of Ọ̀run. Àjẹ́ are heralded as those who know when life will cease to exist because they hold the umbilical cords, long livers, and spiritual life lines of humanity in their hands. Àjẹ́'s knowledge of the duration and their control of the sovereign's life is evident in the rituals essential to king-making and king-termination and in the royal mother who bears the title Ìyá Aláàfin Ikú, Mother of the Aláàfin's Death. What is more, certain Àjẹ́ have duties that place them on par with Orò's executioners. In *The History of the Yorubas*, Samuel Johnson reveals that Ìyá Mọnari's duties include executing "by strangling any Shango worshipper condemned to capital punishment, as they are not to die by the sword."[118] Clearly, these titles are not empty honorifics; these positions can only be held by phenomenally and multiply empowered Àjẹ́.

Women such as Erelú and Yèyé Olorí, the latter being the king's elder counselor, adjudicate matters and act as intermediaries between the king, the Ìrúnmọlẹ̀, and Ògbóni. The Ògbóni society forms the crux of state governance, and Anyebe elaborates on the society's power and the centrality of Àjẹ́ therein:

> Ogboni wielded political, judicial, and religious powers in Yoruba land. This means, in effect that the governance of the Yoruba kingdom as a whole rested with that cult. Its meetings were held within the Palace. *The Alafin, again strangely, participated in the meetings through a woman member.* The priest[s] of Ogboni played a vital role in the installation ceremonies of a new Alafin.

Their duties included ensuring that the powers of the ancestors of the Alafin were transmitted to him.[119]

The vaguely referenced "woman member" is Ọbagùntẹ, who, quite simply, is the king as far as Ògbóni is concerned. Samuel Johnson reveals that "Obagunte . . . represents the King in the Ògbóni house on ordinary occasions, her work being strictly connected with that fraternity. She enters the Ògbóni chamber on all occasions and acts in the King's name, reporting to his majesty the events of each day's sitting. Whenever the King wishes to entertain the Ogbonis, she has to undertake that duty."[120] The fact that Ọbagùntẹ is the link connecting the king to Ògbóni speaks volumes about the degree to which women exert power and represent reserve, respect, and influence on every level of Yoruba politics.

The roles of Àjẹ́ in molding and maintaining sovereigns, spiritual systems, and societies are fully interconnected, and they are comprehensive and include all aspects of existence. Adediran elucidates the indispensability of women to Yoruba religious, social, political, and spiritual life. He finds that "[a]ll shrines had female officials attached to them whether or not they had priests. The duty of the female officials was usually to represent the king's interest and ensure that the deities in the care of men were properly propitiated. In many other cases, the female officials themselves performed the propitiation ceremonies."[121] Everywhere one finds a shrine, an Ilédì, an ojúbọ, a sacred grove, or a God—from Ṣàngó to Ògún from Yemọja to Ọṣun—one finds a woman; indeed, one *must* find a woman. Even when the care of a God has been placed in the hands of a man, a Mother is present to monitor his efforts.

The significance of Àjẹ́ is evident throughout all political and spiritual strata. Adediran makes the important observation that "although the worship of *Ifa* was basically a male affair, the *Iya Mole* was the *Alaafin's* personal *Ifa* priestess and head of all *Ifa* priests."[122] It is fitting that the title of this royal supreme iyaláwo is Ìyá Mọlẹ̀, for she is the mother who oversees all oaths taken, and she holds all mysteries. Ìyá Mọlẹ̀ provides more evidence as to the logicality and necessity of iyaláwo in the Yoruba ethos. The fact that Ìyá Mọlẹ̀ is the head of all royal babaláwo emphasizes my contention that every man, no matter how old, wise, or powerful, is but a son before every woman.

That the matrifocality of Yoruba society did not end with patrification but merely assumed a different form, one that protected the mothers, is evident in the diverse and important roles of Palace Women who exercise varying degrees of power depending upon the societies in which they rule. The women of the Ondo Empire are especially noteworthy in this regard. The Lobun of Ondo boasts her own separate palace, holds court independent of the Osemawe (male ruler), and has a court that consists of joint male-female chiefs. The Lobun is more than the equal of her male counterpart; as Adediran reveals, the Lobun "not only reigned with the *Osemawe* but actually ruled."[123]

The Yoruba kingdom of Idaisa in present-day Benin Republic also boasts a palace filled with Àjẹ́. The Ina, "mothers of the kings," of Idaisa can become kings in their own right.[124] However, an Ina does not need to be a crowned sovereign in order to rule: Her rule is an inherent aspect of the government. Adediran describes Àjẹ́'s role in Benin politics as central and essential:

> No male chief could voice an opinion without prior consultation with his female counterpart. For instance, any state decision that emanated from the palace was the consensual opinion of the male chiefs headed by the *Jagun* and the female cabinet headed by the *Ina-Jagun*. This is because of the belief that the female chiefs had the control of the inner essence (*Ori*) of the male chiefs. Given this situation, female chiefs actually formulated state policy, since what the male chiefs expressed as their opinion was often the opinion of the *Ina* [Mothers]. Even the king as head of state could not discountenance with the opinion of the *Ina-Jagun*. Usually the oldest woman in the palace, the *Ina-Jagun* was the embodiment of the history and customs of the royal lineage.[125]

The Ina oversee a carefully tiered, fully articulated, and socially and politically comprehensive system of governance that perfectly displays the classic Mother-son Àjẹ́ dynamic.

Before they occupy positions of privilege in the palace, Yoruba females are necessarily introduced to, initiated into, and steeped in the powers that they will wield. According to Adediran: "In different parts of Yorubaland women, especially those above the age of puberty, are initiated into powerful cultic groups such as *Egungun* (*Iya Agan*), the bull roar cult (*Iya Oro*), the *Gelede* cult (*Iyanla*), the *Ogboni Erelu*, etc."[126] Adediran offers additional confirmation that women are not barred from sacred societies but are the Mothers (Ìyá) of those societies. He goes on to assert that "[w]hether a female ruler was on the throne or not, the female chiefs constituted an important fulcrum of state administration. For instance, the affairs of the dynastic group were almost totally left in the hands of the female chiefs."[127]

The power of Àjẹ́ is so obvious, ubiquitous, and undeniable in the Yoruba world that it becomes clear that the myth of male domination is nothing more than smoke and mirrors that, like the lies about Àjẹ́, are the work of patriarchal myth makers. It seems to be the case that certain individuals created a Yoruba "history" that was designed to subjugate or eliminate Yoruba women—especially Àjẹ́—and what they wrote was echoed so often by so many that blatant lies became accepted truths which became stereotypes. It may also be the case that Àjẹ́ looked centuries ahead, saw eras of cyclic destructions swirling, and decided that the best way to preserve their control, exercise their influence, and guide their nations was through òdì. With a patriarchal figurehead in place and serving as a resplendent distraction, the Mothers could attend to the real business of state maintenance.

Àjẹ́: The Creators of Kings

The power of Àjẹ́ in the Yoruba palace is revealed in stunning detail in the rituals for making and deposing kings. Because of their control over and knowledge of the span of human existence, Àjẹ́ know when a sitting ruler will "go to sleep" and when to begin preparations for the next ruler to ascend the throne. The rituals for king-making are inextricably bound to the rituals for king-termination, and this reveals the eternal power of curvilinearity which is a cornerstone of the African ethos. Whether their termination is mandated by political necessity or physical decline, deposed kings do not die in the Western sense of the word: They go to sleep, and they awaken physically and spiritually through a series of rituals that bind them to all of their predecessors and that connect them to all of their successors. Such unification may take place through a ritual described by Ulli Beier, who finds that in certain Yoruba kingdoms, the Ọba-to-be "is made to eat the heart of the deceased Oba, during the installation ceremonies."[128]

The Ìyálásẹ̀ plays a profoundly important role in the making of kings. Ìyálásẹ̀ is the Mother of the Gẹ̀lẹ̀dẹ́ shrine; Lawal describes her as "the highest priestess and . . . overall head of the [Gẹ̀lẹ̀dẹ́] society," as well as "the intermediary between Ìyá Nlá and members of the society and community at large."[129] Any major undertaking or event must be approved by Ìyálásẹ̀. Ìyálásẹ̀ is the linchpin of some the most powerful Yoruba organizations: She is the head of the Gẹ̀lẹ̀dẹ́ society; Orò must have her permission before undertaking its rituals; and she is central to Egúngún society, because she ensures the dead reach full transmigration as ancestors. In line with her work of catalyzing power and fomenting actualization, Beier finds that it is the Ìyálásẹ̀, the supreme embodiment of àṣẹ and Àjẹ́, "who takes out the heart of a deceased Oba and gives it to the new one. Thus the 'mothers' also control the installation of kings, and the king must become a member of the Gelede Society himself."[130] This information has relevance beyond the role of Àjẹ́ in king-making; it reveals that rather than Orò, Ògbóni, Egúngún, and Gẹ̀lẹ̀dẹ́ being isolated esoteric cults or entertaining frolics, these institutions are inextricably interconnected by the Àjẹ́ who empower and administer them, and each of these societies is essential to the political, social, cultural, and spiritual evolution and elevation of Yoruba society.

The making of Yoruba rulers is an intricate process that varies depending upon the empire and the title of the ruler. Awo Fatunmbi states that the Ọ̀ọ̀ni of Ifẹ̀'s ascendancy to the throne involves initiation into Ògbóni and multiple initiations into "the mysteries of Odù."[131] This process is likely overseen by Palace Women called the Odù Council, who Fatunmbi finds exercise "considerable power within the court."[132] Below, Peter Morton-Williams describes the process by which Ògbóni ensure continuity among the sovereigns of Ọ̀yọ́:

> The Ogboni priests have a part in the ceremonies following the death of a king and during the installation of his successor. In Oyo they are summoned to the palace as soon as an Alafin has died and attend while the corpse is washed, then they cut off its head and take it to clean all the flesh from the skull. A palace official removes the heart and puts it in charge of the Otun Ẹfa, the titled eunuch responsible for the Ṣango cult. During his installation the succeeding Alafin is taken by the Otun Ẹfa to make a sacrifice to Ṣango and while with him is given a dish containing the heart of his predecessor, which he must eat. Later, he is taken to the Ogboni shrine where the Oluwo hands him the skull of his predecessor, which has been filled with a corn gruel which he must drink. This rite is said to enable his ears always to discriminate between the true and the false, and to give compelling power to his words. Thus, the death of an Alafin cannot be concealed from the Ogboni, and his successor cannot be properly installed without their acceptance and collaboration.[133]

In a curvilinear unification rite that marries the literal and the symbolic, the succeeding ruler ingests not only the power and wisdom of his predecessor, but that of all of the Ọba of the lineage, each having undergone the same ritual as directed by Àjẹ́.

In *Aké: The Years of Childhood*, Wole Soyinka discusses king-making in Aké. He reveals that the process is called "'je oba', and this, we informally gathered was to be taken literally. When the old king died, his heart and liver were removed and the new king was required to eat them."[134] Jẹ ọba reveals another technique by which Àjẹ́ extend the livers of humanity beyond their physical use and the terrestrial sphere into the cosmic realm where the Mothers hold, control, direct, and protect every aspect of existence. The fact that Yoruba rulers must undertake the same acts that are widely attributed to the Mothers—eating human liver and much more—is rather ironic. However, it is important to understand that these rituals cannot be defined as cannibalism; they are sacred rites that certain individuals must undertake to become part of an eternal coterie. These rituals also serve to place every ruler directly under the command of the Mothers who are the literal and cosmic holders of the long livers, hearts, and souls of every Yoruba sovereign.

The fact that the rituals necessary to make kings are not meant to be understood by the general populace is evident in Soyinka's description of his consternation and disbelief that the Aláké, the same person who "had taken me on his lap and claimed I was his *yekan* [*yèkan*, relative] had actually eaten human flesh."[135] To add to his confusion, instead of finding gore and blood on the Aláké's mouth, Soyinka finds only lips stretching into a "warm, crinkly smile."[136] The smile that so mystifies Soyinka is powered by the mirth of every Aláké to ascend the throne. However, as I discuss in chapter five, neither his genial smile nor the power of his progenitors can protect the Aláké when Àwọn Ìyá Wa unite, make Orò, and introduce the Aláké to his Mother, the Law.

King-making involves many rigorous and important rituals besides jẹ ọba. Using the tone and language with which a son would discuss his mother, fine artist and royal family member James Isola Adedayo reveals that Àjẹ́ are the indispensable overseers and administrators of these rites:

> The palace women are regarded as the kingmakers because the king can never make himself, and no other person can make a king. So, these women are powerful, superior. They can do and undo. They give authority. . . . If you don't follow the orders of these people, those women, there isn't anything that is possible. . . . We don't neglect them at all. We can't overlook them. We regard them as our mothers, as the elderly women. So they are very important in the making of the king as well as performing traditional rites and performing rituals to the deities and ancestors.[137]

Adedayo reveals that when a new Ọba is selected, he must go into confinement for three months. The confinement period is called Olófi and the secret and sacred place where Olófi occurs is also called Olófi. Olófi means The Source of All Laws. Olófi has also been described as being synonymous with Olófin, which means Law Giver, which shares stations with, but is distinct from, Aláàfin, which means "king, one who owns the palace."[138] To be clear, *òfin* is translated as "law, commandment," whereas *ààfin* is "king's place, court."[139] It would appear, then, that before a person can reside in and preside over a palace or be trusted to articulate and enforce law, he or she must go to and receive authorization from the Law Giver, Olófi.

Every aspect, ritual, and detail of Olófi is overseen and administered by Àjẹ́, and only Àjẹ́ can direct these rites because they are the guardians and representatives of the law of Onílẹ̀, Odù, Ẹdan, and Orò. Àwọn Ìyá Wa guide the Ọba-to-be to Olófi where he will "be made to know his ancestors, he'll be made to see them, hear them talk to them converse with them. There he'll be given the power of authority to rule. Until an Ọba is given such things, he's not yet an Ọba."[140] As Adedayo elucidates, the Ọba candidate meets his royal Ìṣẹ̀ṣe: including past rulers, Egúngún, and Gods. With the act of meeting and gaining wisdom from one's Ìṣẹ̀ṣe, one's progenitors, the centrality of Onílẹ̀, the Mother and Owner of the Earth, comes to the fore yet again. The third party who witnesses everything is not at all symbolical or metaphorical: She is real; she is accessible; she is Olófin. The ancestors resident within the womb of Ilẹ̀ become one with Her and Àwọn Ìyá Wa, and together they constitute The Law and confer the ultimate authority.

Adedayo reveals that the Palace Women conduct rituals to determine the nature of the Ọba's reign. They prepare numerous àrokò of culturally and spiritually significant symbols such as corn, iron, eggs, and snails. These àrokò are knotted into white cloths and enclosed in from seven to twenty-one calabashes. The Mothers blindfold the Ọba-initiate and place before him a calabash filled with knotted àrokò. The candidate selects a knot, and the Mothers interpret its contents before they offer him another calabash from which he chooses another sign of rule. When this process is complete, the Mothers will know precisely what is in store for the society.

Following the determination of the ruler's reign, the Ọba undergoes a ritual that provides him with the opportunity to "talk to the past Ọbas about their time of Ọbaship, problems, encounters."[141] With this revelation Adedayo provides stunning evidence that those who "sleep" do, indeed, awaken in other realms and continue their curvilinear work. In addition to consulting with his predecessors, Adedayo reveals that the Ọba-to-be learns the "days of divinities, when to worship the Òrìṣà, what kind of ritual will be given them, [and] the time to perform it. Then he will agree to be pleasing these divinities every day of the year except one day only in the year where there is no sacrifice, no worship of divinities, and it is the Ọba alone who knows this day. So these women will be in charge of all these things."[142]

The Palace Women oversee every aspect of the sovereign's consecration and preparation. They divine to determine how long the Ọba will rule. They educate him on what is taboo for him to eat or even touch. The Mothers give the Ọba-initiate a ritual bath and cleanse and anoint him. His head undergoes an additional process in which the mothers shave it, and after seven days, they bathe it in snail water so that the Ọba will have the calm and discerning temperament essential for his office. Adedayo emphasizes that "[o]nce he is given the power and authority to rule, it will be through these people [the Palace Women]. They are always there."[143] Indeed, Àjẹ́ prepare and empower the Adénlá, the Great Crown, itself, and Ìyá Moṣade must be "present at the installation of any chief," for she alone can crown the Ọba.[144]

Royal crowns are intricate spiritual-material constructions, and their empowering elements are hidden from view and from the knowledge of the sovereign. While the Ọba can never know what empowers his orí through òdì, the owners and controllers of that power are evident to all, for Ẹyẹ Àjẹ́ are stationed all about the crown, and they watch the actions of the Ọba, his court, and his constituents. The Ẹyẹ Àjẹ́ that adorn the Adénlá represent the fact that the Ọba rules only with the support of the Mothers. Just as the Ẹyẹ Àjẹ́ crown his Orí, the ruler's closest allies are, logically, the Mothers who created him. In a profound system of checks and balances and multilayered protections of multiple levels of powerwielders, the Ọba has a collective of Mothers who can prognosticate, articulate, and answer his every query.

While the Yoruba maxim states that a king who does not have a woman by his side will not be respected, it appears to be the case that no king can exist unless he is selected, molded, crowned, and directed by Mother Creators. The fact that only the Mothers can create a king is a logical extension of the fact that only a mother can birth a son. And the phrase "king-making" should be taken literally, for the Palace Women are carefully creating an entity with rules, mores, customs, and needs that differ from those of a mere mortal, and this divine creation is truly and necessarily made in his Mothers' image.

Colonization and the forced implementation of destructive puppet governments led to a decline in the powers of Ọba, Aláàfin, and Ọ̀ọ̀ni and their courts. The reader will note that in many cases when historians discuss the traditional Yoruba judiciary they do so in the past tense. I use the present tense because while the traditional forms of governance and the power of the palace may not be what they once were, in many cases they still exist and remain active, vital, and central elements of Yoruba society. Even with the changes wrought by time, one can be sure that if a Yoruba society has a throne, the Mothers are the power that is either behind or upon it. Furthermore, whether there is a throne or not, Àjẹ́ will always constitute the cornerstone and compass of Yoruba society.

Egúngún

The process by which Àjẹ́ create rulers reveals that the man who is made by the Mothers is able to stand with confidence on the wisdom and with the approval of the Ancients. The roles of the Ancients in king-making highlight the abiding presence and indisputable power of Egúngún in Yoruba cosmontology. Egúngún is an inherently gender-balanced force because human parents are of both genders. Odù is credited with founding the ritual worship of Egúngún, and she ensured gender harmony by decreeing that men would wear the mask and embody Egúngún while women would dance unadorned along with Egúngún. Odù also decreed that Àjẹ́ must authorize Egúngún's appearance and oversee its every move, and this reflects the fact that "Women have more power on the earth."[145]

Despite Odù's attempt at ensuring gender balance, some supporters of patriarchy attempt to depict women as being excluded from Egúngún. In *Egúngún among the Ọ̀yọ́ Yoruba*, S. O. Babayemi argues, "Few women know its mysteries and such women are not to divulge the secrets of the cult. . . . They adhere to the saying b'óbìnrin mawo, kò gbọ́dọ̀ wi (If a woman knows cult secrets, she must never tell)."[146] Attempts to obfuscate women's knowledge of and participation in Egúngún are intriguing because Àwọn Ìyá Wa are as integral to Egúngún as they are to Ògbóni, Orò, and existence. Not only is Egúngún dependent on Ẹyẹ Ọ̀rọ̀, but, were it not for the Mothers, there would be no Egúngún. As the Odù Ifá and biology make clear, "Women brought you into this world[;] this is what makes us human."[147] Women are necessary participants in the worship and rituals of Egúngún because they are essential to existence. Babayemi asserts: "[E]verybody has at least one ancestor to call upon."[148] We have that ancestor—and any and all others—because of the choices made by our mothers.

Babayemi moves beyond the patriarchy's proverbs and power grabs to confirm not only that women are full participants in Egúngún rituals and celebrations, but also that some females enter the world as members of the society while others are titled office holders:

> Iyámode and Yèyésòrun are the most senior women titles in the cult. Ato is an initiated member of the cult. There is a tradition that every female child born with her cord placed on the chest like Atori whip is called Ato. Another tradition says that Ato is the child born with membranes covering her head like a masque, if a male, he will be called Amusan. In Egbado, the female title-holders in the cult are the Iya Agan, Otun Iya Agan and Iyameko. Yet another tradition says that the third child of a triplet is called Ato if female, while the first and the second are called Tayewo and Kehinde respectively. The third child of a triplet is naturally an initiated member of egúngún cult.[149]

The various ways by which daughters, in particular, are literally born into Egúngún debunks the assertion that "few women know its mysteries." Àjẹ́ *is* Egúngún's mystery; indeed, while children are in the womb and making their way to the world, Àjẹ́ are in the birth canal with them determining who among them shall be honored with special roles in Egúngún.

The Òrìṣà Àjẹ́ who oversees the selection and preparation of newborn daughters for their roles in Egúngún is most likely Yemòó. Yemòó is symbolized by the egg and "the womb that gives birth to all."[150] John Mason states that the umbilical cord and navel are sacred to Yemòó, and, echoing the findings of Babayemi, Mason also asserts that Yemòó's placement of the umbilical cord on the child's belly determines if the child has come to Earth as Egúngún and the name that child should bear.[151]

Yemòó is also credited with formalizing takọ tabo, eéjì wà po by decreeing that women should not live in gender-exclusive relationships and communities if male counterparts are available.[152] That such a decree would be necessary speaks to the ease and apparent frequency with which Àjẹ́ establish harmonious and thriving societies apart from men. While it is possible for everyone to benefit from a balanced heterogeneous society, the only people who suffer when women form gender-exclusive communities are men. Yemòó's injunction is designed to benefit men; and her consideration for her sons is similar to that of Odù, who granted men Egúngún to appease them and give them a vestige of women's all-encompassing power. Yemòó's decree ensures that men have an honored role in the establishment and protection of the mother-child dyad that results in empowered Egúngún.

Odù and Yemòó are not the only Àjẹ́ who empower Egúngún. As I discuss in *Our Mothers, Our Powers, Our Texts*, Ọya is recognized as the literal mother of Egúngún. In her quest to have children, Ọya sacrificed a multi-colored cloth, which is the hallmark of both Àjẹ́ and Egúngún, and she gave birth to nine children, all of whom emerged from the womb encased in the caul or amniotic sac in the way of Ato and Amusan.[153] Ọya's signature and signifying number is nine, so it is fitting that Ọya's ninth child became Egúngún.[154]

The relationship between mother Ọya and child Egúngún is so close that these two entities amalgamate into a fearsome force, as J. Olumide Lucas describes in *The Religion of the Yorubas*:

> Of all the Egunguns, Ọya is the most dreaded. Whenever he appears he is accompanied by a large band of Atọkuns or Escorts, and elderly men carrying whips. In front of the Egungun goes a band of women who are clad up to their waist, the remaining part being left bare.[155]

Ọya is heralded as the wife who is fiercer than the husband and who grows a beard on account of war.[156] But Ọya is not a man; she is the ultimate woman, and her empowered daughters, looking as if they just arrived from Ìlú Ọmú, the Town of Breasts about which Ibie writes, lead her Egúngún in the expansive regalia of Àjẹ́. With their breasts signifying the elemental creative, nutritional, and cosmic power they wield, Àwọn Ìyá Wa warn the community that oblivion awaits those foolish enough to violate or even gaze at length upon the force that is Woman.

When she is enraged and seeking vengeance, Ọya's face "is so terrible that none dare behold it, her wrath so devastating that it must be absolutely avoided."[157] This manifestation of Ọya is identical to Àgan, who is also known as Mafojukanmi (Do Not See My Face) and boasts a power indistinguishable from that of Orò. A divination verse introduces Àgan in the following manner:

> You must not see my face
> No one can ever see Orombo [Orò m bọ̀ lit.: Orò is coming]
> Whenever the Agan comes out at noon
> (A gale will rage) toppling trees upon trees
> And palms falling upon palms
> Dense forests are set ablaze
> And savanna fields are burnt down completely
> This Ifa divination is cast for Mafojukanmi
> Don't see my face – Who is called Agan.[158]

Àgan is Ọya-in-action, and like Orò, Àgan is Àjẹ́ and àṣẹ. As is customary of most powerful forces in the Yoruba world, it is Àjẹ́, manifest in this context as Ìyá Àgan and Ìyá Ọ̀tún Àgan, who determine when pure power need be summoned to cleanse the community. Àgan's similitude to Orò is evident in Babayemi's assessment that Àgan "rids the society of all forces of instability."[159] While there are distinct and obvious differences between Orò and Egúngún, Babayemi finds that they have the same origin and perform identical social and political functions.[160]

Similar to the Òrìṣà who have myriad origin texts, Egúngún boasts diverse ìtàn. In addition to the texts featuring divine Mothers, Egúngún boasts a human mother in Ìyámọ̀ṣè, an elder woman who, like Ọya was originally childless. Ìyámọ̀ṣè met Amusan who predicted that, despite her age, she would indeed bear a child. "Iyamose became pregnant and gave birth to Egun Anumi who founded the first Igbórí."[161]

The assertions that women have limited roles in Egúngún ring especially hollow in the light of the fact that ìtàn after ìtàn attribute Egúngún's existence and continuity to women—and to women alone. As is the case with the majority of Yoruba Gods and societies, the role of a "father" is nonexistent or negligible. By contrast, the womb and the Mothers recur in discussions of Egúngún's origin because without them Egúngún could not and would not exist—no ancestors can exist and no children can be born without Àjẹ́. What is more, the worship of Egúngún includes the celebration of mothers of Ọ̀run and Ayé and of the past and the present. Curvilinear reverence ensures that the unborn can be born, that they can manifest their destiny, and that they can become Egúngún, themselves.

Egúngún rituals revolve around Ọ̀rọ̀, Power of the Word, which is the birthright of women as a result of their ownership of Àjẹ́. During the Egúngún festival, male maskers tour the community and bestow blessings. The highlights of the festival are the dazzling, intricate, and complex feats of the Egúngún, who are guided by male directors and motivated by male drummers. This display of masculine creativity and prowess is complemented by women who use the palm-fronds sacred to Ògún and Nana Bùrúkù to clear and ritually cleanse the path for Egúngún and who "render melodious songs as the Egúngún dances, and when the Egúngún is relaxing or resting in a relative's compound."[162]

Egúngún festivals, which are gender-balanced and incorporate all community members, are a grand elaboration of the everyday rituals of mothers who bear in their mouths and memories the complete history of their families down to the oríkì of each relative. These mothers, who use their Ọ̀rọ̀ to transmit the oríkì, ìtàn, and orin of the lineage to their children, are absolutely essential to Egúngún. Without the mothers' history-rich odes, children would not know their ancestors or their ancestors' contributions to art, history, politics, science, medicine, and culture; children would not know the heights that they can and are expected to reach; and children would not know the most effective ways to instill expectations of excellence in their progeny.

As Babayemi reveals, Ọ̀rọ̀ and Egúngún are not mere sources of entertainment; they are utilitarian forces that invigorate, heal, and educate:

> Every wife of the lineage is expected to memorise as much as possible the lineage Oríkì. Each of them is to recite the portions she knows whenever her child is crying or is sick. This is meant to put life and vigour into the sick child and to assuage the child's pain. Old women in the lineage recite the Oríkì to greet young members. This is meant to inspire such lineage members to noble deeds. At festivals and in wars, women recite the lineage to invoke the spirits of the ancestors to support their survivors on earth.[163]

The recitation of oríkì through Ọ̀rọ̀ is more than a history lesson or roll call. The Àjẹ́ and àṣẹ that are resident in the chanter of the oríkì and in each word spoken also suffuse the names and deeds of the ancestors and the recipient of the utterance. The recitation of oríkì becomes not merely a prayer but the answer to a prayer. It marries sign to signifier, for when a mother sings an oríkì she is joined by the ancestors she invokes, and, together, they protect and prepare their child. The child whose existence is framed by her oríkì boasts knowledge of both her terrestrial forebears and celestial progenitors. The child possessed of her oríkì walks through life with her Egúngún surrounding her. And while her mother is not the only source for this elemental knowledge, she is its primary repository.

Rather than being ostracized from Egúngún, women can be found at all levels of the institution. Dele Layiwola confirms that "some of the highest initiates of the Egungun cult are still women. In the political headquarters of ancient Yoruba – Oyo – the head of the Egungun cult is the *Iyamode*. She is in charge of the royal mausoleum, she worships the spirits of dead kings and invokes their Egungun. . . . She is generally acknowledged as 'Father' and the king refers to her as his father."[164] Samuel Johnson in *The History of the Yorubas* further elucidates the relationship between the Ìyá Mọdẹ and the sovereign:

> The King looks upon her as his father, and addresses her as such, being the worshipper of the spirits of his ancestors. He kneels in saluting her, and she also returns the salutation kneeling, never reclining on her elbow as is the custom of the women in saluting their superiors. The King kneels for no one else but her, and prostrates before the god Sango, and before those possessed with the deity, calling them "father."[165]

The Ìyá Mọdẹ does not simply oversee the worship of the ruler's ancestors: She *is* those ancestors. The significance of Àjẹ́ is clear here: No man boasts the completion and perfection necessary to house, embody, and be the father—and all ancestors—of the king. Only the Ìyámọdẹ, the quintessential Àjẹ́, can fulfill these duties.

Johnson's reference to Ṣàngó takes one further into Yoruba history, deeper into the ellipsis of curvilinear time, and straight to the intersection of humanity and Divinity, as Ṣàngó is credited with appointing the first Ìyá Mọdẹ and placing her in charge of the worship of his father. Babayemi describes how Ṣàngó marshaled the powers of Àjẹ́ and àṣẹ to solidify his father's immortality:

> Ọràńyàn is believed to have died at Ifẹ̀ and his body turned into stone. Stone carving and terracotta were means of immortalizing the dead in Ifẹ̀ and this is believed to be the earliest personification of the spirits of ancestors in Yorùbáland. . . . Ṣàngó could not carry

> the corpse ofỌ̀rànyàn to Ọyọ, he is said to have therefore designed funeral obsequies for Ọ̀rànyàn at Ọyọ. He is reported to have brought the incarnated spirit of Ọ̀rànyàn to Bàrà (the royal mausoleum). He put the Iyámọ̀dé as the chief priestess and some other old women in the palace whom he termed Bàbá Bàrà (Fathers in Bàrà). The duty of Iyámọ̀dé and her associates Bàbá Bàrà was first to worship the spirit of Ọ̀rànyàn. Iyámọ̀dé was to communicate the wishes of Ọ̀rànyàn to Ṣàngó, and she was to call Ọ̀rànyàn's masquerade from a room called Ilérun, in Bàrà.[166]

Similar to the women who accompany the Ọya Egúngún processional, the women of Bàrà are chosen to be and to represent Ọ̀rànyàn because of the magnitude of their Àjẹ́. Furthermore, the term "Father" does not encompass all that these women are, for each is a Mother in whom a father is housed, in much the same way that the iron particle is contained in and protected by a womb of brass.

Babayemi goes on to reveal the origin of Ìyámọ̀dẹ and the Bàbá Bàrà, and his discussion offers evidence of yet another Ìlú Àjẹ́:

> Other traditions collected in Ọyọ say that Ṣàngó looked upon the women in Bàrà with great reverence for he is reported as prostrating for them. These women shaved their heads clean like men; they did not wear the bùbá (the Yoruba women's upper blouse), and the upper part of the wrapper they put on were tied to the body just above the breasts, the lower part touching the ground. Whenever they happened to leave Bàrà people treated them with awe. Whenever they visited the market, they looted any foodstuff they wanted, and whenever they visited the palace, palace women on their approach, pour water on the ground, shouting that their 'fathers' had come to visit them. Whatever these women demanded would be brought out with respect.[167]

From Babayemi's account, the women of Bàrà appear to have established an Ìlú Àjẹ́ just outside of the Ọ̀yọ́ Empire. Rather than wage war on them, Ṣàngó heralded these fully self-possessed women, who found the world deep and rich enough to nourish their divinity and way of life, as the most potent and important entities in his vicinity.

Ìlú Bàrà is yet another example (along with the Ìlú Ọmú/Ìlú Ẹléyẹ discussed in *Ifism*, the Ìlú Obirin detailed in *Sixteen Cowries*, and the town where women marry women discussed in *My Life in the Bush of Ghosts*) of an Ìlú Àjẹ́ in Yorubaland. While in some traditions Ọ̀ṣun or Ọ̀rúnmìlà are able to lure the women back to the heterogeneous society and other traditions find Yemòó enjoining women to find balance with men, it seems to be the case that many women routinely come to the realization that there are more fulfilling ways to live than navigating the truncated arc of existence hewn by patriarchal insecurity and inadequacy.

Given Àjẹ́'s diverse roles and profound impact on Egúngún, it is ironic that individuals would attempt to disassociate women from the society and even assert that Egúngún is a "witch hunter." If Egúngún is hunting "witches" and if "witch" is code for Àjẹ́, Egúngún is hunting and seeking to destroy its source and its self. However, the efforts to patrify Egúngún and paint it a supporter of misogyny are both recent and transparent. Dele Layiwola bucks the trend instituted by ideologues: In "Womanism in Nigerian Folklore," Layiwola describes Egúngún as originally being "a political tool used by women to boost and protect their status."[168]

After Egúngún was given to men by Odù, or was taken by men, depending on the mythistory, Akinwumi Isola asserts that women simply created another secret society—perhaps in the same way that after one Ìlú Àjẹ́ is reintegrated into the heterogeneous society another materializes. Isola records a "secular [song] used by women in solidarity rallies" that offers another version of the events that led to men's overt roles in Egúngún and that heralds the establishment of a woman-only and Àjẹ́-exclusive Egúngún:

> If you may be initiated into all other ancestor cults,
> You cannot be initiated into ours.
> Bundles of clothes belong to the masquerade
> Our mother controls the ancestors' cult
> Traitors!
> Traitors allowed men
> Into the sacred grove that fateful day
> If you may be initiated into all other ancestor cults,
> You cannot be initiated into ours.[169]

By declaring, "Our mother controls the ancestors' cult," the singers make it clear that while men may claim to have usurped it, Egúngún is still controlled by Àjẹ́. The song also contends that while men take center stage at Egúngún festivals, Àjẹ́ continue their sacred work in another society which, according to Isola, is called Nana Bùrúkù after the powerful Earth Mother God with Pan-African appeal.[170] The assertion that there is another Àjẹ́-exclusive Egúngún is not at all surprising given the discussions of an all-woman Orò and all-women towns. Perhaps Àjẹ́ have been using the myth of patriarchal usurpation and domination of Egúngún as a boisterous but protective shield for the mother of all secret societies.

Dance for Your Life

The campaign to remove women from Yoruba culture, secret societies, sacred institutions, politics, and life and to trivialize those women who are indispensable to these institutions has even made its way to Gẹ̀lẹ̀dẹ́, the society that is devoted to praising Àwọn Ìyá Wa. Babatunde Lawal's and Ulli Beier's findings on the specific roles of women in Gẹ̀lẹ̀dẹ́ reveal to outsiders what community members have always known: Women are not mere spectators; they are necessarily active agents in every stage of Gẹ̀lẹ̀dẹ́ festival. Indeed, Gẹ̀lẹ̀dẹ́ cannot be performed without the approval and participation of the Mothers. The centrality and indispensability of women to Gẹ̀lẹ̀dẹ́ is analogous to their roles in existence and in society.

Beier finds that "the most important [Gẹ̀lẹ̀dẹ́] dance is held in connection with the annual festival of ODUA."[171] Once again, the significance of Odúà, who is "the mother of all" and "the pure orisha" who "turns blood into children," is brought to the fore.[172] It is fitting that Gẹ̀lẹ̀dẹ́ reaches its apex when honoring Odúà. The Earth becomes an ojúbọ to receive full-throated praises from the men and women who were once blood-enriched eggs awaiting the spark of fertilization. As the men and women sing, spin, swirl, and converge perhaps they recall the journeys they took as eggs coursing through fallopian tubes seeking solace in the womb made velvet with fortifying blood. Perhaps they recall the single-minded urgency of sperm traversing silken vaginal walls and seeking justification. They may even be remembering the bliss of being twins dancing Gẹ̀lẹ̀dẹ́ in the womb: Gẹ̀lẹ̀dẹ́ is more than a celebration; it is a re-membering of how lives are conceived, how destinies are shaped, and how heads are molded to glowing perfection.

Babatunde Lawal finds that in many Yoruba towns, elder Gẹ̀lẹ̀dẹ́ officials assert that the ceremony "has evolved from ancient fertility dances staged by women in honor of Òrìṣà ọlọ́mọwẹ́wẹ́, the generic name for patron deities of small children."[173] Lawal states that during ceremonies for Òrìṣà Ọlọ́mọwẹ́wẹ́, "[M]others, spinsters, and youths, carrying woodcarvings and ritual pots on their heads and adorning their bodies with beads, dance round the town, singing and praying for female fertility, male virility, safe delivery of children, long life, and prosperity."[174] From the first festival to its contemporary incarnations, during Gẹ̀lẹ̀dẹ́ women use the classic symbols of Odù, which are also emblematic of their own wombs, to harness their individual, collective, and cosmic power to ensure the continuity and evolution of society.

Òrìṣà Ọlọ́mọwẹ́wẹ́ are essential to existence because they endow parents with the most tender, important, and precious of blessings—babies. To protect the lives of these children, Òrìṣà Ọlọ́mọwẹ́wẹ́ manifest themselves as terrestrial Àjẹ́ who are the expert gynecologists, obstetricians, pharmacists, and pediatricians who ensure that babies grow to become healthy productive adults who, in turn, create more children.

As Lawal's research reveals, Òrìṣà Ọlọ́mọwẹ́wẹ́ are multitudinous, and these Gods' names reflect their manifestations of Àjẹ́ and, often, the children and mothers whom they embody: Ìbejì (Twins); Dàda (children born with knotted hair and the God who protects them); Ẹgbẹ́ (Collective, a term that signifies Àjẹ́); Ará'gbó ("a being from the forest," "a spirit child"); Koórì; Kónkóto; Eléríkò (Àbíkú); Ẹgbẹ́run, "the association of heavenly comrades"; and Ẹgbẹ́ Ògbà, literally, a Collective of Equals, also, "women who worship the spirit double as a special divinity."[175]

The literal translation of Ẹgbẹ́ Ògbà as a Collective of Equals offers important insight into the structure and principles of Àjẹ́, who are extolled as "the gods of society."[176] Rather than the racially-skewed hierarchy that portrays some Àjẹ́ as white and good and others as black and evil or a bizarre assertion that the universe is divided into good and evil realms over which superior and inferior entities preside, Ẹgbẹ́ Ògbà confirms that all Àjẹ́ are equals; they all undertake works and acts that are crucial to human existence and evolution.

Ẹgbẹ́ Ògbà also appears to signify the original Mọlẹ̀ way of life and worldview which are rooted in egalitarianism. The significance of social equality is evident in the founding of Ògbóni, in which all members of the nation, without distinction, were collectively initiated; in the rules that Àjẹ́ must "share everything" and must not engage in displays of wealth; in the edict that babaláwo are in service to their communities and cannot use their gifts to generate personal wealth; and in the monarchal façade that shields the careful labors of an intricately interconnected network of Àjẹ́-rich power wielders. The Mother-son dynamic of Àjẹ́ also signifies egalitarianism, because Mother has milk, love, and protection for all of her offspring, and all of her progeny, ọmọ Onílẹ̀, are working for the fortification and glorification of Onílẹ̀, who fortifies and glorifies humanity.

As a nation of Mothers and sons respecting, protecting, and defending themselves and the Earth, it is easy to understand why, as Opeola reveals, enslaving capitalist colonizers "hated" Mọlẹ̀. While oppressors have done everything in their power to destroy Mọlẹ̀, including attempting to turn the Land of Equals into a "Slave Coast," the Onímọlẹ̀ continue their careful and, in this era of overwhelming capitalism, viciousness, and selfishness, often overlooked efforts to repair the Earth.

Ẹgbẹ́ Ògbà also signifies those who "worship the spirit double as a special divinity"; that exceptional doubling Deity may very well be Ẹgbẹ́run. Lawal describes Ẹgbẹ́run as "the association of heavenly comrades,"[177] which signifies a collective of Mothers whose work in the Cosmos mirrors the Ẹgbẹ́ Ògbà's terrestrial efforts. Opeola sheds more light on Ẹgbẹ́run, a term that, like Àjẹ́, signifies both a God and her society:

> Ẹgbẹ́run is related to Àjẹ́ but a slightly different concept. . . . [Worshipers of Ẹgbẹ́run] chant to Àwọn Ìyá Wa and say "Ìyá OOOOO!" It is not an actual mother but a spirit. This Mother oversees *everything*, every human being born, and she controls those going to earth and those going to heaven. It is these women [the Ẹgbẹ́run] who let you know the state of the deceased, the fortune and the misfortune. In Ẹgbẹ́run, these women have a record of the destiny of each person. They see spiritual things surrounding the death of a person.[178]

Given their cosmic administration of creation and existence and of life and afterlife, it is likely the case that Ẹgbẹ́run is a compound construction of "Ẹgbẹ́" (Collective) and "Ọlọ́run." The phrase "Collective of Ọlọ́run" would situate the Àjẹ́ of Ẹgbẹ́run within the Source—which is Ọ̀run, which is the womb of Odù.

Oyeronke Igbinola expounds on the dynamic between Àjẹ́ and Ọlọ́run: "Ìyàmi Òṣòròngà will call on Ọlọ́run for whatever they want to do. They ask Ọlọ́run, and Ọlọ́run gives them power. Anything they ask for they get answered from Ọlọ́run."[179] Not only are all of Àjẹ́'s actions sanctioned and empowered by the ultimate Source, but the ultimate Source is part of the Ẹgbẹ́ Ògbà of Àjẹ́. Ọlọ́run is Odù: the Mother whose womb is the expansive, generous, and unlimited Cosmos; the Mother who just so happens to also be her very own divine cosmontological collective of equals.

While the understated nature of the term "Òrìṣà Ọlọ́mọwẹ́wẹ́" belies the immeasurable significance of this network of Divinities and Divine Collectives to existence in general and the Yoruba world in particular, it is fitting and important that the sons, the most favored beneficiaries of these Mothers' and their ceaseless efforts, honor them with the grand spectacle that is the Gẹlẹdẹ́ festival.

Gẹlẹdẹ́ is a celebration in òdì, for male maskers are the center of attention. They execute with aplomb meticulous moves that delight and inspire. Dancing for the Mothers as the Mothers is a rigorous ritual that is literally its own reward, for the men who mask are, themselves, the gifts of Àwọn Ìyá Wa, and by dancing, men ensure that Òrìṣà Ọlọ́mọwẹ́wẹ́ will continue to endow the community with life. Gẹlẹdẹ́ also offers, for one day, the opportunity for a man to bear the weighty power that is Mother.

Who better than men, who owe their existence and continuity to the Mothers, to undertake the arduous and laborious celebratory ritual that is Gẹlẹdẹ́? After carrying them in the womb for nine months; risking their lives to push them through the birth canal and into the world; tying them securely to their backs; curing all of their illnesses; not to mention cooking, cleaning, singing, and braving abuse for them; as well as comforting, assuaging, disciplining, and educating them; and teaching them life, social, spiritual, and relationship skills, the very least men can do is "carry" their Mothers in the ritual tribute of Gẹ̀lẹ̀dẹ́. The multitudinous cloths, the elaborate masks, the symbolic breasts and rotund bellies; the rhythmic force of the dance, the four-and-much-more-part harmony vibrating with Òrò is the closest man can come to being God. And so, men dance.

The sons' dance remembers the mollifying and seductive gyrations of Òrúnmìlà who coaxed his warring Mothers back home to reunite with his short-sighted and foolish fathers.[180] The men dance and re-member the harmonizing song of Òṣun whose Gẹ̀lẹ̀dẹ́ concretized the sociopolitical power that women wield in the palace "until today."[181] Thanks to Òṣun, "[W]omen became the husbands, and have more power than men in the presence of the king."[182] Òṣun's Gẹ̀lẹ̀dẹ́ resulted in a communal acknowledgement of Àjẹ́ as the containers and controllers of Yoruba political power.

When a man dons the mask and dances the dance of the Mother, his power is, arguably, at its apex for he becomes òdì. For one day, he is son and Mother, praisesinger and praisesong: He is the prayer and its answer. During Gẹ̀lẹ̀dẹ́, the horizontal undulations and sweet sweaty exertions that produce life's activator are reconceived vertically and reconstituted as a celebration that disseminates joy, abundance, and blessings to the entire community. Through Gẹ̀lẹ̀dẹ́, the owner of the penis morphs into the receiving mother; the penis remembers when it once boasted the concentrated elegance of the clitoris and for one exultant moment, man re-members himself to God.

So, yes, let the sons dance, sweat, and spin in recognition of and respect for the Mothers: "The woodcarvings carried by the women during the Yemọja festival are the real Gẹ̀lẹ̀dẹ́,"[183] as are the actual mothers who are the living models who inspired the woodcarvings who are the Gods who are the Mothers who are elegantly and faithfully reproduced in wood. It is neither possible nor necessary to differentiate the Mother Gods from the God Mothers because They are She is All.

CHAPTER FIVE

THE MOTHERS AND THEIR POWERS AND THEIR SONS:
THE INFLUENCE OF ÀJẸ́ ON OLATUBOSUN OLADAPO, WOLE SOYINKA, FELA ANIKULAPO KUTI, AND TOYIN FALOLA

In *Gẹlẹdẹ: Art and Female Power among the Yoruba*, Drewal and Drewal assert that Àjẹ́ is "a generally pejorative term" that is "used rarely and with caution" and that no one would address a person by that term because of its connotations.[1] In line with their assertions, whenever Drewal and Drewal define Àjẹ́ in their book they use "the destructive power of women" or similar phrasing.[2] When quoting Yoruba informants, Drewal and Drewal routinely translate Àjẹ́ as "destructive women" and "destructive mothers" which reifies their definition of Àjẹ́ as a force that is covert and cloaked in mystery because it is nefarious.[3] However, it appears that Drewal and Drewal are in error.

While living and researching in Nigeria I found Àjẹ́ to be readily used in various contexts including 1) the original and literal sense of phenomenally-empowered, just, and divine entities, including Àwọn Ìyá Wa, Ìyàmi Òṣòròngà, and Odù; 2) metaphorically, to praise a person's achievements or innate abilities (for example: "You must be Àjẹ́ to double-major in astrophysics and molecular biology!"); and 3) the Caucasian-originated "African witch" construct. In many cases, as was the intention of the creators of the "African witch" construct, Àjẹ́ and "witch" are used interchangeably, much to the detriment of Àjẹ́. In fact, Àjẹ́, as conflated and confused with "African witchcraft," is one of the most popular tropes in Nigerian mass media entertainment. Herbert Ogunde's classic film *Aiye* set the standard in depicting Àjẹ́ as stereotypical, bloodthirsty, hell-raising "witches." The vast and lucrative Nigerian video entertainment industry, nicknamed "Nollywood," is so "witch"-driven that some Kenyan filmmakers have described the Nigerian film industry and its consumers as being obsessed with fairytales.[4]

In contrast to the commercially lucrative Caucasian-based depictions of "African witchcraft" are the reaffirming, resonant, and mutually empowering invocations, oríkì, and ìtàn that are offered to Àjẹ́ spontaneously and ritually in various settings in Yoruba life, worship, and art. Babaláwo invoke and pay homage to Ìyàmi Òṣòròngà along with other

Òrìṣà to commence certain ritual ceremonies, and the Mothers' praise is offered with the same tone, tenor, and respect that is shown all other Òrìṣà.⁵ In casual and academic discussions, members of the general Yoruba populace with whom I discussed Àjẹ́ often spontaneously recited oríkì of the Mothers and shared various orature and data about either Àjẹ́ specifically or the inherent power of women in general. I did not find it to be the case that discussions about Àjẹ́ and its sister systems in other African regions inspired either terror or shame. What is more, when I would share examples of manifestations of Àjẹ́ in African America, I was usually inundated with recollections, proverbs, orature, testimonies, and advice. This type of knowledge sharing proved immensely helpful to me, and it was facilitated by frank, free-flowing, and fear-free discussions about Àjẹ́.

One could even argue that celebration of the Àjẹ́ of creation, in particular, is an organic aspect of the Yoruba ethos. For example, a traditional Yoruba song extols:

Orisa bi iya ko si
Iya la ba ma a bo

[There is no deity like mother
It is the mother that is worthy of being worshipped]⁶

While this praisesong does not mention Àjẹ́ explicitly, its lines make it clear that the ultimate Creator is the one from whose womb you came. Furthermore, by giving you life, your mother and you, together, exponentially magnify her divinity. This song also affirms that it is not necessary to gather in particular buildings, memorize certain scriptures, mouth assertions of belief, or twist one's life into a pretzel of hypocrisy to accommodate incongruous dogma to find God: One need only look at one's mother, at a mother, or within one's self.

Far from being shunned and shrouded in taboo, reverential knowledge of Àjẹ́ and recitation of orature regarding Àjẹ́ appear to be organic aspects of the Yoruba consciousness that can be found in all strata of society. In "Calling Àjẹ́ Witch in Order to Hang Her," Ayo Adeduntan analyzes, among other important issues, the ways in which contemporary Yoruba artists publicly praise the "multivalent female force" of Àjẹ́ in their art.⁷ Adeduntan quotes the opening invocation of the song "E Kilo F'Omo Ode" in which King Sunny Ade pays homage to Àjẹ́. Adeduntan also offers as evidence the opening of King Sunny Ade's "Moti Mo," which includes a version of a well-known oríkì Àjẹ́: "Iba awon iya mi ajiginni, aringinni, aringinniginni woja ti kii je k'eru o b omode titi d' ojo ale. [Homage to my mothers who wake up smartly and walk smartly into the market place, who assure the little child of lasting protection]."[8] Adeduntan also analyzes Kola Akintayo's reverence of Àjẹ́ in his popular radio show "Ode Akoni," which explores "the encounters of hunters with the supernatural in the forest."[9] The show's title returns the word "akọni" to the spotlight. Clearly, Akintayo's title celebrates "Brave and Strong Hunters" and not "Hunters of a Violent Character," which is what Verger's translation would yield.[10]

As I detail in *Our Mothers, Our Powers, Our Texts*, hunters have a close and crucial association with Àjẹ́.[11] Given their bond, it is fitting and important that before the brave hunters' exploits are elucidated, Akintayo praises the Mothers:

> Mo se ba eyin aje teeri te njaye
> Eyin abapa wen, ab'ese wen
> Abirin asa lese mejeeji
> Eni ki nmaa 'lo' ko si nkan.

> [I pay homage to you the *aje* owners of the world
> You the sleight-handed
> And fleet-footed ones
> Have assured me of safety][12]

Rather than being terrified into silence, these artists herald Àjẹ́ for providing safety and "lasting protection" to their "children," who include Kola Akintayo and King Sunny Ade and general humanity.

Akintayo and Ade could have omitted reverence of the Mothers, but they did not: They chose to publicly praise Àjẹ́ and are not censured for it. Invocations to Àjẹ́ in popular culture are neither rare nor are they anomalies. Appreciative sons-of-the-soil are moved to praise their Mothers in the same way that a Muslim might praise Muhammad or a Christian might thank Jesus: It may even be the case that the worshipful son of the Mothers is a Muslim or Christian. Adeduntan reveals that Akintayo is a Muslim. His religion does not prevent him from praising the Mothers because he does not consider his religion and his spiritual system to be in competition. Although organized religions often gain converts through terrorism and heinous ultimata, Africans—across the Continent and in the Ìtànkálẹ̀—have always harnessed African spiritual systems' inherent flexibility and syncretism which made it possible for them to covertly and overtly access the power of their indigenous wisdom systems despite terroristic religious mandates. Heartfelt praise to the Mothers by various individuals through multiple media offers evidence of the facts that Àjẹ́ is the undeniable essential and that it is difficult, dangerous, and unnecessary to disavow one's source.

Verbal, visual, and literary tributes to Àjẹ́ flow freely from the mouths, souls, and pens of Yoruba men. The images of Àjẹ́ that emerge from the portraits painted by Olatubosun Oladapo, Wole Soyinka, Fela Anikulapo Kuti, and Toyin Falola are those of political powerhouses who critique and speak truth to power and take oppressors to war to ensure their and their progeny's inherent right to full self-actualization. These men depict Mothers of Compassion who use every tool in their cosmic and terrestrial arsenals to ensure that their progeny are whole, healthy, and purposefully-directed forces in this world. These sons describe Mothers of the Crossroads who access their Àjẹ́ with the same rapidity, resourcefulness, and resolve with which others load guns. These studious biological and spiritual sons absorb the knowledge, strength, and holistic love of Àjẹ́ that suffuses their lives and environments, and then they share with the world the wisdom and workings of the Gods.

"What Will You Do With Your Own Àjẹ́?"[13]

Olatubosun Oladapo is a renowned Yoruba verbal artist who is also known as Odídẹrẹ́ Ayékòótó, the African Grey Parrot which is a favorite of Àjẹ́. The African Grey is cherished for its red tail feathers, but it is also highly regarded for its intelligence and ability to reproduce human speech. The African Grey's penchant for speaking its mind and speaking the truth earned it the nickname Ayékòótó which means The World Does Not Like the Truth.[14] Cognizant that the most unpleasant truths are often the ones that are essential to healing and evolution, Oladapo, as Odídẹrẹ́ Ayékòótó, is a lyrical physician whose words take the form of medicines that sting, soothe, stimulate, and educate, as necessary.

With titles such as *Orin Odídẹrẹ́: Àjẹ́ Ọlọ́mọ* (*The Ballad of Odídẹrẹ́: Àjẹ́: The Mothers of All Children*) and *Emi Lo Ó Máa Fàjẹ́ẹ̀ Rẹ Ṣe?* (*What Will You Do With Your Own Àjẹ́?*),[15] it is evident that Oladapo is not only confident in the Mothers' power and that he has a ready audience desirous of hearing about that power, but also that he is motivated to use his artistry to move his audience to self-analyze and self-actualize. In his own response to the query he raises, Ayékòótó states that he will use his Àjẹ́ to "sanitize the nation."[16] As George Olusola Ajibade elucidates in his article "Endogenous and Exogenous Factors in National Development: Inferences from the Metaphor of Witchcraft (Àjẹ́) in Ọlátúbọ̀sún Ọládàpọ̀'s Poetry," Oladapo's Ọ̀rọ̀ is an effective cleanser and cauterizer. Once sanitized, Oladapo infuses his nation with political and cultural truths that are designed to promote healing and also to inspire, delight, and ignite.

The holistic force of Oladapo's art is on grand display in *Orin Odídẹrẹ́: Àjẹ́ Ọlọ́mọ*. The term "Àjẹ́ Ọlọ́mọ" specifies that Àjẹ́ are, indeed, the

Architects of Existence, the Creators of Life. In his tribute to the Architects, Oladapo defines Àjẹ́ in a comprehensive manner that reveals the depth and breadth of the Mothers' powers and describes how those powers flow seamlessly from the Cosmos to the Earth to human beings and back:

> Ẹyẹ ni:
> Gbogbo awọn ẹ̀bùn àràmọ̀ndà
> Tó bá tí ń jẹ́ bí idán làjẹ́ láyé
> Ayé lẹyẹ: Àjẹ́ ni Talẹnti.
>
> [This is Ẹyẹ:
> All extraordinary endowments are gifts
> As those skills are mastered, they become the àjẹ́ of the world
> The entire world is the mystery of Àjẹ́: Àjẹ́ is Talent manifest.][17]

Oladapo describes Àjẹ́ as a holistic force indispensable to civilization. Indeed, despite the title of his article, Ajibade confirms that Oladapo's Àjẹ́ has no relationship to the "witch" stereotype: "Rather he presents him or her as a citizen on the verge of becoming a mystic by being initiated as an Àjẹ́."[18] The initiation that Oladapo oversees is a comprehensive affair; for, through his artistry, Ayékòótọ́, effectively initiates every member of his audience into the truths of their powers and their selves.

Oladapo confirms that his own Àjẹ́ is evident not only in his mastery of verbal arts, the skill for which he is renowned, but also because he *is* Odídẹrẹ́ Ayékòótọ́. Consequently, the poet speaks from a position of dual Àjẹ́-authority, and to forestall any senseless accusations of "witchcraft," as well as to further clarify and contextualize Àjẹ́ and reveal its scope, Oladapo offers to his reader a simple truth oft-uttered in Yorubaland: "Ẹyin Ẹlẹyẹ: Emi Ẹlẹyẹ (You are Àjẹ́: I am Àjẹ́)."[19] What appears to be a stunning affirmation/accusation is actually logical when one acknowledges with Oladapo that everything is the product of Odù's Àjẹ́-rich womb.

With the assertion that everyone possesses some degree of Àjẹ́ which is manifest in unique talents and abilities, the issues of concern become "What will you do with your own Àjẹ́?" and "What have you done with your own Àjẹ́?" Because the use of Àjẹ́ depends on the ìwà, orí, and motivations of its wielder, the possibilities are endless.

Odídẹrẹ́ describes the Àjẹ́ that is manifest throughout the terrestrial world in human beings, flora and fauna, and objects thought to be inanimate:

> Ọgbọ́n féfééfé, n làjẹ́ ẹ ti Ifá
> Ìmọ̀ràn àmọ̀jù, n làjẹ́ ẹ t'Ọ̀pẹ̀lẹ̀

[Wisdom that is enduring and undeniable is the àjẹ́ of Ifá
Intelligent advice is the àjẹ́ of Ọ̀pẹ̀lẹ̀ (the Ifá divination chain)][20]

Just as such Òrìṣà as Ògún, Èṣù, and Ọbàlúaiyé must have Àjẹ́ in order to successfully undertake their work of creation, growth, expansion, and healing, Ifá, Ọ̀pẹ̀lẹ̀, Igbádù, menstrual blood, and Òkèbàdàn all must have Àjẹ́ as well. Rather than attempting to differentiate metaphorical manifestations of Àjẹ́ from physical women and powers, Oladapo makes it clear that there is no metaphorical Àjẹ́: Àjẹ́ is Àjẹ́. And all manifestations of Àjẹ́ find their origin in the warm womb and rich blood of Odù.

As pure power and creative energy, Àjẹ́ can take infinite forms. Odídẹrẹ́ describes the force of Àjẹ́ manifest in oníṣègun; in Oṣó, who are the "husbands" of Àjẹ́; in such Òrìṣà as Ọya, Ṣàngó, Agẹmọ, and Ògún; in Òṣùpá (the Moon); in the "Àjẹ́-ò-bàlé" tree; and in inventors, technologists, and scientists around the world. Odídẹrẹ́ also devotes several stanzas to corrupt leaders who use their Àjẹ́ to disenfranchise and defraud their constituents while amassing stupendous personal wealth.

Rather than struggling to conceal a covert power in mists of mystery, Oladapo's proclamations about Àjẹ́ are bold and clear. At the zenith of his lyrical demystification, Oladapo likens Àjẹ́ and Odídẹrẹ́ and their creations to complex works of art, the gloriousness of Ọ̀run, and the brilliance of a shining light.[21] Emphasizing the unity and amalgamated force of Yoruba powers, in addition to celebrating his Àjẹ́, Odídẹrẹ́ reveals that he is an Oṣó, and not just any Oṣó, but "Ó n foṣó tirẹ̀ ẹ pèdè ìjìnlẹ̀ (He is an Oṣó who utters words of deep meaning and wisdom)."[22]

Oladapo carefully distinguishes Àjẹ́ from the "African witchcraft" myths that were concocted to destroy its works and worth with a song of affirmation:

Àjẹ́ Awúrelà ló wèmi o
Àjẹ́ Awúrelà ló wèmi o
Èmi ò lè mùjẹ̀ ènìyàn
Èmi kò gbẹ́yẹ lógànjọ́ o
Àjẹ́ Awúrelà ló wèmi o

[Àjẹ́ of Infinite Blessings supports and protects me
Àjẹ́ of Infinite Blessings supports and protects me
I cannot drink the blood of a human being
I do not fly around at midnight
Àjẹ́ of Infinite Blessings supports and protects me][23]

An ogre from a fairytale cannot be compared to the Mother of Power. Oladapo reemphasizes the truth of Àjẹ́ for his audience by ending *Orin Odídẹrẹ́* with a different version of the defining and differentiating song:

Àjẹ́ ọlọ́mọ làjẹ́ àwa
Awa kò lè mùjẹ̀ ènìyàn
Awa kì í gbẹyẹ lọ́ gànjọ́ o
Àjẹ́ ọlọ́mọ làjẹ́ àwa

[The Àjẹ́ which is the mother of all children is our Àjẹ́
We do not drink the blood of human beings
We do not fly around at midnight
The Àjẹ́ manifest in us is that which loves and supports
   all children][24]

Oladapo's verses make it clear that Àjẹ́ is not some closeted "evil" power: It is the source of existence; it is accessed by numerous entities in infinite ways; and it is celebrated and is used to critique and restructure communities. The fact that Oladapo takes seriously his relationship with and responsibilities in his community is abundantly apparent throughout his work, especially in his decision to share his art in Yoruba. His verses are not written for or directed at Western audiences. Odídẹrẹ́ Ayékòótọ́ uses his Àjẹ́ to foment critical analysis, cohesion, and elevation in the Yoruba world first and foremost.

Sisters of the Struggle

Àjẹ́ has many praisesinging sons, and they are not mumbling in the shadows; they are offering resonant melodies in the public square, in books, and in studio recordings with choruses that inspire community harmonization. Fela Anikulapo Kuti and Wole Soyinka are two such sons, and their lives and works reveal not only how they have been inspired by Àjẹ́ but also how they have harnessed the power to motivate others.

Fela Anikulapo Kuti and Wole Soyinka appear to have been cut from completely different bolts of cloth. Soyinka is the elder statesman and Nobel Laureate whose literature and polemics are integral parts of the Nigerian national consciousness. Fela Anikulapo Kuti, who is affectionately known as Fela, is the immortal musician who founded his own liberated African empire. Fela's eviscerating political attacks, the profundity of his wit, and his musical genius made him a terrifying pariah to some and a sensation to many others. Despite their divergent life paths, Fela and Soyinka are united by the facts that they are tireless opponents of corruption and oppression, and that they achieved immortalization while living. In addition to sharing political values and electrifying artistry, Fela and Soyinka are cousins, and although they both were reared in stultifying Christian homes they were also nurtured, educated, and politicized by Àjẹ́.

Caught at the crossroads of British imperialism and Yoruba culture, Soyinka's parents' paradoxical success at adopting Western and Christocentric values is apparent in their nicknames. Soyinka's father, Samuel Ayodele, a clergyman and school headmaster, is known as S. A. or "Essay"; his mother, Grace Eniola, is given the nickname "Wild Christian." Their mastery of English letters and religious practices aside,[25] when the British forced Soyinka's forebears, along with people all over the globe, to adopt a surname to facilitate the British colonization and raping of the world, the name they chose was "Soyinka," which means "I am surrounded by Oṣó."[26] Oṣó are empowered males who work closely with Àjẹ́. While Oṣó do not have Àjẹ́'s scope or power, they are part of Onílẹ̀'s intricate system of checks and balances that is designed to ensure harmony, justice, and order. Soyinka is the product of deep and diverse progenitors: His Christianized parents represent paragons of the mastery of colonial mores and values; while other relatives, such as his grandfather, who appears to be a surrounding and protecting Oṣó, and his aunt Funmilayo, a widely heralded and revered Àjẹ́, impress upon a young Soyinka the power, depth, and profundity of Yoruba culture.

Soyinka was raised in the heart of Yorubaland within an oasis of Eurocentria, and cultural dissonance is abundantly evident. When Soyinka's elders ask him why he does not prostrate when greeting them as is customary, Soyinka astonishes them with his response: "If I don't prostrate to God, why should I prostrate to you? You are just a man like my father aren't you?"[27] When his grandfather mentions Òrìṣà Ògún to him, Soyinka, as if reciting a memorized response titled CAUCASIAN-APPROVED RESPONSE TO QUERIES ABOUT ÒGÚN says, "Ogun is the pagans' devil who kills people and fights everybody."[28] Soyinka's retort reveals an important fact that many Yoruba people and dictionaries can verify: Every Yoruba God who was not linked to Islamic-Judeo-Christian Gods was labeled a jinn, a devil, a witch, or a whore. The issue is not one of misunderstanding but of carefully orchestrated attempts to assassinate character, consciousness, culture, and Gods.

Soyinka's grandfather ensures that his progeny understands the degree to which "Ogun protects his own" by having his grandson ritually infused with the medicinal and empowering forces of Ògún and possibly Oṣó.[29] Soyinka undergoes *gbẹ́rẹ́*, a Pan-African surgical procedure in which hundreds of incisions are made on the body—in Soyinka's case, around his ankles and wrists—and protective and empowering medicines are rubbed into the incisions so that they travel through the bloodstream and suffuse the patient's body, soul, and destiny. While Soyinka's gbẹ́rẹ́ operation appears to be a male-exclusive affair involving Òrìṣà Ògún, Soyinka, Soyinka's grandfather, the physician, and the physician's apprentice, Soyinka emphasizes the fact that, throughout the excruciating ordeal, the physician keeps Soyinka's foot firmly affixed to the ground—ever in contact with Onílẹ̀, the Mother of the Earth.

When the surgery is complete, Soyinka finds that his senses have become acutely sharpened and no detail escapes his attention. His grandfather alerts him to the fact that his heightened awareness will provide him with invaluable assistance: "Whoever offers you food, take it. Eat it. Don't be afraid, as long as you heart says, Eat. If your mind misgives, even for a moment, don't take it, and never step in that house again."[30] Soyinka's grandfather instructs his progeny to never run from a fight. While he may be beaten twice by an opponent, the third time Soyinka will conquer. Whether his patriarch is revealing the by-laws of ọmọ Ògún or those of Oṣó is not disclosed, but the physical and verbal empowerment bestowed on Soyinka has a definite effect on his relationship with his extremities, on his destiny, and on his cultural awareness.[31]

Grandfather's calming, protective, surrounding Oṣó is juxtaposed to the actions of Wild Christian, who is called such because she appears to be the type of devotee who is more zealous than Christ about Christianity. She follows the standard Christian template of standing on a pillar of self-righteousness and from there sighting the "devil." She routinely asserts that her charges are possessed by "emi esu": the spirit (ẹ̀mí) of Èṣù, who is the Yoruba Trickster, Divine Linguist, and Mediator, who Christians, wild and tame, called the devil. As her miseducation demands, Wild Christian expends massive amounts of energy attempting to literally beat the "emi esu," or the "devil," out of children.[32]

Soyinka and Fela both express amazement at the ease and zeal with which their parents mete out Christian authorized brutality on their own children and all children in their care. In his analysis of the pathology that mandates the use of barbaric ritual violence—especially that which is sanctioned by religion—against those who are the most vulnerable, Soyinka muses: "I had now assumed a definite position with regards to the rational shortcomings of grown-ups, marveling how, for instance, an educationist and experienced traveler like Daodu could behave like Wild Christian who obtained all her authority from that section of the Bible which said, 'Spare the rod. . .'"[33] While he does not reveal precisely what his "definite position" is, after his uncle Daodu beats him, Soyinka silently wishes that his uncle be condemned to "Hitler's concentration camp."[34]

While Daodu only beats him once, Soyinka endures years of brutal beatings from Wild Christian and perhaps other relatives as well. However, the Christian and Caucasian colonial sanctioned violence does not crush his spirit. In fact, Soyinka's Ẹ̀mi Èṣù, his support from Oṣó, and his union with Ògún appear to expand exponentially to protect and guide him. It is not the case that Soyinka's spiritual development occurs in spite of or in response to Wild Christian's actions and decrees; Àjẹ́, Oṣó, the Òrìṣà, and the Ìṣẹ̀ṣe are part of the natural order of existence, and their influence is organic. Throughout his memoir, Soyinka contrasts the fluidity of Àjẹ́, Oṣó, the Òrìṣà, and the Ìṣẹ̀ṣe on his psyche and consciousness to an intrusive, abusive, and ineffectual Christianity, and he muses, "I had long lost faith in the efficacy of Wild Christian's prayers. There were several of her wards over whom she prayed night and day. She took them to church and prayed over them, found any excuse, any opportunity at all to drag them before the altar and pray over them. They continued to steal, lie, fight or do whatever it was she prayed against."[35]

The voids Christianity leaves in Wild Christian's life are most apparent when she gives birth to Folasade, who suffers in agony every day of her short life. Because Christianity has trained her to ferret out "devils" and scapegoats, Wild Christian accuses and interrogates a maid, who is most likely an adolescent *au pair*. Wild Christian blames the maid for her daughter's illness, and though she vehemently denies harming the baby, the caregiver is ostracized by the entire household.[36] Although the words are neither written nor spoken, the Christian household has branded the girl a "witch." With this indictment, a child with everything to lose—her reputation, her future, and her and her parents' hopes that by working for the Soyinkas she could attain an education or master a trade—struggles to defend herself against an impossible accusation while little Folasade struggles with an equal lack of success to survive an unknown ailment that could be sickle cell anemia.

In every respect, life in Aké is life at the crossroads—be those roads physical, religious, cultural, social, or political. Indeed, one need not attend school to obtain a rich education because every conflict and confluence at the crossroads is educative. Soyinka's instruction at Aké reaches graduate school intensity thanks to the political Àjẹ́ of his aunt Funmilayo Ransome-Kuti, who is supported in her endeavors by Wild Christian and her husband and "deputy," Israel Oludotun, known as "Daodu." In the 1940s Funmilayo distinguished herself as the premier Nigerian activist, scholar, world traveler, and an indefatigable warrior for the oppressed, including and especially Yoruba women who found themselves in the stranglehold of British economic imperialism.

Rather than use their status as an excuse to segregate themselves from the proletariat, Funmilayo and Wild Christian used their influence to foster comprehensive gender elevation and solidarity. Funmilayo's gathering of upper-middle class Yoruba women, who met to discuss and strive to prevent the degradation of culture, morals, and values, morphed into a communal networking site for Yoruba women of all classes, and that knowledge-sharing collective transformed into a political ẹgbẹ́ Àjẹ́ of unprecedented power. As Soyinka recalls, "The movement of the *onikaba* (upper class women), begun over cups of tea and sandwiches to resolve the problem of newly-weds who lack the necessary social graces, was becoming popular and nation-wide. And it became all tangled up in the move to put an end to the rule of white men in the county."[37]

Although Fela intimates that Funmilayo's work as an international freedom fighter destroyed his parents' marriage, Soyinka depicts Fela's father as a covert guide and committed organizer. Soyinka describes his uncle as listening in on the women's discussions and then strolling by and offering important suggestions as if the thoughts had just crossed his mind. For example, Soyinka describes his uncle musing on the fact that the original women's group did not have any representatives from the working class and was incomplete. After the women integrated their proletarian sisters into the collective, Daodu wondered aloud about the ability of the Western educated women to teach all of the members of their collective to read and write by devoting a mere thirty minutes of each meeting to literacy. Soyinka portrays Daodu as a husband who is so supportive of his wife—and of all women—that he gives them dominion over his ideas—and his ideas are centered on their empowerment.

Daodu and Funmilayo appear to have the quintessential Oṣó-Àjẹ́ relationship, as they work together as true "partners in progress" for the elevation and evolution of the community.[38] The power of their union is extolled in one of the ẹgbẹ́ Àjẹ́'s commemorative songs:

> Béère [Funmilayo], go on enjoying your life,
> All your plans have yielded successful results
> Daodu is deputizing for Kuti
> Just as the stars deputize for the moon
> Daodu is deputizing for Kuti[39]

"Bẹ́ẹ̀rẹ̀" means first born female child, and "Daodu" means first born male child.[40] "Bẹ́ẹ̀rẹ̀" and "Daodu" are also titles that signify the preeminence of their bearers among their peers, and Funmilayo and Israel are distinguished by their educations, their activism, and their commitments to their people. However, the subject of the song is Funmilayo, and she is accorded multilayered praise and reverence.

In the song quoted above, Funmilayo is heralded as "Kuti." Not only does the word Kuti signify her immortality, but the song's lyrics position her as the superior of her husband. Rather than being the anonymous wife whose identity is "property of husband," "Kuti," her husband's surname, becomes Funmilayo's identity: *She* is the defining force who names and claims. Rather than sulk, attack his partner, or make sacrifices to denude her of power, Daodu deputizes for his wife in the same manner that Oṣó deputize for and undertake the actions decreed by Àjẹ́. Israel and Funmilayo's relationship is not unusual; its balance is reflected in Essay and Wild Christian's union. During the height of the struggle for liberation, Soyinka finds his father living up to his nickname by transcribing Wild Christian's polemics into "essays" that are distributed to the masses.[41]

Funmilayo and Wild Christian's love for and commitment to their cause and their enviable support from their husbands and children established the perfect foundation for them to launch a war against the British colonial administration that had decided to tax Ẹgbá women without representation or consideration in the 1940s. With a ruthlessness and greediness that would stun Satan, the British government stretched its tentacles around the world and demanded that people who had lived in harmony with the Earth for millennia pay tribute in a foreign currency to a race of alien thieves. The Ẹgbá women found, as did their Igbo sisters who fought the colonial administration in the 1920s, that the British were astute in enlisting local men as their lackeys. Consequently, while Funmilayo was defending the interests of Ẹgbá women during a visit to England, the colonizers were forging alliances with the Aláké and his council.

The first salvo is fired upon Funmilayo's return from England, when late at night a naked woman is caught outside the Ransome-Kuti compound. The woman bears a calabash that contains palm oil, money, and a dog cut in half from the head to the tail. Ransom-Kuti's comrades discern that the naked woman had been girded with *àfẹ́ẹ̀rí*, a preparation that makes one invisible, but that the medicine evaporated before she could deposit the sacrifice.[42] The force that revealed and thwarted this heinous action is thought to be Funmilayo's Àjẹ́.[43] With this incident, the egbẹ́ understands that the battle they must fight will encompass various realms and will require diverse weaponry, including that which is astral. In this war of spiritual-political wills and powers, the Aláké has the British district officer, Ẹgbá chiefs, Ògbóni officials, and wealthy personages of all ranks to aid him. By contrast, the women have only their Àjẹ́.

A perfect opportunity to compare the power of a woman who is an Àjẹ́ to a man who has Àjẹ́ along with rank and title and perhaps Oṣó, occurs when a Balógun, or War-Leader, who is also an Ògbóni member, derides the women for refusing to pay taxes and surmises that what the women actually need is a kick in their rumps. When he tries to give an example of the force such a kick should carry, he collapses. The felling of the Balógun is also attributed to Funmilayo's Àjẹ́, as Soyinka recalls: "[N]o one could doubt the collective psychic force of the women, and specifically, of the Beere. She was now rumoured to exert supernatural powers."[44] There is neither fear nor condemnation of Beere's Àjẹ́ or that of any other member of the collective. The women are described as simply undertaking the ancient work that signifies their gender and power. Further stressing the significance of gender is the fact the ẹgbẹ́'s Àjẹ́ is galvanized by an insult to the female anatomy. Before his collapse, the Balógun claimed that the manner in which women urinate signifies their inferiority. The Mothers issue the Balógun a reminder that those who squat to urinate also kneel to give birth to men and can alter men's destinies whether standing, sitting, reclining, or squatting.

Before describing the women's attack, Soyinka paints a reverential portrait of Ògbóni that depicts them as the solemn carriers of Ẹ̀gbá history and wisdom, the political power-wielders and controllers of Orò, the *real* power of the Ẹ̀gbá nation: However, power has a Mother. After being insulted and seeing Onílẹ̀ paralyze the Balógun, the ẹgbẹ́ strike the most obvious agents of oppression and corruption and "naked" any Ògbóni member unlucky enough to cross their path.[45] Soyinka describes how the ẹgbẹ́ literally denudes an Ògbóni of his power: "His shawl was snatched, shredded, his wrapping cloth was stripped off him—fan, office staff, cap all had long disappeared. The *ogboni* were flogged with their shawls, fans, and were left only with their undershorts when finally let through a gauntlet of abuse into the palace or back in the direction of their homes."[46] Mother's milk is sweet, and her wrath is astonishing. In this stunning display of the power of the body, rather than the women removing their clothes to curse their male antagonists, the Mothers strip their sons to reveal who gave birth to whom and who is the elder and the owner and controller of all power and all life. The ẹgbẹ́'s act of stripping the Ògbóni returns the men to the status of infants and toddling boys whose existence depends—solely and exclusively—on their Mothers.

The ẹgbẹ́ Àjẹ́ grows in power and rage until it becomes the ancient Orò. When Orò assumes her original form and descends on the community to begin her work, it is men who flee, just as "Something Scarce" taught them to; for rather than stripping trees, Orò strips Ògbóni of the shawls, Ẹdan, caps, and other decorations that they use to signify their relationship with Àjẹ́. Soyinka recounts an especially significant song that the ẹgbẹ́ sing as they catalyze in their power:

> *Oro o, a fe s'oro*
> *Oro o, a fe s'oro*
> *E ti'lekun mo'kunrin*
> *A fe s'oro*
>
> [Orò o! we are about to perform Orò
> Orò o! we are about to perform Orò
> Lock up all the men
> We are bringing out Orò.][47]

With this invocation, Funmilayo transforms into Onílẹ̀, the Mother Earth. She is the Ìyá Àjẹ́ who can "do," "make," and "cause" Òrò "to be." Although Soyinka translates "ṣe" as "perform" the ẹgbẹ́ Àjẹ́ is not concerned with entertainment but upheaval as a precursor to justice.

Àjẹ́ boasts infinite truths, faces, and facets, and during the women's war, Wild Christian offers a moving portrait of compassion. Soyinka finds that despite his mother's ardor for beating children, she abhors violence among adults. Therefore, when she sees an oblivious Ògbóni elder headed to the palace while Òrò is whirling, she provides him with sanctuary. After Wild Christian successfully protects the Ògbóni member from twenty warring women, *he* prostrates to *her*. Although she would decry any association with Àjẹ́, Wild Christian's act of securing her Ògbóni elder/son in her womb of safety to prevent him from being humiliated is very much the work of a loving Àjẹ́ Ọlọ́mọ.

The only men who need not flee Òrò are Daodu, Essay, and their sons. Perhaps more than any other male, Soyinka is stationed at the heart of the women's movement. He proves himself to be a supportive son, a faithful comrade, a shining Oṣó, and an eager student of revolutionary Àjẹ́. What he learns from his aunt Funmilayo and the women she organizes is that Àjẹ́ is supreme. As a testament to the power of Woman, Soyinka writes about the significance of the fact that in the midst of the revolt, a mother gives birth to a baby girl: "Nothing could have happened of such a profound propitiousness as the birth of the child—and a female!"[48] Even from his distant vantage point, Soyinka is able to clearly recognize the crown of eternal power as it emerges from the womb of continuity.

Ọmọ Ìyá Àjẹ́

Funmilayo Ransome-Kuti's battles against the Aláké were successful; he was dethroned and sent into exile as a result of the effort that she spearheaded: But he returned. The hydra-headed beast of colonialism would not be killed so easily. It continued to morph and mutate so that Funmilayo and the Nigerian Women's Union found that they were not fighting a few corrupt rulers but the nation of England, which headed an international collective of usurpers, as well as multitudinous Nigerian puppets and lackeys. But just as new oppressors were born and were created to disenfranchise Africans, so too did Mother continue to give birth to warriors. Funmilayo gave birth to an activist who would become one of the most storied personalities in the world.

Funmilayo Ransome-Kuti left an indelible impact on the mind and spirit of Soyinka and how he viewed women in general and Àjẹ́ in particular. She also had a phenomenal impact on her son Fela. In *Fela:*

This Bitch of a Life, Fela waxes nostalgic about the "ingenious" tactics that his mother used to dethrone the Aláké:

> She got all the women together and told them: "Now, we are going to take over the Alake's house." Everybody hated the Alake. There was a huge courtyard outside his house. So my mother said, "Let's all go and take over the entire house." About 50,000 women went, with my mother at the head. . . . The Alake couldn't get out of his own house. You know what that means? What would you do? You would flee too."[49]

In "The Yoruba Image of the Witch," Raymond Prince discusses what may very well be the historic routing of which Fela speaks:

> There is some obscure fundamental relationship between witchcraft and menstrual blood. The menstruating woman and the witch both have power to render magic and the native doctor's medicines powerless. On one recent occasion in the town of A. the women of the town had risen in revolt against the payment of certain taxes which they considered to be unfair. Their power was so great that they forced the ruling chief of the town to retire to the provinces for a year. They camped in hordes in front of the chief's palace singing and causing a disturbance. When police were sent to disperse them the women brandished their menstruation cloths. This caused the police to take to their heels, for it is believed that if a man is struck by a woman's menstrual cloth he will have bad fortune for the rest of his days.[50]

Prince also finds that in certain Yoruba communities Àjẹ́ were protected and respected despite Christianization and colonization. He reveals that the "king of town A." would not allow the Atinga "witch hunters," who originated in present-day northern Ghana, "to practise their arts in his town because he said that many of the pillars of the community were witches."[51] If the sovereign in question is the Aláké of Abẹ́òkúta, it is important to note that his battles against Àjẹ́ did not alter his reverence of Àjẹ́. He had no choice but to revere those who gave birth to him and who crowned him: Indeed, in *Fela: This Bitch of a Life*, the Aláké is pictured in full regalia, including his crown upon which numerous Ẹyẹ Àjẹ́ perch.[52]

Framing Fela's proud recollections of his mother's might are intimations of how confusing it was to be the child of a firebrand mother whose father was, apparently, pleased to deputize on her behalf. Fela also struggled to understand the Christian-motivated violence of his parents which resulted in brutal beatings that shook the foundations of his love for them. By his count, Fela received no less than 3000 lashes, and these merciless beatings scarred Fela's childhood, body, and psyche.[53] Rather than educate or discipline him, this steady diet of violence made loving or respecting his father so difficult that he could feel little else but relief when his patriarch died.[54] Another source of conflict for Fela was the fact that despite his mother's battle against English oppression, taxation, and colonization, she encouraged Fela and all of her children to study in England, attain Western success, and hold the banner of "*Ransome*-Kuti" on high.

The confused fledgling musician may have fallen into complete obscurity or pop culture oblivion had it not been for a dynamic African American intellectual and revolutionist named Sandra Iszador (née Smith) who conscientised Fela while he was in the United States. It is often the case that people overlook the magnificence in which they are steeped and by which they are surrounded; as a case in point, Sandra introduced Fela to Africa when he lived in California. By doing so, she welcomed him into a world of Pan-African revolutionary power that had been awaiting his arrival. Sandra is the first Àjẹ́ to recognize and catalyze Fela's Àjẹ́. Fela would not be the international sensation and immortal force that he is without the Àjẹ́ of Sandra. She saw the various gifts that were waiting inside of him, and she helped him develop those gifts artistically and politically. Fela's transition from singing about soup to serving lyrical meals of educational soul food, his lacerating tongue spiced liberally with the word "motherfucker," his resolute Black Power salute, and his scathing *yab* sessions, or political harangues, can all be traced to the rhetoric, signs, philosophy, and teachings of Sandra and the Black Panther Party.

When Fela met Sandra, he met a woman who was more than his equal or peer. As a musician, a Black Panther, a scholar of African American political and wisdom systems, and a confident woman who expressed herself in myriad ways (Sandra would cuss out Fela as quickly as she would a corrupt Nigerian diplomat or a racist pig), Sandra was Fela's educator, mentor, and cultural-political catalyst. Fela describes how astounded he was to watch Sandra, at a Black Panther protest rally, kick a "policeman's ass. . . . Whaaaaam!"[55] Sandra was jailed for three months, and Fela expressed his amazement: "How can a woman do that and a man can't do it, a man like me?"[56] Fela's admiration for Sandra's revolutionary Àjẹ́ activated his own. He would eventually be arrested hundreds of times, more than 300 times by some estimates, for his political beliefs and convictions as well as on charges that came straight from the imaginations of Nigerian government officials.[57]

It is not possible to overstate the influence of Sandra and her Àjẹ́ on Fela. With an effusiveness with which he is rarely associated, Fela confesses:

Sandra gave me the education I wanted to know. She was the one who opened my eyes. I swear, man! She's the one who spoke to me about . . . Africa! For the first time I heard things I'd never heard before about Africa! Sandra was my adviser. She talked to me about politics, history. She taught me what she knew and what she knew was enough for me to start on. Yeah, Sandra taught me a lot, man. She blew my mind really. She's beautiful. Too much. Nothing about my life is complete without her. Sandra was the woman . . . I swear.[58]

Àjẹ́ is a malleable and indestructible force. It permeated Africa and survived the Middle Passage intact and flexible enough to orchestrate liberation movements of all kinds in America, Jamaica, Brazil, Cuba, Surinam—wherever Africana people found themselves enslaved and oppressed. Consequently, Sandra's Àjẹ́ is indistinguishable from Funmilayo's, and the women have the same love for and make the same investment in Fela. However, because of the nature of their relationship, Sandra was able to reach Fela in ways his mother could not. Indeed, above and beyond the books, principles, and politics she shared with him, Sandra, in and of herself, was an education for Fela. While Fela loved and respected his mother before he met Sandra, after his conscientization, he better understood his mother and the force he inherited from her.

Fela is candid about his feelings, growth spurts, stagnations, and revelations in *Fela: This Bitch of a Life*. He reveals the mental struggle he faced when his myth of patriarchal supremacy ran headfirst into the Womb of Truth. When Sandra, who was suffering and smiling with him in California, demanded he name a song in honor of her commitment, Fela balked and said like any male chauvinist: "I hated to give women any fucking credit."[59] But he was forced to admit: "Oh, this woman, she has helped me in America-o. She has fed me for five months. There are telephone bills I've run up; they've even cut one telephone line of their house. . . . I've almost made her family bankrupt. . . . I've spoiled their cars. [. . . .] So I said to myself, if I'm gonna sing about any one woman, I would sing about this one."[60] Giving birth to genius is an arduous task: "Frustration of My Lady" is Fela's tribute to Sandra's determination and devotion—the title also alerts other women to the struggles they will encounter if they dare to help a God grow.

Fela was not alone in respecting the power of Sandra's Àjẹ́; the Nigerian government also understood her force and tried to prevent her from visiting the country. When she entered Nigeria, the government tried to expel her. Sandra likens the time she spent in Nigeria to being trapped in a theater of the vicious and absurd. She was attacked by what Fela would call "government magic" and harassed by Fela's Queens. When she realized that she was also being antagonized astrally, Sandra turned to her own Ìyánlá for assistance and told her mother to protect her.[61] Perhaps Sandra's mother's Àjẹ́ communicated to Fela's mother that her daughter needed help, because Fela sent Sandra to stay with his mother in Abẹ́òkúta to avoid arrest by the Nigerian authorities. The "Lioness of Lisabi," as Funmilayo was called, and the Panther of California were united by a loving son, spiteful wives, and intimidated authorities. In Abẹ́òkúta, Sandra sipped from the Source: Mother Funmilayo. As Funmilayo extended her umbrella of protection over Sandra, it is likely that Sandra's presence revealed to Funmilayo that her son's burgeoning political-spiritual ideology and struggle were extensions of her own.

In 1970 Fela established the Kalakuta Republic, the commune named after the first cell in which he was incarcerated. Sandra recalls that when she visited Fela in Nigeria in 1971, he had neither interest in nor knowledge of the Gods. By 1976, Fela was Chief Priest of the Africa Shrine. Both the Kalakuta Republic and the Shrine were built on foundations of reverence for the cosmic, political, and eternal forces that ensure continuity, vindication, and immortality. In 1975 Fela dropped the European "Ransome" from his name and embraced "Anikulapo," which means "He Who Carries Death in His Pouch," as his true identity. Funmilayo also dropped "Ransome" from her name and adopted Anikulapo, further solidifying, along with her son, her true identity and destiny as an Eternal Immortal.

The deeper Fela journeyed into the crossroads where the spiritual and political meet, the more he understood his mother and the force that surrounded, undergirded, and empowered them both. One of the clearest and most resonant testaments to the force of their dyad and the power from which it springs is the fact that Fela adorned himself with the oríkì Ọmọ Ìyá Àjẹ́, the Child of the Mother of Àjẹ́, and confirmed for everyone that the sacred ancient Mother-son Àjẹ́ dyad was alive, thriving, and beating drums of war.

As is brilliantly elucidated in the palace system, in Yoruba politics and ontology, the man who surrounds himself with women surrounds himself with the power of Àjẹ́. In 1976, Fela, who was encircled by a devoted ẹgbẹ́ Àjẹ́, relocated his mother from Abẹ́òkúta to the Kalakuta Republic in Lagos so that she could take her rightful position as the biological, physical, and political Ìyá Ọba. Fela discusses the significance of their political unification:

> I'd seen her operating, running about the country with other women, agitating in the streets, talking, traveling everywhere. . . . and I see me now believing in the same things she believed in then,

even on higher things, me working on the things she believed in. [. . .] I had to bring her to Lagos to stay with me, man.[62]

The combined powers and reputations of Funmilayo and Fela constituted a juggernaut. Here were two political activists inspiring generations through the force of their spirits and words.

Fela, Funmilayo, and the commune of free, unarmed, politically astute artists were a threat to the Nigerian government and to the governments of Britain, South Africa, and America as well. In 1977, Nigerian soldiers stormed Kalakuta. While everyone was assaulted—Fela and his brother Beko were thrown out of a window[63]—the women, with their unique powers, attributes, and vulnerabilities, were specially targeted, and they bore the brunt of the assault. The women were raped, had their pubic hairs ripped off, and had guns, bottles, stones, and knives lodged into their vaginas.[64] Fehintola had to have a bottle and a knife surgically removed from her vagina.[65] Najite's neck was broken, and Kevwe was sodomized with a stick and blinded with gunpowder.[66] Soldiers threw Funmilayo Anikulapo-Kuti, the 78 year old "Mother of Nigeria," out of a window. Although the Lioness of Lisabi eventually died from the injuries she sustained, she left 27 leopards to surround and support her son.

Many people describe Fela's Queens as a novelty, a backdrop, or an exhibition of sexism on steroids; however, Fela thought quite a bit more of the female gender. He defined "women," in general, as "three things: source of power, inspiration, and pleasure,"[67] and Fela maintained a special reverence for his Queens. He praised them as "fearless," "good," "wild motherfuckers," and he stated that their ability to withstand heinous attacks by the Nigerian federal government and remain steadfast in the mission of Kalakuta earned his admiration and pride.[68]

While marrying twenty-seven women at once is one of the things that catapulted him into international notoriety, the reason Fela married the women in a public spectacle in 1978 was to celebrate their survival of the razing of the Kalakuta Republic in 1977. Furthermore, because the Nigerian government was accusing Fela of kidnapping the women and using these false charges to justify periodic raids of his empire, which led to assaults and imprisonment, marriage protected all parties and formally established the fact that the female artists performing and living with Fela were with him because *they* desired to be with him.[69] It is also important to note that Fela chose to build a life with these women. He respected their characters, destinies, lives, gifts, artistry, and futures; this is why he married them. While Fela is roundly criticized (and secretly admired) for marrying twenty-seven women, it is helpful to compare his respect for the women in his life to the alternative model offered by rock and roll and rap stars who famously use and immediately discard women by the thousands.

Fela's Queens are one of the world's most maligned groups, and their widespread condemnation is directly related to their melanin, their gender and their personal and political relationships with Fela. Individuals have manufactured various rationales in their attempts to explain why the Queens chose this particular king. The most prevalent justification offered is that the Queens were prostitutes and drug addicts. While these allegations place the Queens squarely within the cage of abomination built by Caucasian supremacist ideologues to house Africana women, these allegations are not true.

Fela: This Bitch of a Life reveals that the Queens hailed from diverse backgrounds: Many were born into middle-class and upper-class families with parents who were lawyers, physicians, nurses, entrepreneurs, Postmaster Generals, traders, and teachers. Many of the women, like Fela, were raised in homes where Christian hypocrisy and religion-sanctioned violence were the parents' teaching tools of choice and tyranny was the norm—in other words, their parents treated them the same way that racist British colonizers treated Africans, which sheds light on the impact of the colonial mentality on the colonized and the neocolonized. Fela and the Kalakuta Empire stood as a bastion of freedom for these young women—and for hundreds of young men, as well—who did not want to be imitation Caucasians, who did not want to adopt a colonial mentality, and who refused to live lives defined by mental and physical slaveries. The female and male residents of Kalakuta envisioned a free, united, strong Africa and were willing to work with Fela to build it.

Fela's relationship with Queen Kevwe provides an excellent example of the type of consideration, reciprocity, support, and love upon which Kalakuta was built. After being blinded and horrifically outraged during the attack of 1977, Fela, himself, tried unsuccessfully to heal Kevwe. He sent her home to the Delta region of Nigeria for medical attention, and, after a year of treatment by a female traditional physician, Kevwe was healed and her vision was restored. Once Kevwe had fully recovered, she returned to Fela and resumed her mission at Kalakuta of her own volition.[70] While Fela's fame, sex appeal, and notoriety were magnetic to women, the reason the Queens stayed with him after being beaten, raped, brutalized, and humiliated repeatedly by soldiers was because of mutual respect, admiration, and love.

In *Fela: This Bitch of a Life*, Carlos Moore interrogates each Queen in hopes of finding out what Fela has that makes fifteen women (the number who were living with Fela at the time of the interviews) brave raids and attacks by armed soldiers to be with and stay with him. As evidence of the degree to which Africana people, themselves, have been trained to devalue Africana women, Moore prefaces his interview of each woman with a physical appraisal and psychological assessment. The actual interviews are no less disturbing for Moore is clearly fishing for information about sex. Such a fascination with something that is as normal and as necessary as intercourse—a fascination that has been globalized and commercialized—speaks to the degree to which the self-loathing and ignorance-based "values" of organized religions have perverted minds internationally.

While most of the Queens are reticent and resist Moore's prying, Omolara tells him precisely what he wants to hear, leaving Moore to feign shock.[71] Aside from this, the Queens reveal the simple truth that Fela is no different from any other man: They are with him because they respect his "ideas" and because "he fights for African freedom."[72] Omowunmi states that she respects "everything with the [Kalakuta] organization," and when Moore asks Fehintola if she considers Fela to be a brother, father, or husband, she responds: "I see him as my father, as my husband, as my mother because he takes care of everything in life."[73] The relationship between Fela and the Queens was undergirded by reciprocity. But while these women could have married any men and could have left Fela at any time, and many did leave Fela to establish new relationships or to seek success and safer lives abroad, to Fela, the Queens were indispensable.

In the documentary *Music is the Weapon*, Fela's views on Àjẹ́ are in full accord with those of the Ancients, and he gives praise where it is due—to the Queens:

> In the African community there're some special women: We call them Ìyàlájẹ́. It means women who have special powers to see, to see the future, you know, to see front and back. You know, these are the special women. . . . Important people always have them around, you know, in the African home. Like, I have my own Ìyàlájẹ́ in the house . . . who advises me what to do.[74]

This elucidation perfectly illustrates the dynamics of Kalakuta and the reciprocity and power-sharing at work among Fela and the Queens. Fela's terminology is also important: By using Ìyàlájẹ́—and using it fluidly and unapologetically—Fela is not only heralding the power of Àjẹ́ in an organic way, he is also reminding all Africana women, especially Yoruba women, of their birthright and inherent power.

Fela's life boasts three primary phases of Àjẹ́-empowerment: The awakening orchestrated by Sandra in 1969; the solidification with Funmilayo in the mid-1970s; and the crowning of the Queens in 1978. But the roots of Fela's Àjẹ́, Pan-African consciousness, and activism run deep. His maternal great-great-grandmother, Sarah Taiwo, who was born in the early nineteenth century, was kidnapped and enslaved. In *For Women and the Nation: Funmilayo Ransome-Kuti of Nigeria* Cheryl Johnson-Odim and Nina Emma Mba discuss the ordeal of Fela's progenitor:

Sarah Taiwo was only a child at the time, yet old enough to remember her native land and to be remembered by the family she left behind. She was called simply Taiwo then, a Yoruba name signifying that she had been born a twin. The slave ship on which she was eventually boarded was surely headed across the Atlantic Ocean, but fate intervened. In 1807, England had outlawed the slave trade.[75]

The ship that was carrying Taiwo was intercepted, and, like many Africans who shared her fate, Taiwo was liberated in Freetown, Sierra Leone.

While many discussions about trans-Atlantic exile and enslavement imply that Africans took an "out of sight; out of mind" approach to the loss of their kin, Johnson-Odim and Mba's findings show that the opposite is true: "It was not unusual for families of captives to send messages to Badagry to ascertain if they had relations living among the returnees or if anyone knew if their kin were still in Sierra Leone."[76] With spiritual and scripted messages beckoning her, Taiwo made her way back to Nigeria. After living in the coastal town of Badagry, she journeyed to Abẹ̀òkúta where she lived the remainder of her life. There is a monument erected in Abẹ̀òkúta in honor of Sarah Taiwo.[77]

Sarah Taiwo's captivity and her family's reaction to it dispel many myths regarding enslavement in Africa. Far from "selling their own people," Taiwo's family used every tool in their arsenal to facilitate their stolen daughter's return. However, Sarah Taiwo's journey also offers a poignant example of how Àjẹ́ came to suffuse the globe. During the era of trans-Atlantic exile and enslavement, of the many millions of Africans who were chained in ships of slavery from the 1440s until the 1860s, tens of millions jumped or were tossed into the ocean, and while some survivors were emancipated in Sierra Leone in the 1800s, millions of Africans wound up enslaved all over the globe. Given the number of Yoruba people who were stolen from what Europeans casually and callously christened the "Slave Coast," Sandra could have closer ties to the Anikulapo-Kuti family than one might imagine.

In the effort to understand Pan-Africanism, African holism, and the scope of Àjẹ́, one must have a global consciousness. The children of Onílẹ̀ are acknowledged as being perfectly positioned all over the Earth: While some sailed around the globe of their own volition; others were victims of this world's most monumental crime against humanity. Ironically, the tragedy of exile and enslavement emphasizes the foresight of Onílẹ̀ and the resilience of Àjẹ́, for there is clear continuity linking Sarah Taiwo's Àjẹ́ to that of Funmilayo to that of Sandra to that of the Queens. This confluence of Àjẹ́ is the source of Fela's existence, creativity, and development.

For more than a century before he was born, Fela was being molded, prepared, and inspired by his progenitor's Àjẹ́. But in a magnificent irony, in *Fela: This Bitch of a Life*, Fela describes Sarah Taiwo as a "grandfather" who walked from Sierra Leone to Lagos.[78] Fela is very proud of his "grandfather" and "his" accomplishments. How Fela's pride might have increased or decreased had he known Taiwo's gender, is impossible to determine. One also must wonder if Fela patrified Taiwo or if her ìtàn was transmitted to him in an altered state. No matter the source, Fela's valiant "grandfather" provides clear proof of the persistence of patrification.

Fela's entire life, like the lives of his progenitors, is a study of growth in the midst of contradiction, complexity, and confinement. Fela is one of the most arrested human beings in the history of the world. While his arrests were inspired by the courage of Sandra, they also recall to the temerity of Funmilayo, who was arrested during her battle against the Aláké, and the tragedy of Sarah Taiwo, who was abducted and held captive in a slave ship. Like many incarcerated people, especially freedom fighters, Fela's confinement inspired introspection and self-analysis and social-critique. The depth of the political revelations that Fela gained during his most lengthy incarceration are elucidated in his global indictment titled "Beasts of No Nation," but being incarcerated for 18 months also granted him wisdom about gender and marriage that he applied to his life.

Fela emerged from prison to find that life had proceeded without him; some of his Queens had found new kings. Fela analyzed the situation and realized that the Caucasian-founded institution of marriage was created for men to establish ownership and control of "their" women and children. Fela stated what he knew all too well: "Marriage brings jealousy and selfishness," and he resolved, "I just don't agree to possess a woman. I just don't want to say: 'This woman is mine, so she shouldn't go out with other men.'"[79] This is a revelation that many so-called feminists and womanists are yet to have, but Abàmi Ẹ̀dá, the Extraordinary One, was not finished. He continued to expose marriage as a destructive farce:

> The marriage institution for the progress of the mind is evil. I learned that from prison. Why do people marry? Is it to be together? Is it to have children? People marry because they are jealous. People marry because they are possessive. People marry because they are selfish. All this comes to the very ugly fact that people want to own and control other people's bodies. I think the mind of human beings should develop to the point where that jealous feeling should be completely eradicated.[80]

Prior to his incarceration Fela asserted that African women are trained not to be jealous, and one of Fela's Queens confirmed, "Jealousy is not an

African word."[81] The difference between African American and Yoruba women's reactions to man-sharing is evident when one compares how Sandra goes off (as only an African American woman can) on Fela for inviting a woman on a date at the same time and place that Fela was hosting Sandra and her parents,[82] to the nonchalant reaction of Remi, Fela's first wife, to Fela's numerous relationships. Remi went on to reveal, "I don't believe in women's lib at all. . . . These women in Europe, I don't agree with at all."[83] And she need not agree with them, not with her culture having provided her with resounding confirmations that there are endless ways to manifest one's womanhood and harness one's Àjẹ́.

When a woman's vision is not narrowed to the desire to "have" or the struggle to "keep" a man, she can focus on protecting and developing the most significant dyad—that of mother and child. Consequently African women's purported lack of jealousy is not only important to a smoothly-running polygamous home, but it places men in their proper position of secondary to the union of mother and child. The significance of motherhood *vis-à-vis* marriage is evident in the fact that, traditionally, an African woman does not take her husband's name upon marriage: This is a Caucasian custom, rooted, as Fela correctly surmises, in possession, economics, and the demented concept of legitimizing life. When a woman in a traditional African society becomes a mother, she is granted a new name that heralds her as the mother of her child. With the child elevating a woman's status, it is not the social construct of marriage, but the biological fact of motherhood that confers glory, divinity, and immortality on a woman.

More than anything else, Fela's revelation on marriage displays his level of personal development, because when he describes the institution of marriage fomenting jealousy, selfishness, and possessiveness he is addressing faults he found within himself. With his pronouncement, Fela breaks his own chains of codependency. In 1986 Fela adopted a wholly egalitarian and logical relationship with the Queens, stating that as inherently free people, the Queens were free to conduct their lives as they wished—with or without him. However, this is not a grand advancement. Each female and male citizen of Kalakuta had come to Fela's empire of his or her own volition and had stayed or left as she or he had seen fit anyway. Fela's denunciation of marriage can be best understood as a return to the fluidity that had characterized his relationships before the need for Western formalization arose.

While many seek to define Fela by narrow and inappropriate Western standards, Fela was a complex man and his complexity is evident in his relationships with women and in his relationship with Àjẹ́. His love and admiration for his mother could be described as reverential. One can imagine Fela's awe at watching Funmilayo go to war against the Aláké, network with the Polish proletariat, or share wisdom with Kwame Nkrumah and Mao Tse Tung. Rather than the submissive woman that British missionary colonizers tried to invent, Funmilayo was a traditional Yoruba Àjẹ́ in every way. While Fela embraced his mother's Àjẹ́ and basked in its power, he refused to follow the in the footsteps of his father and deputize for a woman. It is telling that Fela transitioned from Sandra, a woman very much like Funmilayo in her prime, to his Queens, women who Fela could mentor, mold, and teach in the same what that Sandra had guided him.

While Fela fought against the colonial mentality from the moment of his political awakening, his struggles with gender relationships and dynamics boast a layered intricacy. Indeed, in some of the songs that most critics point to as examples of shameless sexism, Fela weaves threads of irony and sews swatches of truth. Critics often point to Fela's songs "Lady" and "Mattress" as bold exhibitions of chauvinism. "Lady," however, is better understood when it is juxtaposed with "Gentleman," for both songs offer critiques of the West's influence on and perversion of African mores and concepts of self, gender, propriety, and power. Furthermore, when the songs "Gentleman" and "Lady" are contextualized by "Shakara (Oloje)" one becomes aware of the evenhandedness with which Fela attacks what he considers to be hypocritical, aberrant, and dissonant behavior in both genders and in Western as well as in Yoruba culture.

"Mattress," which appears to be a particularly crass comparison of a woman to a mattress, is a song swaddled in truth. During my life as a fiercely independent womanist scholar, I would have found "Mattress" to be inexcusably insulting. As a mother, I understand Fela's lyrics perfectly. Before I heard of or heard "Mattress," I marveled at how my baby finds new and expedient uses for me. I noted that, at any given time, Ìyá is a ladder, stool, pillow, mattress, chair, ledge, and towel. In addition to these, I am my child's professor, student, entertainer, umbrella, life preserver, and aggressor killer. I am the foundation and means of elevation, and I provide comfort beyond compare. With my child having taught me about myself, when I first listened to "Mattress" on 05 March 2012 at 8:07 pm when I began writing this chapter, I had to laugh and concur with Fela's Queens whose back-up chants include the affirmation, "You no lie, my friend" to Fela's proclamation that a woman is a mattress.

My understanding of "Mattress" aside, the validity of Fela's intended meaning of the song is evident in the millions of women around the world—especially in the West—who cater to grown men with a devotion and diligence that should be reserved for their children and in the social decadence and decay that leads babies of Western and Westernized societies to learn to make do with formula, self-soothing rituals, and isolation so that women's bodies are free to provide physical entertainment (read: be mattresses) for grown men.

Critics are quick to mention "Condom Scallywag and Scatter" ("Condom") as evidence of Fela's disregard for human life in the face of a surging AIDS epidemic, but this association may prove problematic. In the early 1990s, Fela decided to stop recording his music. He realized that the public had pigeon-holed him as the eccentric firebrand who was celebrated—"Fela, you done come again!" "Fela, what ting you go sing about?"—but not heeded and followed. I do not think it is a coincidence that Fela's refusal to record his music coincided with Moshood K. O. Abiola, a bitter enemy and antagonist of Fela, winning the Nigerian presidential election in 1993. Because Fela would not record his compositions but would perform them only as he desired at the Shrine, few people who mention "Condom" actually quote the song's lyrics.

In *Afrobeat: Fela and the Imagined Continent*, Sola Olorunyomi includes some of the lyrics of "Condom," and in the song, Fela invokes Yemọja and Ògún. He praises Yemọja's èrò and procreative power, and he honors Ògún as the God who is the "enemy of oppression" and the "enemy of injustice."[84] While all of the lyrics of "Condom" are not available at the time of this publication, it could be the case that the song's impetus is not in irresponsible sexual abandon but in encouraging his audience to embrace the eternal powers of life and abundance signified by Yemọja and to protect the sanctity of life with the righteous ferocity of Ògún. Such a call would ring with resounding resonance given the myriad threats that have been manufactured to delimit and destroy Africana life.

When critics are seeking songs to illuminate Fela's thoughts on gender, no one mentions "Frustration of My Lady," his ode to Sandra; no one mentions "Water No Get Enemy," which is encoded praise to Yemọja and her utilitarian and global èrò; and no one mentions "Unknown Soldier," which is a testament to the strength and resilience of the male and female Kalakutans—especially his mother—who were attacked by the Nigerian military in 1977.

In "Unknown Soldier," while Fela describes the soldiers destroying Kalakuta and beating and raping its citizens, the Queens, who are chanting along with him, are reliving being horrifically outraged. But the song is more for Funmilayo than anyone else. In the song, Fela praises her as "Ideological Mama / Influential Mama" and "The only Mother of this country."[85] His voice trembles as he recalls, "Dem throw my Mama out of a window / Dem kill my Mama."[86] Fela concludes his lyrics by describing the absurd objectives and senseless motivations of the Nigerian government: "Them turn green into red / Them turn blue into white," and by this time, Fela is weeping openly.[87] The Queens, who know exactly who raped them and beat them and who threw their mother out of a window, bear up Fela as they indict the lie of the "Unknown Soldier." At the conclusion of the song, Fela, as if a mere child completing a task, looks up to Funmilayo and says, "I'm finished, Mother."[88]

But he was not finished. Funmilayo died in 1978 from the injuries she sustained in the Kalakuta War, but in 1979 she paid a visit to her killers. Fela took his mother's coffin to Dodan Barracks where General Olusegun Obasanjo, the Head of State, resided. Fela honored and obtained justice for his mother the only ways he could: by placing her coffin at the home of the general who sanctioned her killing, and, in the process, revealing the identity of one "unknown soldier"; and by documenting his retributive act in the classic song "Coffin for Head of State" and its album art. After the Head of State received his coffin, Funmilayo metamorphosed into the Spirit of Rain, and, through that medium, she continued to communicate with her son. While Fela's views on gender, relationships, and women grew and developed as he did, his views on and respect for Àjẹ́—and Àjẹ́'s guidance and support of Fela—were consistent.

When one undertakes a comprehensive examination of Fela's political motivations, articulations, and edifications, it is clear that he is extending the power, struggle, Àjẹ́, Ọ̀rọ̀, and Orò of his mother. Fela's political organizations, Movement of the People and Young African Pioneers, are reconstitutions of Funmilayo's Nigerian Women's Union. There is a clear line of continuity that connects Funmilayo invoking Orò to terrify men, her threats to male adversaries that "vagina's head will seek vengeance," and her calling the Aláké a "big man with an ulcer" and a "thief" to the political artistry and attacks of her son's songs.[89]

Fela condemns neocolonial power wielders as "Beasts of No Nation" and as "Vagabonds in Power." In the song "I.T.T.," Fela gives Olusegun Obasanjo and Moshood K. O. Abiola a new oríkì, "International Thief Thief." Obasanjo ruled Nigeria as a military dictator and persecutor of Fela from 1976 to 1979.[90] Abiola was a business tycoon who held various powerful positions, including chief financial officer of International Telephone and Telegraph (I.T.T.) from 1969 to 1988. Abiola also tried to use his influence to destroy Fela. Fela retaliated against Obasanjo and Abiola in many ways including deliberately using the acronym of the telecommunications company as a code to define their characters and to inform Nigerians of the "shit" that they were carrying because of Abiola's and Obasanjo's greed and lust for power.[91]

Fela, his Queens, and the other artists of his band castigated Nigerian heads of state and the world's wealthiest, most lauded, and most influential figures with no weapons or defenses other than the truthfulness of their words. The Kalakuta Empire (Fela declared it an empire when he was informed that it was unlawful to establish a republic within Nigeria's own republic[92]), which continued to rise from the ashes despite curvilinear raids and razings, was a haven where capitalism, materialism, and corruption held no sway. Cognizant that racial, political, economic, and ideological corruption, oppression, and destruction are rooted in and replenished by democracy, capitalism, and organized religion, Fela practiced "Africanism" and recreated in Kalakuta the type of holistic, balanced, communal society that existed before the concept of Europe was conjured. While Fela lived, all Kalakutans—male and female—were guaranteed food, clothing, shelter, respect, camaraderie, and a place to develop their crafts and do the work that they enjoyed.

Fela was mystifying to a world gleefully enslaved by capitalism, colonialism, and consumerism. He had no interest in the fame and fortune that most musicians crave. As a true artist, he was not interested in becoming a commercial hit factory. He used his music to open minds and to attack hypocrisy, corruption, and racism. In a Nigeria that finds more weakness than strength in ethnocentrism, Fela made it clear that he was an *African* and a true Pan-Africanist, as is reflected in his Queens, band, artistry, and Black Power politics. In a world of capitalistic excess, sycophantism, and Europhilia, Fela, who, decried all of that, was truly Abàmi Ẹ̀dá, The Exceptional One. Rather than live in a secluded gated mansion, Kalakuta was a haven where anyone was welcome to visit, live, eat, learn, and do the work that they loved. Instead of a fleet of luxury vehicles, he had ragged Volkswagen bugs and buses. Rather than signing multimillion naira or dollar contracts to churn out mindless pop hits, Fela refused to sing songs once he recorded them. Abàmi Ẹ̀dá is often translated as "The Weird One,"[93] and Fela truly did appear as weird as Mọlẹ̀ to narrow minded mortals focused on the superficial and the material.

While human beings' physical growth may stop, their intellectual growth should continue eternally: Fela is emblematic of eternal development and evolution. Near the end of his life Fela was sharing wisdom with the Ancients in preparation for his soul's next journey. Fela's son Seun describes him as being "in a godlike state" during this time.[94] In what is thought to be his last interview, Fela, with his surgical wit and probing mind, discusses politics, revolution, intergalactic travel, talking trees, and the inadequacy of the concept of Jesus Christ with Femi Sanyaolu.

Sanyaolu offers his impression of the legend: "I sensed someone who truly loved himself and all peoples, but who has been persecuted for speaking truth, by the very same people it was designed to uplift."[95] Despite his decades-long persecution, Fela remained a firebrand. In his interview with Sanyaolu, Fela reveals the gaps in what the West terms science and technology, and he describes how Europeans stole technology from Africans. With the cunning and patience of a seasoned prosecuting attorney, Fela uses Ronald Reagan's battle with Alzheimer's disease to critique the political hypocrisy and resolute thuggishness that led Reagan to invade sovereign nations.[96]

Rather than "mellow with age" or modify or compromise his principles, Fela found that current events confirmed the validity of his early assertions. For example, in "Perambulator," Fela warns his audience that the model of success defined by Caucasians, (neo)colonialism, and capitalism is dependent on Africans volunteering to become "certified slave[s]."[97] Having spent his career refusing to become a volunteer slave for the recording industry, Fela used his Àjẹ́-enhanced analytical powers and his liberated and liberating voice to reveal the true motivations of Motown Records:

> Motown came here some time ago to sign me up. In the first place the deal they were offering me was so ridiculous. These bastards came all the way from America to come and talk this shit? I said to people: "Look at this name 'Motown.' That word is Yoruba: mo-ta-ohun, it literally means 'I sell my voice.'" [Laughter.] I said: "Anybody who goes with these people will be finished." Then later Motown collapsed or the head was sacked or something like that. They had been found out![98]

Fela relished exercising his power to name, claim, and define, and, as is evident in his translation of "Motown," he found that Yoruba encoded with the wisdom of Àjẹ́ was the perfect language to reveal the true meaning of English words and phonemes.

Using his unique system of lexical deconstruction, Fela reveals that the headquarters of the only and actual "witches" is where one might imagine it is, in Windsor Castle. He avers, "When people say 'Wind-sor,' it's actually a Yoruba word: iwin so (the witch is speaking) because that is the headquarters of the witches; that was where Queen Victoria and Queen Elizabeth belong. And now they have reincarnated in Margaret Thatcher and Elizabeth II."[99] This system of linguistic explication is the same one that Fela used to decipher the truth about democracy and reveal why democracy has never been successfully implemented anywhere and why countries yoked to the concept of democracy are mired in debt, racism, poverty, and violent upheaval.[100]

After dismissing "democrazy" because it deliberately impedes and undermines holistic progress, Fela turns to the cosmontological and philosophical.[101] Observing that archeologists go to Egypt to find the tombs of the sovereigns who were "the gods of that era," Fela asserts that the Gods of this era are "now down on earth walking on two or four legs just like everybody else."[102] The concept of a four-legged God is laughable until one recalls the anthropomorphism of African cosmology, including Àjẹ́'s Spirit Bird, Ọya's buffalo, Heru and his hawk, and the sacred cow of

Hathor. Fela's understanding of the limitless ubiquity of the Gods is in complete consonance with his ancient Nubian, Kemite, Igbo, and Yoruba ancestors.[103]

After submerging himself in the infinite wisdom of Odù's depths; after traversing the endless expanse of Ọ̀run; after studying ancient African philosophy, physics, science, mathematics, and technology; after investigating the Earth's interactivity and symbiosis with the Moon and the Cosmos, Fela realized what every holistic wisdom keeper also comes to know, that the biggest impediments to human beings obtaining the comprehensive knowledge necessary for evolution and elevation are the Caucasian constructs of "science," "religion," and "physics" which are dependent on geocentric, capitalist-driven, religion-sanctioned ignorance. Arguing that rather than helping humanity evolve, "science . . . is scattering the world from what it is supposed to be," Fela encourages an eradication of everything that human beings are taught in Caucocentric, Christocentric, capitalism-based educational and social systems.[104]

Having risen far beyond and above nationless beasts and their pseudo-scientists, Fela greeted the end of his life as a Divinity who was looking forward to the next life. Sanyaolu describes Fela in his last days precisely as he is depicted in the last known videos of him, as a slim hoary-headed elder who had simply outgrown Nigeria and a tiny simple-minded world captivated by pseudo-puritanical retrogressive pigshit.[105]

Fela was an inheritor and a conduit of Àjẹ́, and the power of his elders, ancestors, and partners surged within and through him to catalyze, educate, and energize the world. Fela shared his numinosity artistically, biologically, spiritually, and politically, and having fully manifested his destiny, Fela journeyed to the other side having attained the immortality that was his birthright, that his identity always signified, and that is the perfect manifestation of a complete existence. Mo júbà Òrìṣà Olufela!

A Son of Many Mothers

Singer Seyi Sodimu makes it clear: "There will never be another Fela!"[106] Fela was truly a divine original, but as Olatubosun Oladapo informs us, the world is filled with the Mothers' remarkable creations. While indoctrination, colonization, disinformation, and miseducation attempt to crush the richness of Ọbàtálá's carefully wrought individuality into lockstep conformity and mediocrity, the optimum balance of Àjẹ́, àṣẹ, Orí, and ìwà results in countless irrepressible spirits.

Toyin Falola, like Oladapo, Soyinka and Fela, came of age in a Nigeria throbbing with diverse cultural, social, religious, political, and familial intricacies and dynamics. But unlike Fela and Soyinka, Falola was raised in a home of many mothers. Despite the colonizers' attempts to force everyone to adhere to their nuclear family model, which often breeds isolation, exhaustion, hypocrisy, cheating, and nihilism, Falola was raised in a polygamous home, and the benefits of the system that Àjẹ́ founded are evident. Falola and all of his siblings are supported and surrounded by mothers of varying titles, powers, positions, and affiliations, and each mother contributes to all children's growth and development and that of the familial unit.

Falola's memoir also depicts the invaluable benefits of intergenerational childrearing. Rather than one mother and one father struggling to juggle work, daycare, meals, cleaning, and "quality time" with their children, with the latter often considered optional, the African traditional home is rich with mothers and grandparents who are indispensable. Falola's grandmother Ìyá Àgbà, alone, reveals the essentiality of the family members that the West deems optional and terms "extended," for she is the wisdom keeper who knows and recites the oríkì of every member of the household. Every morning she instills in Falola his glory:

> Isola, the scion of Agbo
> He who dreams daily of wealth
> He who thinks daily of the good things of life
> He who looks unto the sky and says, "I can hold you if I want to"
> Isola, spare the sky.
> ....
> Isola, the scion of Agbo
> The Agbo who cages the tiger
> Isola, the mighty tiger
> ....
> Isola who says he is not ready to marry
> When he is ready
> Girls will line the street from here to Hausaland.[107]

Àjẹ́, who are the repositories and custodians of familial power and lore, bathe each of their progeny in the inestimable wealth of the ages every morning so that they know both the force of the Egúngún who support them and the heights that they are expected to reach. The wisdom that Falola gains from Ìyá Àgbà alone is sufficient to remake worlds, and she is one of many mothers.

In addition to the four mothers of the house and two younger mothers who are Falola's elder brothers' wives, there are other mothers who visit periodically. Falola receives gifts, instruction, chores, meals, love, and discipline from all of his mothers equally. He can sleep with any of his mothers, but his "official bed" is with Mama One. Falola is surrounded by mothers, and his formative years are framed by their life-bearing bellies, their nutrient-rich breasts; their strategies, tears, and rotational meals (from which the perceptive child can benefit); their profits from industry; and their lessons, loves, and conflicts. Surrounded by so much Mother, Falola is not introduced to the concept of a "biological mother" until he is ten years old, and once he is introduced to the concept, he does not know who she is. Falola's enviable familial support reveals the seamless and infinite protections offered by the Àjẹ́-founded compound system.

While Falola is encircled by multiple mothers wherever he lives, when he meets Ìyá Lekulẹja, he meets the Mother of mothers. "Lekulẹja" is routinely translated as "traditional pharmacist," but the term literally means "One who has rats and fish." Lekulẹja is a title that is indicative of the holistic nature of African pharmacology, and it might also synecdochically infer that the Mother's range of knowledge and her tools and skills encompass the land and the sea. With her seemingly mundane name, the Mother who has Rats and Fish is actually capable of providing a person with everything he needs to thrive.

After learning that the entity he originally thinks is an iwin, or spiritual being, is actually a bona fide woman, Falola remains intrigued; indeed, he appears to be irresistibly drawn to Ìyá Lekulẹja and her shop, which, Falola reveals, actually does seem to have everything anyone could possibly need:

> I doubt if Leku herself could have known the number of items in the store. Arranged in a way known only to her, they comprised an assortment of all known herbs, dried leaves, roots of many kinds of trees and shrubs, fresh and dead plants, bones of various animals (including tigers, leopards, and hyenas), skulls of various animals, dried rats, rodents, other animals, dry and living insects such as millipedes and centipedes, reptiles (including parts of snakes, lizards, and alligators), rocks and soils, and ritual lamps and pots. Tortoises, snails, and small cats walked around, and they, too, were for sale. Dangerous scorpions in bottles, as well as snakes in cages, were waiting for food and ready to bite.[108]

Ìyá Lekulẹja's shop is Onílẹ̀'s dispensary where all flora and fauna are maintained, and within Ìyá Lekulẹja's small frame is Ọgbọ́n Ayé, the Wisdom of the World.

Ìyá Lekulẹja's only concern is healing and dispensing wisdom and tools that facilitate healing. Falola notes that despite being an elder, Ìyá Lekulẹja does not concern herself with the typical goings-on of townsfolk, and she is absent from events in which elders are usually showcased: "[S]he never got involved in any issue, never showed up for any celebration, never commented on any issue, and she would never give advice, rebuke, complain, or even talk."[109] Ìyá Lekulęja has no interest in ceremonial or social activities, and she does not care what members of the community think of her. She is Ayé, a world unto herself.

Ìyá Lekulęja is the literal personification of Onílę̀. Similar to the Mother who used herself to create the world, Ìyá Lekulęja is both the world and its custodian. Because of the significance of her work, Ìyá Lekulęja has no distractions, obligations, or duties other than to fully manifest her destiny as the guardian of healing wisdom. As Falola observes: "Her only passion was the store, not as a space in which to make money but one in which to make herbs and medicine available to whoever wanted them."[110] Nigerian women are renowned for their control of economies and domination of trade, but because she is the world, Ìyá Lekulęja has neither need nor desire to acquire temporal constructs of worldly power or wealth. Consequently, while Ìyá Lekulęja appears to be running a business, she has no profit motive—her shop thrives on òdì-economics. Ìyá Lekulęja is one of the few elders who uses money—as nothing more than the tool it is—to provide herself only with the sustenance necessary to continue acquiring and cataloging the pharmacological infinitude of Onílę̀'s medicine chest.

Cognizant of currency's corrupting influences, Ìyá Lekulęja handles money in the same manner as other traditional Africana wisdom keepers: She directs the token payment be placed on or in some object and avoids, as much as possible, contact with money. Falola notices that when a client produces payment for a service, Ìyá Lekulęja does not check the money to see if the correct amount has been deposited—she does not look at or touch the money at all. Most telling, "If the woman had no money, Leku would still give her the medicine and refused to reply or respond to the long statement of gratitude. It was not that the gratitude was wasted or the beneficiary should not thank her; it was as if she were saying that her help was rendered on behalf of some higher forces."[111] Ìyá Lekulęja is a conduit through which cosmic and terrestrial powers flow to the community to ensure continuity. And as further evidence of her integrity, directives, and motivations, if Ìyá Lekulęja is unable to determine the cure for a particular ailment, she refers the client to an oníṣẹ̀gun, a babaláwo, or a Western-educated physician. Rather than place people on a merry-go-round of psychological, physiological, or chemical dependency, she utters laconic lifesaving truths that ensure societal health and vitality.

Ìyá Lekulęja is an Àjẹ́ and, even though her portrait is in profile as a result of her single-minded devotion to her life's work, her character boasts a dimensionality that suffuses Falola's narrative. With his description of the elder it is easy to see why Àjẹ́ are often the subjects of wild rumor and speculation: The most evolved see through the distracting, destructive, and delimiting preoccupations of mortals and live a life of submergence in the spiritual realm. Ìyá Lekulęja's richest discourse is between herself and the flora and fauna and Gods who communicate to her their powers, medicines, and gifts. Ìyá Lekulęja's pharmacological knowledge is so vast that Falola recalls his school headmaster comparing Western education to the Wisdom of the World and informing his students that "what the teachers wanted us to learn was nothing compared to what Leku knew."[112] This is an important admission from a guardian of Western education.

Ìyá Lekulęja is a perfect example of an iyaláwo—a humble divinity whose sole mission is to fully spend herself in service to her community. Ìyá Lekulęja reveals the level of intensity and life-long focus it takes to be a true wisdom keeper. She is a walking spiritual, pharmacological, linguistic, terrestrial encyclopedia who not only knows the names of thousands perhaps millions of flora and fauna, but who knows their oríkì as well. As Yoruba cosmontology makes clear, knowledge of oríkì is essential: Just as Falola's oríkì helps illuminate his identity, define his character, and prepare him to attain excellence, so too do the oríkì of flora and fauna detail their characteristics, identities, specializations, and applications. By chanting their oríkì, Ìyá Lekulęja galvanizes and activates the àșę and Àję́ of the flora and fauna. Indeed, some medicines become effective only with the utterance of oríkì.

Falola's fascination with and attraction to Ìyá Lekulęja make him privy to another aspect of her existence. Falola helps her carry her load to her bedroom; and rather than seeing the usual items one would expect to find there, Ìyá Lekulęja's bedroom is an extension of her shop with more herbs, skulls, feathers, seeds, and roots. Falola notes that although her shop has electricity, in her room, Ìyá Lekulęja has a simple clay lamp with five wicks that burns red oil, and "[b]ehind the lamp was a wooden statue, a representation of a god or goddess."[113]

The simplest things can hold multifold meaning. The importance of Ìyá Lekulęja's work and the focus with which she undertakes it are directly reflected in the simplicity of her shrine. Ìyá Lekulęja is clearly the Child and Mother of the Earth, and her worship of Àję́ is simple and employs elemental objects including a clay pot hewn from the red laterite of the Earth that is fueled by the palm oil of Àję́ and illuminated by five wicks.

Five is a number of great physical and spiritual significance. The human body's major and minor extremities are numbered in fives. Ifá and Mę́rìndilogun divination both describe five types of blessings and five misfortunes that will impact human beings.[114] The number five recurs in Àję́'s rituals and symbolism; indeed, the number represents Ọ̀șun, who is heralded as "the leader of Àję́."[115] To better understand the cosmontological significance of the number five, it is helpful to examine ęsę associated with the number in Mę́rìndilogun divination.

When one sees five elders on the Mę́rìndilogun divination tray, one has divined Ọșę, and the verses of Ọșę recorded in *Sixteen Cowries* all relate to attaining one's destiny, founding towns, enjoying success, and transforming imperfections into glory. In the fourth ẹsẹ of Ọṣẹ, Osinnido offers the following things to found the town of Ìbàdàn: five pigeons, five snails, and five cocks; ọdúndún and tètè leaves, which are used to make omi èrọ̀; an àtòrì tree, which is known for its strength and is used for making the àtòrì whip of Egúngún; pèrègún, a tree "used as a landmark" and for determining the optimal place for offering sacrifice;[116] and a banana, which is a phallic symbol rich with procreative seeds. The highly symbolic snails that Osinnido sacrifices are essential to the founding of Ìbàdàn because the distance that they travel in their respective directions determines the limits of Ìbàdàn which "is the largest indigenous city in West Africa."[117] The same verse reveals Osinnido's identity which further elucidates the connection to Àjẹ́: "He is the one we call Ibadan Hill."[118] Here, Òkèbàdàn, the God of the Hill of Ìbàdàn, whom I discuss in the introduction, has been patrified. But rather than obliterating Òkè's abundant maternal qualities, patrification affirms Òkè's snail-like holism and provides a context by which to appreciate Òkè's "tough" and "active" penis which hits men and penetrates women.[119] Òkè offers vibrant proof of the fact that God must be Everything—She certainly is.

Important exploits of Òṣun are recorded in the ẹsẹ of Ọṣẹ including Òṣun instituting peace and gender balance by dancing the warring Àjẹ́ of the "Town of Women" back into the town of Òjògbòmẹkùn and Òṣun sacrificing a ladder with five steps to be successful in battle against Ìlájẹ́, The Town of Wealth.[120] In the tenth ẹsẹ, Òṣun grants healthy children to the people of Òṣogbo, but, in a gentle reminder customary of Àjẹ́, she gives the children fevers to remind the people of Òṣogbo to worship and praise her. The people of Òṣogbo learn to offer sacrificial items in fives every fifth day to Òṣun.[121]

The verses of Ọṣẹ are rich with entities, ìtàn, and symbols that relate to Àjẹ́, and to ensure that these subtle references are not dismissed as coincidental, the eleventh ẹsẹ of Ọṣẹ recounts the glorification of Odídẹrẹ́, the king's favorite. When Odídẹrẹ́'s sacrifice to heal her buttocks turns her tail feathers red, she is mortified. The king not only reassures her verbally, "I say that in my eyes you are glorious," but he also organizes a "dance in the nude" at the annual festival to showcase her crimson attributes.[12] As a result of her glorification, ikó oódẹ became the signature adornment of Àjẹ́ and rulers and initiates as well.[123] Odídẹrẹ́ is also featured in the twelfth verse of Ọṣẹ which describes how Ọbàtálá's efforts to establish a farm are thwarted by African Grey Parrots who eat his corn. Ọbàtálá and his disabled servant devise a strategy to capture and the parrots which saves Ọbàtálá's corn crop and provides him with Odídẹrẹ́ to keep as pets and ikó oódẹ to use and sell.[124]

All of the paradox, power, and profundity of creating and ending life; of being humiliated but later being honored; and of healing, harming, and making whole that is revealed in Ọṣẹ also glows in Ìyá Lekulẹja's humble clay lamp. While the exact name of her God is unknown, Falola reveals that Ìyá Lekulẹja visits Òkèbàdàn to procure the hill's omi èrò which can cure barrenness, grant children, and heal sicknesses. Ìyá Lekulẹja's unnamed God could very well be Òkè, or she could be Mọlẹ̀, Ìyàmi Òṣòròngà, Odù, or Ìyá Lekulẹja, herself, for they are all the same.

It is important to note that Ìyá Lekulẹja's God does not demand specific types of gin and cigars or certain denominations of currency. The needs of Òrìṣà Ìyá Lekulẹja are as humble as those of Ìyá Lekulẹja because neither she nor her God are self-interested capitalists who are thrilled by glitzy gewgaws or ego-building tributes. In fact, Ìyá Lekulẹja, herself, offers a riveting portrait of a true and living God dwelling amongst mortals, and she differs from many of the recorded portrayals of Òrìṣà and rulers in that she has no interest in wealth, ego, prestige, spouses, or glory. Ìyá Lekulẹja's clothing is solely what is sufficient to cover her body. She probably offers her God more food than she feeds herself. Ìyá Lekulẹja does not adorn herself in sumptuous robes or station herself on golden thrones; she does not organize expensive initiations or charge a cow or its equivalent in exchange for information. Ìyá Lekulẹja is, quite simply, the truth. And the truth, like the bounty and wisdom of the Earth is free.

A simple and stunning example of an Onímọlẹ̀, Ìyá Lekulẹja adheres to the three laws of Àjẹ́ as detailed by Opeola: Her life revolves around the expert application of flora and fauna; she shares freely with the community; and, as it regards displays of wealth, Ìyá Lekulẹja seems to know well the words Ọbàtálá shared with his three brothers:

> Money is the death
> Money is the trouble
> Money is all evil
> He said, "Since you have broken the taboo
> And you all love money
> Whoever's interested in these kinds of things
> Will not live long."[125]

Ìyá Lekulẹja is aware that capitalism's wealth is actually worthless, and the confusions it creates are soul-stymieing distractions. Consequently, she quietly works to cure the insanities, illnesses, and depravities born of an aberrant way of life.

Ìyá Lekulẹja's focus on healing her community is so complete that her vocation *is* her identity. She does not have lengthy titles of honor or respect; she does not proselytize or preach; she does not stand on the necks of others so that she can appear to be taller than she is. She simply harmonizes and harnesses the powers of the Earth. Although she is shunned by many, those with open ojú inú know her power. Falola, for example, does what no one else dares or cares to do—sit in her shop and observe her while she works. Falola is so impressed with her that he asks her to teach him to harness the power of flora and fauna. In response, "She removed the pipe from her mouth, smiled, and said nothing": Falola concludes, "I forgot about my request."[126] One wonders if Ìyá Lekulẹja's smile is saying: "What do you think we have been doing?" or if she is thrilled to have a sound vessel in whom to pour her wisdom. Falola's response is no less mystifying. Does her smile astonish him into forgetfulness, does he simply forget, or does his Orí direct him towards other pursuits? The author leaves a charged space between the lines in which he and Ìyá Lekulẹja continue their spiritual dialogue.

The charged space in which Ìyá Lekulẹja shares wisdom, power, and secrets with Falola attains high voltage when Falola strays into the arena of misuse of power. When Sali, Falola's eleven-year-old friend, decides to win the love of a twelve-year-old class prefect named Risi, Falola is appointed head of the advisory board of love. The boys draft love letters and graduate to potions when words fail. When Falola, Sali, and the rest of the board go to Ìyá Lekulẹja to obtain the necessary herbs to place Risi under the command of Sali's devotion, Falola unconsciously makes an appointment for rebirth and baptism in the waters of Àjẹ.

The actions of these children are repeated all over the world by children and adults who attempt to create and manipulate a fictional concept of "love" that they are convinced they cannot live without. The children's acts would be considered harmless to many. But by breaking the rule of Àjẹ forbidding the indiscriminate use of ewé, the children could unknowingly create a concoction that maims or kills Risi or that drives her insane. In seeking tools of manipulation from Ìyá Lekulẹja, the children make her complicit in their actions: Such an association could result in the lynching of a Mother. The children's single-minded devotion to mastering the art of manipulation presages the type of corruption, abuse of power, and treachery for which Nigerians have become infamously stereotyped. Because of the seriousness the children's actions and because of Ìyá Lekulẹja's bond with Falola, Ìyá Lekulẹja does everything in her power to redirect Falola's misdirected Orí.

A cadre of elders, including his biological mother, his mother's mother, and his mother's father in addition to other relatives, corner Falola. After they hold him down and shave his head, Ìyá Lekulẹja performs gbẹ́rẹ́ on Falola: "Leku came with a new blade and made over a hundred incisions on my head. She opened a small container and rubbed a dark looking powder on the small cuts, speaking in tongues as she did."[127] After Falola's head is cleansed, anointed, and remolded, Ìyá Lekulẹja uses *eku*, a rat, her synecdochal signifier, to mix the surest and most potent of all medicines: "She removed her cloth, and stood naked for all to see. She moved in circles many times, uttering archaic words in rapid succession. Then she knelt over the bowl and washed her breasts and vagina into its contents."[128] By removing her clothes and assuming the posture of ìkúnlẹ̀ abiyamọ, Ìyá Lekulẹja opens her sacred Igbádù and accesses her Àjẹ́ and àṣẹ for the benefit of Falola who drinks her rarified liquefied power.

The ritual suckling of the breasts that Abiodun describes is expanded by Ìyá Lekulẹja who charges the omi ẹ̀rọ̀ of her breasts with the cleansing waters of her vagina and the cauterizing power of her clitoris. By drinking his medicine, Falola is effectively reborn and baptized in Ìyá Lekulẹja. He literally tastes his mother; and as a result, he is placed under her protective auspices for life. It is important to note that Ìyá Lekulẹja's actions are performed at the request and under the watchful eyes of Falola's relatives including his mother, grandmother, and grandfather. His progenitors know the power and guidance that Ìyá Lekulẹja offers, and they know that a child can never have too many loving mothers. Indeed, it appears that even with all of the various degrees and dimensions of mother-love in which Falola is steeped, the undiluted Àjẹ́ of *the* Mother is essential for his safety and self-actualization.

After his rebirth, Falola assumes the status of a newborn and is made to stay in Ìyá Lekulẹja's store and as close to her as possible. To further facilitate the permeation of Ìyá Lekulẹja's ritual waters and protective medicines into his being, Falola eats minimally and is not allowed to bathe. While incubating in Ìyá Lekulẹja's external womb, Falola comes to better know his Mother:

> When she was not smoking her pipe, she was talking to unseen strangers, appealing to gods, cursing witches, praising herbs, and begging gods. . . . she was obsessed with appealing to the gods and all universal forces not to make impotent the plants, roots, bones, and other items in the store. The Yoruba she used to communicate, to talk to herself, and to say all these strange things was not the language we used at home or school. Leku was so strange that I began to believe Sali, who claimed that the woman had twenty-four eyes.[129]

Ìyá Lekulẹja is the classic Àjẹ́: a person with two bodies, a being of two spheres, one who can see inside and outside, a mother with two tongues. Perhaps Ìyá Lekulẹja is using the language of the original inhabitants of Ifẹ̀, the Onímọlẹ̀, when communicating with the spirit realm. The only thing that is clear is that the depths of Odù's Ọ̀rọ̀ are infinite.[130]

With Falola having truly become Ìyá Lekulẹja's son, she reveals her soul to him, and her soul is Àjẹ́:

> Leku had completely overwhelmed me, showing me her other side, which was more secretive, more frightening, more threatening, and more powerful. . . . Eventually, I was able to claim, and then only privately, that I fully understood her essence, her representation in the realm of the living and the underworld. I never said that I understood her power or its sources. I could only know bits and pieces.[131]

What Falola experiences—from the tasting of and rebirth through Ìyá Lekulẹja to his tutelage at her knee—is the closest equivalent to an initiation into Àjẹ́ that there could ever be.

Ìyá Lekulẹja teaches Falola and his readers the difference between a "witch" and an Àjẹ́. Had she been a "witch," we would never have heard of Falola, because Ìyá Lekulẹja would have made ọmọ stew out of Falola and his companions, and, if caught, she would have been tried for murder and sentenced to death. But Ìyá Lekulẹja is not some fairy tale fabrication designed to terrorize, she is Mother Divine, who without a word establishes a psychic bond of care and respect with Falola, who appears to have been called to her as if their relationship were born in another realm and came of age during Falola's terrestrial youth. Falola becomes both a son and a tool capable of revealing some of the verses of Ìyá Lekulẹja's epic ìtàn. What is more, rather than a mistake, Falola's attempt at conjuring Risi is revealed to be an essential step in consecrating his bond with Ìyá Lekulẹja. Had he not gone to such lengths, he would not have been reborn, purified, and united with Ìyá Lekulẹja through omi ẹ̀rọ̀ gidigidi and Àjẹ́.

Ìyá Lekulẹja rises from the margins of obscurity to become Falola's warrior and hero, and her love and wisdom expand to envelope Falola's family as well. When Falola's grandfather, known as "Pasitor" in respect to his occupation, struggles to obtain justice for the wronged, he drags Falola with him on visits to various chiefs and to the Reformed Ogboni Fraternity lodge only to find that the persons from whom he seeks assistance are part of a cadre of corruption. The pair consults Ìyá Lekulẹja, and she confers with authorities higher than chiefs and lodge members; she holds counsel with those who keep and embody the ancient laws of Onílẹ̀. Ìyá Lekulẹja reports that the ẹgbẹ́ Àjẹ́, who are referred to in the text as "awon aiye" and "awon agba,"[132] offer a clear solution to the problem: "They said you must all fight."[133] With this solution, the responsibility for righting wrongs is placed in the hands of the wronged. Those who seek to end corruption, oppression, and wickedness must, themselves, be active agents of sanitization and liberation. Those who want justice must do what Fela,

Funmilayo, Thomas Sankara, Patrice Lumumba, Yaa Asante Waa, El Hajj Malik El Shabazz, Ganga Zumba, the Deacons for Defense, the Black Panther Party, Nyabinghi, the Mau Mau, Jean-Jacques Dessalines, Boukman, Robert Williams, and many more warriors did: They must risk their lives and take lives as necessary.

Àjẹ́ works in many ways, including doing nothing at all, to move human beings out of stasis, self-pity, and finger pointing and into direct action and full actualization of their own power, their own Àjẹ́. Perhaps Oladapo is making reference to Àjẹ́'s passive-aggressive approach to sparking revolution and inspiring change in *Orin Odídẹrẹ́: Àjẹ́ Ọlọ́mọ* when he observes,

> *Alujìbìtì, wàyó*
> *Wọ́n bẹ nílẹ̀:*
> *Ẹyẹ ri won kò leè mùjẹ̀ ẹni jìbìtì*

> [Wicked deceitful people
> They are controlling the land:
> Ẹyẹ sees them but does not drink the blood of the wicked][134]

Like the child carried òdì, the Mothers see everything. They watch the few oppress the many who acquiesce in their subjugation. The Mothers see their empowered children falling on their knees and praying instead of standing tall and taking action. The Mothers do not pass judgment; they patiently facilitate the awakening and arrival of the warriors.

In their efforts to galvanize the masses, Oladapo and his loquacious Odídẹrẹ́ are siblings of Fela and his "Basket Mouth,"[135] which leaks truth everywhere. In the way of his countryman, Oladapo calls out and condemns Nigeria's leaders who use their powers to foment destruction, hostility, death, and negativity: "*Ẹ̀jẹ̀ ọmọ ènìyàn / N lẹyìn fi í ṣorò láìsùn!!!* (The blood of children / Is what you use to gather wealth every single moment of the day!!!)."[136] The real "African witches" are the wealthy leaders and magnates: They are the ones who are—figuratively and, in some cases, literally—harvesting the blood, potential, and power of youths to pad their wealth and solidify others' destitution. How to dispatch these thieves provides revolutionaries with a curvilinear riddle for the ages because there are no easy answers or magic bullets. As Falola and Pasitor come to learn, there is no covert coven sucking up souls at night. Those who seek to change society must do what freedom fighters have always done—Fight.

Revealing her special regard for her Falola, Ìyá Lekuleja reveals that while Pasitor's perambulations have made the child a target, she has protection waiting in her pocket. In addition to giving Pasitor more medicine to apply to Falola through gbẹ́rẹ́, which will make it impossible for anyone to harm him, she reveals that she also gave Falola "ogun isoye" a medicinal technology used throughout Africa "to permanently invigorate the brain to attain excellence."[137] Ìyá Lekulẹja, as the quintessential Àjẹ́, girds her son in the perfect protections that can only be granted by The Wealth of the Earth.

. . .

The women discussed in this chapter—Ìyá Lekulẹja, Funmilayo Anikulapo Kuti, The Queens, Ìyá Àgbà, Wild Christian, Sandra Iszador, Òkèbàdàn—offer a rich representative sample of Àjẹ́'s great depth, dimension, diversity, and devotion in Yoruba life. As their courageous sons reveal, these women are the very definition of Àjẹ́ Ọlọ́mọ. They are mothers protecting, loving, teaching, molding, and feeding children, whether those children are their biological issues or not. Àjẹ́ is the mother who glories in the successes of her children and who gives them the technologies and techniques to fully self-actualize. Àjẹ́ is the Mother with the ability to do the impossible with ease and without motivation of inheritance or accolades of recognition.

Now, who *wouldn't* want a Mother of Power? Who *wouldn't* want to be Ọmọ Ìyá Àjẹ́?

CONCLUSION

THE VERY DEFINITION OF EVIL

It is altogether bizarre that Africana women who are mothers, sisters, wives, daughters, and, yes, Gods would be casually and routinely vilified in academic studies of various fields and in nearly every facet of the entertainment industry as "witches." When they are not being maligned as "witches," Africana women are being condemned or celebrated, depending upon the context, as "bitches" and/or "whores." The dehumanization of Africana women is so prevalent and virulent that it could be described as a pathological festival of defamation. The debasement of Africana womanhood impacts all strata of existence, from infants to Gods; in fact, one of the most widely denigrated/celebrated Àjẹ́ is Òrìṣà Òṣun.

Òṣun is a God who knows, controls, and enjoys her body and her sexuality. In that the human genitals are designed to feel fantastic so as to make the biological creation of life enjoyable and inevitable, Òṣun boasts a knowledge of self that any normal right-minded human being or God also enjoys; indeed all of the Òrìṣà are quite comfortable with their abilities to create life cosmically and biologically (Èṣù's love of sex and his massive penis come to mind).

I have never heard an indigenous Yoruba devotee of Òṣun describe her as a whore: This is because Òṣun is not a whore, sex worker, slut, or anything similar to these constructs. Indeed, there is no indigenous Yoruba word for "prostitute" because the concept is an alien one in traditional Yoruba society. Prostitution was introduced to Africa by Caucasians long after Òṣun had enjoyed her terrestrial existence and solidified her immortality as iyaláwo, nation builder, peace bringer, and divine mother of thriving children. However, with the Caucasian colonial, missionary, and intellectual rape of Africa, constructs that did not exist in Africa and that are not appropriate for African culture became convenient tools of defilement. In the puerile antilife Caucasian worldview, Àjẹ́ are "witches," Èṣù is the "devil," and Òṣun is a "harlot."

William Bascom's *Sixteen Cowries* offers insight as to the origin of the academic reification of Òṣun's denigration. Bascom's informant Salako reveals that "Oshun is fonder of intercourse than all other women."[1] Given the physical and physiological make-up of human beings, being fond of sex is logical: It is the opposite that is unnatural—unless one's indoctrination has led one to believe that intercourse and the genitals are "dirty" and "sinful." To help his repressed Caucasian Christian intended audience understand the phenomenon of a God who is an African who is woman who enjoys sex, Bascom adds with no substantiation, "Because of her promiscuity her worshipers describe her as a harlot, but they take pride in her amorous adventures because they add to her reputation for beauty and desirability."[2] With one sentence, Bascom turns the God of children, fertility, political authority, and sensual bliss, who ensures human continuity and abundance and who protects her progeny with Àjẹ́ and guides them to self-actualization into a pornographic comic book superhero.

The character assassination of Ọ̀ṣun and the desire to associate her with prostitution is part of a centuries-old scheme that was originally employed to justify the perpetual rape and denigration of enslaved and exiled African women and that is constantly revivified through Western popular culture.[3] The Eurocentric packaging and consumption of Ọ̀ṣun as a prostitute is also the forerunner of the unrelenting efforts to defile, disgrace, and condemn Fela's Queens, despite the fact that none of them were prostitutes.

The concerted effort to reduce African cultural, biological, technological, and spiritual magnificence to "witchcraft," "sorcery," "whoredom," and the like is designed to facilitate one of the most stultifying disconnects in the Cosmos. This disconnect is not a theoretical one, nor is it the result of accidental erroneous definitions or attributions. The disconnect is that which seeks to sever children from their mothers. The goal is to turn the Owners of the Earth into the scourge of the Earth. The aim is to replace Gods, Mothers, Wives, and Warriors with prostitutes, bitches, and sluts. The goal is to remove the crown of a queen and replace it with an acronym: AIDS.[4]

To gain a full understanding of how Caucasians orchestrated the defilement of Africana women, mothers, and Gods and why such defilement was essential to their culturally, economically, and sexually exploitative agenda, it is helpful to journey to the land of the Ookun-Yoruba.

Z. O. Apata's "Women Cults and Colonial Responses 1897 – 1960: The Case of Okun-Yoruba People" is an important and illuminating study of the Aruta, Ofoṣi, and Ogun secret societies of the Ookun-Yoruba of contemporary Kogi State.[5] Apata states that his efforts to undertake an exhaustive study of these institutions were thwarted by a policy of "Wogbe Woku," which means "Say it and Die." The societies' members are fiercely protective of their mysteries and powers because they have suffered and survived savage Christian and colonial attacks. However, the members did reveal to Apata important information about the societies' origins and about the introduction of evil and the devil to the land of the Ookun-Yoruba.

Oral tradition reveals that a man who is called Amugbagewo by some informants travelled from his home in Olle to neighboring Gbobe and found there a group of women executing unique rituals and dances and singing songs in a language unfamiliar to him. Similar to Òrúnmìlà's struggle to be as close as possible to Àjẹ́ and become initiated into their àṣírí, Amugbagewo stayed with the women and became one with them. When he left them, he did so carrying on his head a "pot wrapped in a white cloth."[6] African art is replete with images of women carrying pots on their heads; it is an image that represents women's various labors—domestic, economic, biological, and spiritual—all of which are essential to existence. Amugbagewo bearing Odù's pot is an evocative image that at once recalls the Igbádù on the head of the babaláwo and also confirms that man's role is to fertilize and disseminate the divinity of woman, and this is precisely what Amugbagewo did.

The women of Olle turned out *en masse* to greet Amugbagewo upon his return, and they performed essential sacrifices that released and disseminated divinity: "The women could not relieve him of the pot until the blood of a ram, goat, and tortoise was poured on the pot. As soon as the pot was dislodged, the women were instantly possessed by a spirit which drove them into the forest for thirteen days."[7] Africana wisdom workers often sojourn in the wilderness—by choice or by force—to learn and become one with the dynamics and àṣẹ of the Earth's flora, fauna, and spiritual forces.[8] It seems to be the case that Amugbagewo's pot contained Onílẹ̀'s own spirit, and, once released, she drove the women into the womb of the Earth so that she could steep them in a unique aspect of Àjẹ́. On the fourteenth day, the women were found unconscious and wrapped in white cloth. Amugbagewo revived the women by anointing them with a mixture of palm oil and shea butter, which is a soothing, enriching, and empowering approximation of menstrual fluid.

The women emerged as the same mothers, daughters, and wives as before but with profound spiritual accentuation. The Àjẹ́ that they came to Earth with was magnified and enriched, and to better harness their power and ensure its holistic judicial application, the women formalized the language, dances, rituals, and codes of their new identity and power before returning to their homes and families:

> They however retained in them the mysterious spirit which could be induced or activated whenever suitable spiritual atmosphere prevailed such as coronation, burial ceremonies, or important festivals. The news of strange happenings at Olle soon spread to

other parts of Okun-Yorubaland. Some of the communities sent delegates to procure the strange "medicine".[9]

Ookun-Yoruba communities clamored for the pot of power to be brought to and electrify the Àjẹ́ of their women, and the Ofoṣi society spread rapidly.

Apata finds that Ofoṣi's course runs parallel to that of a society called Ogun. Similar to Amugbagewo's role in disseminating power, a man named Obayelu is credited with founding the Ogun sacred society. He "made some incantation to the deity of egun (masquerade) and called the names of some women into the pot of medicine. The women became possessed by the Ogun spirit, and rushed into the forest."[10] Palm oil, ginger, and kola nuts were offered to the "sacred pot" of medicine and used to revive the women. The Ogun society also spread swiftly, as several women were empowered simultaneously by having their names uttered into the odù of sacred medicine.

A sister society called Aruta was founded using a similar methodology as Ofoṣi and Ogun. Employing gender balance as the platform for female spiritual empowerment, titled elder men would submit the names of female relatives, often daughters, to the "Iye Aruta (the head of the Aruta cult). She, in turn[,] called their names into a specially prepared medicine."[11] The females whose spirits had been invoked would not know of the rituals performed on their behalves, but when their male progenitors died, the Aruta spirit would possess the females, who would experience physical and psychic alterations which would increase until the women were fully manifesting the mannerisms, speech, knowledge—the complete identity—of the titled men who had selected them for initiation into Aruta. Similar to Ṣàngó who knew the women of Bàrà were the only entities worthy of guarding and guiding his father's soul, Ookun-Yoruba men acknowledged the spiritual supremacy of their daughters, and before they died, the men arranged for their curvilinear return through their divine daughters.

The Aruta, Ofoṣi, and Ogun sacred societies were highly esteemed. Members of these institutions were exalted, and their communities "accepted them as superior to the non-members."[12] Women were not the only beneficiaries: Entire communities thrived under the auspices of these societies; consequently, men would nominate their daughters and wives for deification, and bachelors sought initiates for brides. Aptata reveals that men who were married to members were expected to exhibit exemplary character because their wives were not ordinary mortals:

> Their husbands had to treat them almost as a special species. Since the adherents were commonly known to be transparently honest and faithful, their husbands were expected to reciprocate by

treating them well. In fact, it was considered a very serious offense for the husbands to beat, slap, or physically assault in any way their wives, who were members of the cults. Any husband who ignored this injunction and maltreated his wife paid very dearly for it.[13]

One would think that men would choose less intimidating, phenomenal, and majestic partners for wives, but Apata finds that initiates were highly sought after: "Rather than this rigid observance scaring men away, it propelled them to place the cults' members on their priority list as wives. Men preferred to marry the adherents as they were considered trustworthy and dependable."[14]

The gender dynamics of the Ookun-Yoruba are profoundly important: In addition to men being credited with bringing these institutions to the Ookun-Yoruba, fathers ensured their daughters were nominated and, therefore, protected, revered, glorified, and deified, and men chose to establish families and build futures only with divine initiates. Here is ample evidence of a nation of men who not merely facilitated but demanded the full empowerment and deification of their wives, daughters, and mothers. While some ẹsẹ Ifá and babaláwo suggest ways to weaken and delimit women, I think the Ookun-Yoruba's response to Àjẹ́ and female empowerment is reflective of the gender relations that prevailed in Yoruba and other African societies prior to the patriarchal shift and the destruction wrought by slavery, colonization, and Christianization.

The Ookun-Yoruba offer rich portraits of healthy harmonious societies that are centered on holistic personal and community elevation and deification. It is rather easy to imagine the character of societies undergirded by Aruta, Ofoṣi, and Ogun. Abuse of any kind would be rare, as would dishonesty, theft, debauchery, and the myriad social ills that are popularized and promoted in the West and in nations infected with Western mores. While Ookun-Yorubaland was not a utopia, it seems a close approximation of one.

When from the late 1800s to the mid-1900s Caucasian Christians infested the hinterland of West Africa, they brought with them and began spreading the world's most virulent disease—evil. As Apata reveals, "The christian[15] converts of the various denominations described the women cults as devil created, and the spirit that descended on the adherents of Ofoṣi, Ogun, and Aruta was described as an evil spirit. The secrecy surrounding some of the activities of the cults was roundly condemned."[16]

The Christian assessment of and response to these peaceful balanced societies are important for many reasons, the chief among them being that they elucidate the origin, meaning, and methodology of evil. There were neither "devils" nor "evils" in the Ookun-Yoruba nation until the arrival of

Christians. "Evil" and "the devil" were nonexistent because African societies are founded on empirical knowledge acquisition, reciprocity, balance, and propriety as opposed to ignorance, judgment casting, scapegoating, belief, "othering" and vilifying. The only way that the aliens could justify their totalitarian and barbaric religion was by first introducing the individuals they sought to convert to their narrow, racist, and ignorance-dependent and xenophobia-drenched constructs of "evil" and "devil."

While reading Apata's article I had the epiphany that Caucasians are the source of all of the evil in this world: This is not a race-based condemnation but an etymological observation. The word "evil" is wholly Caucasian and does not have a source beyond Old English.[17] The word "devil" can be traced to the Late Greek and Greek words *dialoblos* and *diaballein* which mean "slanderer" and "to slander," respectively.[18] The relationship between "devil" and "slander" is important because slandering other Gods, religions, and peoples is precisely what Caucasian Christians and Caucasian Christianity have done the world over. One could argue that slandering the "other" is an essential weapon in the Christian missionary arsenal, because the only way Christianity can appear to make sense is not merely by making other ways of life appear nonsensical or different, but by denigrating them completely by defining them as evil.

In traditional African cosmogony, cosmology, ontology, and philosophy, the concepts of sin—especially as associated with the human body and sex—evil, and devil do not exist. These concepts do not exist because they are antihuman, antilife, and antiscientific. The concepts of "evil" and "devil" also stymie self-actualization because they prevent human beings from learning the lessons and acquiring the skills that lead to numinosity. Manifesting one's divinity is a vital and inextricable aspect of African ontology, cosmology, and identity, and of the many ways there are to create Gods, sex is one of the most important.[19]

Caucasians, swaddled in pseudo-scientific superstition and misogynist-based ignorance, considered the womb to be a wandering pollutant. By contrast, Yoruba scientists understood eons ago that the womb is literally Ilé Ọlẹ̀, The Home of Embryos. Rather than the source of original sin, Woman in Yoruba cosmontology is the Keeper of the Home of Embryos, and, therefore, the literal Lord of Destiny, Eternity, and Divinity. The job of the man is to inseminate, disseminate, protect, and project Mother's Divinity, and, thereby, ensure divine continuity. Man's job is made fulfilling through the thrill of sex and by seeing the energies that he expends in the creative process literally take on new lives that extend his own life and solidify his immortality.

Yoruba cosmontology is simply too deeply rooted in scientific and biological facts for such concepts as devil, sin, witch, witchcraft, and evil to have developed organically. These concepts had to be literally beaten, lynched, and branded into the Yoruba and into everyone else that Caucasian missionary colonizers came in contact with. Not only did Caucasians indoctrinate peoples all over the world to believe in outlandish concepts that were born of their superstitions and complete misunderstandings of life, biology, cosmology, and ontology, but they also convinced people all over the world that not only were they backward if they did not believe in racist juvenile Caucasian concepts of good, evil, sin, god and devil, but also that their indigenous cultures and divine selves were sinful and evil and that their Gods and ancestors were devils.

The Christian world is dependent on dichotomy. Without the concepts of evil, devil, death, and sin, the concepts of good, savior, salvation, and holiness are irrelevant. Christianity is so inextricably linked to and dependent upon evil and the devil that Christianity could be considered synonymous with evil, and Jesus could be defined as a codependent complement of Satan, who is known in some circles as Lucifer. The importance of bifurcation to Christianity and the Western worldview is evident in the fact that Jesus and Lucifer share a home in and identification with the same bright and morning star (the planet Venus). This seemingly oppositional pair must co-exist in the Christian world, for without one the other has no significance.

The Devil/Satan/Lucifer construct has proven itself to be an essential terroristic tool for solidifying indoctrination and coercing obedience to a Jesus construct that looks, surprisingly, exactly like the enslaver/colonizer/missionary/rapist. But it is important to note that Lucifer literally means "Bearer of Light," which implies knowledge, wisdom, and elevation of consciousness—attributes that are the enemies of organized religion and such psychological crutches as faith and belief. Indeed, when one has wisdom and knowledge and is enlightened, faith and belief are irrelevant as is the need to "rely" on or be "bound" to any religion.[20]

Knowledge and illumination are also anathema to colonization and imperialism. Had Christian Caucasians simply engaged in knowledge sharing, scientific discussions, or intellectual debates with the indigenous peoples they met all over the world, they would have gained few if any converts and the Christian religion would have been useless as a tool of economic, political, and social control. Only after terrorizing innocent people and then bombarding them with the lies that their customs, practices, powers, science, technology, secrets, mothers, and they, themselves, were "evil" could the lie of an ironically enslaving, oppressing, and disenfranchising "savior" make sense and be considered necessary.

The most illogical, heinous, racist, ignorant, and bloodthirsty God ever fabricated condemned the Ofoşi, Ogun, and Aruta as "evil" and declared war on them. Caucasians shrewdly placed Christianized Africans on the frontlines of their battle to destroy Africa's soul. A convert named James Orisadare Olorunyomi, despite his names, was happy to wield a sword for his Caucasian lord, and he discussed the multi-tiered nature of attack:

> First to expose the secrets of this doctrine to the christians so that they may be able to wage war against the worshippers so that they may repent and accept a religion capable of salvation. Second when these idol worshippers realise that their secrets have been published . . . they will be convinced that their doctrine is without foundation and one without truth. They will then repent in shame.[21]

It is perplexing that a religion that styles itself as "the way, the truth, and the life" would feel the need to "wage war" and slaughter those to whom it claims to offer salvation. If theirs is, in fact, *the* way, wouldn't there be no other way? If theirs is *the* truth, why are there so many other truths? If their religion signifies life, why did Christian crusades anoint the world in rivers of the blood of innocent people? If salvation is so important, why did it only become necessary when Christian savagery suffused the planet? These questions raise other questions: If Christianity traces sin to women's wombs, how much disgust must Caucasian men feel for their counterparts? How much must Caucasian men loathe themselves? Why did Christians choose to spread self-loathing and hatred externally rather than undertake self-inspection and work to establish internal harmony, balance, and peace? Rather than simply and blindly believe, many Ookun-Yoruba queried their oppressors, examined the actual facts, and fought back. They fought for their lives and against the God of sin, hate, evil, slavery, prostitution, and submission. Apata finds that "[b]etween 1930 and 1955, frequent and prolonged clashes were reported between the adherents of these cults and the christians. Rumours of some christians dying mysteriously spread like wildfire. This was attributed to the mystical powers of the cults. Peace and order were upset in the region leading to the intermittent disruption of colonial administration."[22]

This Christian crusade was a brutal and gory distraction. Caucasian colonizers were not concerned with "saving" the very people they were slaughtering. These missionaries were the scouts and running dogs of colonizers; their job was to rid the land of dissidents so that the wealth of the Continent could more easily flow to England. While the Christians waged a flashy and boisterous war on the divine Ookun-Yoruba, the colonizers waged a quiet economic war. When the crusade was over, the Ookun-Yoruba found that the land that they had lived with harmoniously since the birth of time; land that nurtured them as surely and securely as a mother nurtures her embryos, was now—somehow—"owned" by an alien people and nation. These usurpers claimed to own not only the land but everyone and everything on it as well. The oppressors also asserted that the Ookun-Yoruba had to pay taxes to them in thanks for and in order to continue their existence. To facilitate the taxation, commercialization, and domination of human beings, Caucasian colonizers forced the Ookun-Yoruba, and nearly everyone in the world, to dam the inherent fluidity of their identities and adopt a surname.

While they have been packaged to appear as both natural and necessary, currency and surnames are recent inventions that Caucasian colonizers made mandatory all over the world to facilitate global colonization and capitalist oppression primarily through taxes and debt. Surnames are not indigenous aspects of many world cultures, including that of the Yoruba. In the article, "Etymological Evolution of Yoruba Names," Adebayo Faleti discusses the primary names that a Yoruba person can bear and they include *orúkọ àmútọ̀runwa*, the name one came from Ọ̀run with; *orúkọ àbísọ*, one's birth name; *oríkì*, the name with which one is praised; and *orílẹ̀*, the name signifying one's totem.[23] Faleti asserts that these four names reveal a person's "unmistakable full identity," and none of these names represents a surname.[24] In fact, unlike the names mentioned above, which are rich in power, identification, and significance, the Yoruba term for "surname" is *àpelé*, which means nothing more than "that which is added."[25]

As it relates to the Caucasian custom of a wife taking her husband's name, which signifies ownership, Samuel Johnson makes it clear that in Yoruba culture, "A married woman cannot adopt her husband's totem, much less his name."[26] The married woman, identical to the single woman, the married man, and the single man, has her own specific names, oríkì, totem, and spiritual-cultural identifiers.

In "Sexism, English and Yoruba," Yisa K. Yusuf confirms that because Yoruba names relate to identity and destiny, the surname concept and its attendant sexism and ownership are not part of the traditional Yoruba worldview:

> In normal Yoruba culture, children are not given surnames. Instead, they are given only personal names which may be feminine, masculine, or gender neutral. . . . A Yoruba child carries their personal names throughout their life. In other words, marital re-naming does not take place in traditional Yoruba culture. The question of marking marital status as *Miss* and *Mrs* . . . does not therefore arise. The wife may be described (not labeled) as the wife of X, while the husband may equally be described as the husband of Y. In other words, Yoruba naming practices, like its pronoun system and word formation principles, are unlike those of English [and are] non-sexist.[27]

Traditional Yoruba naming practices are characterized by respect, age, and familial and community contextualization and status. The fluidity of African naming is evident in Ìyá Lekulẹja whose name is her vocation. To illustrate the reverence with which identity and names are treated in the traditional Yoruba world, in *A Mouth Sweeter than Salt* Toyin Falola discusses an elderly woman who showed so much respect for her husband that when he fell ill and she was asked his name to complete hospital paperwork her response was simple: "We never mention the name in vain."[28] This powerful statement confirms that respect and tradition, also known as ìṣèṣe, are more important than Western forms and mandates. The elder's statement also stands as a clear confirmation that her husband's divinity is equal, if not superior, to that of an aliens' God.

Undaunted by such concepts as respect, consideration, and propriety, Caucasian oppressors named enslaved Africans any foolishness that flowed through their stunted minds, and they continued this practice during the colonization of Africa. Not only did British colonial officials force Africans to create and adopt surnames but, as Falola reveals, "The British officials and their agents . . . actually gave people last names if they failed to come up with one. Those who gave their *oriki* found that these had been converted to their last names. For hundreds of others, the British simply converted their towns and cities into their last names, as in the case of Tafawa Balewa."[29] While dislocated Africans often covet "African names," with Falola's revelation it is apparent that "slave names" and racist misnaming are *pan*-African realities. Those idealized "African names" may actually be brand names (pun intended) of African neo-servitude.

Having been defined as evil and then renamed to truncate, alter, or obliterate identity and destiny and, most important to colonizing capitalists, to facilitate taxation, the Ookun-Yoruba—like victims of colonization and neocolonization the world over—were forced to work in Caucasian created and controlled factories and industries. Rather than working to manifest their divinity and immortality, people were introduced to a new form of slavery in which they had to "work for a living," as refusal to pay taxes resulted in death. The Caucasian world order, which remains in effect to this day, resulted in a global colonization that compels the masses to labor all of their diminished lives to provide luxuries for the only devils this world has ever known.

It is very important for human beings to probe the concept of currency and understand why it was created. Many people assume that they need money to live. However, the Earth is designed to provide every human being who has ever lived and who will ever live with everything he or she needs. Neither human beings nor any of the Earth's innumerable organisms can be honestly or accurately valued in any form of currency; so how did the abstract constructs of currency and capital come to rule the world? A people with a bottomless void in the place of a cultural foundation created a mythical construct of supremacy and cloaked themselves in it in hopes of concealing their soullessness. After either slaughtering or terrorizing and indoctrinating the peoples of the world, Caucasian colonizers enforced their economic order. Oppressors placed their images on both their savior and their money and demanded tributes of the latter to the former in the form of taxes and tithes as well.

Colonization strove to alter the very ìwà and orí of the African continent and all of its inhabitants. Everything—the land, the waters, the air, the flora and fauna, the minerals, and, most of all, the shining people—was perverted, twisted, polluted, raped, or destroyed to fit the Caucasian pro-capital—antilife mandate. Caucasians decreed that communally necessary and ecologically balanced agrarian labor be abandoned for the cultivation of "cash crops" that destroyed the land and starved the people but rained riches on colonizers. Animals were slaughtered in record numbers so that their carcasses could become trophies. Lush forests were leveled. Human beings and human lives were utterly devastated. Whatever could not be bent to serve the colonial order was broken. Having their homes completely defiled was not enough: Africans, like peoples all over the world, had to pay their oppressors to live in wastelands created by depravity. And because only Caucasians had access to the pieces of paper that they created and declared had value, Africans had to work for Caucasians in industries created for African destruction to pay for their existence and to purchase what Africans had harvested and fashioned themselves prior to slavery and the camouflaged slaveries of colonialism and neocolonialism.

Like so many millions of people all over the world, the Ookun-Yoruba could not pay taxes in the currency that was fabricated by their oppressors but backed by stolen African gold.[30] The divine mothers, wives, and daughters of the Ookun-Yoruba—women who occupied positions of power, prominence, and esteem in their communities—were forced to leave their homes and shrines and labor in towns born of the betrayal of humanity. It is in this social abyss that Caucasians introduced African women to the "profession" that Caucasians celebrate as the oldest in the world and in which the Caucasian cultural identity and economy are rooted: prostitution.

The members of Aruta, Ofoṣi, and Ogun were laid low by the systematic gang rape of Christianity, Cauconomics, and the tragic irony of being natally alienated in their own homelands. Their divinity, their names, their social and political powers, and their whole and healthy families were attacked, derided, and decimated. They gained a sadistic religion, the economics of the impoverished, and the gift from the Caucasian man to himself, prostitution.

All over Africa and all over the world, Caucasian imperialists and missionaries have worked together to transform African Queens and Gods into witches, bitches, and whores for their amusement and gratification and for the glorification of their religious myths. Christian colonizers have been so successful globally that today it is common and acceptable to associate Africana women in general and African Queens and Gods in particular with witchery, whoredom, and/or some manner of depravity, viciousness, and/or destitution. Those individuals who know and hold the truth of the Africana woman are rarely heard against the cacophony of hate-mongers. When they are heard, they are promptly vilified, pushed to the margins, or dismissed as reactionaries. Consequently, many wisdom keepers can be found submerged in silence with Mother's Truth locked, as safely as her ova, in the cores of their beings.

Aruta, Ofoṣi, and Ogun, like Ògbóni and Àjẹ́, were not founded as secret societies. Originally, these institutions were embraced as organic social structures that were beneficial and essential for personal empowerment, community actualization, and holistic evolution. Ẹdan initiated every member of ancient Ifẹ̀—men, women, and children—into Ògbóni. Mothers and fathers nominated their daughters for initiation into Aruta, Ofoṣi, and Ogun, and men chose to build lives with women who had been initiated into those societies and who had become those Gods. Àjẹ́, as the mothers, wives, kingmakers, physicians, oríkì chanters, educators, enforcers of justice, and foundation of the Yoruba nation, enjoyed complete community regard and reverence.

It is with the persecution initiated by Caucasian missionary colonizers and enforced by the African missionary colonized that a policy such as "Wogbe Woku" would have to be erected to surround the surviving Divinities of Okun-Yoruba in a wall of empowered silence. The concerted and relentless attacks on Ògbóni, spurred by its eternal reverence of Divine Mother Mọlẹ̀, necessitated both the protective submersion of the original society and the birth of the self-consciously Christocentric "Reformed" Ògbóni Fraternity. The cyclical harvest of blood and innocent bodies reaped by Christian fanatics moves Àjẹ́ to declare themselves "white" if they reveal their divinity at all.

Verily, there is no evil in the world more virulent than that which seeks to destroy the soul of a people through religion-sanctioned savagery.

While Caucasian oppressors have brainwashed billions of people the world over to believe that they are worshippers of "devils" and supporters of "evil," the constructs of evil, witchcraft, devils, and witches can all be traced to Caucasian people and culture and to those peoples' specific fears, vapidity, inadequacies, greed, and self-hatred. The impact of the hatred generated by the Caucasian ethos is global. Consequently, what may be packaged as elaborations on indigenous African concepts, whether in academic tomes or in Africana communities, are, in many cases, centuries of Caucasian slander, filth, fear, inadequacy, jealousy, viciousness, opprobrium, and self-loathing. When one reads or listens to analyses about African "witches," "sorcerers," and "witchdoctors" one is really reading and hearing testaments to Caucasian envy, sadism, racism, and barbarism which, having festered internally for so long, explode like a corpse during summer's dog days and infect everyone and everything in its vicinity with ignorance and pestilence.

A tremendous amount of effort, ink, film, and paper has been expended in the concerted attempt to devalue Àjẹ́ and its wielders, works, and activators, which include Africana mothers, menstrual blood, Yoruba Gods, and Yoruba ontology, cosmogony, cosmology, medicine, and science. Many careers and fortunes have been made at the expense of the Mothers. As I write, hate-filled songs, vile videos, bogus books, and outlandish articles are being published all in the effort to undo She who cannot be undone: We who cannot be undone.

. . .

To understand the truth about one's self, one's relationship with the Cosmos, one's weighty responsibilities, and one's infinitely expansive arc of actualization, one must desire to know and must actively seek knowledge about one's source, lineage, powers, destiny, and, for the most evolved, knowledge of one's inherent divinity. Many individuals avoid such holistic wisdom acquisition. Some shun their histories because they are afraid of what they will find. Others have resigned themselves to an evolution from apes, while others glorify their Neanderthal ancestors.[31] Some people are so terrified of the immensity, the truths, and the infinitude of the Cosmos that they claim that nothing is there. Àjẹ́ and their sons do not have these problems. They behold in their daughters' tender bodies the perfect containers of eternity—Olódù Ilé Ọlẹ̀: Whole, perfect, growing, glowing Àjẹ́. They gaze at their Mothers and see Gods glistening with power. They look to the Cosmos and find the cervix of immensity expanding to accommodate the births of all creation. They look within; they find Her shining; and they know

We
are
Àjẹ́
is
Eternal.

NOTES

Mo ní Mọlẹ̀: Mọlẹ̀ ní mi

[1] I thank Cee-Lo Green for this wonderful phrase. *Cee-Lo Green and His Perfect Imperfections* (La Face 2002), CD. The errors you find in this book are the result of my passion and exhaustion and not the machinations of a racist masquerading as some type of "editor."

Introduction: The Womb is a Cosmos / The Cosmos is a Womb

[1] Aseret Sin, "Momma's Original Pot Likka," *Eyeball Literary Magazine: In Love & Revolution* (2003): 18.
[2] Toni Morrison, *Beloved* (New York: Plume, 1988), 191.
[3] Marimba Ani, *Yurugu: An African-Centered Critique of European Cultural Thought and Behavior* (Trenton: Africa World Press, 1994).
[4] See Paul Avis, *Eros and the Sacred* (Harrisburg, PA: Morehouse), 50–52; 100–102.
[5] Susan Griffin makes this point as well in *Pornography and Silence: Culture's Revenge Against Nature* (New York: Harper and Row, 1981) 89n*.
[6] Martyn Stubbs is a Canadian who was employed at a cable television station. His interest in astronomy and his job provided him with the opportunity to film the live raw-feed transmissions of NASA's space walks and journeys to the international space station. The footage Stubbs recorded was also broadcast live on C-SPAN. Many people, including Stubbs, documented interesting occurrences on several broadcasts. So much interest was generated by the activity and active participants of "space" that NASA stopped broadcasting live transmissions. Thanks to Stubbs, everyone can view and analyze NASA's recordings and better appreciate Earth's position as one small part of an infinite system of organic dynamism. See *The Secret NASA Transmissions: 'The Smoking Gun,'* directed by Graham W. Birdsall (Quest Publication, 2001). See also <http://www.snagfilms.com/films/title/the_secret_nasa_transmissions> accessed 24 March 2011.
[7] See the transmission of NASA shuttle mission STS-80 Columbia, 19 November 1996. NASA's video provides a window into the activating agents of certain African spiritual technologies. Lydia Cabrera describes a BaKongo technology which is called the Seven Stars because "the stars come down to this charm. There is an hour in the night when the nkisi is left by itself in the forest, so that the stars may come down, to enter into its power. When you see

something brilliantly coming down—it is a star, entering an nkisi." Quoted in Robert Farris Thompson, *Flash of the Spirit* (New York: Vintage, 1983), 124.

[8] Anthony T. Browder, *Nile Valley Contributions to Civilization: Exploding the Myths*, volume one (Washington, D.C.: Institute of Karmic Guidance, 1992), 242.

[9] Milan Zaviačič and Richard J. Ablin, "The Female Prostate," *Journal of the National Cancer Institute* 90:9 (6 May 1998): 1 <http://jnci.oxfordjournals.org/content/90/9/713.1.full.pdf> accessed 14 May 2012.

[10] Radha Chitale, "Will Chromosome Y Go Bye-Bye?" *ABC News* 17 July 2009 <http://abcnews.go.com/Health/MensHealthNews/story?id=8104217&page=1> 18 December 2011.

[11] Babatunde Lawal, *The Gèlèdé Spectacle: Art, Gender, and Social Harmony in an African Culture* (Seattle: University of Washington Press, 1996), 39, 71, 74, 97.

[12] "'Mitochondrial Eve' Research: Humanity Was Genetically Divided For 100,000 Years," *Science Daily* 15 May 2008 <http://www.sciencedaily.com/releases/2008/05/080515154635.htm> accessed 26 March 2012.

[13] Titles such as *The Rise and Fall of the Yoruba Race: 10,000 BC–1960 AD* by Ayoade Oluwaseun Olubunmi; *The Glory of the Yoruba Race: Past, Present, and Future* by Femi Ade Ogbontiba; *The Cradle of a Race: Ife from the Beginning to 1980* edited by I. A. Akinjogbin; *Ife: The Genesis of Yoruba Race: An Anthology of Historical Notes on Ife City* by M. A. Fabunmi; and Political *History of Ile-Ife (Cradle of Yoruba Race) 1900 – 1980* by Olubayo Okelola prove illustrative. Also, see Seun Ayoade, "Do Yorubas Have An Origin Different From Other Africans?" guest editorial, *Indian Journal of Physiology and Pharmacology* 55:4 (2011): 295–296.

[14] Benjamin F. Voight, Sridhar Kudaravalli, Xiaoquan Wen, and Jonathan K. Pritchard, "A Map of Recent Positive Selection in the Human Genome," *PLOS Biol* 4:3 (2006) <http://www.plosbiology.org/article/info:doi/10.1371/journal.pbio.0040072> accessed 17 April 2013. While the popular pseudohumanist cliché claims "we are all the same underneath," we are not. Different members of the human family boast distinct and significant biochemical and genetic differences.

[15] Ayoade, "Do Yorubas Have An Origin Different From Other Africans?" 295–296. One can even trace the migrations of this Yoruba group by using Hemoglobin C as an indicator.

[16] The Kemetic Kahun Papyrus is thought to be the source of the "wandering womb" myth, but the Kahun Papyrus offers only a superficial gloss of ailments and cures for the convenience of physicians. The information in the papyrus is meant to be understood within the context of holistic Kemetic wisdom. For a more complete understanding of the causes, effects, and cures that relate to the womb, woman, humanity, Gods, flora, and fauna, read R. K.

Ritner, "A Uterine Amulet in the Oriental Institute Collection," *JNES* 43:3 (1984), 209–221. To compare Kemetic to Yoruba medicine—especially the roles of Gods, spiritual entities, and the power of invocation in healing and harming—compare Ritner's findings to chapter five of Moses A. Makinde, *African Philosophy, Culture and Traditional Medicine* (Athens, OH: Center for International Studies, 1988).

[17] "Hystera," *A Dictionary of Medical Science*, edited by Robley Dunglison and Thomas Lathrop, 23rd edition (Philadelphia: Lea Brothers and Co., 1903), 560.

[18] Susan Perry, "Theories abound about conversion disorder and illnesses in LeRoy, N.Y.," *Minnpost* 5 March 2012 <http://www.minnpost.com/second-opinion/2012/03/theories-abound-about-conversion-disorder-and-illnesses-leroy-ny> 14 May 2012.

[19] For an example of the problems that arise when one attempts to apply Judeo-Christian patriarchal insecurities, myths, and fallacies to Yoruba culture read Phillips Stevens, Jr.'s "Women's Aggressive Use of Genital Power in Africa," *Transcultural Psychiatry* 43:4 (2006): 594. For Stevens, the "polluting power of the genitals" is a given; he asserts that "corrupted" àṣẹ becomes Àjẹ́; and he casually connects Àjẹ́ to such Caucasian fictions as witchcraft and "cannibalism and vampirism" (594).

[20] Basil Davidson, *The African Genius* (New York: Atlantic Monthly Press, 1969), 125.

[21] Davidson, *The African Genius*, 125.

[22] "Calling Àjẹ́ Witch In Order to Hang Her: Yorùbá Patriarchal Definition And Redefinition Of Female Power," Global African Spirituality, Social Capital And Self-Reliance, Centre For Black And African Arts and Civilization (CBAAC), Casa Del Papa, Ouidah, Republic Of Benin, November 2007, manuscript shared with the author.

[23] James Wan, "Exorcising Witchcraft in Ghana," *Think Africa Press* 10 November 2011 <http://thinkafricapress.com/ghana/exorcising-witchcraft-gambaga> 14 December 2011.

[24] Clair MacDougall, "Ghana moves to ban 'witchcraft,'" *The Christian Science Monitor* 15 Sep 2011 <http://www.csmonitor.com/World/Africa/2011/0915/Ghana-aims-to-abolish-witches-camps> 1 July 2013.

[25] Mark Oppenheimer, "On a Visit to the U.S., a Nigerian Witch-Hunter Explains Herself," *NY Times* 21 May 2012 <http://www.nytimes.com/2010/05/22/us/22beliefs.html> accessed 21 June 2012.

[26] "Return to Africa's Witch Children," directed by Mags Gavan and Joost van der Valk, (Dispatches, 2009) <http://topdocumentaryfilms.com/return-to-africas-witch-children/> accessed 21 June 2012. See also "Abuse and Persecution of Akwa Ibom children on Account of Witchcraft – Petition," *Akwa Ibom News Online* 21 November 2008 <http://www.akwaibomnewsonline.com/petition/petition-against-akwa-ibom-children-

witchcraft-abuse.php> accessed 21 June 2012.

[27] Toyin Falola, *A Mouth Sweeter Than Salt* (Ann Arbor: University of Michigan Press, 2004), 226.

[28] Falola, *A Mouth Sweeter Than Salt*, 221.

[29] Falola, *A Mouth Sweeter Than Salt*, 221.

[30] Falola, *A Mouth Sweeter Than Salt*, 221.

[31] Falola, *A Mouth Sweeter Than Salt*, 223.

[32] Michael Castleman, "So THAT'S How It Feels…," *All About Sex: The Best Sex Ever* in *Psychology Today* 1 July 2012 <http://www.psychologytoday.com/blog/all-about-sex/201207/so-thats-how-it- feels> accessed 8 December 2012.

[33] Falola, *A Mouth Sweeter Than Salt*, 223.

[34] Falola, *A Mouth Sweeter Than Salt*, 226.

[35] Falola, *A Mouth Sweeter Than Salt*, 222.

[36] Oyeronke Olajubu "The Effect Of Taboos On The Health Of African Women: The Yoruba Experience," *Unilorin* 2 July 2012 <http://www.unilorin.edu.ng/publications/olademoo/OYERONKE%201.dot> accessed 21 December 2012.

[37] Kathleen Doheny, "Oxytocin More Than Mere 'Love Hormone,'" *WebMD* 15 November 2010 <http://www.webmd.com/news/20101114/oxytocin-more-than-mere-love-hormone> accessed 15 May 2012.

[38] Taiwo Makinde, "Motherhood As A Source Of Empowerment Of Women In Yoruba Culture," *Nordic Journal Of African Studies* 13(2): (2004): 165 <www.njas.helsinki.fi/pdf-files/vol13num2/makinde.pdf> accessed 16 August 2012.

[39] Malidoma Patrice Somé, *Of Water and the Spirit: Ritual, Magic, and Initiation in the Life of an African Shaman* (New York: Penguin Compass, 1994), 44.

[40] *Daughters of the Dust*, directed by Julie Dash, director's commentary (1991; New York: Kino, 2000), DVD.

[41] Toni Morrison, *Song of Solomon* (New York: Plume, 1977), 14.

[42] *Essential Visual History of World Mythology* (Washington, D.C.: National Geographic, 2008), 92. A gilded silver Kushite amulet from the Napatian period (743–712 BCE) depicts a God, perhaps Mut, the patron Deity of Nubian royal women, embracing and nursing Kushite Queen Nefrukakashta. This amulet reveals that access to the breast's divine protections and powers is unlimited and eternal. See MFA for Educators, "Amulet of Hathor nursing a queen," Harvard University—Boston Museum of Fine Arts, *MFA* <http://educators.mfa.org/ancient/amulet-hathor-nursing-queen-27520> accessed 31 December 2014.

[43] "Harms of Cesarean Versus Vaginal Birth," *Childbirth Connection* 10 March 2006 <http://www.childbirthconnection.org/article.asp?ck=10271> accessed 09 April 2012.

1. Odù: The Mother with a Womb Filled with Gods

[1] Samuel M. Opeola, personal interviews, Obafemi Awolowo University, Ile-Ife, Nigeria, 1997.
[2] Awo Fá'lokun Fatunmbi, *Ìwa-pẹ̀lẹ́: Ifá Quest: The Search for the Source of Santería and Lucumí* (Bronx: Original, 1991), 85.
[3] Peter Morton-Williams, William Bascom, and E. M. McClelland, "Two Studies of Ifa Divination. Introduction: The Mode of Divination," *Africa: Journal of the International African Institute*, 36:4 (Oct. 1966): 423.
[4] Browder, *Nile Valley Contributions to Civilization*, 243.
[5] Glenn Elert, editor, "Speed of the Milky Way in Space," *The Physics Factbook 2000* <http://hypertextbook.com/facts/1999/PatriciaKong.shtml> accessed 21 May 2012.
[6] See Thomas G. Brophy, *The Origin Map: Discovery of a Prehistoric, Megalithic, Astrophysical Map and Sculpture of the Universe* (Bloomington: iUniverse, 2002); and see "Magical Egypt III" Descent 1, 2, 3 *You Tube* <http://www.youtube.com/watch?v=dWMKMT4CCJI>, <http://www.youtube.com/watch?v=C4nB3RyrrgY&feature=related>, and <http://www.youtube.com/watch?v=huXAqcVeQWA&feature=related>, respectively, accessed 29 June 2009.
[7] Browder, *Nile Valley Contributions to Civilizations*, 242.
[8] "Cosmontology" is the author's compound neologism that melds the words cosmology, ontology, and logic. This neologism is the closest approximation possible in English of the holistic Yoruba spiritual system.
[9] Fatunmbi, *Ìwa-pẹ̀lẹ́: Ifá Quest*, 119.
[10] Fatunmbi, *Ìwa-pẹ̀lẹ́: Ifá Quest*, 186.
[11] Modupe Oduyoye, "The Spider, the Chameleon and the Creation of the Earth," in *Traditional Religion in West Africa*, edited by E. E. Ade Adegbola (Accra: Asempa, 1983), 383.
[12] Fatunmbi, *Ìwa-pẹ̀lẹ́: Ifá Quest*, 38.
[13] Fatunmbi, *Ìwa-pẹ̀lẹ́: Ifá Quest*, 38.
[14] Fatunmbi, *Ìwa-pẹ̀lẹ́: Ifá Quest*, 102.
[15] J. Olumide Lucas, *The Religion of the Yorubas* (1948; reprint, Brooklyn: Athelia Henrietta Press 1996), 95.
[16] Lucas, *The Religion of the Yorubas*, 95.
[17] Oduyoye, "The Spider, the Chameleon and the Creation of the Earth," 383.
[18] E. Bolaji Idowu, *Olódùmarè: God in Yoruba Belief* (1962; reprint, New York: Wazobia, 1994), 25.
[19] Noel Baudin, *Fetichism and Fetich Worshippers*, translated by M. McMahon (St. Louis: Benziger Brothers, 1885), 13.
[20] Reverend S. Crowther, *A Vocabulary of the Yoruba Language*, 1852, *Internet Archive* <http://www.archive.org/stream/vocabularyofyoru00crow/vocabularyofyoru00crow_djvu.txt> accessed 31 July 2011.

[21] Ulli Beier, *Yoruba Poetry* (Bayreuth, Germany: Eckhard Breitinger, 2002), 31.
[22] Beier, *Yoruba Poetry*, 31.
[23] In *The Gẹ̀lẹ̀dẹ́ Spectacle* Lawal states that in Ìlaró, Ìyánlá is called Alakàá Ìkó "owner of a chamber full of red parrot feathers" (241). Ìyánlá's chamber could very well a room in Odùduwà's home.
[24] Babatunde Lawal, "Ejiwapo: The Dialectics of Twoness in Yoruba Culture," *African Arts*, 2008 *Free Online Library* <http://www.thefreelibrary.com/Ejiwapo%3A+the+dialectics+of+twoness+in+Yoruba+art+and+culture.-a0175443008> accessed 15 January 2012.
[25] Teresa N. Washington, *Our Mothers, Our Powers, Our Texts: Manifestations of Àjẹ́ in Africana Literature*, revised and expanded edition (Oya's Tornado, 2015), 25–29.
[26] Fatunmbi, *Ìwa-pẹ̀lẹ́: Ifá Quest*, 121; diacritics are retained from the original.
[27] Beier, "Gelede Masks," 8.
[28] Beier, *Yoruba Poetry*, 30.
[29] Thomas Jefferson Bowen, *Grammar and Dictionary of the Yoruba Language* (Washington, D.C.: Smithsonian Institution, 1858), xvi.
[30] I write of áre's *probable* influence in deference to Idowu's analysis of *má rè* and *arè* in *Olódùmarè* (35).
[31] Washington, *Our Mothers, Our Powers, Our Texts*, 42–43.
[32] Fatunmbi, *Ìwa-pẹ̀lẹ́: Ifá Quest*, 84; diacritics are retained from the original.
[33] Fatunmbi, *Ìwa-pẹ̀lẹ́: Ifá Quest*, 85.
[34] Idowu, *Olódùmarè*, 143.
[35] Opeola, personal interviews, Obafemi Awolowo University, Ile-Ife, Nigeria, 1997.
[36] Lawal, "Ejiwapo: The Dialectics of Twoness in Yoruba Culture."
[37] Lawal, "Ejiwapo: The Dialectics of Twoness in Yoruba Culture."
[38] Washington, *Our Mothers, Our Powers, Our Texts*, 37–38.
[39] Henry John Drewal and Margaret Thompson Drewal, *Gẹlẹdẹ: Art and Female Power among the Yoruba* (Bloomington: Indiana University Press, 1983), 9.
[40] Pierre Fatumbi Verger, "The Rise and Fall of the Worship of Ìyàmi Òṣòròngà (My mother the sorceress) Among the Yoruba," in *Articles*, volume one, translated by Chris Brunski (1965; reprint, Montclair, N.J.: Black Madonna Enterprises, 2007), 144.
[41] It is unclear if the incongruous information in the ẹsẹ is the work of Verger's informants, or of his transcribers, or of Verger himself. I discuss issues regarding Verger's intentional mistranslations and academic ventriloquism in chapter three.
[42] Verger, "The Rise and Fall," 136.
[43] Verger, "The Rise and Fall," 136.
[44] Verger, "The Rise and Fall," 134.

[45] Verger, "The Rise and Fall," 134.
[46] Verger, "The Rise and Fall," 134.
[47] Verger, "The Rise and Fall," 76–77.
[48] Verger, "The Rise and Fall," 135.
[49] Verger, "The Rise and Fall," 139.
[50] Verger, "The Rise and Fall," 139.
[51] Verger, "The Rise and Fall," 135, emphasis added.
[52] Verger, "The Rise and Fall," 138.
[53] Verger, "The Rise and Fall," 139, 152.
[54] Verger, "The Rise and Fall," 144, 145, 146.
[55] Verger, "The Rise and Fall," 146.
[56] Verger, "The Rise and Fall," 147.
[57] Verger, "The Rise and Fall," 147 and 159. I have changed the translation of "Ọgbọ́n aiyé" from "intelligence of the earth" to the more recognizable phrase "wisdom of the world."
[58] Verger, "The Rise and Fall," 168.
[59] Verger, "The Rise and Fall," 168.
[60] Verger, "The Rise and Fall," 169.
[61] Verger, "The Rise and Fall," 172.
[62] Verger, "The Rise and Fall," 172.
[63] Verger, "The Rise and Fall," 172.
[64] Verger, "The Rise and Fall," 171.
[65] Verger, "The Rise and Fall," 172.
[66] Bascom, *Sixteen Cowries*, 219.
[67] Bascom, *Sixteen Cowries*, 219.
[68] Bascom, *Sixteen Cowries*, 221. Bascom, like many scholars, mistranslates Ẹléyinjú ẹgẹ́, as "One who has dainty eyes." The correct translation is the "Owner of Protruding and Ensnaring Eyeballs," and this is an oríkì of Ẹdan whose eyes behold everything and ensnare and entrap violators and offenders.
[69] See Teresa N. Washington, chapter three, *Manifestations of Masculine Magnificence: Divinity in Africana Life, Lyrics, and Literature* (Ọya's Tornado, 2014).
[70] Bascom, *Sixteen Cowries*, 9.
[71] Drewal and Drewal, *Gẹlẹdẹ*, 9.
[72] Bascom, *Ifa Divination*, 81.
[73] Adefioye Oyesakin, "The Image of Women in Ifá Literary Corpus," *Nigeria Magazine* 141(1982): 16. Tone marks have been altered for consistency.
[74] Oyesakin, "The Image of Women in Ifá Literary Corpus," 16n4. Tone marks have been altered for consistency.
[75] Wande Abmimbola, *Ifá Will Mend Our Broken World: Thoughts on Yoruba Religion and Culture in Africa and the Diaspora* (Roxbury, MA: Aim, 1997), 62.

[76] For more examples of the ẹsẹ see Drewal and Drewal *Gẹlẹdẹ*, 9; and Bascom, *Sixteen*, 217–223.
[77] John Mason, *Orin Òrìṣà: Songs for Selected Heads*, revised second edition (1992; Brooklyn: Yoruba Theological Archministry, 1997), 240–241.
[78] "Igbá," *Dictionary of the Yoruba Language*, part two (1950; reprint, Ibadan: University Press Limited, 1991), 110.
[79] C. L. Adeoye, *Ìgbàgbọ́ àti Ẹ̀sìn Yorùbá* (Ibadan: Evans Bros., 1985), 362.
[80] For more on Oya's marriages see Washington, *Our Mothers, Our Powers, Our Texts*, 168–170. I discuss women-only towns and Àjẹ́'s relationship to Orò in chapters three and four, respectively, of *The Architects of Existence*.
[81] Adeoye, *Ìgbàgbọ́ àti Ẹ̀sìn Yorùbá*, 362.
[82] Adeoye, *Ìgbàgbọ́ àti Ẹ̀sìn Yorùbá*, 363–364.
[83] Verger, "The Rise and Fall," 188.
[84] "Àpẹ̀rẹ," *A Dictionary of the Yoruba Language*, part two, 39; "sign" *A Dictionary of the Yoruba Language*, part one, 168; Verger, "The Rise and Fall," 177; and Rowland Abiodun, "Verbal and Visual Metaphors: Mythical Allusions in Yoruba Ritualistic Art of Orí," *Ifẹ̀: Annals of the Institute of Cultural Studies* (1986): 15.
[85] Adeoye, *Ìgbàgbọ́ àti Ẹ̀sìn Yorùbá*, 356.
[86] Verger, "The Rise and Fall," 180.
[87] William Bascom, *Ifa Divination: Communication between Gods and Men in West Africa* (Bloomington: Indiana University Press, 1969), figure 21A.
[88] Verger, "The Rise and Fall," 182.
[89] Verger, "The Rise and Fall," 183.
[90] Verger, "The Rise and Fall," 183.
[91] Fatunmbi, *Ìwa-Pẹ̀lẹ́: Ifá Quest*, 100.
[92] Bascom, *Ifa Divination*, 83.
[93] Quoted in Bascom, *Ifa Divination*, 83.
[94] Henry John Drewal, "Art and Ethos of the Ijebu," in *Yoruba: Nine Centuries of African Art and Thought*, by Henry John Drewal, John Pemberton, III, and Rowland Abiodun, edited by Allen Wardell (New York: The Center for African Art: 1989), 136.
[95] Lawal *The Gẹ̀lẹ̀dẹ́ Spectacle*, xxii; and see also Babatunde Lawal, "À Yà Gbó, À Yà Tó: New Perspectives on Edan Ògbóni," *African Arts* 28:1 (Winter, 1995): 40–41.
[96] Quoted in Drewal and Drewal, *Gẹlẹdẹ*, 9.
[97] Adeoye, *Ìgbàgbọ́ àti Ẹ̀sìn Yorùbá*, 358.
[98] Adeoye, *Ìgbàgbọ́ àti Ẹ̀sìn Yorùbá*, 358.
[99] Adeoye, *Ìgbàgbọ́ àti Ẹ̀sìn Yorùbá*, 358.
[100] Adeoye, *Ìgbàgbọ́ àti Ẹ̀sìn Yorùbá*, 358.
[101] Adeoye, *Ìgbàgbọ́ àti Ẹ̀sìn Yorùbá*, 358.
[102] Adeoye, *Ìgbàgbọ́ àti Ẹ̀sìn Yorùbá*, 359.

[103] Cromwell Osamaro Ibie, *Ifism: The Complete Works of Orunmila*, volume one (Lagos: Efehi, 1986), 48.
[104] Fatunmbi, *Ìwa-pèlé: Ifá Quest*, 158.
[105] Adeoye, *Ìgbàgbọ́ àti Ẹ̀sìn Yorùbá*, 359.
[106] Adeoye, *Ìgbàgbọ́ àti Ẹ̀sìn Yorùbá*, 359.
[107] Ibie, *Ifism*, 93.
[108] Ibie, *Ifism*, 133.
[109] Ibie, *Ifism*, 154.
[110] Bascom, *Ifa Divination*, 155.
[111] Bascom, *Ifa Divination*, 155.
[112] Bascom, *Sixteen Cowries*, 347.
[113] For a full analysis of the proliferation of ẹsẹ Ifá through African American folktales see Teresa N. Washington, "*Mules and Men* and Messiahs: Continuity in Yoruba Divination Verses and African American Folktales," *Journal of American Folklore* 125:497 (Summer 2012): 263–285.
[114] Bascom, *Ifa Divination*, 429–433.
[115] Bascom, *Ifa Divination*, 436–441.
[116] Bascom, *Ifa Divination*, 433, 439.
[117] Fatunmbi *Ìwa-pèlé: Ifá Quest*, 85.
[118] Bascom, *Sixteen Cowries*, 55.
[119] Bascom, *Ifa Divination*, 267.
[120] Adeoye, *Ìgbàgbọ́ àti Ẹ̀sìn Yorùbá*, 326–327.
[121] Bascom, *Sixteen Cowries*, 55.
[122] Fatunmbi, *Ìwa-pèlé: Ifá Quest*, 85, 186.
[123] Bascom, *Sixteen Cowries*, 213, 215.
[124] Bascom, *Sixteen Cowries*, 215.
[125] "Grandeur et décadence du culte de *iyámi òṣòròngà* (ma mère la sorcière) chez les *Yoruba*," in *Journal de la Societé des Africanistes* 35:1 (1965): 157; see also Verger, "The Rise and Fall," 70. Find a similar but shorter version in Peter Morton-Williams, William Bascom and E. M. McClelland, "Two Studies of Ifa Divination. Introduction: The Mode of Divination," *Africa: Journal of the International African Institute*, 36:4 (Oct. 1966): 423.
[126] Ibie, *Ifism*, 247–248.
[127] Ibie, *Ifism*, 249.
[128] Ibie, *Ifism*, 249.
[129] Ibie, *Ifism*, 250.
[130] Quoted in A. P. Anyebe, *Ògbóni: The Birth and Growth of the Reformed Ògbóni Society* (Lagos: Sam Lao, 1989), 18.
[131] Adeoye, *Ìgbàgbọ́ àti Ẹ̀sìn Yorùbá*, 341.
[132] Opeola, Personal Interviews, Obafemi Awolowo University, Ile-Ife, Nigeria, 1997.
[133] Opeola, Personal Interviews, 1997.

2. The Vagina Gives Birth to the World

[1] Opefeyitimi, "Women of the World in Yoruba Culture," 16. See also Washington, *Our Mothers, Our Powers, Our Texts*, 29–30.
[2] Pierre F. Verger, *Ewé: The Use of Plants in Yoruba Society* (Sao Paulo: Odebrecht, 1995), 721.
[3] Lawal, *The Gèlèdé Spectacle*, 128–129.
[4] Raymond Prince, "The Yoruba Image of the Witch," *Journal of Mental Science* 107:449 (July 1961): 797.
[5] Washington, *Our Mothers, Our Powers, Our Texts*, 18.
[6] Abiodun, "Woman in Yoruba Religious Images," 15.
[7] Washington, *Our Mothers, Our Powers, Our Texts*, 24, 34.
[8] Beier, *Yoruba Poetry*, 98.
[9] Adeoye, *Ìgbàgbó àti Èsìn Yorùbá*, 337–341.
[10] Quoted in Lawal, *The Gèlèdé Spectacle*, 73.
[11] Lawal, *The Gèlèdé Spectacle*, 73.
[12] Beier, *Yoruba Poetry*, 138.
[13] Beier, *Yoruba Poetry*, 19.
[14] Rowland Abiodun, "Woman in Yoruba Religious Images," *African Languages and Cultures* 2:1 (1989): 11.
[15] Pemberton, "The Oyo Empire," in *Yoruba: Nine Centuries of African Art and Thought*, 175, 177.
[16] Alice Walker, *Possessing the Secret of Joy* (New York: Harcourt, Brace, Jovanovich, 1992).
[17] Olabode Ibironke, personal interview, Obafemi Awolowo University, 1997.
[18] Makinde, "Motherhood As A Source Of Empowerment Of Women In Yoruba Culture," 169.
[19] Makinde, "Motherhood As A Source Of Empowerment Of Women In Yoruba Culture," 170.
[20] Lawal, *The Gèlèdé Spectacle*, 39.
[21] Makinde, "Motherhood As A Source Of Empowerment Of Women In Yoruba Culture," 169n5.
[22] Agbo Folarin, "Maternal Goddess in Yoruba Art: A New Aesthetic Acclamation of Yemoja, Osun, and Iya Mapo," *Passages* 1993 <http://quod.lib.umich.edu/p/passages/4761530.0006.005?rgn=main;view=full text> accessed 8 December 2012.
[23] Folarin, "Maternal Goddess in Yoruba Art."
[24] Folarin, "Maternal Goddess in Yoruba Art."
[25] Adeoye, *Ìgbàgbó àti Èsìn Yorùbá*, 344.
[26] Robert Farris Thompson, *Black Gods and Kings: Yoruba Art at UCLA* (Bloomington: Indiana University Press, 1971), CH 6/2.
[27] Robert Farris Thompson, *Flash of the Spirit* (New York: Vintage, 1983), 142.

[28] Bascom, *Ifa Divination*, 287.
[29] Drewal and Drewal, *Gẹlẹdẹ*, 75.
[30] Chief Oludare Olajubu, "References to Sex in Yoruba Oral Literature," *The Journal of American Folklore* 85:336 (April–June 1972): 156.
[31] Drewal and Drewal, *Gẹlẹdẹ*, 71.
[32] Olajubu, "References to Sex in Yoruba Oral Literature," 158.
[33] "Odù-Ifá: Òwọ́nrín Ògùndá explains; Ìṣẹ̀ṣe (Primordials / Ones Progenitors) *Ifa Speaks* 02 September 2011 <http://www.ifaspeaks.blogspot.com> accessed 24 December 2011.
[34] Olajubu, "References to Sex in Yoruba Oral Literature," 156.
[35] Olajubu, "References to Sex in Yoruba Oral Literature," 156.
[36] Olubayo Oladimeji Adekola, "Èṣù Ẹlẹ́gbára in Yorùbá Spiritual and Religious Discourse," in *Èṣù: Yoruba God, Powers, and the Imaginative Frontiers*, edited by Toyin Falola (Durham, NC: Carolina Academic Press, 2013), 70.
[37] Adekola, "Èṣù Ẹlẹ́gbára in Yorùbá Spiritual and Religious Discourse," 70.
[38] Quoted in Cheikh Anta Diop, *The Cultural Unity of Black Africa* (reprint; 1959, Chicago: Third World Press, 1963), 62.
[39] Beier, *Yoruba Poetry*, 47.
[40] Beier, *Yoruba Poetry*, 152.
[41] Beier, *Yoruba Poetry*, 47.
[42] Beier, *Yoruba Poetry*, 47.
[43] Lisa Collier Cool, "Could You Be Forced To Have A C-Section?" *Advocates for Pregnant Women* May 2005 <http://www.advocatesforpregnantwomen.org/articles/forced_c-section.htm> accessed 30 December 2012.
[44] Field research, St. Francis Medical Center, Monroe, LA, 2010.
[45] Tom Wilemon, "Lower TennCare rates for C-sections upset obstetricians," *The Tennessean* 25 March 2011 <http://www.wbir.com/rss/article/163251/2/Lower-TennCare-rates-for-C-sections-upset-obstetricians> accessed 27 May 2012.
[46] In 2012, New York City, NY launched the "Latch-On NYC" initiative which makes it unlawful for hospitals to give mothers and newborns formula. Kudos to New York for putting children, mothers, and families before corporate greed. (Mothers who choose to formula-feed can simply bring their formula with them to the hospital.)
[47] Abiodun, "Woman in Yoruba Religious Images," 11.
[48] Abiodun, "Woman in Yoruba Religious Images," 11.
[49] Abiodun, "Woman in Yoruba Religious Images," 12.
[50] Abiodun, "Woman in Yoruba Religious Images," 12.
[51] Abiodun, "Woman in Yoruba Religious Images," 7.
[52] Abiodun, "Woman in Yoruba Religious Images," 15.
[53] Adeoye, *Ìgbàgbọ́ àti Ẹ̀sìn Yorùbá*, 359.
[54] Beier, *Yoruba Poetry*, 81.

⁵⁵ Verger, *Ewé*, 113.
⁵⁶ Quoted in Edward Kofi Quashigah and Obiora Chinedu Okafor, *Legitimate Governance in Africa: International and Domestic Legal Perspectives* (Cambridge, MA: Kluwer Law International, 1999), 57.
⁵⁷ Alfred Burdon Ellis, *The Yoruba-Speaking Peoples of the Slave Coast of West Africa* (London: Chipman and Hall, 1894), 7–8. See also Anthony Okion Ojigbo, "Conflict Resolution in the Traditional Yoruba Political System," *Cahiers d'études africaines* 13:50 (1973): 285.
⁵⁸ For more information on àrokò read Philip Adeotun Ogundeji, "The Communicative and Semiotic Contexts of àrokò among the Yoruba Symbol-Communication Systems, *African Languages and Cultures* 10:2 (1997): 145–156.
⁵⁹ Patrick J. Ebewo, "History and Dramatic Fiction: Rotimi's *Kurunmi* and the Nineteenth Century Ijaiye War," *Yoruba Creativity: Fiction, Language, Life and Songs*, edited by Toyin Falola and Ann Genova (Trenton: Africa World Press, 2005), 129.
⁶⁰For a visual example of such a transformation in Bambara culture see the film *Yeelen*, directed by Souleymane Cisse (1987; New York Kino, 2002), DVD.
⁶¹ Rowland Abiodun, personal email communication, 1 January 2012.
⁶² Beier, "Gelede Masks," 6.
⁶³ Wole Soyinka, *Idanre and Other Poems* (1967; reprint, New York: Hill and Wang, 1987), 72.
⁶⁴ Washington, *Our Mothers, Our Powers, Our Texts*, 20.
⁶⁵ Olajubu, "References to Sex in Yoruba Oral Literature," 156; Drewal and Drewal, *Gẹlẹdẹ*, xv; and Lawal, *The Gẹ̀lẹ̀dẹ́ Spectacle*, 75n10.
⁶⁶ Drewal and Drewal, *Gẹlẹdẹ*, 79.
⁶⁷ Drewal and Drewal, *Gẹlẹdẹ*, 15.
⁶⁸ Drewal and Drewal, *Gẹlẹdẹ*, 75.
⁶⁹ Raymond Prince, "The Yoruba Image of the Witch," *Journal of Mental Science* 107 (July 1961): 798.
⁷⁰ Griffin, *Pornography and Silence*, 27–28.
⁷¹ Beier, "Gelede Masks," 8, emphasis added.
⁷² Fatunmbi, *Ìwa-pẹ̀lẹ́: Ifá Quest*, 38; and Bascom, *Ifa Divination*, 35.
⁷³ Verger, *Ewé*, 274–275.
⁷⁴ Verger, *Ewé*, 274–275.
⁷⁵ In *Sixteen Great Poems of Ifá*, Wande Abimbola asserts that palm oil, red in color is a signature staple of sacrifices to Àjẹ́ (106).
⁷⁶ Washington, *Our Mothers, Our Powers, Our Texts*, 20.
⁷⁷ Fatunmbi, *Ìwa-pẹ̀lẹ́: Ifá Quest*, 38–39. I have altered the original diacritical marks to distinguish Ọ̀rọ̀ from Orò.
⁷⁸ Washington, *Our Mothers, Our Powers, Our Texts*, 25–29.

[79] Rowland Abiodun, "Identity and the Artistic Process in Yoruba Aesthetic Concept of Ìwà," *Journal of Cultural Inquiry* 1:1 (December 1983): 15. For examples of the Kemites' respect for the power of pure melanin, and for divine erection as well, as actualized and activated in the immortalization of King Tutankhamun, please see Owen Jarus, "King Tut's mummified erect penis may point to ancient religious struggle," *Live Science* 3 January 2014 <http://www.nbcnews.com/science/king-tuts-mummified-erect-penis-may-point-ancient-religious-struggle-2D11850882?lite&lite=obnetwork> accessed 4 January 2014.
[80] Verger, "The Rise and Fall," 168.
[81] Rowland, Abiodun, "Hidden Power: Òṣun: the Seventeenth Odù," in *Òṣun Across the Waters*, edited by Joseph Murphy and Mei Mei Sanford (Bloomington: Indiana University Press, 2001), 25–26.
[82] S. O. Babayemi, *Egúngún among the Òyó Yoruba* (Ibadan: Board Publications, 1980), 50.
[83] "Ãró," "arò," and "àró," *A Dictionary of the Yoruba Language*, part two, 41.
[84] "Oku," *A Dictionary of the Yoruba Language*, part two, 171
[85] "Oku-áyamọ," *A Dictionary of the Yoruba Language*, part two, 171.
[86] Babayemi, *Egúngún among the Òyó Yoruba*, 50.
[87] Babayemi, *Egúngún among the Òyó Yoruba*, 50.
[88] Babayemi, *Egúngún among the Òyó Yoruba*, 50.
[89] Verger, "The Rise and Fall," 127.
[90] Verger, "The Rise and Fall," 127.
[91] Verger, "The Rise and Fall," 128.
[92] Please see chapters one and five of Washington, *Manifestations of Masculine Magnificence*.
[93] Moses A. Makinde, *African Philosophy, Culture and Traditional Medicine* (Athens, OH: Center for International Studies, 1988), 93.
[94] Makinde, *African Philosophy, Culture and Traditional Medicine*, 93.
[95] Verger, "The Rise and Fall," 128.
[96] Verger, "The Rise and Fall," 129.
[97] Verger, "The Rise and Fall," 129.
[98] Samuel M. Opeola, personal interviews, Obafemi Awolowo University, Ile-Ife, 1998.
[99] Benedict M. Ibitokun, *Dance as Ritual Drama and Entertainment in the Gèlèdé of the Kétu-Yorùbá subgroup in West Africa* (Ile-Ife: Obafemi Awolowo University Press, 1993), 90.
[100] Ibitokun, *Dance as Ritual Drama and Entertainment in the Gèlèdé of the Kétu-Yorùbá subgroup in West Africa*, 87–88.
[101] Fatunmbi, *Ìwa-pèlé: Ifá Quest*, 121.
[102] Ibie, *Ifism*, 14.
[103] Ibie, *Ifism*, 16.

[104] Ibie, *Ifism*, 249. One can compare transportation via Ìyá Màpó's palm to the Future Sign tree ushering Tutuola's protagonist in *My Life in the Bush of Ghosts* into and out of the spiritual realm. Amos Tutuola, *My Life in the Bush of Ghosts and The Palm-Wine Drinkard* (reprint; 1954, New York: Grove, 1984), 21, 166.
[105] "Entry for Croton zambesicus," *JSTOR Plant Science* <http://plants.jstor.org/upwta/2_105> accessed 13 January 2012.
[106] Verger, *Ewé*, 300, 301.
[107] Verger, *Ewé*, 293, 306–309
[108] Drewal and Drewal, *Gẹlẹdẹ*, 81.
[109] Susan Mullin Vogel, "Rapacious Birds and Severed Heads: Early Bronze Rings from Nigeria," *Art Institute of Chicago Museum Studies* 10 (1983): 330–357.
[110] Drewal and Drewal, *Gẹlẹdẹ*, 22.
[111] Washington, *Our Mothers, Our Powers, Our Texts*, 23.
[112] Opefeyitimi, "Women of the World in Yoruba Culture," 1, 16.
[113] Washington, *Our Mothers, Our Powers, Our Texts*, 23–24.
[114] Bascom, *Ifa Divination*, 269.
[115] Bascom, *Ifa Divination*, 271.
[116] Eleburuibon, *The Adventures of Obatala*, 9, emphasis added.
[117] Bascom, *Ifa Divination*, 441.
[118] Bascom, *Ifa Divination*, 273.
[119] Wande Abimbola, *Ifá: An Exposition of the Ifá Divination Corpus* (Ibadan: Oxford University Press, 1976), 206.
[120] Drewal and Drewal, *Gẹlẹdẹ*, 134; and Lawal, *The Gèlèdé Spectacle*, 54.
[121] Drewal and Drewal, *Gẹlẹdẹ*, 116.
[122] Lawal, *The Gèlèdé Spectacle*, 241.
[123] Drewal and Drewal, *Gẹlẹdẹ*, 74
[124] Bascom, *Ifa Divination*, 469.
[125] Bascom, *Sixteen Cowries*, 85.
[126] Lawal, *The Gèlèdé Spectacle*, 241.
[127] Abiodun, "Woman in Yoruba Religious Images," 3.
[128] Abiodun, "Woman in Yoruba Religious Images," 8.
[129] Robert Sydney Smith, *Kingdoms of the Yoruba*, third edition (Madison, WI: University of Wisconsin Press, 1988), 51.
[130] Abiodun, "Hidden Power," 13–14; Plates 2.2, 2.3a, 2.3b; and "Igogo festival in owo ondo state 1," *You Tube* 6 December 2012 <http://www.youtube.com/watch?v=SLrdEUwggR4> accessed 23 December 2012.
[131] Abiodun, "Hidden Power," 14; and Jacob K. Olupona, "Yorùbá Goddesses and Sovereignty in Southwestern Nigeria," in *Goddesses Who Rule* edited by Elisabeth Benard and Beverly Moon, (New York: Oxford University Press,

2000), 125. Abiodun calls the beaded garment "pàkatò" whereas Olupona calls it "patako." See also "Igogo festival in owo ondo state 1"; Taiwo Abiodun, "11 is my mystery number—Oba Olateru Olagbegi," *Taiwo's World* 9 April 2011 <http://taiwosworld.blogspot.com/2011/04/11-is-my-mystery-number-oba-olateru.html> accessed 23 December 2012; and Taiwo Abiodun, "Behold a festival of love!" *The Nation Online* 30 September 2011 <http://thenationonlineng.net/new/sunday-magazine/arts-life/behold-a-festival-of-love/> accessed 23 December 2012.

[132] Washington, *Our Mothers, Our Powers, Our Texts*, 19.
[133] "Liver Diseases," *Medicine Plus* <http://www.nlm.nih.gov/medlineplus/liverdiseases.html> accessed 15 January 2012.
[134] Washington, *Our Mothers, Our Powers, Our Texts*, 281–282.
[135] Washington, *Our Mothers, Our Powers, Our Texts*, 24, 20, 34.
[136] Washington, *Our Mothers, Our Powers, Our Texts*, 19, 21.
[137] Washington, *Our Mothers, Our Powers, Our Texts*, 21.
[138] Washington, *Our Mothers, Our Powers, Our Texts*, 20.
[139] Washington, *Our Mothers, Our Powers, Our Texts*, 34.
[140] Washington, *Our Mothers, Our Powers, Our Texts*, 34.
[141] Verger, "The Rise and Fall," 120.
[142] Washington, *Our Mothers, Our Powers, Our Texts*, 35.
[143] Ibie, *Ifism*, 47.
[144] Washington, *Our Mothers, Our Powers, Our Texts*, 35.
[145] Opeola, personal interviews, Obafemi Awolowo University, Ile-Ife, Nigeria, 1997; and Dr. Samuel Modupeola Opeola, *Napatian Society: A Society in Search of Ancient African Knowledge* 1 (1993): 15.
[146] Ibie, *Ifism*, 48.
[147] Ibie, *Ifism*, 171.
[148] See Washington, "*Mules and Men* and Messiahs," 263–285.
[149] Ibie, *Ifism*, 148.
[150] See also Abimbola, *Sixteen Great Poems of Ifá*, 106.
[151] Lawal, *The Gèlèdé Spectacle*, 129.
[152] Lawal, *The Gèlèdé Spectacle*, 243.
[153] Drewal and Drewal, *Gẹlẹdẹ*, 22.
[154] Ibie, *Ifism*, 85–86.
[155] Bascom, *Ifa Divination*, 433.
[156] Bascom, *Ifa Divination*, 469.
[157] Bascom, *Ifa Divination*, 469; see also 405.
[158] Ibie, *Ifism*, 196–197.
[159] Ibie, *Ifism*, 246 and 248.
[160] Ibie, *Ifism*, 139.
[161] Ibie, *Ifism*, 143.
[162] Ibie, *Ifism*, 176. Eji Oko's cure for infertility is stunningly similar to that Miranda devises in Gloria Naylor's *Mama Day* (1988; reprint, Vintage, New

York, 1993), 139–140. For an analysis of the impact of Àjẹ́ in *Mama Day* see Washington, *Our Mothers, Our Powers, Our Texts*, 113–140.
[163] Ibie, *Ifism*, 179.
[164] Washington, *Our Mothers, Our Powers, Our Texts*, 34, 281.
[165] Verger, "The Rise and Fall," 120.
[166] An example of the influence that the son's tears have on the Mothers in African America occurs in the folktale "How Jack Beat the Devil." The folktale is an exhibition of power between two of African American orature's master tricksters: Jack and Devil. Jack is clearly possessed of Alamiyo's wisdom for whenever Devil gives him an impossible task to complete, Jack sits down and cries. Devil's daughter, Beatrice, completes the tasks while Jack rests his head in her lap. See Zora Neale Hurston, *Mules and Men*, 47–53.
[167] Oyeronke Igbinola, personal interviews, Ile-Ife, Nigeria, 1998.
[168] Verger's *Ewé* includes a preparation that claims to endow one with Àjẹ́, but this is most likely a preparation to stimulate latent Àjẹ́.
[169] Opeola, personal interviews, Obafemi Awolowo University, Ile-Ife, Nigeria, 1997.
[170] Samuel M. Opeola, "A Common Sense Way of Understanding Yoruba Belief in Witchcraft," Institute of Cultural Studies seminar, Obafemi Awolowo University, Ile-Ife, Nigeria, 1997.
[171] Opeola, "A Common Sense Way of Understanding Yoruba Belief in Witchcraft."
[172] Opeola, personal interviews, Obafemi Awolowo University, Ile-Ife, Nigeria, 1997.
[173] Opeola, personal interviews, 1997.
[174] Opeola, personal interviews, 1997.
[175] Opeola, personal interviews, 1997.
[176] Opeola, personal interviews, 1997.
[177] Opeola, personal interviews, 1997.
[178] Leslie Lyon, "Race, gender and sexuality in African art," *Know* 28 February 2011 <http://www.utexas.edu/know/2011/02/28/okediji_moyo/> accessed 5 July 2012.
[179] Lyon, "Race, gender and sexuality in African art."
[180] Lyon, "Race, gender and sexuality in African art."
[181] Cheikh Anta Diop, *The Cultural Unity of Black Africa* (1959; reprint, Chicago: Third World Press, 1963), 120.
[182] Opeola, personal interviews, Obafemi Awolowo University, Ile-Ife, Nigeria, 1998.
[183] Washington, *Our Mothers, Our Powers, Our Texts*, 37–38.

3. Àwọn Ìyá Wa in the Ẹsẹ Ifá

[1] Verger, *Ewé*, 10.

[2] Due to inconsistencies in the Black Madonna Enterprises edition of "The Rise and Fall," which is the only English translation available to date, I use Verger's orthography from the original French publication, P. Verger, "Grandeur et décadence du culte de ìyámi òṣòròngà (ma mère la sorcière) chez les Yoruba," in *Journal de la Societé des Africanistes* 35:1 (1965): 141–243.

[3] Verger, "The Rise and Fall," 54.

[4] Adeoye, Ìgbàgbọ́ àti Ẹ̀sìn Yorùbá, 341.

[5] Verger, "The Rise and Fall," 74.

[6] Verger, "The Rise and Fall," 40. Verger, who was initiated into Candomblé and various sects of Ifá and "reborn" as Fatumbi in 1952, introduces "The Rise and Fall" with the following statement: "It has generally been proposed that witchcraft, since antisocial by its very nature, is not part of the religions of a human (civilized) community." Although Verger assures his intended Caucasian audience that he can give evidence that the Yoruba are, indeed, human, such a supposition and premise is extraordinarily insulting (it is also a criteria for a society that I have never heard of before and one that would reduce the witch-filled societies of Europe and America, past and present, to the status of sub-human or non-human). For a Caucasian who claims to be "reborn by Ifá" to begin an article written in 1964 and published in 1965—when the Civil Rights Movement and Pan-African Movements were in full-swing and the Black Power Revolution was entering its first cycle—with such a statement speaks volumes.

[7] Verger, "The Rise and Fall," 40–41.

[8] "Akọni," *Dictionary of the Yoruba Language*, part two, 28.

[9] For a very similar oríkì for Èṣù that also uses akọni and emphasizes its positive meaning, see Adekola, "Èṣù Ẹlẹ́gbára in Yorùbá Spiritual and Religious Discourse," 60.

[10] Verger, "The Rise and Fall," 46–47.

[11] Verger, "The Rise and Fall," 73–74.

[12] Verger, "The Rise and Fall," 47.

[13] Verger, "The Rise and Fall," 60. Verger's original in French reads: "Ha! Àgbà, l'ancienne a exagéré, elle refuse de faire les offrandes prescrites par *ifá*, d'écouter ses conseils, d'agir avec calme et prudence (Verger, "Grandeur et décadence du culte de ìyámi òṣòròngà (ma mère la sorcière) chez les Yoruba," 152).

[14] Verger, "The Rise and Fall," 67.

[15] See, Washington, *Our Mothers, Our Powers, Our Texts*, 58.

[16] Verger, "The Rise and Fall," 70.

[17] Verger, "The Rise and Fall," 70–71.

[18] Verger, "The Rise and Fall," 71.

[19] Verger, "The Rise and Fall," 71.

[20] Verger, "The Rise and Fall," 73.

[21] Wande Abimbola, *Sixteen Great Poems of Ifá* (UNESCO, 1975), 10, 131.

[22] Wande Abimbola, "The Image of Women in the Ifá Literary Corpus," *ANNALS New York: Academy of Sciences* 810 (1997):404.

²³ Abimbola, "The Image of Women in the Ifá Literary Corpus," 409–411.
²⁴ Abimbola, "The Image of Women in the Ifá Literary Corpus," 411.
²⁵ Ibie, *Ifism*, 4.
²⁶ Ibie, *Ifism*, 5.
²⁷ Ibie, *Ifism*, 5.
²⁸ Ibie, *Ifism*, 9.
²⁹ Bascom, *Ifa Divination*, 88.
³⁰ Ama Ata Aidoo, *Anowa* in *The Dilemma of a Ghost and Anowa* (1965; reprint, London: Longman, 1987), 71.
³¹ Bascom, *Ifa Divination*, 88–89.
³² Idowu, *Olódùmarè*, 80, emphasis added. Compare Idowu's discussion to that of Piet Meyer, "Divination among the Lobi of Burkina Faso," in *African Divination Systems: Ways of Knowing*, edited by Philip M. Peek (Bloomington: Indiana University Press, 1991), 93; and Ngugi wa Thiong'o, *Wizard of the Crow* (New York: Pantheon, 2006), 295.
³³ Ibie, *Ifism*, 17.
³⁴ Ibie, *Ifism*, 42.
³⁵ Ibie, *Ifism*, 42.
³⁶ Ibie, *Ifism*, 47.
³⁷ Bascom, *Ifa Divination*, 176–177.
³⁸ Bascom, *Sixteen Cowries*, 263–265; and Bascom, *Ifa Divination*, 176–177.
³⁹ Bascom, *Ifá Divination*, 557.
⁴⁰ Bascom, *Ifá Divination*, 479–481.
⁴¹ Bascom, *Ifa Divination*, 459.
⁴² Adeoye, *Ìgbàgbọ́ àti Ẹ̀sìn Yorùbá*, 104.
⁴³ Ibie, *Ifism*, 49.
⁴⁴ Washington, *Our Mothers, Our Powers, Our Texts*, 21.
⁴⁵ Washington, *Our Mothers, Our Powers, Our Texts*, 23.
⁴⁶ Verger, "The Rise and Fall," 76.
⁴⁷ Verger, "The Rise and Fall," 78.
⁴⁸ "Ogbó," and "ògbó," *A Dictionary of the Yoruba Language*, part two, 188.
⁴⁹ Verger, "The Rise and Fall," 70, and Bascom, *Sixteen Cowries*, 221.
⁵⁰ "Oje" and "Òjé," *A Dictionary of Yoruba Language*, part two, 166.
⁵¹ Ulli Beier, *Yoruba Myths* (New York: Cambridge University Press, 1980), 1.
⁵² Verger, "The Rise and Fall," 70.
⁵³ Verger, "The Rise and Fall," 82.
⁵⁴ Washington, "*Mules and Men* and Messiahs," 278.
⁵⁵ Verger, "The Rise and Fall," 84–85.
⁵⁶ Verger, "The Rise and Fall," 82.
⁵⁷ Verger, "The Rise and Fall," 89.
⁵⁸ "You Can't Win," *The Wiz: Original Soundtrack* (1978; MCA, 1997).
⁵⁹ Verger, "The Rise and Fall," 92.
⁶⁰ Verger, "The Rise and Fall," 93.

[61] Washington, *Our Mothers, Our Powers, Our Texts*, 66.
[62] Verger, "The Rise and Fall," 94, emphasis added.
[63] Verger, "The Rise and Fall," 92.
[64] Beier, *Yoruba Poetry*, 29.
[65] Beier, *Yoruba Poetry*, 29.
[66] Fatunmbi, *Ìwa-pèlé: Ifá Quest*, 27.
[67] For a detailed analysis of the role of Devil and other tricksters in African American orature, see Washington, "*Mules and Men* and Messiahs."
[68] Hurston, *Mules and Men*, 47–53.
[69] Hurston, *Mules and Men*, 155–156.
[70] Hurston, *Mules and Men*, 118–119.
[71] Verger, "The Rise and Fall," 100.
[72] "Ẹgẹ́" and "Ẹlẹgẹ́," *A Dictionary of the Yoruba Language*, part two, 74 and 76, respectively.
[73] Verger, "The Rise and Fall," 103–104.
[74] Verger, "The Rise and Fall," 103–104.
[75] Verger, "The Rise and Fall," 105.
[76] Verger, "The Rise and Fall," 102.
[77] Verger, "The Rise and Fall," 117.
[78] Verger, "The Rise and Fall," 120.
[79] Verger, "The Rise and Fall," 121.
[80] Verger, "The Rise and Fall," 120.
[81] Verger, "The Rise and Fall," 122.
[82] Audre Lorde defines *Zami: A New Spelling of My Name* as a "biomythography" because her life is a melding of history and myth that features herself, her contemporaries, her relatives, her ancestors, and her Gods. Audre Lorde, *Zami: A New Spelling of My Name* (Freedom, CA: Crossing Press, 1982.
[83] Ibie, *Ifism*, 47.
[84] Ibie, *Ifism*, 48.
[85] Ibie, *Ifism*, 48.
[86] Bascom, *Sixteen Cowries*, 417–419.
[87] Amos Tutuola, *My Life in the Bush of Ghosts*, in *the Palm-Wine Drinkard and My Life in the Bush of Ghosts* (1954; reprint, New York: Grove, 1984), 123.
[88] Emily Wax, "A Place Where Women Rule," *The Washington Post* 9 July 2005 <http://www.washingtonpost.com/wp-dyn/content/article/2005/07/08/AR2005070801775.html> accessed 28 Sept-ember 2012; and "History," *Umoja Women* 9 July 2012 <http://www.umojawomen.org/index.php/about-us/history-for-umoja.html> accessed 28 September 2012.
[89] Rowland Abiodun, "Identity and the Artistic Process in Yorùbá Aesthetic Concept of Ìwà," *Journal of Cultural Inquiry* 1:1 (December 1983): 23, 14.

[90] Ibie, *Ifism*, 89.
[91] Ibie, *Ifism*, 89.
[92] Ibie, *Ifism*, 85.
[93] Ibie, *Ifism*, 85–86. Also see the first verse of Ogbe-Meji in *Ifa Divination* (141–143) for an incomplete variant. Bascom states that the meaning of the ẹsẹ is "obscure probably because no story accompanies it" (143). Ibie's contribution fills in the blanks.
[94] Ibie, *Ifism*, 100.
[95] See also Verger, "The Rise and Fall," 117; and Afolabi A. Epega and Philip John Neimark, *The Sacred Ifa Oracle* (New York: Harper, 1995), 88–89.
[96] Ibie, *Ifism*, 100.
[97] Ibie, *Ifism*, 101, emphasis added.
[98] Ibie, *Ifism*, 134.
[99] Washington, *Our Mothers, Our Powers, Our Texts*, 19–20.
[100] Ibie, *Ifism*, 135.
[101] For an African American orature in which phenomenal boasts become reality see "The Fortune Teller" in Hurston, *Mules and Men*, 80–82.
[102] Ibie, *Ifism*, 136.
[103] Ibie, *Ifism*, 137.
[104] Ibie, *Ifism*, 141.
[105] Ibie, *Ifism*, 142.
[106] Ibie, *Ifism*, 142.
[107] Ibie, *Ifism*, 142.
[108] Ibie, *Ifism*, 142.
[109] Ibie, *Ifism*, 143.
[110] Ibie, *Ifism*, 144.
[111] The obvious problems that arise with infants ruling nations may have moved Àjẹ́ to institute the highly advanced system of governance in which Àjẹ́, themselves, make the kings and surround and guide them throughout their tenure. See my full discussion in chapter four.
[112] Ibie, *Ifism*, 159.
[113] Ibie, *Ifism*, 159.
[114] Washington, *Our Mothers, Our Powers, Our Texts*, 86.
[115] Ibie, *Ifism*, 160.
[116] Lawal, *The Gẹ̀lẹ̀dẹ́ Spectacle*, 34; see also Taiwo Makinde, "Motherhood As A Source Of Empowerment Of Women In Yoruba Culture," 172.
[117] Abimbola, *Ifá: An Exposition of Ifá Literary Corpus*, 152; see also Abimbola, *Sixteen Great Poems of Ifá*, 293.
[118] Ibie, *Ifism*, 146–147.
[119] "Elénìní," *Dictionary of the Yoruba Language*, part two, 70.
[120] Ibie, *Ifism*, 147.
[121] Ibie, *Ifism*, 147–148.
[122] Ibie, *Ifism*, 148.

[123] Abimbola, *Sixteen Great Poems of Ifá*, 292–293.
[124] Ibie, *Ifism*, 192.
[125] Ibie, *Ifism*, 192.
[126] Abimbola, *Sixteen Great Poems of Ifá*, 292.
[127] John S. Mbiti, *African Religions and Philosophy*, second edition (Portsmouth, New Hampshire: Heinemann, 1969), 177–178.
[128] By finding a "womb to enter," Ọ̀sá Méjì's soul enters the body of an *in vitro* fetus in a manner identical to that Malidoma Somé describes in his autobiography, *Of Water and the Spirit* (272–282).
[129] Ibie, *Ifism*, 194.
[130] Ibie, *Ifism*, 194.
[131] Ibie, *Ifism*, 194.
[132] Ibie, *Ifism*, 193.
[133] Ibie, *Ifism*, 193.
[134] Ibie, *Ifism*, 194.
[135] Ibie, *Ifism*, 197.
[136] Verger, "The Rise and Fall," 163.
[137] Bascom, *Ifa Divination*, 459.
[138] Abimbola, *Sixteen Great Poems of Ifá*, 312–322.
[139] "Ọ̀rọ̀," *A Dictionary of the Yoruba Language*, part two, 187; and Abimbola, *Sixteen Great Poems of Ifá*, 323.
[140] Rowland, Abiodun, "Verbal and Visual Metaphors: Mythical Allusions in Yoruba Ritualistic Art of Orí," *Ife: Annals of the Institute of Cultural Studies* (1985): 8–9; and Fatunmbi, *Ìwa-pẹ̀lẹ́: Ifá Quest*, 38–39.
[141] Abiodun, "Verbal and Visual Metaphors," 8–9.
[142] Abiodun, "Verbal and Visual Metaphors," 8–15.
[143] Fatunmbi, *Ìwa-pẹ̀lẹ́: Ifá Quest*, 38. I have altered the diacritical marks of the original from "*Oro*" to "*Ọ̀rọ̀*" for clarity.
[144] Adeoye, *Ìgbàgbọ́ àti Ẹ̀sìn Yorùbá*, 340–341.
[145] Olawole Francis Famule, "Art And Spirituality: The Ijumu Northeastern-Yoruba Egúngún," dissertation, University of Arizona, 2005, 144 <Arizona.openrepository.com/arizona/.../1/azu_etd_1372_sip1_m.pdf> accessed 3 January 2013.
[146] Abimbola, *Sixteen Great Poems of Ifá*, 327.
[147] Abimbola, *Sixteen Great Poems of Ifá*, 327.
[148] Abimbola, *Sixteen Great Poems of Ifá*, 333.
[149] Ibie, *Ifism*, 37.
[150] Ibie, *Ifism*, 199.
[151] Ibie, *Ifism*, 199.
[152] Ibie, *Ifism*, 199.
[153] Ibie, *Ifism*, 200.
[154] Solagbade Popoola, *Practical Ifa Divination: Ifa Reference Manual*, volume three (New York: Athelia Henrietta Press, 1997), 370.

[155] Popoola, *Practical Ifa Divination*, 371.
[156] Popoola, *Practical Ifa Divination*, 372.

4. "The Left is for the Gods"

[1] Opeola, Personal Interviews, Obafemi Awolowo University, Ile-Ife, Nigeria, 1997.
[2] Biodun Adediran, "The Early Beginnings of the Ife State," *The Cradle of a Race: Ife: From the Beginning to 1980*, edited by I. A. Akinjogbin (Sunray: Lagos, 1992), 89.
[3] Idowu, *Olódùmarè*, 27.
[4] Adeoye, *Ìgbàgbọ́ àti Ẹ̀sìn Yorùbá*, 341.
[5] Adeoye, *Ìgbàgbọ́ àti Ẹ̀sìn Yorùbá*, 340.
[6] Adeoye, *Ìgbàgbọ́ àti Ẹ̀sìn Yorùbá*, 356.
[7] Adeoye, *Ìgbàgbọ́ àti Ẹ̀sìn Yorùbá*, 337.
[8] Adeoye, *Ìgbàgbọ́ àti Ẹ̀sìn Yorùbá*, 337.
[9] Adeoye, *Ìgbàgbọ́ àti Ẹ̀sìn Yorùbá*, 341.
[10] Adeoye, *Ìgbàgbọ́ àti Ẹ̀sìn Yorùbá*, 341.
[11] Adeoye, *Ìgbàgbọ́ àti Ẹ̀sìn Yorùbá*, 340.
[12] Anyebe, *Ògbóni*, 37.
[13] Adeoye, *Ìgbàgbọ́ àti Ẹ̀sìn Yorùbá*, 341.
[14] Adeoye, *Ìgbàgbọ́ àti Ẹ̀sìn Yorùbá*, 359–360; and Famule, "Art And Spirituality: The Ijumu Northeastern-Yoruba Egúngún," 64–65.
[15] Famule, "Art And Spirituality: The Ijumu Northeastern-Yoruba Egúngún," 64.
[16] Famule, "Art And Spirituality: The Ijumu Northeastern-Yoruba Egúngún," 65.
[17] Famule, "Art And Spirituality: The Ijumu Northeastern-Yoruba Egúngún," 115.
[18] Famule, "Art And Spirituality: The Ijumu Northeastern-Yoruba Egúngún," 98.
[19] Babatunde Lawal, "*À Yà Gbó, À Yà Tó*: New Perspectives on Edan Ògbóni," *African Arts* 28:1 (Winter, 1995): 36. Unless otherwise noted, diacritics from quotations are retained from Lawal's original.
[20] Adeoye, *Ìgbàgbọ́ àti Ẹ̀sìn Yorùbá*, 343; and Lawal, *The Gẹ̀lẹ̀dẹ́ Spectacle*, 293.
[21] Taiwo Makinde, "Motherhood As A Source Of Empowerment Of Women In Yoruba Culture," 170.
[22] Washington, *Our Mothers, Our Powers, Our Texts*, 280, 281.
[23] Washington, *Our Mothers, Our Powers, Our Texts*, 281.
[24] Opeola, Personal Communications, Obafemi Awolowo University, Ile-Ife, Nigeria, 1997; and A. P. Anyebe, *Ògbóni*, 21.
[25] Lawal, "*À Yà Gbó, À Yà Tó*," 46.

[26] Lawal, "À Yà Gbó, À Yà Tó," 46.
[27] Lawal, "À Yà Gbó, À Yà Tó," 46.
[28] Bascom, *Ifa Divination*, 273.
[29] "Oxytocin," "Pathophysiology of the Endocrine System," *Colorado State University* 12 July 2010 <http://www.vivo.colostate.edu/hbooks/pathphys/endocrine/hypopit/oxytocin.html> accessed 14 March 2012; and Lillian Presti, "The Benefits of Natural Childbirth," *Naturally Savvy* 30 June 2008 <http://www.naturallysavvy.com/natural-pregnancy/the-benefits-of-natural-childbirth> 04 June 2012.
[30] Amy M. Romano, "Research Summaries for Normal Birth," *The Journal of Perinatal Education* 15:4 (2006 Fall): 46–49, *US National Library of Medicine National Institutes of Health* <http://www.ncbi.nlm.nih.gov/pmc/articles/PMC1804302/> accessed 24 December 2012.
[31] Abiodun, "Woman in Yoruba Religious Images," 14.
[32] Philip Ogundeji, "The Communicative and Semiotic Contexts of Àrokò among Yoruba Symbol-Communication Systems," *African Languages and Cultures* 10:2 (1997): 150–151.
[33] Opeola, personal interviews, Obafemi Awolowo University, Ile-Ife, Nigeria, 1998.
[34] Morton-Williams, "The Yoruba Ogboni Cult in Ọyọ," 364.
[35] Opeola, personal interviews, Obafemi Awolowo University, Ile-Ife, Nigeria, 1997.
[36] Quoted in Washington, *Our Mothers, Our Powers, Our Texts*, 31.
[37] Adeoye, *Ìgbàgbọ́ àti Ẹ̀sìn Yorùbá*, 341.
[38] Lawal, "À Yà Gbó, À Yà Tó," 46.
[39] Adeoye, *Ìgbàgbọ́ àti Ẹ̀sìn Yorùbá*, 344.
[40] "Òdi," *A Dictionary of the Yoruba Language*, part two, 166; and Lawal, "À Yà Gbó, À Yà Tó," 41.
[41] Thompson, *Black Gods and Kings*, CH 6/1.
[42] Thompson, *Black Gods and Kings*, CH 6/1.
[43] Thompson, *Black Gods and Kings*, CH 6/1.
[44] Browder, *Nile Valley Contributions to Civilization*, 38–40, 46. Mercator projection maps distort the sizes of continents and make Africa appear three times smaller than it actually is.
[45] Abimbola, *Sixteen Great Poems of Ifá*, 329.
[46] Thompson, *Black Gods and Kings*, CH 6/2.
[47] Washington, *Our Mothers, Our Powers, Our Texts*, 40.
[48] Thompson, *Black Gods and Kings*, CH 6/2; and Lawal, "À Yà Gbó, À Yà Tó," 43–44.
[49] Henry John Drewal, "Art and Ethos of the Ijebu," 143.
[50] Please see the Odù Ifá, especially those recorded in Ibie's *Ifism*; Malidoma Somé's journeys into the Cosmos as well as the underworld as detailed in his

autobiography, *Of Water and the Spirit*; and Amos Tutuola's *The Palm-wine Drinkard* and *My Life in the Bush of Ghosts*.
[51] Lawal, "*À Yà Gbó, À Yà Tó*," 43.
[52] Lawal, "*À Yà Gbó, À Yà Tó*," 44.
[53] Peter Morton-Williams, "The Yoruba Ogboni Cult in Ọyọ," *Africa: Journal of the International African Institute* 30:4 (Oct 1960): 373.
[54] Lawal, "*À Yà Gbó, À Yà Tó*," 40.
[55] Lawal, "*À Yà Gbó, À Yà Tó*," 41, diacritics are as they appear in the original.
[56] Adeoye, *Ìgbàgbọ́ àti Ẹ̀sìn Yorùbá*, 343.
[57] "Womb," *A Dictionary of Yoruba Language*, part one, 215.
[58] Adeoye, *Ìgbàgbọ́ àti Ẹ̀sìn Yorùbá*, 342–343.
[59] Sue Picton, "The visual arts of Nigeria, "in *Nigerian History and Culture*, edited by Richard Olaniyan (Ibadan: Longman, 1985), 258.
[60] Babatunde Lawal, "Ejiwapo: The Dialectics of Twoness in Yoruba Art and Culture," *African Arts* (Spring 2008), Find Articles <http://findarticles.com/p/articles/mi_m0438/is_1_41/ai_n24327210/> accessed 9 February 2012.
[61] Thompson Drewal, *Yoruba Ritual*, 175.
[62] Thompson Drewal, *Yoruba Ritual*, 176–177.
[63] Lawal, "Ejiwapo."
[64] Hans Witte, "The Secret Ogboni Society," *African Arts* 10:1 (Oct 1976): 75; and Mullin Vogel, "Rapacious Birds and Severed Heads," 333.
[65] Fatunmbi, *Ìwa-pẹ̀lẹ́: Ifá Quest*, 124.
[66] Washington, *Our Mothers, Our Powers, Our Texts*, 36.
[67] Morton-Williams, "The Yoruba Ogboni Cult in Ọyọ," 369n1.
[68] Lawal, "Ejiwapo."
[69] Adeoye, *Ìgbàgbọ́ àti Ẹ̀sìn Yorùbá*, 344–345.
[70] Washington, *Our Mothers, Our Powers, Our Texts*, 25–29.
[71] Morton-Williams, "The Yoruba Ògbóni Cult in Ọyọ," 366.
[72] Quoted in Anyebe, *Ògbóni*, 30.
[73] Anyebe, *Ògbóni*, 22–23, 26.
[74] Vogel, "Rapacious Birds and Severed Heads: Early Bronze Rings from Nigeria," 339.
[75] Lawal, "*À Yà Gbó, À Yà Tó*," 46.
[76] Lawal, "*À Yà Gbó, À Yà Tó*," 45.
[77] Anyebe, *Ògbóni*, 55.
[78] Anyebe, *Ògbóni*, 55.
[79] Anyebe, *Ògbóni*, 55.
[80] Anyebe, *Ògbóni*, 55.
[81] Anyebe, *Ògbóni*, 55.
[82] Anyebe, *Ògbóni*, 55.
[83] Drewal and Drewal, *Gẹlẹdẹ*, 73.

[84] Drewal and Drewal, Gẹlẹdẹ, 90.
[85] Quoted in Washington, *Our Mothers, Our Powers, Our Texts*, 32.
[86] Washington, *Our Mothers, Our Powers, Our Texts*, 34.
[87] J. R. O. Ojo, "The Position of Women in Yoruba Traditional Society," *Department of History: University of Ifẹ Seminar Papers, 1978–79* (Ile-Ife: Kosalabaro, 1980), 128.
[88] Ojo, "The Position of Women in Yoruba Traditional Society," 128.
[89] Bascom, *Sixteen Cowries*, 675.
[90] Bascom, *Sixteen Cowries*, 676.
[91] Bascom, *Sixteen Cowries*, 677.
[92] Bascom, *Sixteen Cowries* 677 and 677n3.
[93] Bascom, *Sixteen Cowries*, 679.
[94] Verger, "The Rise and Fall," 93.
[95] Bascom, *Sixteen Cowries*, 679n5.
[96] Bascom, *Sixteen Cowries*, 265.
[97] Bascom, *Ifa Divination*, 177.
[98] Bascom, *Ifa Divination*, 177.
[99] "Ṣe," *Dictionary of the Yoruba Language*, part two, 212.
[100] "Ọbalùfọ̀n," *Dictionary of the Yoruba Language*, part two, 181.
[101] Bascom, *Sixteen*, 265.
[102] Biodun Adediran, "Women, Rituals, and Politics in Pre-colonial Yorubaland," Unpublished paper, Obafemi Awolowo University, Ile-Ife, 1998, 9.
[103] Beier, "Gelede Masks," 7.
[104] Beier, "Gelede Masks," 7.
[105] Samuel M. Opeola, "A Common Sense Way of Understanding Yoruba Belief in Witchcraft," Institute of Cultural Studies lecture, Obafemi Awolowo University, Ile-Ife, Nigeria, 1998.
[106] Adediran, "Women, Rituals and Politics in Pre-colonial Yorubaland," 2, 3.
[107] O. B. Olaoba, "The Position of Women in Yoruba Palace," *Yoruba Ideas* 1:1 (1997): 106.
[108] Adediran, "Women, Rituals and Politics in Pre-colonial Yorubaland," 5.
[109] Quoted in Biodun Adediran and Olukoya Ogun, "Women, Ritual, and Politics of Pre-colonial Yorubaland," in *Shaping Our Struggles*, edited by Obioma Nnaemeka and Chima Korieh (Trenton: Africa World Press, 2011), 148.
[110] Adediran and Ogun, "Women, Rituals and Politics of Precolonial Yorubaland," 148.
[111] Adediran and Ogun, "Women, Rituals and Politics of Precolonial Yorubaland," 148–149.
[112] Adediran and Ogun, "Women, Rituals and Politics of Precolonial Yorubaland," 148–149; and Samuel H. Johnson, *A History of the Yorubas from the Earliest Times to the Beginning of the British Protectorate* (1921; reprint, New York: Cambridge University Press, 2010), 66.

[113] Johnson, *The History of the Yorubas*, 48.
[114] Adediran, "Women, Rituals, and Politics in Pre-colonial Yorubaland," 7.
[115] Adediran, "Women, Rituals, and Politics in Pre-colonial Yorubaland," 7–8.
[116] Johnson, *The History of the Yorubas*, 63.
[117] Adediran, "Women, Rituals, and Politics in Pre-colonial Yorubaland," 7.
[118] Johnson, *The History of the Yorubas*, 64.
[119] Anyebe, *Ògbóni* 26, emphasis added.
[120] Johnson, *The History of the Yorùbás*, 66.
[121] Adediran, "Women, Rituals, and Politics in Pre-colonial Yorubaland," 7.
[122] Adediran, "Women, Rituals, and Politics in Pre-colonial Yorubaland," 7. See also Layiwola, "Womanism in Nigerian Folklore and Drama," 28.
[123] Adediran, "Women, Rituals and Politics in Pre-colonial Yorubaland," 8.
[124] Adediran, "Women, Rituals, and Politics in Pre-colonial Yorubaland," 8.
[125] Adediran and Ogun, "Women, Rituals and Politics in Precolonial Yorubaland," 151–152.
[126] Adediran, "Women, Rituals, and Politics in Pre-colonial Yorubaland," 8.
[127] Adediran, "Women, Rituals, and Politics in Pre-colonial Yorubaland," 8.
[128] Beier, "Gelede Masks," 7. Please see Diop, *The Cultural Unity of Black Africa*, 153 for information about African societies that put "put their king to death after a reign."
[129] Lawal, *The Gèlèdé Spectacle*, 82.
[130] Beier, "Gelede Masks," 7–8.
[131] Fatunmbi, *Ìwa-pèlé: Ifá Quest*, 98.
[132] Fatunmbi, *Ìwa-pèlé: Ifá Quest*, 100.
[133] Morton-Williams, "The Yoruba Ogboni Cult in Oyo," 371.
[134] Wole Soyinka, *Aké: The Childhood Years* (1981; reprint, New York: Vintage International, 1989), 205.
[135] Soyinka, *Aké*, 205.
[136] Soyinka, *Aké*, 205.
[137] James Isola Adedayo, personal interview, Obafemi Awolowo University, Ile-Ife, Nigeria, 1998.
[138] "Olófin" and "Aláàfin," *A Dictionary of the Yoruba Language*, part two, 172 and 30, respectively.
[139] "Òfin" and "ààfin," *A Dictionary of the Yoruba Language*, 167 and 9, respectively.
[140] Adedayo, personal interview.
[141] Adedayo, personal interview.
[142] Adedayo, personal interview.
[143] Adedayo, personal interview.
[144] Mba, *Nigerian Women Mobilized*, 6.
[145] Verger, "The Rise and Fall," 144–146.
[146] S. O. Babayemi, *Egúngún among the Òyó Yoruba* (Ibadan: Board Publications, 1980), 4.

[147] Verger, "The Rise and Fall," 147.
[148] Babayemi, *Egúngún among the Òyọ́ Yoruba*, 4.
[149] Babayemi, *Egúngún among the Òyọ́ Yoruba*, 4n1; capitalization and tone marks are as they appear in the original.
[150] Mason, *Orin Òrìṣà*, 245.
[151] Mason, *Orin Òrìṣà*, 245.
[152] Adeoye, *Ìgbàgbọ́ àti Èsìn Yoruba*, 318.
[153] Washington, *Our Mothers, Our Powers, Our Texts*, 50–51.
[154] Mason, *Orin Òrìṣà*, 314.
[155] Lucas, *The Religion of the Yorubas*, 138.
[156] Bascom, *Sixteen Cowries*, 45, 459; and Mason, *Orin Òrìṣà*, 314.
[157] Mason, *Orin Òrìṣà*, 314.
[158] Babayemi, *Egúngún among the Òyọ́ Yoruba*, 9.
[159] Babayemi, *Egúngún among the Òyọ́ Yoruba*, 10.
[160] Babayemi, *Egúngún among the Òyọ́ Yoruba*, 8.
[161] Babayemi, *Egúngún among the Òyọ́ Yoruba*, 13.
[162] Babayemi, *Egúngún among the Òyọ́ Yoruba*, 35.
[163] Babayemi, *Egúngún among the Òyọ́ Yoruba*, 46.
[164] Dele Layiwola, "Womanism in Nigerian Folklore and Drama," *African Notes* XI:1 (1987): 28.
[165] Johnson, *The History of the Yorubas*, 65.
[166] Babayemi, *Egúngún among the Òyọ́ Yoruba*, 20. Tone marks of "Bàrà" altered for consistency.
[167] Babayemi, *Egúngún among the Òyọ́ Yoruba*, 20. Tone marks of "Bàrà" altered for consistency.
[168] Layiwola, "Womanism in Nigerian Folklore and Drama," 29.
[169] Akinwumi Isola, "Oya: Inspiration and Empowerment," 7–8. Isola dramatized this mythistory in his play *Madam Tinubu: The Terror of Lagos* (Ibadan: Heinemann, 1998), 99, 115–116. The version that Isola includes in *Madam Tinubu* patrifies the Mother.
[170] Akinwumi Isola, "Oya: Inspiration and Empowerment," Institute of Cultural Studies seminar and paper, Obafemi Awolowo University, Ile-Ife, 1998.
[171] Beier, "Gelede Masks," 8.
[172] Beier, "Gelede Masks," 8.
[173] Lawal, *The Gèlèdé Spectacle*, 43.
[174] Lawal, *The Gèlèdé Spectacle*, 46.
[175] Lawal, *The Gèlèdé Spectacle*, 43–46, 53–55, 62, 67, 261, 292.
[176] Drewal and Drewal, *Gẹlẹdẹ*, 8.
[177] Lawal, *The Gèlèdé Spectacle*, 51, 261.
[178] Opeola, Personal Interview, Obafemi Awolowo University, Ile-Ife, Nigeria 1998, emphasis is Opeola's.
[179] Igbinola, personal interviews, Ile-Ife, Nigeria, 1998.
[180] Ibie, *Ifism*, 48.

[181] Bascom, *Sixteen Cowries*, 419.
[182] Bascom, *Sixteen Cowries*, 419.
[183] Lawal, *The Gẹ̀lẹ̀dẹ́ Spectacle*, 43. See the power of Lawal's plate 3.1.

5. The Mothers and Their Powers and Their Sons

[1] Drewal and Drewal, *Gẹlẹdẹ*, 9.
[2] Drewal and Drewal, *Gẹlẹdẹ* 9, 14, 74, 203.
[3] Drewal and Drewal, *Gẹlẹdẹ*, 14 and 203, respectively.
[4] Benjamin Njoku, "Nollywood Celebrates Witchcraft, Voodoo Say Kenyan Film Makers," *Vanguard* 24 October 2009 <http://www.vanguardngr.com/2009/10/nollywood-celebrates-witchcraft-voodoo-say-kenyan-film-makers/> 14 April 2012.
[5] Field research, Ifá Yorùbá Kabbalah Centre, Ilé-Ifẹ̀, Nigeria, 1999.
[6] Quoted in Taiwo Makinde, "Motherhood As A Source Of Empowerment Of Women In Yoruba Culture," 165.
[7] Adeduntan, "Calling Àjẹ́ Witch in Order to Hang Her,"19.
[8] Quoted in Adeduntan, "Calling Àjẹ́ Witch in Order to Hang Her," 18. Compare King Sunny Ade's invocation to lines 154–160 of the *Ìtàn-Oríkì Ìyàmi Òṣòròngà* in Washington, *Our Mothers, Our Powers, Our Texts*, 282.
[9] As quoted in Ayo Adeduntan, "Calling Àjẹ́ Witch in Order to Hang Her," 17. Also see Adeduntan's article "Yoruba Hunter and the 'Sin' of Narrative Performance," *Text and Performance Quarterly* 30:2 (2010): 103–121.
[10] Verger, "The Rise and Fall," 41. See the discussion of this term in chapter one of this book.
[11] Washington, *Our Mothers, Our Powers, Our Texts*, 24, 32–35.
[12] Quoted in Ayo Adeduntan, "Calling Àjẹ́ Witch in Order to Hang Her," 17.
[13] George Olusola Ajibade, "Endogenous and Exogenous Factors in National Development: Inferences from the Metaphor of Witchcraft (Àjẹ́) in Ọlátúbọ̀sún Ọládàpọ̀'s Poetry," *Tydskrif Vir Letterkunde* 48:1 (2011): 167 <http://www.ajol.info/index.php/tvl/article/viewFile/63827/51646> accessed 28 April 2012. I am very appreciative of Ajibade's thorough analysis and translation of Oladapo's rich poetry: His work assisted my efforts.
[14] Lawal, *The Gẹ̀lẹ̀dẹ́ Spectacle*, 243.
[15] Ajibade, "Endogenous and Exogenous Factors in National Development," 167.
[16] Ajibade, "Endogenous and Exogenous Factors in National Development," 178.
[17] Olatubosun Oladapo, *Orin Odídẹrẹ́: Àjẹ́ Ọlọ́mọ* (Ibadan: Ọmọ Ogúngbọlá Ventures, 1994), 6.
[18] Ajibade, "Endogenous and Exogenous Factors in National Development,"170.
[19] Oladapo, *Orin Odídẹrẹ́*, 6, 7. The full saying is, "You are Àjẹ́; I am Àjẹ́. We all have Àjẹ́ in our pockets."

[20] Oladapo, *Orin Odídẹ́rẹ́*, 7.
[21] Oladapo, *Orin Odídẹ́rẹ́*, 12.
[22] Oladapo, *Orin Odídẹ́rẹ́*, 12.
[23] Oladapo, *Orin Odídẹ́rẹ́*, 8.
[24] Oladapo, *Orin Odídẹ́rẹ́*, 12.
[25] Christianity is not of European/Caucasian origin. I refer here to the version that was crafted by enslavers, colonizers, and capitalists to facilitate their attempts to subjugate, rape, and control the world.
[26] Washington, *Our Mothers, Our Powers, Our Texts*, 32.
[27] Soyinka, *Aké*, 128.
[28] Soyinka, *Aké*, 140.
[29] Soyinka, *Aké*, 140.
[30] Soyinka, *Aké*, 147.
[31] Soyinka, *Aké*, 148.
[32] The phrase "I will beat the devil out of you" is a staple in many African American families and is routinely used to threaten a child with a beating or to justify a beating that is taking place. Like so many destructive and crippling elements of Africana existence, the assertions that there is a devil; that he dwells within someone, especially a child; and that he can be exorcised through violence is the product of Caucasian thought and behavior. It is rather telling that the phrase appears to originate with oppressors seeking justification to enslave and beat enslaved human beings. In Alfred J. Swann's "A Slave Caravan," enslavers claim that only enslaved Africans "who become possessed with the devil try to escape"; consequently, when enslavers catch runaways, they beat the "devil" out of them. Alfred J. Swann's "A Slave Caravan," in *Africa: Selected Readings*, edited by Fred Burke, revised edition (New York: Houghton Mifflin, 1974), 124.
[33] Soyinka, *Aké*, 177.
[34] Soyinka, *Aké*, 173.
[35] Soyinka, *Aké*, 105.
[36] Soyinka, *Aké*, 96–97.
[37] Soyinka, *Aké*, 199–200.
[38] For more on Oṣó, see Washington, *Our Mothers, Our Powers, Our Texts*, 31–35.
[39] Cheryl Johnson-Odim and Nina Emma Mba, *For Women and the Nation: Funmilayo Ransome-Kuti of Nigeria* (Chicago: University of Illinois Press, 1997), 83.
[40] Adelami Feyisetan, "The Name is Dawodu (not David)—Part II," 24 February 2012 <http://yemitom.wordpress.com/tag/david/> 20 April 2012.
[41] Soyinka, *Aké*, 198.
[42] "Àfẹ̀rí," *A Dictionary of the Yoruba Language*, part two, 8, I have replaced "ẹ̀" with "ẹ́ẹ̀" to better represent the word; and Soyinka, *Aké*, 212.
[43] Soyinka, *Aké*, 212.
[44] Soyinka, *Aké*, 212.

⁴⁵ Similar to the African American linguistic dexterity that verbalizes nouns, to "naked" someone is an expression and act that occurs routinely in West Africa in various contexts. Fighters—especially females—attempt to strip the clothes off of, or "naked," their adversaries during battle; thieves, once caught, may be punished with public stripping so as to shame them and prevent future crimes from both the thieves and onlookers.
⁴⁶ Soyinka, *Aké*, 213.
⁴⁷ Soyinka, *Aké*, 213. Tone marks have been altered for clarity.
⁴⁸ Soyinka, *Aké*, 217.
⁴⁹ Moore, *Fela*, 45.
⁵⁰ Raymond Prince, "The Yoruba Image of the Witch," 798.
⁵¹ Prince, "The Yoruba Image of the Witch," 801.
⁵² Carlos Moore, *Fela: This Bitch of a Life* (1982; reprint, Chicago: Lawrence Hill Books, 2009), 44.
⁵³ Moore, Fela, 36–39.
⁵⁴ Moore, *Fela*, 52.
⁵⁵ Moore, *Fela*, 84–85.
⁵⁶ Moore, *Fela*, 84–85.
⁵⁷ Robyn Dixon, "Fela Kuti's voice still rings loud and true," *Los Angeles Times* 05 June 2011 <http://articles.latimes.com/2011/jun/05/entertainment/la-ca-fela-kuti-20110605> accessed 10 March 2012.
⁵⁸ Moore, *Fela*, 85.
⁵⁹ Moore, *Fela*, 88.
⁶⁰ Moore, *Fela*, 88.
⁶¹ Moore, *Fela*, 103–104.
⁶² Moore, *Fela*, 240.
⁶³ Johnson-Odim and Mba, *For Women and the Nation*, 169.
⁶⁴ Moore, *Fela*, 200–201, 208, 216, 223.
⁶⁵ Moore, *Fela*, 227.
⁶⁶ Moore, *Fela*, 208, and 188–189.
⁶⁷ "Fela Kuti & Egypt 80 [Arsenal TV3 Catalonian TV 1987-08-04]," <http://www.youtube.com/watch?v=gFY-6x1qTzU> accessed 28 December 2013. In this interview, Fela also discusses women's significant roles and powers in African spiritual arts and sciences. He makes many of the same points that Opeola makes.
⁶⁸ Moore, *Fela*, 158 and 128.
⁶⁹ Moore, *Fela*, 127.
⁷⁰ Moore, *Fela*, 188–189.
⁷¹ Omolara first states that she likes Fela's mind. After further prodding from Moore, she admits that she likes "his prick": "It be good-o. Na sweeter than sugar-o" (Moore, *Fela*, 223).
⁷² Moore, *Fela*, 217, 208.
⁷³ Moore, *Fela*, 220, 227.

[74] *Fela Kuti – Music is the Weapon*, directed by Jean-Jacques Flori, Stéphane Tchalgadjieff (Universal Import, 1982).
[75] Johnson-Odim and Mba, *For Women and the Nation*, 21.
[76] Johnson-Odim and Mba, *For Women and the Nation*, 23.
[77] A photograph of the monument is included with a group of photographs at the end of chapter one of Johnson-Odim and Mba's *For Women and the Nation*.
[78] Moore, *Fela*, 32.
[79] Quoted in Moore, *Fela*, 278.
[80] Quoted in Moore, *Fela*, 278.
[81] Outtakes from *Fela Kuti – Music is the Weapon*, and Moore, *Fela*, 165.
[82] Moore, *Fela*, 98.
[83] Moore, *Fela*, 173.
[84] Sola Olorunyomi, *Afrobeat! Fela and the Imagined Continent* (Trenton, NJ: Africa World Press, 2003), 95.
[85] Fela Kuti, "Unknown Soldier," *Coffin for Head of State/Unknown Soldier* (MCA, 2000), CD.
[86] Kuti, "Unknown Soldier."
[87] Kuti, "Unknown Soldier."
[88] Kuti, "Unknown Soldier."
[89] Johnson-Odim and Mba, *For Women and the Nation*, 82–83.
[90] Obasanjo was also the democratically elected president of Nigeria from 1999 to 2007.
[91] Fela Anikulapo Kuti and Africa 70, "V.I.P." *V.I.P* (Jofabro/Kalakuta, 1979) LP; and Fela Anikulapo Kuti and Africa 70, "I.T.T." *I.T.T.-International Thief Thief* (Kalakuta, 1979), LP.
[92] Cathy Nolan "Pop Star (and Ex-Polygamist) Fela Anikulapo Kuti Sets His Sights on Nigeria's Presidency," *People* 26:22 (01 Dec 1986) <http://www.people.com/people/archive/article/0,,20095158,00.html> accessed 3 March 2012.
[93] "Abàmi," *A Dictionary of the Yoruba Language*, part two, 2.
[94] Alex Hannaford, "He was in a godlike state," *The Guardian* 24 July 2007 <http://www.guardian.co.uk/music/2007/jul/25/popandrock.worldmusic> accessed 29 June 2012.
[95] Femi Sanyaolu (Keziah Jones), "When You Kill Us, We Rule," *Black Avant-Garde* 12 December 2008 <http://africangirlinparis.blogspot.com/2008/12/when-you-kill-us-we-rule- fela-kutis.html> accessed 13 March 2012.
[96] Sanyaolu, "When You Kill Us, We Rule."
[97] Fela Anikulapo Kuti and Egypt 80, "Perambulator," *Perambulator* (Lagos International, 1983), LP.
[98] Sanyaolu, "When You Kill Us, We Rule."
[99] Sanyaolu, "When You Kill Us, We Rule."

[100] Fela Anikulapo Kuti, "Teacher, Don't Teach Me Nonsense," *Teacher, Don't Teach Me Nonsense* (1986; MCA, 2001), CD.
[101] Sanyaolu, "When You Kill Us, We Rule."
[102] Sanyaolu, "When You Kill Us, We Rule."
[103] "Nubian/Egyptian Gods and Goddess," *Dignubia* <http://www.dignubia.org/bookshelf/goddesses.php> accessed 9 May 2012.
[104] Sanyaolu, "When You Kill Us, We Rule."
[105] Mike Smada's video tribute to Fela includes images of Fela during what appear to be his last public court appearances. Rather than the dead-man-walking image fabricated by certain writers, Fela looks calm, condescending, and far, far above the shenanigans of the officials before whom he is standing. He leaves court in a form-fitting salmon outfit and swaggers as he gives the two-fist Black Power salute. See "Fela's Burial," <http://www.youtube.com/watch?v=Q2XJPEFQuzg&feature=channel> accessed 18 August 2012. To better understand how much Fela was loathed in the West and how much he is feared by certain Westerners, take careful note of how certain writers attempt to associate him with AIDS in perpetuity, as if a disease associated with a man by hearsay or truth can obliterate his accomplishments.

While undertaking the research for this chapter, I discovered that some of the most bizarre, incendiary, and outlandish comments attributed to Fela and the numerous descriptions of Fela sporting lesion-scarred skin cannot be traced to any verifiable or credible source at all. Several individuals simply requoted fabricated information from an individual who was fired from *Source* magazine for plagiarizing interviews with Nigerian leaders; other writers quote the outlandish fictions of a "student journalist" from England who wrote her article on Fela's burial two years *after* the burial had occurred. One gets the impression that certain entities decided long ago that the best way to prevent new Felas from being born and establishing empires was to associate the Original with ignominy in life and in death. It is also interesting to note that many of the very people attacking Fela are using him to launch their careers. And yet, much to the consternation of his enemies and despite their best efforts, Fela has become a God. Àikú! Àikú Òrìṣà Fela!
[106] Seyi Sodimu, "Fela the King," *State of Mind* (1997; Goodlife 2003), CD.
[107] Falola, *A Mouth Sweeter than Salt*, 22–23.
[108] Falola, *A Mouth Sweeter than Salt*, 171.
[109] Falola, *A Mouth Sweeter than Salt*, 172.
[110] Falola, *A Mouth Sweeter than Salt*, 172.
[111] Falola, *A Mouth Sweeter than Salt*, 174.
[112] Falola, *A Mouth Sweeter than Salt*, 173.
[113] Falola, *A Mouth Sweeter than Salt*, 175.
[114] Bascom, *Sixteen Cowries*, 8.
[115] Diedre Badejo, *Ọ̀ṣun Ṣẹ̀ẹ̀gẹ̀sí: The Elegant Deity of Wealth, Beauty, and Femininity* (Trenton: Africa world Press, 1996), 1.

[116] "Pèregún," *A Dictionary of the Yoruba Language*, part two, 194; and Bascom, *Sixteen Cowries*, 288–293.

[117] "Ibadan City Profile," *The Federal Republic of Nigeria* <http://ruaf.iwmi.org/Data/Sites/4/PDFs/Ibadan%20Background%20Info%201.pdf> accessed 1 April 2012.

[118] Bascom, *Sixteen Cowries*, 401, 403.

[119] Falola, *A Mouth Sweeter than Salt*, 223.

[120] Bascom, *Sixteen Cowries*, 413–419, 407–411.

[121] Bascom, *Sixteen Cowries*, 421–425. For a discussion of a similar punishment described in fiction in Igboland see Washington, *Our Mothers, Our Powers, Our Texts*, 133.

[122] Bascom, *Sixteen Cowries*, 425, 427, 429.

[123] Bascom, *Sixteen Cowries*, 427.

[124] Bascom, *Sixteen Cowries*, 431–435, Bascom's English translation of this ẹsẹ also reveals the impact that one word can have. His translation reads, "Orisha's children were killing the parrots with knives" (433). This would not only be brutal, unnecessary, and shortsighted but would also echo ẹsẹ that describe Òrúnmìlà, Òsá Méjì, and Ọbàtálá massacring Àjẹ́. However, Ọbàtálá's children do not kill the parrots. The verb "*tẹ*" is mistranslated. Tẹ́ does not mean to kill; it means to level or flatten (*A Dictionary of the Yoruba Language*, part two, 220). The verse states that Ọbàtálá gives his servant the power to render the birds unable to fly; this fits the meaning of tẹ́. After they are rendered incapable of flight, the parrots are covered in cloths, put into cages, and taken to Ọbàtálá's home—which indicates that they were not killed. One can compare this ẹsẹ to the version included in Ifayemi Eleburuibon's *The Adventures of Obatala*. After the servant catches and cages the living birds, he takes their feathers and creates a beautiful cap for Ọbàtálá (41–43).

[125] Eleburuibon, *The Adventures of Obatala*, 69.

[126] Falola, *A Mouth Sweeter than Salt*, 176.

[127] Falola, *A Mouth Sweeter than Salt*, 190.

[128] Falola, *A Mouth Sweeter than Salt*, 190.

[129] Falola, *A Mouth Sweeter than Salt*, 192.

[130] In his autobiography, Malidoma Somé refers often to what he calls "primal language," which is unintelligible except to certain entities and Gods, and can be lethal. Somé, *Of Water and the Spirit*, 19, 47, 197, 213.

[131] Falola, *A Mouth Sweeter than Salt*, 193.

[132] Falola, *A Mouth Sweeter than Salt*, 269.

[133] Falola, *A Mouth Sweeter than Salt*, 268.

[134] Oladapo, *Orin Odídẹrẹ́*, 9–10.

[135] Fela Anikulapo Kuti and Egypt 80, "Beasts of No Nation," *Beasts of No Nation/ODOO* (1989; MCA, 2001). CD.

[136] Oladapo, *Orin Odídẹrẹ́*, 10.

[137] Falola, *A Mouth Sweeter than Salt*, 270.

Conclusion: The Very Definition of Evil

[1] Bascom, *Sixteen Cowries*, 43.
[2] Bascom, *Sixteen Cowries*, 43.
[3] Some examples of the glamorization of the denigration of Africana women in music include The Rolling Stones' "Brown Sugar," LaBelle's "Lady Marmalade" (which was remade in 2001 by Lil Kim, Christina Aguilera, Mya, and Pink to introduce a new generation of girls to Caucasia's oldest profession), Donna Summer's "Bad Girls," Tina Turner's "Private Dancer," and hip hop's tired celebration of pimp and strip club culture.
[4] See Sokari Douglas Camp, "Open and Close (2003)" *sokari* <http://www.sokari.co.uk/art/work/?a=44> accessed 8 June 2012. The character-assassination campaign to which the Kalakutans have been subjected for decades is relentless. I can think of no other persons whose humanity has been erased and replaced with a disease in the manner of Fela and his wives.
[5] Z. O. Apata, "Women Cults and Colonial Responses 1897–1960: The Case of Okun-Yoruba People," *Ifẹ: Annals of the Institute of Cultural Studies* 5 (1994): 30.
[6] Apata, "Women Cults and Colonial Responses 1897–1960," 31.
[7] Apata, "Women Cults and Colonial Responses 1897–1960," 31.
[8] Teresa N. Washington, "Nickels in the Nation Sack: Continuity in Africana Spiritual Technologies," *Journal of Pan African Studies* 3:5 (2010): <http://www.jpanafrican.com/docs/vol3no5/3.5-2newNickelsintheNation.pdf> accessed 28 January 2012.
[9] Apata, "Women Cults and Colonial Responses 1897–1960," 32.
[10] Apata, "Women Cults and Colonial Responses 1897–1960," 32–33.
[11] Apata, "Women Cults and Colonial Responses 1897–1960," 33.
[12] Apata, "Women Cults and Colonial Responses 1897–1960," 35.
[13] Apata, "Women Cults and Colonial Responses 1897–1960," 36.
[14] Apata, "Women Cults and Colonial Responses 1897–1960," 36.
[15] Apata is consistent in not capitalizing the word "Christian" and its cognates. Because his usage is consistent and deliberate, I will not use "[*sic*]" but will respectfully quote his words as he published them.
[16] Apata, "Women Cults and Colonial Responses 1897–1960," 38.
[17] "Evil," *The American Heritage Dictionary of the English Language*, third edition (New York: Houghton Mifflin, 1992), 636.
[18] "Devil," *The American Heritage Dictionary of the English Language*, 511–512.
[19] For a full exposition on Africana divinity, see Washington, *Manifestations of Masculine Magnificence*.
[20] For the etymological relationship between "religion" and the words "bind" and "rely" see "religion," *The American Heritage Dictionary of the English*

Language, 1525. The RZA makes this important observation in Ismael AbduSalaam, "The RZA: Do the Knowledge (Tao of the Wu)," part one, *AllHipHop* 15 October 15, 2009 <http://allhiphop.com/stories/reviews books/archive/2009/10/15/21979105.asp x> accessed 16 August 2011.

[21] Quoted in Apata, "Women Cults and Colonial Responses 1897–1960," 39.

[22] Apata, "Women Cults and Colonial Responses 1897–1960," 39.

[23] Adebayo Faleti, "Etymological Evolution of Yoruba Names," *Ifẹ̀: Journal of the Institute of Cultural Studies* 7 (1999): 31.

[24] Faleti, "Etymological Evolution of Yoruba Names," 31.

[25] "Àpelé," *A Dictionary of the Yoruba Language*, part two, 38.

[26] Johnson, *The History of the Yorubas*, 86.

[27] Yisa K. Yusef, "Sexism, English and Yoruba," *Linguistikonline* 11:2 (2002) <http://www.linguistik-online.de/11_02/yusuf.html> accessed 14 May 2012.

[29] Falola, *A Mouth Sweeter than Salt*, 88.

[30] Falola, *A Mouth Sweeter than Salt*, 88.

[31] Kevin Shillington, *History of Africa*, revised edition (Hampshire, England: Palgrave Macmillan, 1995), 94.

[32] Charles Choi, "The real question: Who didn't have sex with Neanderthals? Sub-Saharan Africans only modern humans whose ancestors did not interbreed with them," *NBC News* 1 November 2012 <http://www.msnbc.msn.com/id/49642484/ns/technology_and_science-science/t/real-question-who-didnt-have-sex-neanderthals/> accessed 24 November 2012.

BIBLIOGRAPHY

Abimbola, Wande. *Ifá: An Exposition of the Ifá Divination Corpus*. Ibadan: Oxford University Press, 1976.
-----. "The Image of Women in the Ifá Literary Corpus." *ANNALS New York: Academy of Sciences* 810 (1997): 401–413.
-----. *Sixteen Great Poems of Ifá*. N. P., UNESCO, 1975.
Abiodun, Rowland. "Hidden Power: Ọ̀ṣun: The Seventeenth Odù." In: *Ọ̀ṣun Across the Waters*. Eds. Joseph Murphy and Mei Mei Sanford. Bloomington: Indiana University Press, 2001. 10–33.
-----. "Identity and the Artistic Process in Yorùbá Aesthetic Concept of Ìwà." *Journal of Cultural Inquiry* 1:1 (December 1983): 13–30.
-----. "Verbal and Visual Metaphors: Mythical Allusions in Yoruba Ritualistic Art of Orí." *Ifẹ̀: Annals of the Institute of Cultural Studies* (1985): 3–38.
-----. "Woman in Yoruba Religious Images." *African Languages and Cultures* 2:1 (1989): 1–18.
"Abuse and Persecution of Akwa Ibom Children on Account of Witchcraft – Petition." *Akwa Ibom News Online*. 21 November 2008. 21 June 2012 <http://www.akwaibomnewsonline.com/petition/petition-against-akwa-ibom-children-witchcraft-abuse.php>.
Adediran, Biodun. "The Early Beginnings of the Ife State." In: *The Cradle of a Race: Ife: From the Beginning to 1980*. Ed. I. A. Akinjogbin. Sunray: Lagos, 1992. 77–95.
-----. "Women, Rituals, and Politics in Pre-colonial Yorubaland." Unpublished paper. Obafemi Awolowo University, Ile-Ife, 1998.
Adediran, Biodun and Olukoya Ogun. "Women, Ritual, and Politics of Pre-colonial Yorubaland." In: *Shaping Our Struggles: Nigerian Women in History, Culture and Social Change*. Eds. Obioma Nnaemeka and Chima Korieh. Trenton: Africa World Press, 2011. 143–162.
Adeduntan, Ayo. "Calling Àjẹ́ Witch In Order to Hang Her: Yorùbá Patriarchal Definition And Redefinition Of Female Power." Global African Spirituality, Social Capital And Self-Reliance, Centre For Black And African Arts and Civilization (CBAAC). Casa Del Papa, Ouidah, Republic Of Benin, November 2007. Manuscript shared with author.
Adekola, Olubayo Oladimeji. "Èṣù Ẹlẹ́gbára in Yorùbá Spiritual and Religious Discourse." In: *Èṣù: Yoruba God, Power, and the Imaginative Frontiers*. Ed. Toyin Falola. Durham, NC: Carolina Academic Press, 2013. 57–76.
Adeoye, C. L. *Ìgbàgbọ́ àti Èṣìn Yorùbá*. Ibadan: Evans Bros., 1985.
Aidoo, Ama Ata. *The Dilemma of a Ghost and Anowa*. 1965. London: Longman, 1987.
Ajibade, George Olusola. "Endogenous and Exogenous Factors in National Development: Inferences from the Metaphor of Witchcraft (Àjẹ́) in

Ọlátúbọ̀sún Ọládàpọ̀'s Poetry." *Tydskrif Vir Letterkunde* 48:1 (2011): 167–183. 17 August 2012 <http://www.ajol.info/index.php/tvl/article/viewFile/63827/51646>.

The American Heritage Dictionary of the English Language. 3rd edition. New York: Houghton Mifflin, 1992.

Ani, Marimba. *Yurugu: An African-Centered Critique of European Cultural Thought and Behavior*. Trenton: Africa World Press, 1994.

Anikulapo Kuti, Fela and Africa 70. "I.T.T." *I.T.T. – International Thief Thief.* Kalakuta, 1979.

-----. "V.I.P." *V.I.P.* Jofabro/Kalakuta, 1979. LP.

Anikulapo Kuti, Fela and Egypt 80. "Beasts of No Nation." *Beasts of No Nation/ODOO*. 1989. MCA, 2001. CD.

Anyebe, A. P. *Ògbóni: The Birth and Growth of the Reformed Ògbóni Society*. Lagos: Sam Lao, 1989.

Apata, Z. O. "Women Cults and Colonial Responses 1897–1960: The Case of Okun-Yoruba People." *Ifẹ̀: Annals of the Institute of Cultural Studies* 5 (1994): 30–44.

Avis, Paul. *Eros and the Sacred*. Harrisburg, PA: Morehouse, 1989.

Ayoade, Seun. "Do Yorubas Have An Origin Different From Other Africans?" Guest Editorial. *Indian Journal of Physiology and Pharmacology* 55:4 (2011): 295–296.

Babayemi, S. O. *Egúngún among the Ọ̀yọ́ Yoruba*. Ibadan: Board Publications, 1980.

Badejo, Diedre. *Ọ̀ṣun Ṣẹ̀ẹ̀gẹ̀sí: The Elegant Deity of Wealth, Beauty, and Femininity*. Trenton: Africa World Press, 1996.

Bascom, William. *Ifa Divination: Communication between Gods and Men in West Africa*. Bloomington: Indiana University Press, 1969.

-----. *Sixteen Cowries*. Bloomington: Indiana University Press, 1980.

Baudin, Noel. *Fetichism and Fetich Worshippers*. Trans. M. McMahon. St. Louis: Benziger Brothers, 1885.

Beier, Ulli. "Gelede Masks." *Odu* 6 (1958): 5–23.

-----. *Yoruba Myths*. New York: Cambridge University Press, 1980.

-----. *Yoruba Poetry*. Bayreuth, Germany: Eckhard Breitinger, 2002.

Bowen, Thomas Jefferson. *Grammar and Dictionary of the Yoruba Language*. Washington, D.C.: Smithsonian Institution, 1858.

Brophy, Thomas G. *The Origin Map: Discovery of a Prehistoric, Megalithic, Astrophysical Map and Sculpture of the Universe*. Bloomington: iUniverse, 2002.

Browder, Anthony T. *Nile Valley Contributions to Civilization: Exploding the Myths*. Vol. 1. Washington, D.C.: Institute of Karmic Guidance, 1992.

Castleman, Michael. "So THAT'S How It Feels...," *All About Sex: The Best Sex Ever. Psychology Today*. 1 July 2012. 8 December 2012 <http://www.psychologytoday.com/blog/all-about-sex/201207/so-thats-how-it-feels>.

Chitale, Radha. "Will Chromosome Y Go Bye-Bye?" *ABC News*. 17 July 2009. 18 December 2011 <http://abcnews.go.com/Health/MensHealth News/story?id=8104217&page=1>.
Choi, Charles. "The real question: Who didn't have sex with Neanderthals? Sub-Saharan Africans only modern humans whose ancestors did not interbreed with them." *NBC News*. 1 November 2012 <http://www.msnb.msn.com/id/49642484/ns/technology_and_science-science/t/real-question-who-didnt-have-sex-neanderthals/>.
Crowther, Rev. Samuel. *A Vocabulary of the Yoruba Language*. 1852. Internet Archive. 31 July 2011 <http://www.archive.org/stream/vocabularyof yoru00crow/vocabulary ofyoru00crow_djvu.txt>.
Daughters of the Dust. Dir. Julie Dash. 1991. Kino, 2000. DVD.
Davidson, Basil. *The African Genius*. New York: Atlantic Monthly Press, 1969.
A Dictionary of the Yoruba Language. 1913. Ibadan: University Press Limited, 1991.
Diop, Cheikh Anta. *The Cultural Unity of Black Africa: The Domains of Matriarchy and of Patriarchy in Classical Antiquity*. 1959. Chicago: Third World Press, 1963.
Dixon, Robyn. "Fela Kuti's voice still rings loud and true." *Los Angeles Times*. 05 June 2011. 10 March 2012 <http://articles.latimes.com/2011/jun/05/entertainment/la-ca-fela- kuti-20110605>.
Doheny, Kathleen. "Oxytocin More Than Mere 'Love Hormone.'" *WebMD*. 15 November 2010. 15 May 2012 <http://www.webmd.com/news/20101114/oxytocin-more-than-mere- love-hormone>.
Douglas Camp, Sokari. "Open and Close" (2003). *Sokari*. 8 June 2012 <http://www.sokari.co.uk/art/work/?a=44>.
Drewal, Henry John. "Art and Ethos of the Ijebu." In: *Yoruba: Nine Centuries of African Art and Thought*. Eds. Henry John Drewal, John Pemberton, III, and Rowland Abiodun. New York: The Center for African Art, 1989.
Drewal, Henry John and Margaret Thompson Drewal. *Gẹlẹdẹ: Art and Female Power among the Yoruba*. Bloomington: Indiana University Press, 1983.
Dunglison, Robley and Thomas Lathrop, eds. *A Dictionary of Medical Science*. 23rd edition. Philadelphia: Lea Brothers and Co, 1903.
Ebewo, Patrick J. "History and Dramatic Fiction: Rotimi's *Kurunmi* and the Nineteenth Century Ijaiye War." In: *Yoruba Creativity: Fiction, Language, Life and Songs*. Eds. Toyin Falola, Ann Genova. Trenton: Africa World Press, 2005. 113–132.
Elert, Glenn, ed. "Speed of the Milky Way in Space." *The Physics Factbook 2000*. 21 May 2012 <http://hypertextbook.com/facts/1999/Patricia Kong.shtml>.

Ellis, Alfred Burdon. *The Yoruba-Speaking Peoples of the Slave Coast of West Africa*. London: Chipman and Hall, 1894.
"Entry for Croton zambesicus." *JSTOR Plant Science*. 13 January 2012 <http ://plants.jstor.org/upwta/2_105>.
Epega, Afolabi A. and Philip John Neimark. *The Sacred Ifa Oracle*. New York: Harper, 1995.
Essential Visual History of World Mythology. Washington, D.C.: National Geographic, 2008.
Faleti, Adebayo. "Etymological Evolution of Yoruba Names." *Ifẹ: Journal of the Institute of Cultural Studies* 7 (1999): 27–40.
Falola. Toyin. *A Mouth Sweeter Than Salt*. Ann Arbor: University of Michigan Press, 2004.
Famule, Olawole Francis. "Art And Spirituality: The Ijumu Northeastern-Yoruba Egúngún." Diss. University of Arizona, 2005. 3 January 2013 <arizona.openrepository.com/arizona/.../1/azu_etd_1372_sip1_m.pdf>
.
Fatunmbi, Awo Fá'lokun. *Ìwa-pèlé: Ifá Quest: The Search for the Source of Santería and Lucumí*. Bronx: Original, 1991.
Fela Kuti — Music is the Weapon. Dir. Jean-Jacques Flori, Stéphane Tchalgadjieff. 1982. Universal Import, 2004. DVD.
Feyisetan, Adelami. "The Name is Dawodu (not David)—Part II." 24 February 2012. 20 April 2012 <http://yemitom.wordpress.com /tag/david/>.
Folarin, Agbo. "Maternal Goddess in Yoruba Art: A New Aesthetic Acclamation of Yemoja, Osun, and Iya Mapo." *Passages*. 1993. 8 December 2012 <http://quod.lib.umich.edu/p/passages/4761530.0006 .005?rgn=main;v iew=fulltext>.
Griffin, Susan. *Pornography and Silence: Culture's Revenge Against Nature*. New York: Harper and Row, 1981.
Hannaford, Alex. "He was in a godlike state." *The Guardian*. 24 July 2007. 29 June 2012 <http://www.guardian.co.uk/music/2007/jul/25/popandrock .worldmus ic>.
"Harms of Cesarean Versus Vaginal Birth." *Childbirth Connection*. 10 March 2006. 09 April 2012 <http://www.childbirthconnection.org/article.asp ?ck=10271>.
Hurston, Zora Neale. *Mules and Men*. 1935. New York: Harper Perennial, 1990.
"Ibadan City Profile." *The Federal Republic of Nigeria*. 1 April 2012 <http:// ruaf.iwmi.org/Data/Sites/4/PDFs/Ibadan%20Background%20Info% 201.pdf>.
Ibie, C. Osamaro. *Ifism: The Complete Works of Orunmila*. Lagos: Efehi, 1986.

Ibitokun, Benedict M. *Dance as Ritual Drama and Entertainment in the Gẹ̀lẹ̀dẹ́ of the Kétu-Yorùbá subgroup in West Africa*. Ile-Ife: Obafemi Awolowo University Press, 1993.
Idowu, E. Bolaji. *Olódùmarè: God in Yoruba Belief*. 1962. New York: Wazobia, 1994.
Isola, Akinwumi. *Madam Tinubu: The Terror of Lagos*. Ibadan: Heinemann, 1998.
-----. "Ọya: Inspiration and Empowerment." Unpublished paper. Institute of Cultural Studies Seminar. Obafemi Awolowo University, Ile-Ife, 1998. Essay shared with author.
Johnson, Samuel H. *A History of the Yorubas from the Earliest Times to the Beginning of the British Protectorate*. 1921. New York: Cambridge University Press, 2010.
Johnson-Odim, Cheryl and Nina Emma Mba. *For Women and the Nation: Funmilayo Ransome-Kuti of Nigeria*. Chicago: University of Illinois Press, 1997.
Lawal, Babatunde. "*À Yà Gbó, À Yà Tó*: New Perspectives on Edan Ògbóni." *African Arts* 28:1 (Winter 1995): 36–49, 98–100.
-----. "Ejiwapo: The Dialectics of Twoness in Yoruba Culture." *African Arts* (2008). *Free Online Library*. 15 January 2012 <http://www.thefreelibrary.com/Ejiwapo%3A+the+dialectics+of+twoness+in+Yoruba+art+and+culture.-a0175443008>.
-----. *The Gẹ̀lẹ̀dẹ́ Spectacle: Art, Gender, and Social Harmony in an African Culture*. Seattle: University of Washington Press, 1996.
Layiwola, Dele. "Womanism in Nigerian Folklore and Drama." *African Notes* XI:1 (1987): 26–33.
"Liver Diseases." *Medicine Plus*. 15 January 2012 <http://www.nlm.nih.gov/medlineplus/liverdiseases.html>.
Lucas, J. Olumide. *The Religion of the Yorubas*. 1948. Brooklyn: Athelia Henrietta Press, 1996.
Lyon, Leslie "Race, gender and sexuality in African art." *Know*. 28 February 2011. 5 July 2012 <http://www.utexas.edu/know/2011/02/28/okediji_moyo/>.
MacDougall, Clair. "Ghana moves to ban 'witchcraft.'" *The Christian Science Monitor*. 15 September 2011. 1 July 2013 <http://www.csmonitor.com/World/Africa/2011/0915/Ghana-aims-to- abolish-witches-camps>.
Makinde, Moses A. *African Philosophy, Culture and Traditional Medicine*. Athens, OH: Center for International Studies, 1988.
Makinde, Taiwo. "Motherhood As A Source Of Empowerment Of Women In Yoruba Culture." *Nordic Journal Of African Studies* 13:2 (2004): 164–174. 16 August 2012 <http://www.njas.helsinki.fi/pdf-files/vol13num2/makinde.pdf>.

Mason, John. *Orin Òrìṣà: Songs for Selected Heads*. Brooklyn: Yoruba Theological Archministry, 1992.
Mbiti, John S. *African Religions and Philosophy*. 2nd edition. Portsmouth, New Hampshire: Heinemann, 1969.
Meyer, Piet. "Divination among the Lobi of Burkina Faso." *African Divination Systems: Ways of Knowing*. Ed. Philip M. Peek. Bloomington: Indiana University Press, 1991. 91–100.
"'Mitochondrial Eve' Research: Humanity Was Genetically Divided For 100,000 Years." *Science Daily*. 15 May 2008. 26 March 2012 <http://www.sciencedaily.com/releases/2008/05/080515154635.htm>.
Moore, Carlos. *Fela: This Bitch of a Life*. 1982. Chicago: Lawrence Hill Books, 2009.
Morrison, Toni. *Beloved*. New York: Plume, 1988.
-----. *Song of Solomon*. New York: Plume, 1977.
Morton-Williams, Peter, William Bascom and E. M. McClelland. "Two Studies of Ifa Divination. Introduction: The Mode of Divination." *Africa: Journal of the International African Institute* 36:4 (Oct. 1966): 406–431.
Morton-Williams, Peter. "The Yoruba Ogboni Cult in Ọyọ." *Africa: Journal of the International African Institute* 30:4 (Oct 1960): 362–374.
Ngugi wa Thiong'o. *Wizard of the Crow*. New York: Pantheon, 2006.
Njoku, Benjamin. "Nollywood Celebrates Witchcraft, Voodoo Say Kenyan Film Makers." *Vanguard*. 24 October 2009. 14 April 2012 <http://www.vanguardngr.com/2009/10/nollywood-celebrates-witchcraft-voodoo-say-kenyan-film-makers/>.
Nolan, Cathy. "Pop Star (and Ex-Polygamist) Fela Anikulapo Kuti Sets His Sights on Nigeria's Presidency." *People*. 26:22 (1 Dec 1986) 3 March 2012 <http://www.people.com/people/archive/article/0,,20095158,00.html>.
"Nubian/Egyptian Gods and Goddess." *Dig Nubia*. 9 May 2012 <http://www.dignubia.org/bookshelf/goddesses.php>.
"Odù-Ifá: Ọ̀wọ́nrín Ògùndá explains; Ìṣẹ̀ṣe (Primordials / Ones Progenitors)." *Ifa Speaks*. 02 September 2011. 24 December 2011 <http://www.ifaspeaks.blogspot.com>.
Oduyoye, Modupe. "The Spider, the Chameleon and the Creation of the Earth." In: *Traditional Religion in West Africa*. Ed. E. E. Ade Adegbola. Accra: Asempa, 1983. 374–388.
Ogundeji, Philip Adeotun. "The Communicative and Semiotic Contexts of Àrokò among the Yoruba Symbol-Communication Systems." *African Languages and Cultures* 10:2 (1997): 145–156.
Ojigbo, Anthony Okion. "Conflict Resolution in the Traditional Yoruba Political System." *Cahiers d'études africaines* 13:50 (1973): 275–292.
Ojo, J. R. O. "The Position of Women in Yoruba Traditional Society." *Department of History: University of Ifẹ̀ Seminar Papers, 1978–79*. Ile-Ife: Kosalabaro, 1980.

Oladapo, Olatubosun. *Orin Odídẹrẹ́: Àjẹ́ Ọlọ́mọ*. Ibadan: Ọmọ Ogúngbọlá Ventures, 1994.
Olajubu, Chief Oludare. "References to Sex in Yoruba Oral Literature." *The Journal of American Folklore* 85:336 (Apr–Jun 1972): 152–166.
Olajubu, Oyeronke. "The Effect Of Taboos On The Health Of African Women: The Yoruba Experience." *Unilorin.* 2 July 2012. 21 December 2012 <http://www.unilorin.edu.ng/publications/olademoo/OYERONKE%201.dot>.
Olaoba, O. B. "The Position of Women in Yoruba Palace." *Yoruba Ideas* 1:1 (1997): 105–110.
Olorunyomi, Sola. *Afrobeat! Fela and the Imagined Continent*. Trenton, NJ: Africa World Press, 2003.
Olupona, Jacob K. "Yorùbá Goddesses and Sovereignty in Southwestern Nigeria." In: *Goddesses Who Rule*. Eds. Elisabeth Benard and Beverly Moon. New York: Oxford University Press, 2000. 119–132.
Opefeyitimi, Ayo. "Women of the World in Yoruba Culture." Unpublished paper. Obafemi Awolowo University, 1993.
Opeola, Samuel M. "A Common Sense Way of Understanding Yoruba Belief in Witchcraft." Institute of Cultural Studies Seminar. Obafemi Awolowo University, Ile-Ife, Nigeria, 1998. Essay shared with author.
-----. *Napatian Society: A Society in Search of Ancient African Knowledge* 1 (1993).
Oppenheimer, Mark. "On a Visit to the U.S., a Nigerian Witch-Hunter Explains Herself." *NY Times.* 21 May 2012. 21 June 2012 <http://www.nytimes.com/2010/05/22/us/22beliefs.html>.
"Oxytocin." "Pathophysiology of the Endocrine System." *Colorado State University.* 12 July 2010. 14 March 2012 <http://www.vivo.colostate.edu/hbooks/pathphys/endocrine/hypopit/oxytocin.html>.
Oyesakin, Adefioye. "The Image of Women in Ifá Literary Corpus." *Nigeria Magazine* 141 (1982): 16.
Perry, Susan. "Theories abound about conversion disorder and illnesses in LeRoy, N.Y." *Minnpost.* 5 March 2012. 14 March 2012 <http://www.minnpost.com/second-opinion/2012/03/theories-abound-about-conversion-disorder-and-illnesses-leroy-ny>.
Philipkoski, Kristen. "Women May Replenish Eggs." *Wired.* 10 March 2004. 20 January 2012 <http://www.wired.com/medtech/health/news/2004/03/62609>.
Picton, Sue. "The visual arts of Nigeria." In: *Nigerian History and Culture*. Ed. Richard Olaniyan. Ibadan: Longman, 1985. 253–283.
Popoola, Solagbade. *Practical Ifa Divination: Ifa Reference Manual*. Vol. 3. New York: Athelia Henrietta Press, 1997.
Presti, Lillian. "The Benefits of Natural Childbirth." *Naturally Savvy.* 30 June 2008. 4 June 2012 <http://www.naturallysavvy.com/natural-pregnancy/the-benefits-of-natural-childbirth>.

Prince, Raymond. "The Yoruba Image of the Witch." *Journal of Mental Science* 107:449 (July 1961): 795–805.

Quashigah, Edward Kofi and Obiora Chinedu Okafor. *Legitimate Governance in Africa: International and Domestic Legal Perspectives*. Cambridge, MA: Kluwer Law International, 1999.

"Return to Africa's Witch Children." Dir. Mags Gavan and Joost van der Valk. *Dispatches*, 2009. 21 June 2012 <http://topdocumentaryfilms.com/return-to-africas-witch-children/>.

Ritner, R. K. "A Uterine Amulet in the Oriental Institute Collection." *JNES* 43:3 (1984): 209–221.

Sanyaolu, Femi (Keziah Jones). "When You Kill Us, We Rule." *Black Avant-Garde*. 12 December 2008. 13 March 2012 <http://africangirlinparis.blogspot.com/2008/12/when-you-kill-us-we-rule-fela-kutis.html>.

The Secret NASA Transmissions: "The Smoking Gun." Dir. Graham W. Birdsall. Quest Publication, 2001. 24 March 2011 <http://www.snagfilms.com/films/title/the_secret_nasa_transmissions>.

Sin, Aseret. "Momma's Original Pot Likka." *Eyeball Literary Magazine*. Special issue: In Love & Revolution (2003): 15–18.

Smada, Mike. "Fela's Burial." *You Tube*. 30 July 2010. 18 August 2012 <http://www.youtube.com/watch?v=Q2XJPEFQuzg&feature=channel>.

Smith, Robert Sydney. *Kingdoms of the Yoruba*. 3rd edition. Madison, WI: University of Wisconsin Press, 1988.

Somé, Malidoma Patrice. *Of Water and the Spirit: Ritual, Magic and Initiation in the Life of an African Shaman*. New York: Penguin Compass, 1994.

Soyinka, Wole. *Aké: The Childhood Years*. 1981. New York: Vintage International, 1989.

-----. *Idanre and Other Poems*. 1967. New York: Hill and Wang, 1987.

Stevens, Jr., Phillips. "Women's Aggressive Use of Genital Power in Africa." *Transcultural Psychiatry* 43:4 (2006): 594.

Swann, Alfred J. "A Slave Caravan." In: *Africa: Selected Readings*. Ed. Fred Burke. Rev. edition. New York: Houghton Mifflin, 1974.

Thompson Drewal, Margaret. *Yoruba Ritual: Play, Performers, Agency*. Bloomington: Indiana University Press, 1992.

Thompson, Robert Farris. *Black Gods and Kings: Yoruba Art at UCLA*. Bloomington: Indiana University Press, 1971.

-----. *Flash of the Spirit*. New York: Vintage, 1983.

Tutuola, Amos. *The Palm-Wine Drinkard and My Life in the Bush of Ghosts*. New York: Grove, 1984.

Verger, Pierre Fatumbi. *Ewé: The Use of Plants in Yoruba Society*. Sao Paulo: Odebrecht, 1995.

-----. "Grandeur et décadence du culte de *iyámi òṣòròngà* (ma mère la sorcière) chez les *Yoruba*." *Journal de la Societé des Africanistes* 35:1 (1965):

141–243. 16 June 2012 <http://www.persee.fr/web/revues/home/ prescript/article/jafr_0037-9166_1965_num_35_1_1393>.
-----. "The Rise and Fall of the Worship of Ìyàmi Òṣòròngà (My Mother the Sorceress) Among the Yoruba." *Articles*. Vol. 1. Trans. Chris Brunski. 1965. Montclair, N.J.: Black Madonna Enterprises, 2007.
Vogel, Susan Mullin. "Rapacious Birds and Severed Heads: Early Bronze Rings from Nigeria." *Art Institute of Chicago Museum Studies* 10 (1983): 330–357.
Voight, Benjamin F., Sridhar Kudaravalli, Xiaoquan Wen, and Jonathan K. Pritchard. "A Map of Recent Positive Selection in the Human Genome." *PLOS Biol* 4:3 (2006). 17 April 2013 <http://www.plos biology.org/article/info:doi/10.1371/journal.pbio.00 40072>.
Walker, Alice. *Possessing the Secret of Joy*. New York: Harcourt, Brace, Jovanovich, 1992.
Wan, James. "Exorcising Witchcraft in Ghana." *Think Africa Press.* 10 November 2011. 14 December 2011 <http://thinkafricapress.com/ ghana/exorcising-witchcraft-gambaga>.
Washington, Teresa N. *Manifestations of Masculine Magnificence: Divinity in Africana Life, Lyrics, and Literature*. Ọya's Tornado, 2014.
-----. "*Mules and Men* and Messiahs: Continuity in Yoruba Divination Verses and African American Folktales." *Journal of American Folklore* 125:497 (2012): 263–285.
-----. *Our Mothers, Our Powers, Our Texts: Manifestations of Àjẹ́ in Africana Literature*. Revised and expanded edition. Ọya's Tornado, 2015.
-----. "Nickels in the Nation Sack: Continuity in Africana Spiritual Technologies." *Journal of Pan African Studies* 3:5 (2010): 5–28. 28 January 2012 <http://www.jpanafrican.com/docs/vol3no5/3.5-2new NickelsintheNation.pdf>.
Wilemon, Tom. "Lower TennCare rates for C-sections upset obstetricians." *The Tennessean.* 25 March 2011. 27 May 2012 <http://www.wbir. com/rss/article/163251/2/Lower-TennCare-rates-for-C-sections-upset-obstetricians>.
Witte, Hans. "The Secret Ogboni Society." *African Arts* 10:1 (Oct 1976): 75–76.
"You Can't Win." *The Wiz. Original Soundtrack*. 1978. MCA, 1997.
Yusef, Yisa K. "Sexism, English and Yoruba." *Linguistik Online* 11:2 (2002). 14 May 2012 <http://www.linguistik-online.de/11_02/yusuf.html.>.
Zaviačič, Milan and Richard J. Ablin. "The Female Prostate." *Journal of the National Cancer Institute* 90:9 (6 May 1998). 14 May 2012 <http://jnci.oxfordjournals.org/content/90/9/713.1.full.pdf>.

Interviews and Seminars

Adedayo, James Isola. Personal Interviews. Obafemi Awolowo University, Nigeria, 1998.
Abiodun, Rowland. Email communication. 1 January 2012.
Faleti, Adebayo. Personal Interviews. Obafemi Awolowo University, Nigeria, 1998.
Ibironke, Olabode. Personal Interview. Obafemi Awolowo University, Nigeria, 1997.
Igbinola, Oyeronke. Personal interviews and communications. Ile-Ife, Nigeria, 1997–1998.
Isola, Akinwunmi. "Oya: Inspiration and Empowerment." Institute of Cultural Studies Seminar. Obafemi Awolowo University, Ile-Ife, 1998.
Opeola, Samuel M. "A Common Sense Way of Understanding Yoruba Belief in Witchcraft." Institute of Cultural Studies Seminar. Obafemi Awolowo University, Ile-Ife, Nigeria, 1998.
-----. Personal interviews. Obafemi Awolowo University, 1997–1998.
Ositola, Kolawole. Personal Interviews. Ibadan, Nigeria, 1998.

INDEX

"*À Yà Gbó, À Yà Tó*" (Lawal), 156, 163–164
Abáàra méjì, 91, 93, 98
Abimbola, Wande, 59, 92, 112, 118–119, 143, 145, 148–149, 150, 151
Abiodun, Rowland, 49, 59, 63, 70, 71, 72, 74–74, 84, 85, 94, 148, 149, 169, 273
Adedayo, James Isola, 186–188
Adediran, Biodun, 152, 179–183
Adeduntan, Ayo, 10, 201–202
Adeoye, C. L., 44, 45, 50, 53, 59, 62, 123, 153–155, 160, 165–166, 177
African Grey Parrot, 26, 74, 81, 94, 131, 203, 234
Àjẹ́ kòbàlé (*also* Àjẹ́ òfòlé), 89–90
Ajibade, George Olusola, 203–204
Aké: The Childhood Years (Soyinka), 185, 206–213
Anikulapo Kuti, Fela, 10, 210, 213–229, 233, 238, 239, 242
Anikulapo Kuti, Funmilayo (Ransome Kuti), 207, 209–214, 216, 217–218, 220, 221, 222, 223–224, 225–226, 238, 240
Anyebe, A. P., 157, 172, 174, 181
Apata, Z. O, 242–246, 248
Àpẹ̀rẹ̀ Ayé, 41–51, 61, 75, 84, 145, 153
Aragamago, 39, 63, 84–85, 90, 125
Àrokò, 58, 61, 74–76, 84, 108, 130, 136, 154, 158–159, 187
Aruta (secret society), 242–245, 247, 251, 252
Àṣẹ, 28, 33, 39, 42, 44, 45, 46, 54, 66, 75, 81, 82–83, 85, 87,

Àṣẹ (cont.), 88, 100, 102, 103, 105, 127, 132, 137, 166, 184, 192–193, 229, 233, 237, 243
Àṣúrín, 87–88
Ausar (Kemetic God of Perfect Blackness), 51, 83
Ayé, *see* Ilẹ̀

Babayemi, S. O., 85, 189, 190–94
Bàrà, 193–194
Bascom, William, 40, 41, 52, 53, 54, 123, 148, 176, 177, 242
Beier, Ulli, 25, 28, 29, 62, 62, 75, 79, 81, 127, 178–179, 184, 196
Bird, *see* Ẹyẹ
Blood, 6, 9, 21, 26–28, 46, 59, 62–66, 72, 75–84, 87, 90, 94, 96, 97, 102–103, 134, 144, 147, 148, 150, 156, 159, 162, 165, 168, 171, 173, 174, 186, 196, 197, 200, 205–206, 214, 239, 243, 247, 252, 253
Breast milk, 15, 70, 96, 106, 157–158
Breastfeeding, 15–17, 70, 95–96, 99, 106, 117, 166–167
Breasts, 4, 7, 13–15, 47, 69, 70, 77, 96, 109, 134, 158, 167, 191, 194, 198, 231, 237

Calabash, 24, 26, 35, 44–48, 73–74, 84–87, 90, 110, 125–126, 127, 132, 153, 165, 180, 187, 211
"Calling Àjẹ́ Witch in Order to Hang Her" (Adeduntan), 10, 201–202
Capitalism, 8, 12, 28, 70, 80, 100–101, 121, 172, 181, 226–228, 229, 235, 249–250, 251
Cesarean section, 69–70

Clitoris, 5, 9, 14, 23, 29, 31, 35, 41, 60, 63–64, 74, 84–85, 89, 93, 109, 126, 148, 164, 167–168, 199, 237
Cosmontology, 21, 22, 26, 27, 31, 32, 43, 48, 49, 51, 56, 57, 65, 66, 79, 83, 84, 85, 93, 109, 115, 143, 149, 163, 167, 172, 174, 189, 198, 228, 233, 245, 246
Cosmos, 1, 3–6, 18, 19–25, 29, 31, 41, 43, 44–45, 48, 50, 51, 52, 57, 60, 61, 63, 72, 82–86, 102, 113, 114, 121, 132, 144, 153, 198, 204, 229, 242, 253

Drewal and Drewal, 34, 36, 78–79, 175, 200
Drewal, H. J., 48
Drewal, M. T., 166

Eggs, 1, 3–5, 20, 54–55, 62, 72–75, 76, 81, 83, 102, 103, 104, 131, 134, 146, 165, 170, 180, 187, 190, 196, 228, 237
Egúngún, 34, 36–37, 40–43, 63, 67, 84–87, 90, 92, 96, 126, 127, 141, 147, 147, 152, 174, 176, 177, 184, 187, 188–195
Èjì Ogbè, 103, 135–137, 140
Eleburuibon, Ifayemi, 92
Èṣù Ẹlẹ́gbára, 29, 55, 92, 104, 105, 108, 122, 129, 139, 141, 142, 143, 146, 150, 241
Ètùtù, 81, 85, 101–105, 134, 146–147
Evil, 7, 9, 11, 12, 15, 27, 32, 35, 39, 40, 44, 77, 82, 83, 93, 99–101, 114, 120, 122, 129–131, 143, 147–149, 155, 170, 171, 174, 178, 197, 206, 222, 235, 241–253
Ewé, 61, 101, 112, 236
Ewé: The Use of Plants in Yoruba Society (Verger), 59, 73, 81, 89, 112

Ẹdan, 33, 40, 50, 55, 56, 62, 65, 71, 97, 100, 126–127,130–131, 153–157, 160–62, 165–175, 177–180, 187, 213, 252, 260n68
Ẹgbẹ́ Ògbà, 197–198
Ẹgbẹ́run, 197–198
Ẹléyinjú Ẹgẹ́, 54, 127, 130, 155
Ẹyẹ and Ẹlẹ́yẹ, 35–37, 39, 84–85, 90–95, 98, 110, 119, 125–127, 148, 173, 188, 189, 197, 204, 214, 239

Faleti, Adebayo, 99, 172, 249
Fatunmbi, Awo F., 21, 22, 25, 27, 30, 47, 50, 53, 81–82, 88, 129, 149, 168, 185
Fela: This Bitch of a Life (Moore), 214–222
Folarin, Agbo, 65

Gèlèdé, 109, 195–199
Gẹlẹdẹ: Art and Female Power Among the Yoruba (Drewal and Drewal), 34, 78, 200
"Gelede Masks" (Beier), 28, 79, 178, 183–184
The Gèlèdé Spectacle (Lawal), 48, 52, 59, 218

Hunters, 53, 60–62, 80, 104, 109, 141, 202

Ibie, C. Osamaro, 50, 55, 89, 99, 102, 112, 119–151
Ifa Divination (Bascom), 41, 52, 53, 123, 148, 151, 177, 191
Ifism: the Complete Works of Orunmila (Ibie), 55, 89, 102, 104, 112, 119, 122, 133–151
Igbá, 24, 35, 41–48, 56, 72, 82, 84, 125, 126, 132, 145, 165, 176, 180, 205, 237, 243
Igbá Ẹyẹ, 84–85, 125–126
Igbádù, 41–48, 56, 72, 74, 84–85, 126, 145, 165, 176, 205, 237

Ìgbàgbọ́ àti Ẹ̀sìn Yorùbá (Adeoye), 44, 49, 62, 121
Igbinola, Oyeronke, 81, 89–90, 105, 124–125, 198
Ìkó oódẹ or ìkóódẹ, 26, 30, 74, 94–95
Ilé Ọlẹ̀ (The Home of Embryos, The Womb; *see also* Womb), 4, 246, 253
Ilẹ̀ (*also* Ayé, Onílẹ̀, Ìyá Ayé), 31, 44, 45, 46, 48–52, 53, 55, 65–66, 84, 103, 124, 129, 134, 137, 143, 145, 146, 153, 154, 160–160, 166, 167, 173, 180, 192, 203, 231, 232
Imọlẹ̀ (*also* Mọlẹ̀), 26, 31, 35, 56, 77, 99, 103 133, 149, 150, 152–156, 160, 170, 165, 172, 177–178, 182, 227, 235, 237, 252
Ìrókò, 52, 87–89, 127, 134, 136, 148
Irosùn, 46, 81, 110, 144
Ìrosùn Méjì, 143–145
Isola, Akinwumni, 195
Iszador, Sandra, 215–217, 220, 221, 222, 223, 224, 225, 240
Ìtàn-Orikì Ìyàmi Òṣòròngà, 31, 96, 97, 98, 105, 124, 151, 281n8
Ìwa-pẹ̀lẹ́: Ifá Quest (Fatunmbi), 21, 129
Ìyá-Àbíyè and Erelú Àbíyè, 156, 181
Ìyá Ayé, *see* Ilẹ̀
Ìyá Lekulẹja, 231–239
Ìyá Màpó, 62–72, 85, 89, 137, 160
Iyaláwo, 39–43, 55, 92, 103, 149, 182, 233, 241
Ìyálóde, 35, 156–126
Ìyàmi Òṣòròngà, 8, 31, 33, 81, 88, 96, 97, 98, 99, 105, 112–118, 124–134, 136, 140, 145, 148, 155, 157, 160, 176, 197, 200, 235

Iyangbà, 24, 29, 31, 51, 52, 158

Jẹ ọba, 184–186

Johnson, Samuel, 181, 182, 193, 249

Lawal, Babatunde, 26, 33, 49, 59, 103, 156, 157, 160, 163, 164, 166–167, 169–170, 173, 184, 196–197
Left, 102, 152, 157, 160, 162, 175, 183
Liver, 93, 96–97, 145, 185
Lucas, J. Olumide, 24, 190

Makinde, Moses, A., 87
Makinde, Taiwo, 64–65
Menses and menstruation, 1, 6, 17, 21, 26, 46–47, 64, 67, 73, 75–83, 89, 94, 95, 144, 148, 165, 168, 173, 205, 214, 243, 253
Morton-Williams, Peter, 160, 171, 173
A Mouth Sweeter Than Salt (Falola), 13–15, 229–240, 250
My Life in the Bush of Ghosts (Tutuola), 135, 194

Nwt, 4, 7, 17, 20, 51

Òdì, 55, 65–67, 110, 160–171, 179, 184, 188, 198, 232, 239
Odùduwà (Odúà), 23–26, 28–32, 44, 45, 46, 50, 56, 82–83, 103
Odù (God), 17, 19–57, 58, 59, 61, 62, 66, 69, 71, 74, 75, 80, 82–89, 90, 92, 102, 109, 110, 114, 116, 117, 124, 125, 127, 131, 135, 136, 137, 138, 143–144, 148, 149, 153, 154, 157, 158, 165, 168, 173, 176, 185, 187, 189, 190, 195, 196, 198, 200, 204, 205, 229, 235, 237, 243

Odù Ifá, 22, 27, 33, 39, 41–43, 46, 52, 81, 92, 104, 108, 121, 123, 132, 133, 134–135, 143–144, 163

Ofoṣi, 242, 244, 245, 247, 251, 252
Ògbóni, 32–33, 40, 50, 52, 55–56, 62, 73, 77, 90, 100, 108, 123, 126–127, 130, 141, 149–189, 211–212–213, 252
Ogun (secret society), 242, 244–245, 247, 251, 252
Ògún, 31–32, 35, 40, 45, 46, 51, 53, 75–76, 94, 104, 126, 132, 147, 157, 168–169, 175, 182, 192, 205, 207–208, 209, 225
Ògúndá Méjì (*also* Eji Oko *also* Alamiyo), 104–105
Òkèbàdàn, 13–15, 205, 234, 235, 240
Olatubosun Oladapo, 20, 203–206, 229, 239
Olódùmarè, 30, 31, 35–39, 53–55, 67, 84, 121, 125, 128, 138, 143, 153
Olódùmarè: God in Yoruba Belief (Idowu), 24
Olófi and Olófin, 186–187
Omi ẹ̀rọ̀, 45, 71, 234–238
Onílẹ̀, *see* Ilẹ̀
Ookun-Yoruba, 156, 242–245
Opefeyitimi, Ayo, 59, 91
Opeola, Samuel M., 19, 32, 41, 56, 88, 101, 106–110, 113, 116, 132, 156, 157, 160, 165, 169, 179, 197, 235
Orin Odídẹrẹ́: Àjẹ́ Ọlọ́mọ (Oladapo), 203–206, 239
Òrìṣà Ọlọ́mọwẹ́wẹ́, 196–198
Orò, 37, 44, 90, 100, 123, 127, 142, 148, 152, 173, 174–179, 181, 184, 187, 189, 191, 195, 212, 213, 226, 239
Òṣùmàrè, 31–35, 52–56, 138, 141

Our Mothers, Our Powers, Our Texts (Washington), 17, 82, 171, 190, 202
Ovaries, 72, 79, 80
Oxytocin, 16, 70, 158

Ọbàtálá, 12–38, 41, 43, 45, 53, 54, 65, 76, 83, 84, 98, 103, 123, 127, 132, 147–148, 150, 151, 157, 177, 229, 234, 235
Ọ̀bàrà Méjì, 104, 138–140
Ọká, 53, 127
Ọ̀kànràn Méjì, 140–141
Ọlọ́run, 24–25, 27, 31, 53, 98, 102–103, 124, 133, 198
Ọ̀rọ̀, 21–22, 29, 37, 41, 42, 48, 58, 68, 81–82, 100, 132, 137, 140, 148–150, 162, 171, 176–177, 189, 192, 198, 203, 227, 237
Ọ̀rúnmìlà, 36, 39–45, 51, 84, 85, 91, 92–93, 102–104, 115, 120–135
Ọsá Méjì, 104, 145–151
Ọ̀sanyìn, 51, 84, 90, 103, 119
Ọ̀ṣun, 31, 33, 40, 42, 51, 53, 65, 91, 92, 108, 128, 132–134, 182, 194, 198, 233–234, 241, 242
Ọ̀wọ́nrín Méjì, 142–143
Ọya, 31, 44, 137, 190–191, 194, 205, 228
Ọ̀yẹ̀kú Méjì, 138–140, 145

Palm oil, 81, 102–103, 105, 127, 144–146, 211, 233, 243, 244
Penis, 1, 5, 14–15, 22, 29, 31, 54, 62, 63, 67, 164, 168, 199, 234, 241
Polygamy, 13, 15, 106, 107
Pot (Odù), 13, 19, 22, 24, 27, 30–31, 33, 35, 37, 50, 53–56, 58, 62, 65, 69, 71, 74, 84–87, 90–92, 102, 106, 110, 129, 140, 146, 151, 159, 161, 168, 169, 173, 196, 231, 243–244

Prince, Raymond, 59, 79, 214

The Queens, 217–237, 240, 242
Queen Fehintola, 218, 220
Queen Kevwe, 218–219
Queen Najite, 218

The Religion of the Yorubas (Lucas), 24, 190
"The Rise and Fall of the Worship of Ìyámi Òṣòròngà (My mother the sorceress) among the Yoruba" (Verger), 33–34, 39, 45, 54, 87, 112–122, 123, 125–133, 134, 142, 146, 147, 178

Sanyaolu, Femi, 227, 229
Sarah Taiwo, 220–222
"Sleep," 73, 74, 173, 180, 184, 187
Sixteen Cowries (Bascom), 40, 41, 51, 53, 54, 93, 123, 175, 177, 194, 233, 241
Sixteen Great Poems of Ifá (Abimbola), 118, 145, 148–149
Soyinka, Wole, 76, 116, 185, 206–213, 229
Sperm, 1, 3, 4, 20, 62, 64, 72, 76, 158, 168

Ṣàngó, 109, 182, 193–194, 205, 244

Thompson, Robert Farris, 66, 161–162

Ugbin Ejo (*Ifism*), 55–56, 89, 103, 149–150

Vagina, 1, 4, 7, 13–17, 20–22, 23, 25, 27, 29, 38, 47, 58, 60–64, 65–72, 74, 77, 79–80, 84, 85, 89, 92, 119, 158, 162, 164,

Vagina (cont.) 165, 167, 170, 196, 219, 226, 237
Vaginal fluid, 62-72
Verger, Pierre F., 33, 34, 36, 39, 40, 54, 55, 59, 73, 81, 87, 112–118, 122, 123, 124, 125, 129, 161, 202

"When You Kill Us, We Rule" (Sanyaolu), 227–229
Wild Christian, 207, 211, 213, 240
Womb, 1–3, 5–8, 13, 15–17, 19–25, 27–30, 32, 33, 35, 37, 38, 41, 43, 45, 46–50, 53, 54, 56, 58, 60, 61, 62, 64, 65–68, 69, 72, 74, 75, 76, 79, 80, 83, 84, 85, 87, 92, 93, 95, 96, 100, 102–106, 109, 110, 111, 113, 114, 118, 119, 126, 140, 144, 145, 149, 153, 158, 159, 164, 164, 167, 168, 173, 180, 187, 189, 190, 191, 194, 196–198, 201, 204, 205, 213, 216, 237, 243, 246
"Women Cults and Colonial Responses 1897–1960" (Apata), 242–246, 247–249, 250, 251, 252
"Witch" (*also* "witchcraft"), 8–12, 27, 44, 62, 63, 79, 82, 89, 91, 98, 103, 113–118, 120, 122, 123, 130, 136, 137, 140, 141–143, 145–147, 151, 155, 171, 172, 195, 200, 201, 203–207, 209, 214, 228, 237, 239, 241, 242, 246, 252–253

X chromosome, 4–5, 6

Y chromosome, 4–5, 169
Yemòó, 148, 190, 194
Yewájọbí, 64
Yèyé Múwọ̀, 143–144,
Yoruba Poetry (Beier), 25, 28, 60
Yusuf, Yisa. K., 249

Teresa N. Washington is the author of *The Architects of Existence: Àjẹ́ in Yoruba Cosmology, Ontology, and Orature*; *Manifestations of Masculine Magnificence: Divinity in Africana Life, Lyrics, and Literature*; and *Our Mothers, Our Powers, Our Texts: Manifestations of Àjẹ́ in Africana Literature*. She is also the editor of *The African World in Dialogue: An Appeal to Action!* Dr. Washington's analyses are published as chapters in *Harold Bloom's Modern Critical Interpretations: Toni Morrison's <u>Beloved</u>: New Edition*; *Yemoja: Gender, Sexuality, and Creativity in the Latina/o and Afro-Atlantic Diasporas*; *Èṣù: Yoruba God, Power, and the Imaginative Frontiers*; and *Step into a World: A Global Anthology of the New Black Literature*. Her articles have been published in many noted journals, including the *African American Review*, the *Journal of American Folklore*, *FEMSPEC*, and the *Journal of Pan African Studies*.

MORE "BOOKS TO BLOW YOUR MIND" FROM ỌYA'S TORNADO!

Ah Jubah! A PleaPrayerPromise (a novel)
Asiri Odu, author
ISBN: 9780991073047 (pbk); also available as a Kindle Book

Six Pan-African collectives organize to unite warring gangs, exterminate "good old boys," turn tables—and barrels—on trigger-happy cops, and heal victims of genital excision, rape, and sodomy. Want a blueprint for complete elevation and liberation? Check out the novel *Ah Jubah!* It's a revolution in ink.

The African World in Dialogue: An Appeal to Action!
Teresa N. Washington, editor
ISBN: 9780991073078 (cloth); 9780991073061 (pbk); 9780991073085 (ebook)

In this contemporary anthology, elders, warriors, scholars, artists, and activists address some of the most significant political, cultural, and social issues facing the African world. What is more, they offer viable solutions to facilitate progress, evolution, and elevation.

The Architects of Existence: Àjẹ́ in Yoruba Cosmology, Ontology, and Orature
Teresa N. Washington, author
ISBN: 9780991073016 (pbk); 9780991073030 (cloth)

The Architects of Existence is the companion to Teresa N. Washington's *Our Mothers, Our Powers, Our Texts: Manifestations of Àjẹ́ in Africana Literature*, and it is the only book-length exposition of the power of Àjẹ́ and the African Gods and Divine Mothers who own and control this power in Yoruba cosmology and ontology.

Manifestations of Masculine Magnificence: Divinity in Africana Life, Lyrics, and Literature
Teresa N. Washington, author
ISBN: 9780991073009 (pbk); 9780991073023 (cloth)

Teresa N. Washington uses a compelling historical and spiritual foundation as a lens by which to analyze the proliferation of humanodivinity in contemporary Africana life, in some of the deepest lyrics ever spit and in some of the richest literature ever written.

Our Mothers, Our Powers, Our Texts: Manifestations of Àjẹ́ in Africana Literature
Teresa N. Washington, author
ISBN: 9780991073054 (pbk)

Using orature and historical documents, this book explores Àjẹ́'s forces and figures throughout the African continuum. From this rich foundation, Teresa N. Washington analyzes the impact and influence of Àjẹ́ in the contemporary literature of Africana writers. Ọya's Tornado is proud to publish the revised and expanded edition of Washington's groundbreaking study!

Ọya's Tornado books are also available wherever fine books are sold!
Visit us at www.oyastornado.com

www.ingramcontent.com/pod-product-compliance
Lightning Source LLC
Chambersburg PA
CBHW031407290426
44110CB00011B/294